AF575177

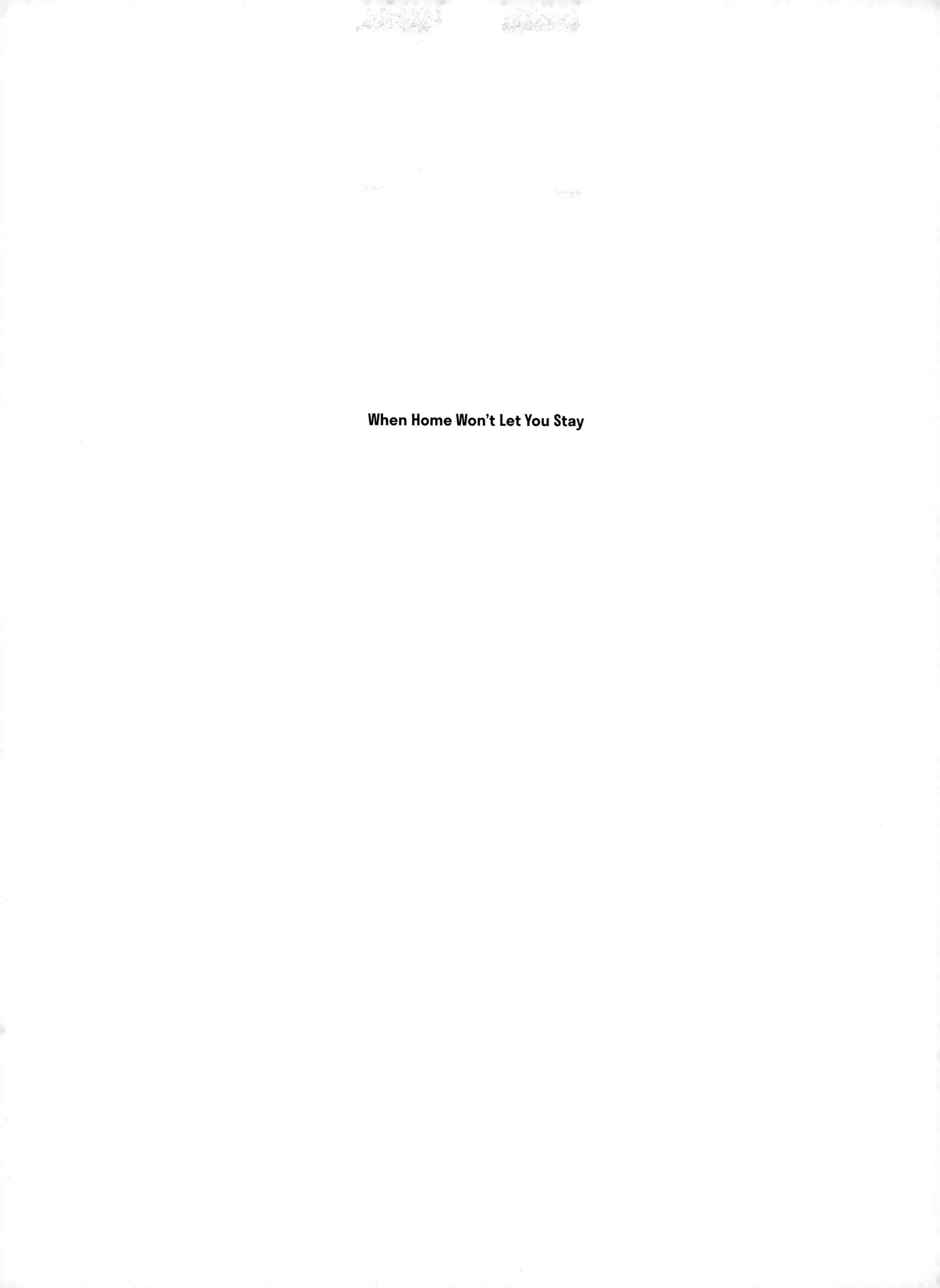

When Home Won't Let You Stay

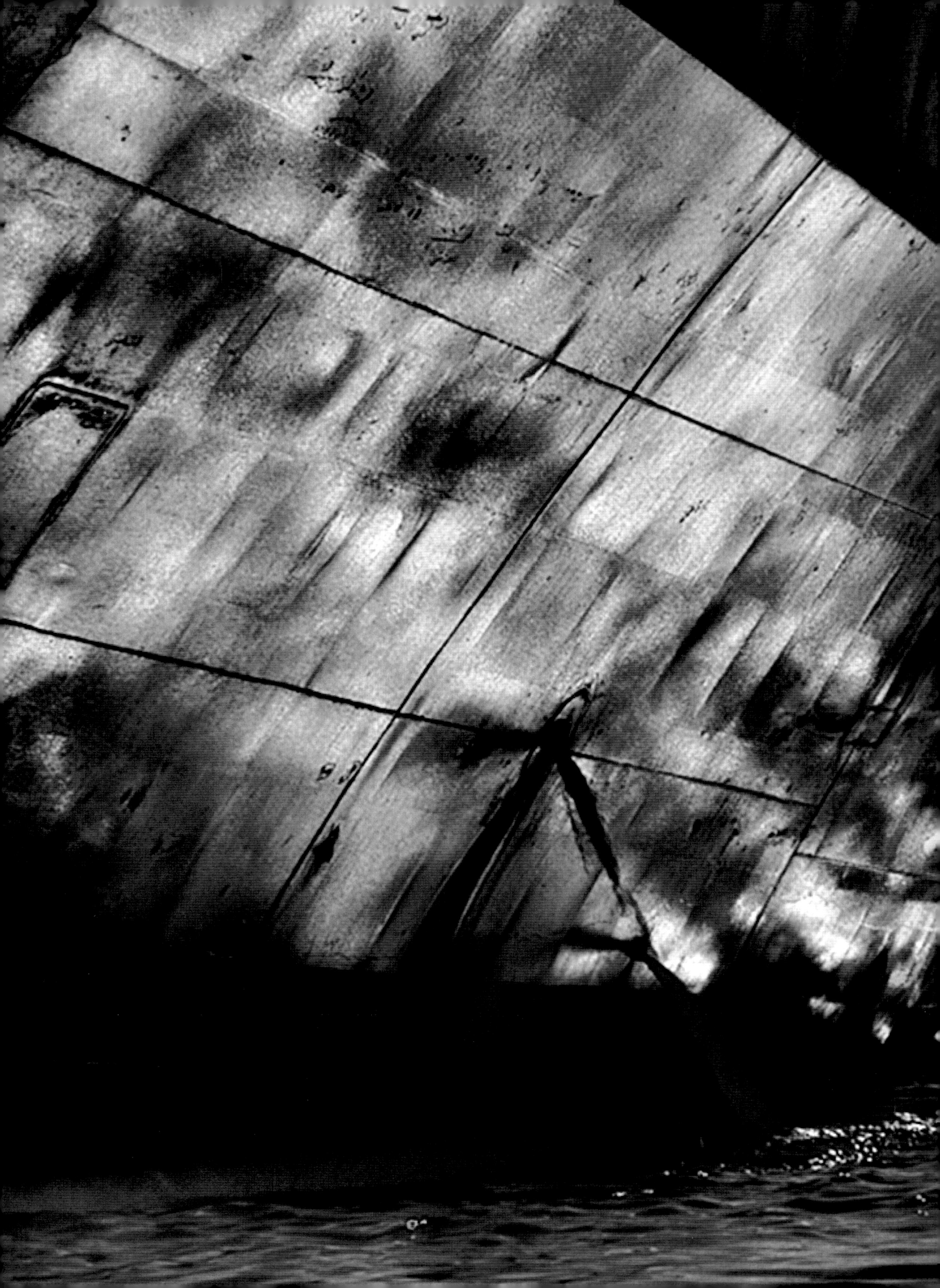

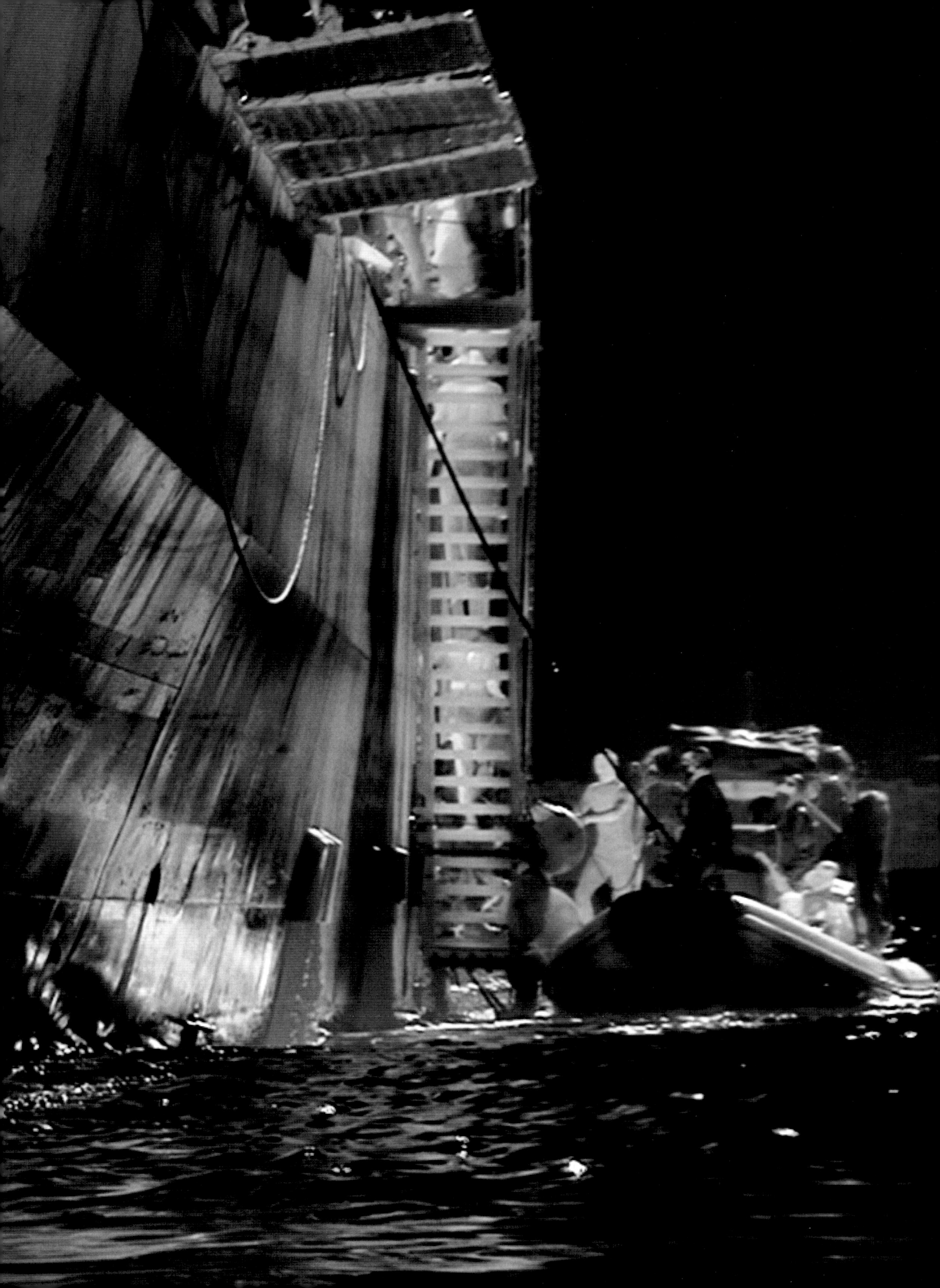

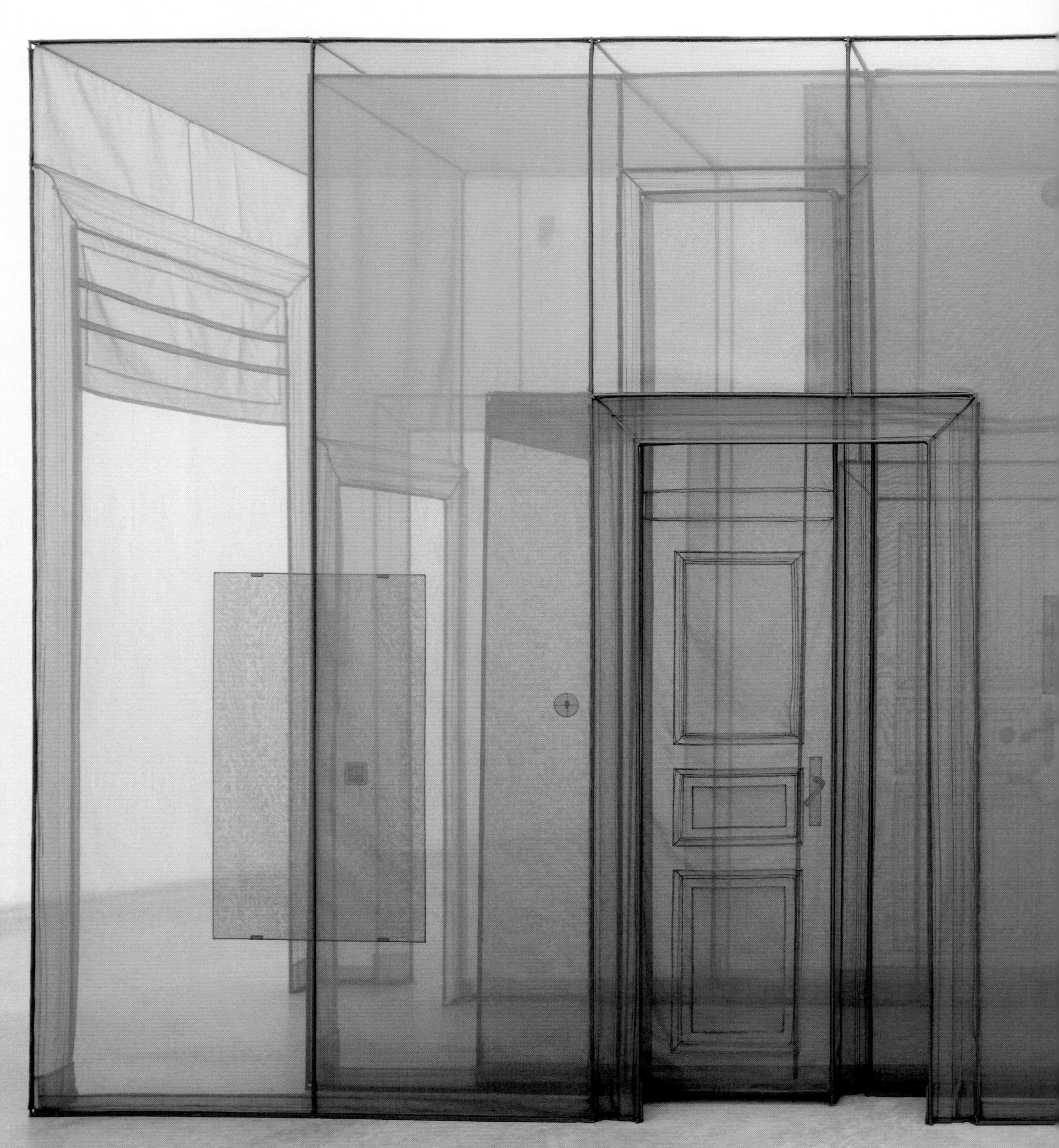

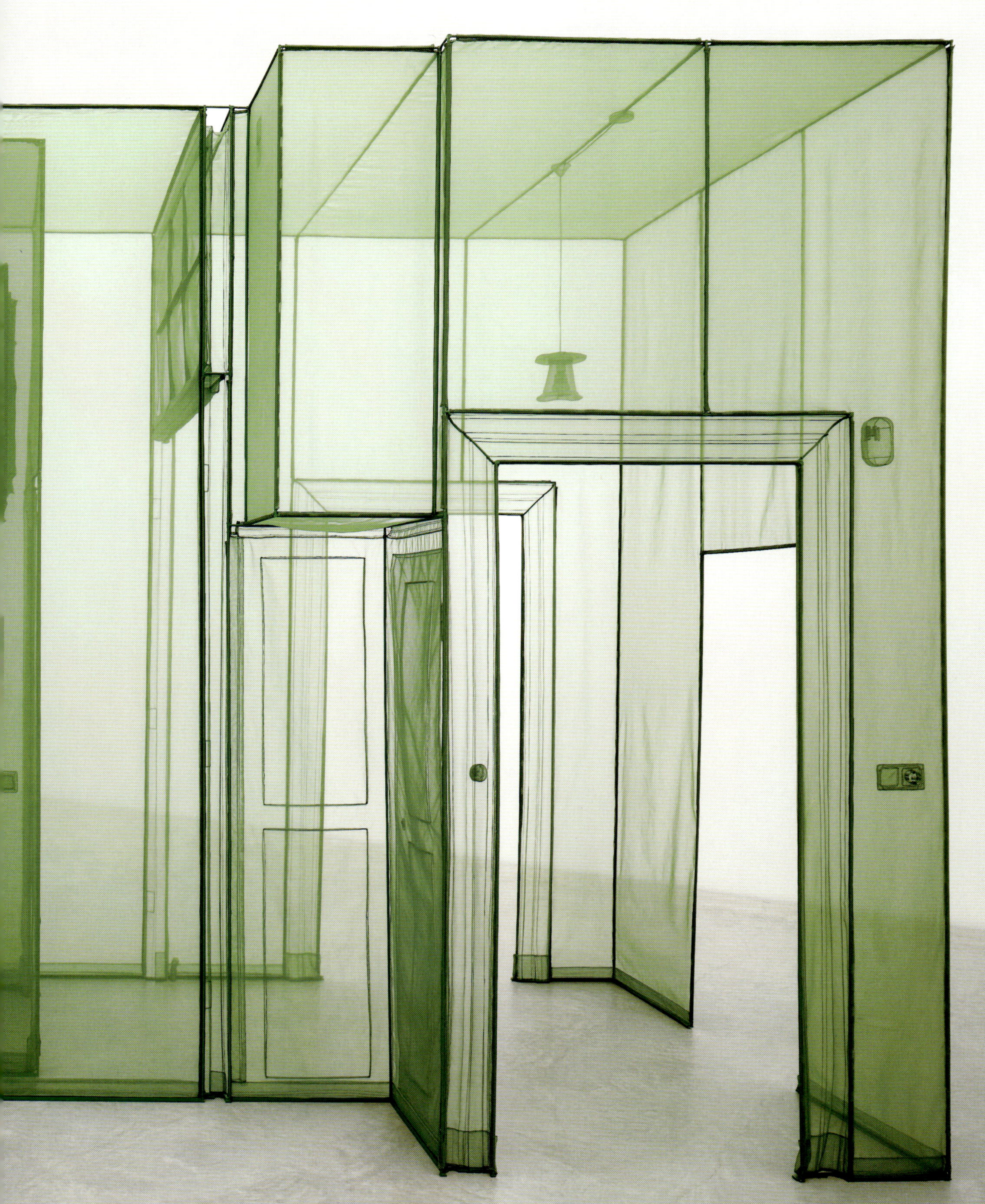

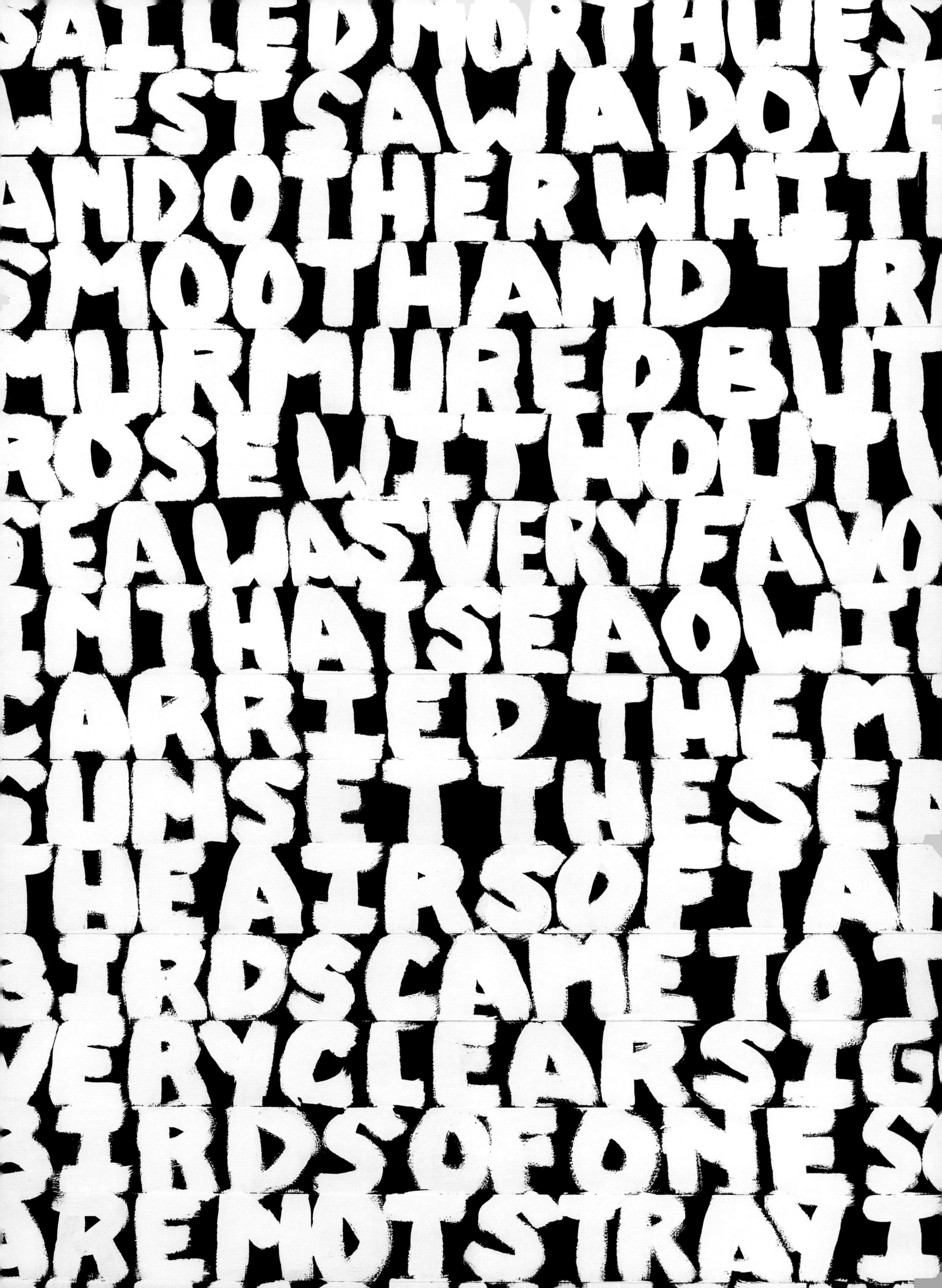
SAILED NORTHWES
WEST SAW A DOV
AND OTHER WHIT
MOOTH AND TR
MURMURED BUT
ROSE WITHOUT
EA WAS VERY FAVO
NTHAT SEA OWI
ARRIED THE M
UNSET THE SE
HE AIRS OF TA
BIRDS CAME TO T
VERY CLEAR SIG
BIRDS OF ONE S
ARE NOT STRAYI

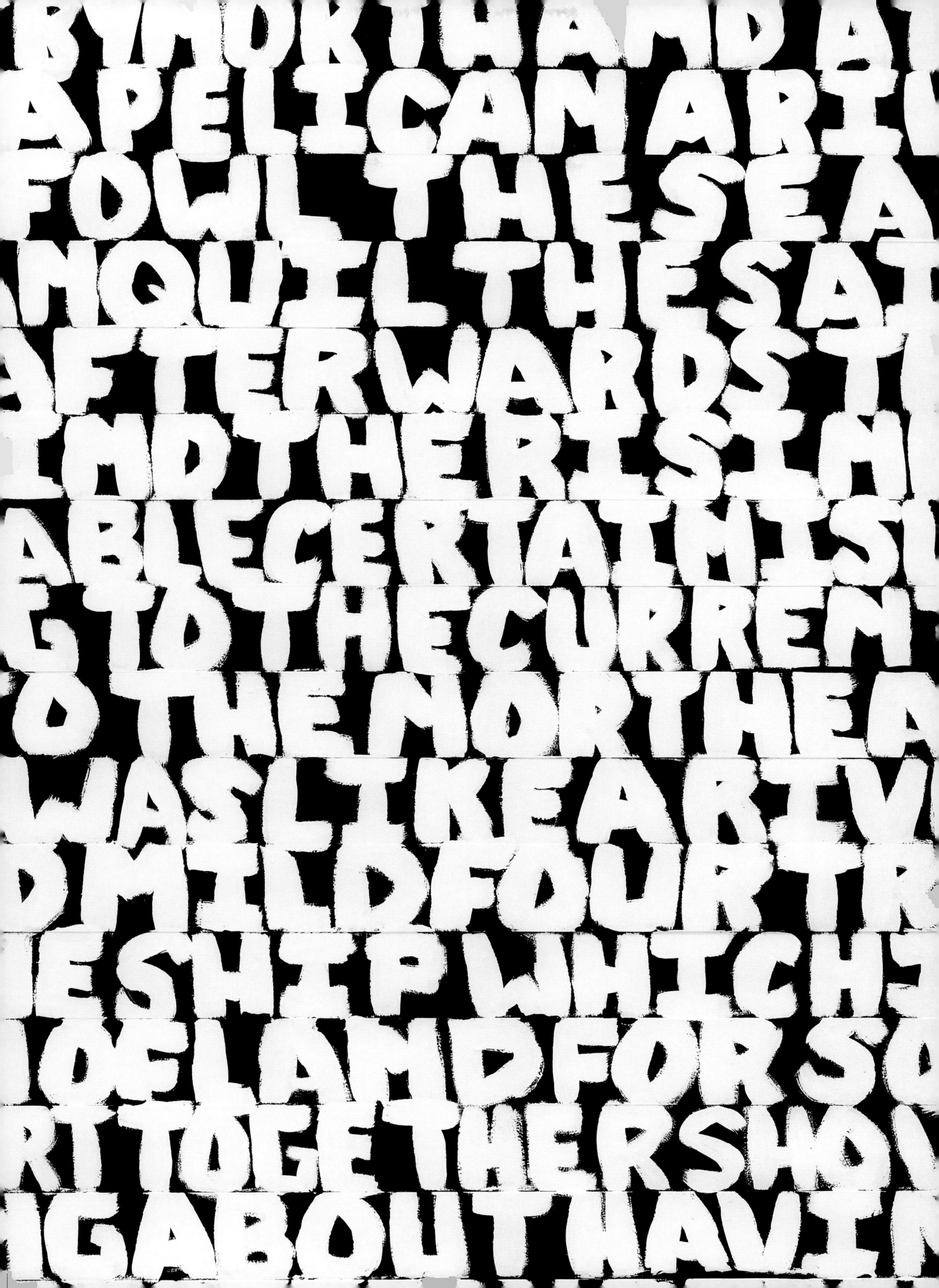
BYNOKTHANDA
APELICANARIV
FOWLTHESEA
NQUILTHESAT
AFTERWARDSTH
INDTHERISIN
ABLECERTAINISL
GTOTHECURRENT
OTHENORTHEA
WASLIKEARIV
DMILDFOURTR
ESHIPWHICHT
OFLANDFORSO
RTTOGETHERSHO
IGABOUTHAVIN

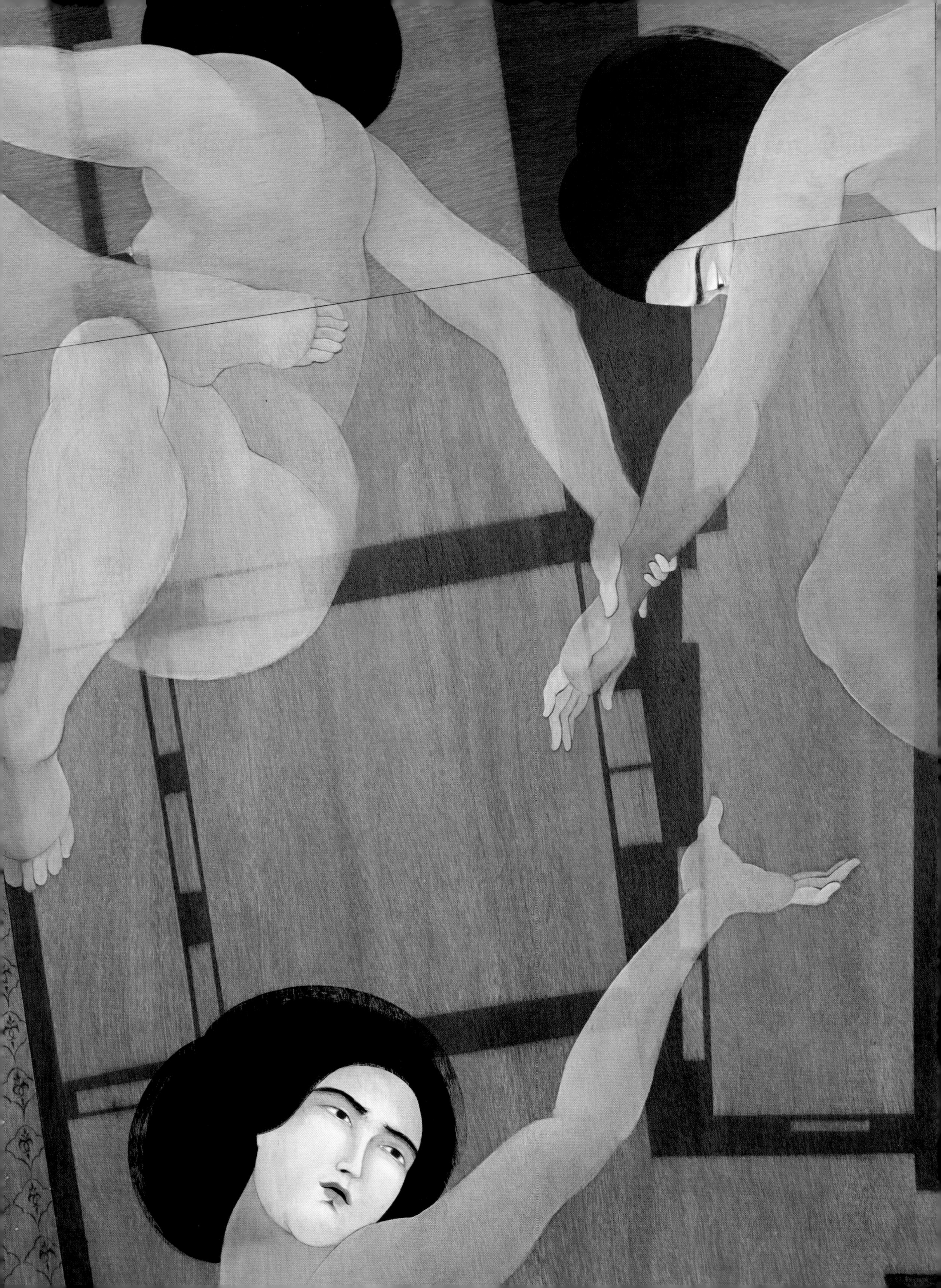

When Home Won't Let You Stay

Migration through Contemporary Art

Edited by
Ruth Erickson and Eva Respini

The Institute of Contemporary Art/Boston
in association with
Yale University Press, New Haven and London

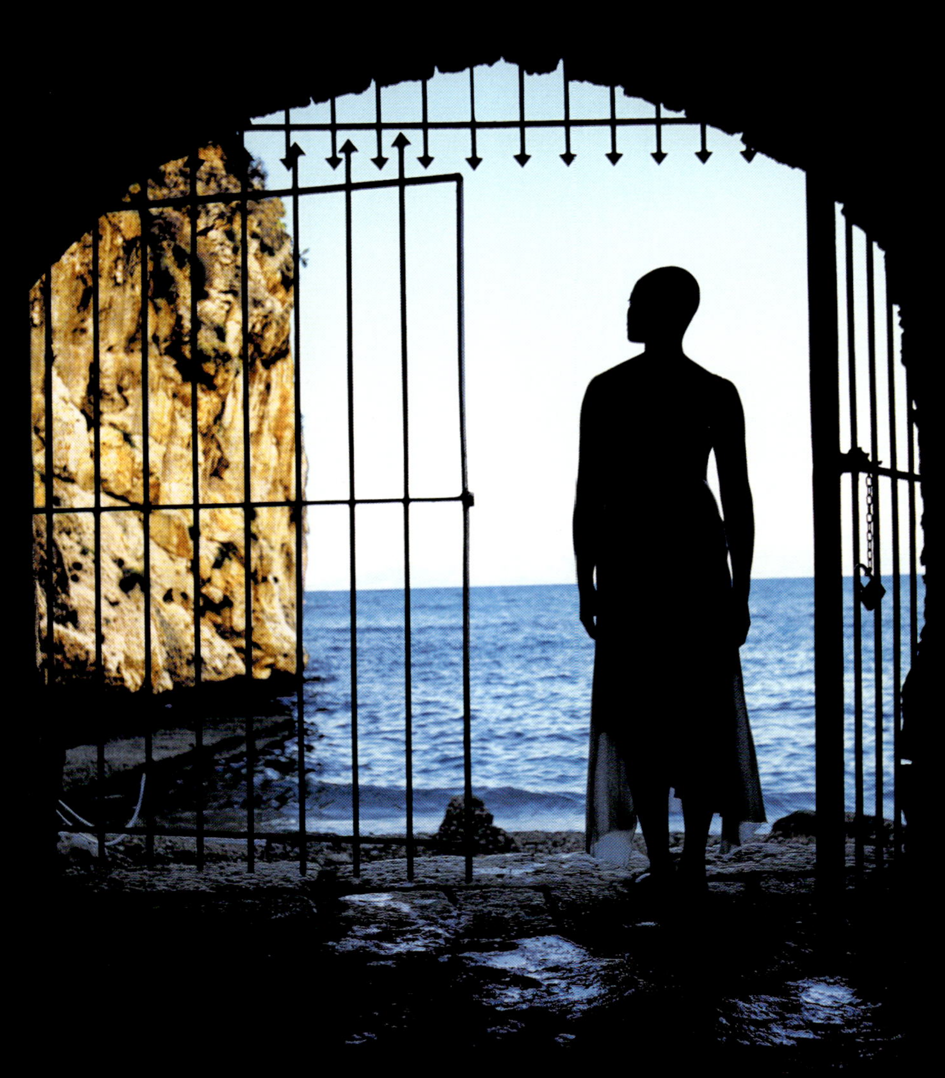

We dedicate this book to Okwui Enwezor (1963–2019), whose incisive and committed work vastly enlarged the horizons of art, scholarship, and museums, and without whom this project is unimaginable.

Conversations

Essays

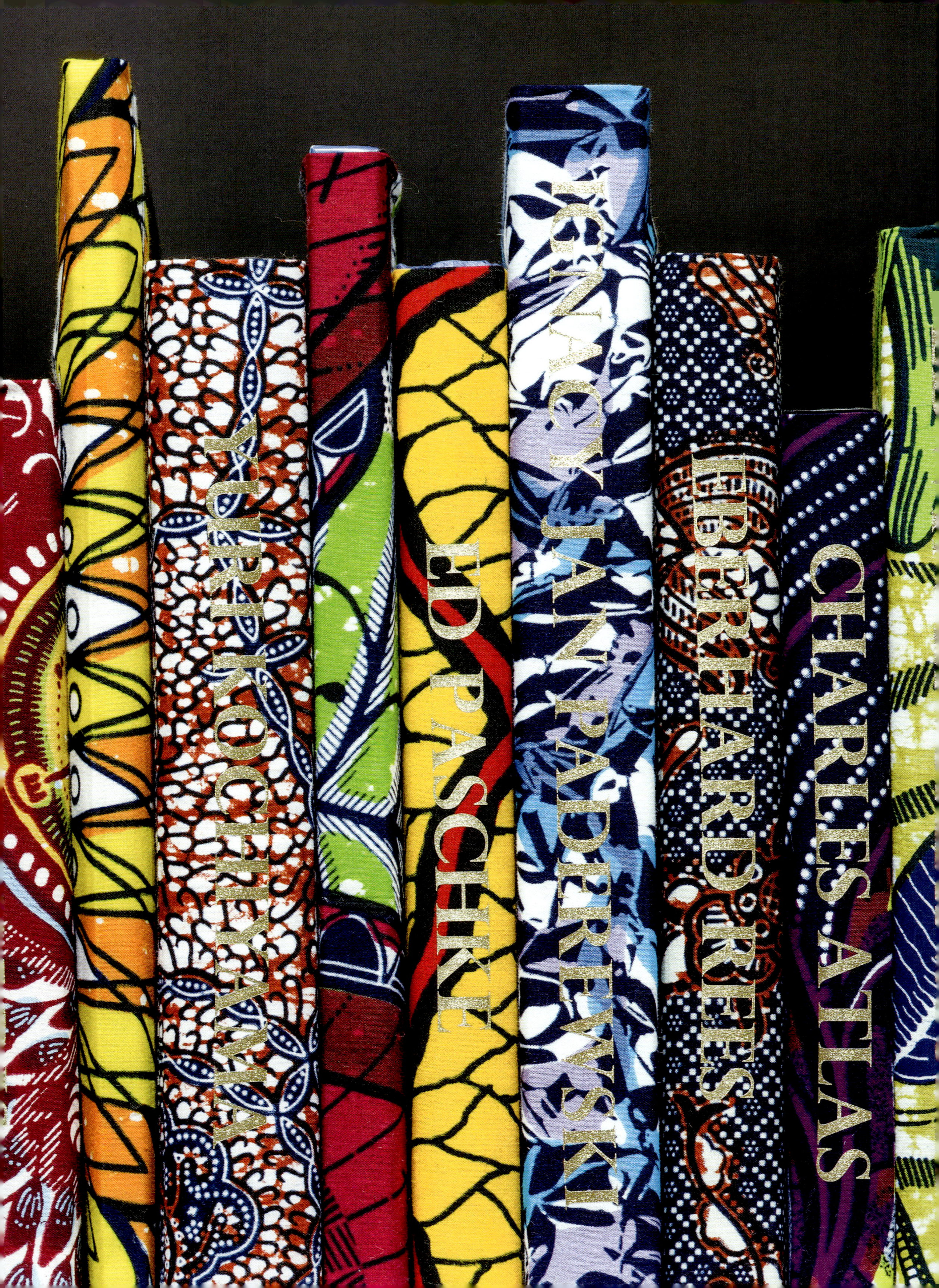
YURI KOCHIYAMA
ED PASCHKE
IGNACY JAN PADEREWSKI
EBERHARD REES
CHARLES ATLAS

Director's Foreword

Throughout history, people have left their homes for many reasons—to flee war, persecution, or environmental disaster, or to seek economic survival and opportunity. In the United States, migration has been a defining experience since before the nation's founding. In the last century alone, the Great Migration affected the lives of over seven million African Americans who moved from the South to the North for economic, social, and political reasons, initiating a complex set of attachments and experiences that continues today.

We are currently witness to the highest levels of global movement on record. The United Nations High Commissioner for Refugees estimates the number of people now forcibly displaced worldwide—internally displaced people, refugees, and asylum-seekers—at 68.5 million. *When Home Won't Let You Stay: Migration through Contemporary Art* considers a group of contemporary artists who have responded to the migration, immigration, and displacement of peoples, and how these artists grapple with upended ideas of home, histories, borders, and belonging.

When Home Won't Let You Stay borrows its title from a poem by Warsan Shire, a Somali-British poet who gives voice to the experiences of refugees. The exhibition shares with Shire's poem the imperative to create a public platform for the jarring realities and experiences of refugees and immigrants, broadly understood. Through artworks made since 2000 by artists from more than a dozen countries, this exhibition and publication examine how the forces of migration and displacement are radically destabilizing the basic structures of belonging, a concept foundational to selfhood.

When Home Won't Let You Stay will travel to the Minneapolis Institute of Art and the Cantor Arts Center at Stanford University. It is accompanied by this richly illustrated scholarly publication, edited by Ruth Erickson, Mannion Family Curator, and Eva Respini, Barbara Lee Chief Curator, here at the ICA. I extend my thanks to Eva, Ruth, Assistant Curator Ellen Tani, and their teams for their magnificent efforts, and to Kaywin Feldman, former Director of the Minneapolis Institute of Art, and Susan Dackerman, John and Jill Freidenrich Director of the Cantor Arts Center at Stanford University, for their partnership. This catalogue includes essays by Aruna D'Souza, Okwui Enwezor, Thomas Keenan, Uday Singh Mehta, and Peggy Levitt, and conversations with artists Hayv Kahraman and Reena Saini Kallat; Guillermo Galindo and cultural historian Josh Kun; and Aliza Nisenbaum and Anthony Romero. We appreciate their time and generosity. Integral to the project is the impressive cohort of advisors assembled by Ruth and Eva, who shared expertise and ideas that greatly helped to shape the exhibition, publication, and related programs. I am grateful to Pedro H. Alonzo, Celina Barrios-Millner, Matt Cameron, Monica Garza, Cheryl Hamilton, Carol León, Noora Anwar Lori, Timothy Patrick McCarthy, Anthony Romero, Adam Strom, and Mehtap Yağcı for their time as advisors. A very special thanks goes to the individual and institutional lenders for sharing their works for this exhibition and allowing us to reproduce them for this publication.

A project of this ambition and scale requires a vast array of artistic, intellectual, organizational, and financial resources. We are grateful to Paul and Catherine Buttenwieser, Steve Corkin and Dan Maddalena, Alan and Vivien Hassenfeld, Kristen and Kent Lucken, the Poss Family Foundation, and Mark and Marie Schwartz, and to the ICA Board of Trustees and Advisory Board, for their generosity and support. It has long been part of ICA's ethos to consider the role of the arts in society and as a connector to civic life. I am honored and grateful to each of the artists whose combined knowledge, experiences, and perspectives have allowed us to explore migration through the lens of art in *When Home Won't Let You Stay*. In every moment, we depend on the work of visionary artists to help us see our changing cultural landscape more clearly and to imagine a more just future.

Jill Medvedow
Ellen Matilda Poss Director
ICA/Boston

Curators' Introduction

Ruth Erickson and Eva Respini

What do we mean when we speak about migration? Moreover, what does the word mean today, in our politically divisive and uncertain time? This exhibition is based on the understanding that migration—the movement of people and cultures—is the default, rather than the exception. Migration is an utterly common aspect of life in the twenty-first century, when millions of people are moving for myriad reasons, from fleeing war and religious persecution to seeking better educational or financial horizons. Migration is not new—people have always migrated—but its character changed dramatically with European colonialism, the displacement of indigenous populations, and the Atlantic slave trade, and reached new heights in the nineteenth and twentieth centuries through the ease of travel and the displacement caused by the World Wars. With every change in how and why people move, notions of borders, nationhood, and citizenship also shift and shape contemporary debates.[1] Today, we live in the era of the highest-ever rate of displacement. The United Nations estimates that one out of every seven people in the world is an international or internal migrant.[2] The development of efficient transportation and new communication technologies has made movement and travel easier and faster. At the same time, new technologies have also emerged to track, regulate, and criminalize the movement of people across borders. Migration and the displacement of people have given rise to new areas of inquiry and study, such as diaspora and postcolonial studies. These fields have shed light on the slippery and increasingly inadequate nature of our common language around experiences of migration, with terms such as "exile," "diaspora," "migrant," "immigrant," "refugee," "asylum," "citizen," "nomad," "border," "belonging," and "home" acquiring new meanings in the short years since the turn of this new century.[3]

The imaginations and critical engagements of artists, art historians, writers, critics, and curators have been sparked by the issue of migration. The art world itself can be understood as both a product of an increasingly peripatetic and globalized world and a complicit agent of globalization, and a number of large international platforms for contemporary art, including documenta, the Venice Biennale, and Manifesta, have featured work exploring issues around migration.[4] Yet never have the complicating factors of national, regional, and cultural identities been so fraught with explosive discussions. "Migration" is one of the most divisive political debates today, and continues to shape many aspects of public rhetoric, opinion, and policy that touch individual lives in very real ways.

While researching this exhibition and book over the last two years, we have contended with a daily barrage of headlines, social-media posts, and news about migration—a topic thrust to the center of U.S. politics by the political agenda of Donald Trump. From the U.S. president's tweets about "banning Muslims" or building walls to news stories detailing Immigration and Customs Enforcement (ICE) arrests, the separation of families, and the "migrant caravan," we grappled with how to calibrate our curatorial project with these current events.[5] We sought the advice of scholars, writers, and others studying the cultural impact of migration, and of those working directly with immigrants, refugees, and asylum seekers.[6] On one of these

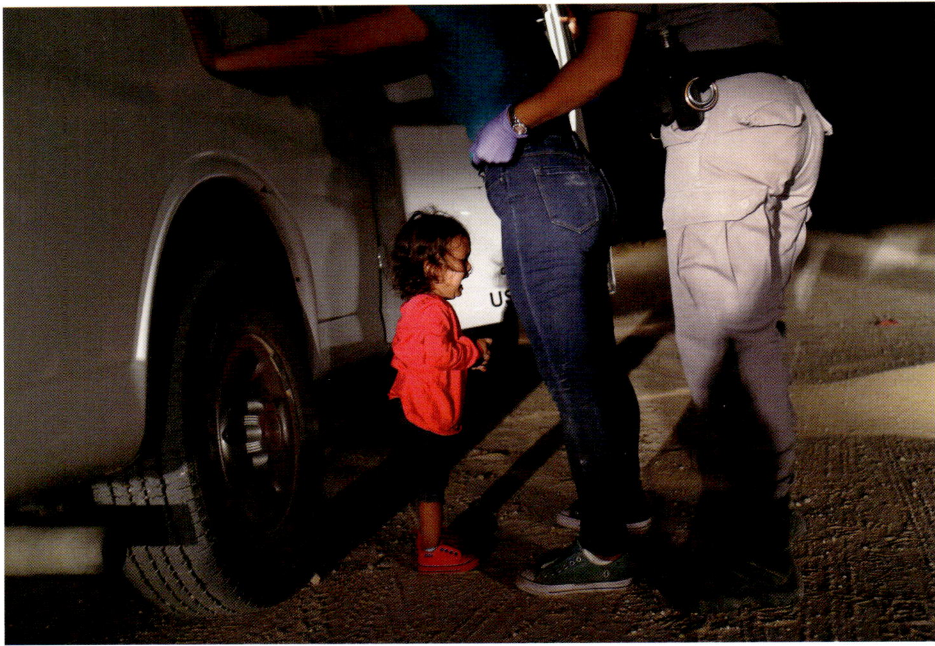

Fig. 1. A two-year-old from Honduras, Yanela Sanchez, cries as her mother, Sandra Sanchez, is searched and detained near the U.S.-Mexico border on June 12, 2018, in McAllen, Texas. John Moore/Getty Images News/Getty Images

visits, after politely listening to our project synopsis, a well-regarded scholar asked bluntly: *What are your stakes?* Indeed, the topic of migration is political, politicized, and has been addressed in many platforms, exhibitions, and books.[7] The questions we posed while working on this project evolved over time and in response to our times. They include: What role does art play in today's evolving understanding of migration? What can this project add to the current discourse? What does contemporary art offer that other forms of information and illustration cannot? Who does this project serve? What is the role of art institutions in confronting immigration issues? How does our work as curators intersect with our own roles as citizen and alien, neighbor and mother?

So, what *are* our stakes? At the center of this exhibition is a belief in the primacy of the artist's role in reflecting on social and political changes today. Understanding that migration is not one thing or one story, we maintain that artistic representations of migration and migrant identities can offer deep and unique insights that compete with the many (mis)understandings of migrants, immigrants, and refugees. We have illustrated this essay with diagrams and news photos—the kinds of images that usually accompany stories about migration, recent and iconic photographs of suffering and violence seared in our minds from the news cycle. The photograph of two-year-old Yanela Sanchez crying as her mother is searched became a rally cry against Trump's family-separation policy in the summer of 2018, winning the photographer John Moore a Pulitzer [fig. 1]. Dangerously overfilled boats crossing the Mediterranean Sea came to represent the so-called "European migrant crisis" around 2015 [fig. 3]. And the most recent image we share here, of Border Patrol agents firing tear gas at migrants near the U.S.-Mexico border at Tijuana, highlighted the intensified militarization of the southern border [fig. 4]. While these images may be front of mind when we talk about migration, you will not find these kinds of images in the exhibition. Rather, we have selected artworks that lead us to more nuanced understandings of the experiences of migration and narratives of belonging. Art's role is to probe the viewer. It can catalyze action and foster contemplation and empathy. It can provide opportunities for publics to reconsider their own positions, perspectives, and experiences. Perhaps, as some artists in this exhibition believe, art and institutions should do more than create representations, platforms, and experiences; they should reallocate resources, shift behavior, be activist, be useful. These calls demand that we think deeply about our institution's civic responsibility in both the short term and the long. With this exhibition, we intend to both harness the power of symbolism in art and use our positions and resources to engage new and underserved communities.

The exhibition's title, *When Home Won't Let You Stay*, is drawn from a line in a poem by Warsan Shire, a Somali-British poet and activist inspired by the stories of refugees and immigrants. (The poem appears on page 29 of this volume). Shire's poem "Home" expresses the vast, visceral, and often violent experiences of migrants, revealing displacement and exile to be both deeply complex and utterly common. The exhibition shares with the poem a desire to bring forward a variety of experiences around migration. Through works made since 2000 by twenty artists from throughout the globe—from countries such as Colombia, Cuba, India, Iraq, Ireland, Mexico, Morocco, Nigeria, Palestine, South Korea, the United States, and the United Kingdom—this exhibition reveals how the forces of migration touch us all. With *When Home Won't Let You Stay*, we hope to unseat expectations of place in migration narratives by exploring ideas of home, sites of transit such as the sea, provisional structures such as borders and refugee camps, and narratives of displacement. The exhibition is not a survey. In eschewing the comprehensive in favor of the specific, it acknowledges the transient and ever-changing times in which we live, knowing that while today's crises will be subsumed by others in the next mass-media cycle, it is crucial to pause and reflect on the events shaping daily life. The artists included in the exhibition, some of whom are immigrants, refugees, or migrants, challenge established ideas of what it means to leave home, and to search and make home in other ways. Their work plays a profound role in understanding this urgent issue and, we hope, in converting interest into investment.

This book seeks to amplify the ideas and experiences evoked by the artworks exhibited. Essays by scholars from a variety of disciplines reflect on migration through distinctive lenses, making arguments centered not on those artworks but on specific practices, experiences, and major sociopolitical shifts both past and present. Thomas Keenan focuses on the visual culture of maps and mapmaking in the context of migration, drawing attention to their many uses by state agencies, migration-rights activists, and migrants. One of the things we learn from these maps is just how circuitous and truncated migrant journeys tend to be. Aruna D'Souza highlights the frequent yet overlooked experience of waiting—and its quiet violence—as migrants and others await the privilege, the paperwork, or the means to move. From their distinctive fields, Okwui Enwezor and Uday Singh Mehta consider the impact of migration on restructuring national and social identities. Peggy Levitt explores the definitions over time and space of such key terms as "border," "nation," and "assimilation." These essays together function as both reader and resource guide, and create a larger context in which to consider the artworks and the exhibition. Shorter texts focused on the artworks provide a close reading of the works, as well as an understanding of each artist's practice and biography. Finally, the conversations between artists included throughout this volume underscore the primacy of the artist's voice to this project. Some artists have been in dialogue for years, while others met for the first time through Skype sessions hosted by the ICA. Together, these essays speak to the layers and nuances at the center of art and migration today.

On the Harbor

The ICA is located in Boston's Seaport neighborhood and its galleries are housed in a dramatic cantilever that hovers over the city's harbor. Visitors to the ICA take in art alongside sweeping views of the busy port, where tankers come and go, and sightings of airplanes arriving and departing from the adjacent Logan International Airport are commonplace. The movement of people and goods is embedded in the very fabric of the ICA's site and building, part of every visitor's experience of the museum.

In the summer of 2018, the ICA opened the Watershed, a seasonal exhibition space located in the Boston Harbor Shipyard & Marina in East Boston, directly across the harbor from the museum [fig. 2]. The ICA's two sites are connected by a short boat ride, so that movement across the water is now an integral part of museum visitors' experience. East Boston is one of Boston's most geographically isolated communities, and is the neighborhood, historically and contemporaneously, of many of Boston's immigrants. In the twentieth century, East Boston was home to primarily

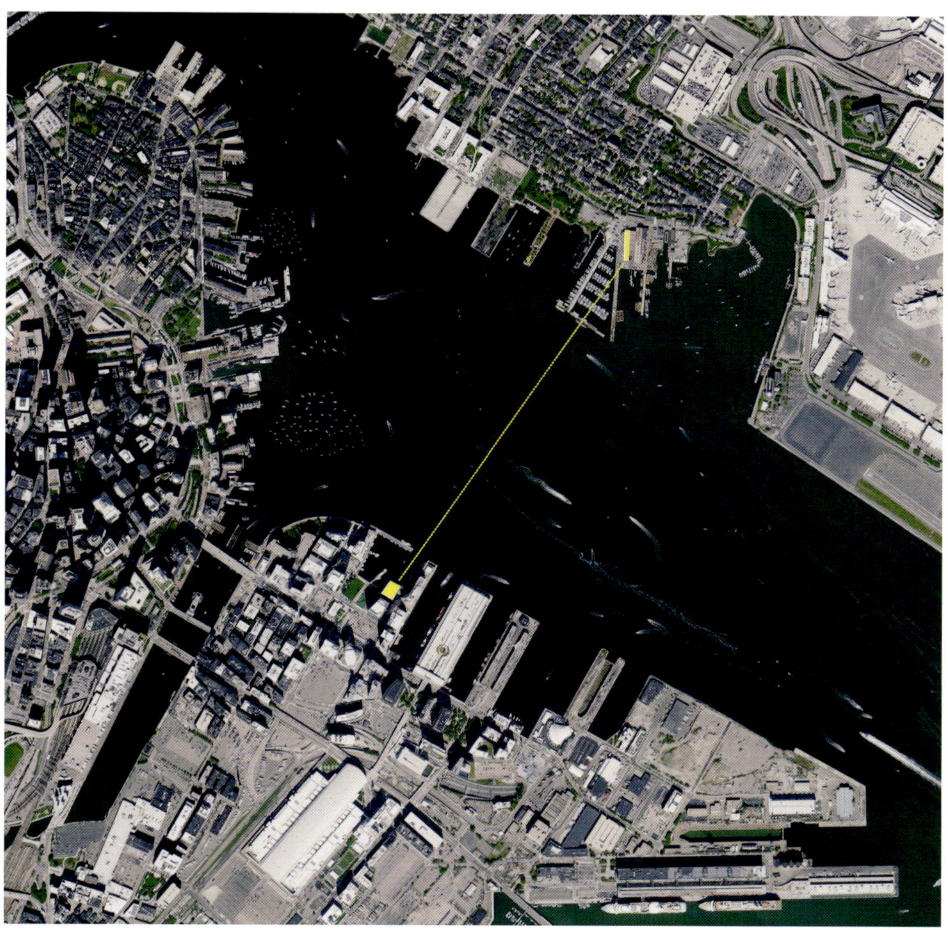

Fig. 2. Apple Maps view of the ICA/Boston and ICA Watershed locations on Boston Harbor, altered to indicate spatial relationships, 2018

Italian and Irish families; its immigrants today hail mostly from Central and South America, as well as from Southeast Asia. Over 50 percent of East Boston households speak Spanish as their primary language.[9] The opening of the Watershed led us to think deeply about the ICA's unique perch on both sides of Boston Harbor.

Museums, of course, are fraught spaces and have been outcomes and expressions of colonialism and white privilege. The territory on which the ICA itself sits has a long history of displacements, land claims, and construction. Before its Euro-American settlement, what we now call Massachusetts was home to several indigenous tribes, including the Mahican, the Massachusett, the Nipmuc, and the Wampanoag.[10] Present-day Boston was at the time comprised of numerous islands and inlets on which native groups supported themselves. As colonial settlements and the resulting violence increased, indigenous peoples were killed by disease, driven out, or forcibly removed, with many interned on remote islands around the Massachusetts Bay. Furthermore, in the colonial period, Boston was a New England center for the Atlantic slave trade, supporting the movement of enslaved people from Africa and the West Indies to the colonies. Over time, and through these intersecting industries, European settlers and colonizers would artificially fill in the many islands and inlets of

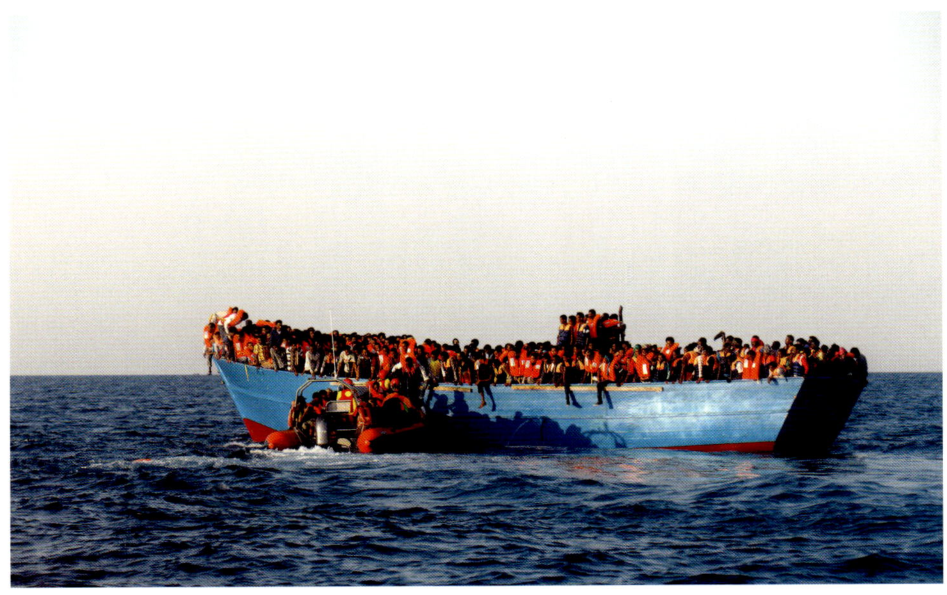

Fig. 3. A rescue boat from the Spanish NGO Proactiva approaches an overcrowded wooden vessel carrying migrants from Eritrea in the Mediterranean off the Libyan coast, August 29, 2016. Giorgos Moutafis/Reuters Pictures

Massachusetts Bay, forming the land on which the city, and the ICA, now stand.[11] This work of building the city—in Boston's case, literally the ground it stands on—devastated and displaced the many surviving native communities, spurring the ongoing political and legal debates on native land-rights claims and recognition in the United States today.

The ICA's site points to this long and complex history of movement from and to Boston, one of the United States' oldest cities. Home to waves of immigrants hailing from Ireland, Italy, China, and Russia, as well as liberated African Americans from the American South, the city is now entering a new era of immigration patterns and policies that will surely shape it for generations to come.[12] *When Home Won't Let You Stay* responds to this history and the present moment, and also to how migration can be read through our unique site. ICA's location on the Boston Harbor played a pivotal role in the conceptualization of this exhibition, which is organized around sites of transit. Bodies of water, crossings, borders, refugee camps, and the shifting idea of home—all of these sites, in both their real and their imagined characteristics, are explored through this exhibition and connected to the ICA's location and local history. By considering place and movement together, *When Home Won't Let You Stay* connects the local with larger global issues shaping the nation and world today.

The Sea

The sea and bodies of water figure powerfully in many narratives and images of migration. It is the fluid element between borders and landmasses, promising freedom and threatening death. It is an international zone, where for many years being stranded meant that you would be saved regardless of the nationality of the vessel discovering you. Difficult to navigate, seas and rivers hold the potential to carry your body faster than your legs ever could, to throw pursuing dogs off your scent, and yet to take your life in one gulp.

The sea is one of the most resonant and recurring sites in the exhibition and museum. It is pictured in Kadar Attia's *La Mer Morte* (The Dead Sea) (2015) [pp. 96–97], a sprawling sculpture, comprised of blue articles of clothing, that evokes the many migrant and refugee lives lost at sea. The sea serves as a leitmotif in Isaac Julien's symphonic three-channel video *Western Union: small boats* (2007) [pp. 100–05], filmed on Italy's southernmost island, Lampedusa. The Mediterranean is rarely pictured but ever present in Yto Barrada's series A Life Full of Holes: The Strait Project (1998–2003) [pp. 90–93], which features poetic images of daily life in Tangier, the gateway to the Strait of Gibraltar. Although the Atlantic Ocean is not pictured, it looms large in Xaviera Simmons's color photograph reflecting on the vestiges of the Middle Passage and the Great Migration in the United States [p. 87], and in her text painting of quotations from Christopher Columbus's journals [pp. 84–85]. The various routes of the movement of people and goods across oceans are mapped via twisted and barbed wires in Reena Kallat's *Woven Chronicle* (2011–16) [pp. 34–37]. These artworks attest to how seas, oceans, and the movement across them are sources of some of the most searing images of migration and endure as symbols inexorably linked to it.

Home

Questions of "home" start many conversations with people who have migrated: "Where do you come from?" or "Where do you live?" Such exchanges put forward an idea of home as singular, fixed, familiar, and a pure expression of our identity. We emerge from home and belong to it, but artists and writers have long conveyed other notions of it. The critic Sara Ahmed has argued against "a model of home as familiarity," which she suggests "projects strangeness beyond the walls of the home." Indeed, she encourages us to recognize the "strangeness and movement within the home itself."[13] Many of the artists in *When Home Won't Let You Stay* invite us to rethink how we understand home, allowing memory, movement, and imagination to be integral acts and processes linked to the idea of home and the sense of belonging.

Do Ho Suh's exacting replicas, in colorful fabric, of the dwellings where he has lived in Seoul, Berlin, New York, and other cities [pp. 72–77] highlight journey, memory, and mobility as constituent parts of home. The psychic qualities of home appear in Hayv Kahraman's large-scale oil painting *Bab el Sheikh* (2013) [pp. 62–63]. Kahraman, who became a refugee from Iraq at the age of ten, describes the "inaccessibility in my own life in relation to a place that I used to call home…a place that I'm supposed to be completely a part of but that at this point in my life I don't understand."[14] Camilo Ontiveros's sculpture *Temporary Storage: The Belongings of Juan Manuel Montes* (2017) [pp. 45–47] gathers together the entire contents of Montes's bedroom after he was deported from the United States, offering an image of home in transit.

Personal narratives of migrants reveal the ways individuals move between homes, forming attachments and reinventing their identities along the way. Whether Rineke Dijkstra's photographs of Bosnian refugee Almerisa, taken over decades [pp. 66–69], or Carlos Motta's video portraits of LGBTQI+ refugees [pp. 130–35], these artworks offer potent stories of displacement and regrounding. Aliza Nisenbaum's portraits of Marissa and her parents depict quotidian scenes of the family in their apartment in New York, the parents' journey from Mexico decades earlier a distant event [pp. 138–41]. These artists reveal how identity and experiences of belonging (and alienation) evolve as individuals move between sites and between homes. No single place is pure; rather, each one possesses a memory of what came before, a reaction to the present, and a vision of what the future holds.

Temporary Sites

Many provisional or temporary sites directly shape the contours of migration: borders, refugee camps, detention centers, and other infrastructure meant to control movement. These are actual places that can be entered or traversed, but they are also potent symbols and fictions that masquerade as real. Indeed, the delineation of a border on a map, and its translation to the land, depends entirely on one's belief in the entity possessing the territory and the power to represent it.[15] Refugee camps and centers are often constructed as temporary settlements for people forced to flee, but some have become extensive permanent cities, housing hundreds of thousands of people for decades.[16] Like the sea and the home, borders and camps are as real and material as they are symbolic and imagined. The power that they wield hinges entirely on the mobility and freedom afforded—or not—by one's status.

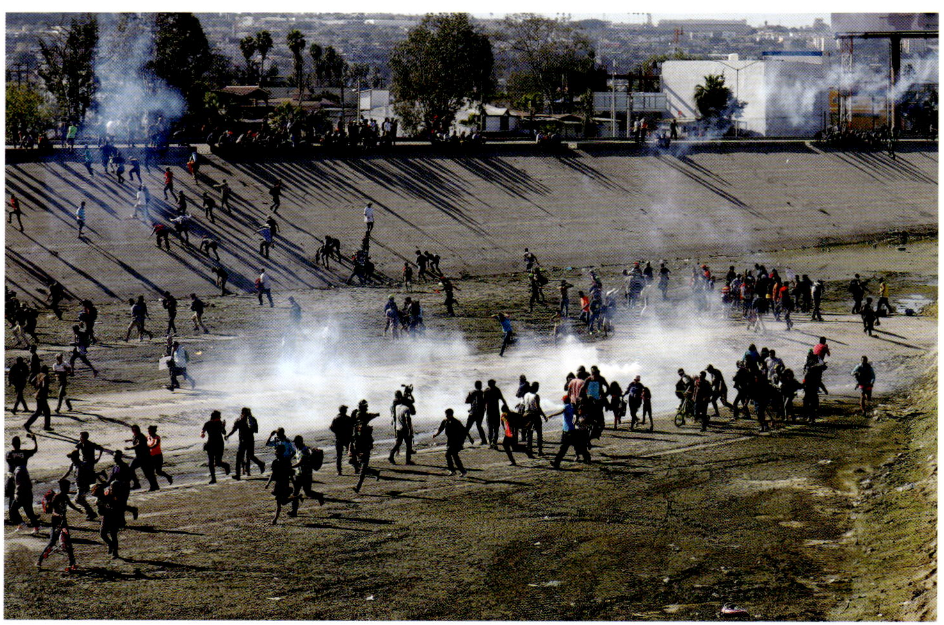

Fig. 4. Migrants in Tijuana, Mexico, run from tear gas fired at them by the U.S. Border Patrol near the border fence between Mexico and the United States. November 25, 2018. Hannah McKay/Reuters Pictures

The U.S.-Mexico border is the focus of Guillermo Galindo and Richard Misrach's multiyear collaboration Border Cantos (2004–16) [pp. 118–23, 126–27]. They bring together images and artifacts gathered at the border, capturing its quality as a no-man's-land, inhospitable territory, and accordingly the distress, and also the determination and resourcefulness, that fuel people's journeys through these borderlands. Richard Mosse's video work *Incoming* (2014–17) [pp. 54–59] documents masses of people moving along some of the busiest global migration routes and inhabiting crowded refugee camps. Michelle Angela Ortiz draws attention to borders within the nation. As part of her *Familias Separadas* project, she has chalked the words of a detained immigrant named Ana ("WE ARE HUMAN BEINGS, RISKING OUR LIVES, FOR OUR FAMILIES AND OUR FUTURE") in front of a U.S. Immigration and Customs Enforcement (ICE) building in Philadelphia, marking its threshold [pp. 152–53]. Tania Bruguera reimages the symbol of the flag as something other than an expression of nationalism and related claims of territory and borders. She joins together the continents to underscore the dignity shared by all humans regardless of nationality or citizenship [pp.114–15].

Conclusion

By the time you read this essay, some of the issues and events referenced in this book will be out of date. However, as evidenced by Okwui Enwezor's timely revisit of his 2005 text "Tebbit's Ghost," included in this volume [pp. 172], countless issues around migration and displacement are recurring, or perhaps never went away. We offer *When Home Won't Let You Stay* as a platform to think about, as Enwezor remarks in his interview here, "the relationship between roots and routes—the convergence of these two things, of people who are rooted but also people who are uprooted, who are en route, who are going somewhere, and whether that somewhere represents a place of hospitality."[17]

We began this project by thinking about the ICA and its site, and we would like to conclude by returning to this museum as it is reimagined through two artworks. The exhibition at the ICA ends with Yinka Shonibare CBE's *American Library* (2018) [pp. 156–59], a room filled floor to ceiling with over 6,000 books bound in Dutch wax cloth and imprinted in gold with the names of individuals who have made a mark on American culture. Many of these names are familiar and all of them have some connection to immigration: they are first- or second-generation immigrants, or descendants of those brought to America by force through slavery. Some are advocates of immigration rights and others oppose them. Shonibare's work also invites visitors to learn more about the individuals named; and they can enter their own immigration stories through a Web interface, establishing the library as an ever expanding, always unfinished archive. The library offers a representation of the United States that foregrounds migration, whether across oceans or within the country, and reveals the project of imagining the nation to be never finished. Like Shonibare's library, the ICA serves as a site of contemporary art and also as a place where the act of representation can be interrogated, corrected, and made more inclusive.

Early on, we recognized that we would also have to reach beyond the museum's walls if we wanted this exhibition to reach the audiences and issues we hope it will. Extending from the ICA's ongoing outreach to schools and surrounding communities, we invited Boston-based artist and educator Anthony Romero to develop a project that he has titled *...first in thought, then in action* [p. 144]. From the spring of 2019 through the run of the exhibition at the ICA in January 2020, Romero will organize a series of community gatherings and performance events at the ICA, the Watershed, and locations in East Boston, offering participants and audiences the opportunity to think through the many impacts of immigration law and policy.[18] The project begins with a series of community listening events and meals with East Boston residents, whose expressed needs and interests will inform a number of legal-empowerment workshops developed by Northeastern University's innovative NuLawLab. It continues with gatherings and performances at the ICA for which Romero will adapt Franz Kafka's novel *The Trial* (1914–15), a surreal tale of judicial bewilderment, confusion, and criminalization, to reflect on the particularities of migrating to and within the United States and navigating its immigration and judicial system. *...first in thought, then in action* brings many of the ideas, images, questions, and provocations posed in the galleries beyond the museum, harnessing the exhibition as a means to invest more deeply in immigrant communities, or, in Romero's formulation, "to build social relations over property relations."[19] The means to do this are relatively simple and begin with a commitment to listen and gestures of hospitality.

When Home Won't Let You Stay posits the museum as another site of migration, one that historically has shaped—and will continue to shape—experiences of belonging. We hope that this exhibition, book, and programs will offer opportunities to reflect on, interrogate, and understand migration through the work of contemporary artists, curators, and museums. None of this would have been possible without the generative and generous work of the artists and scholars included in this book, and of those we encountered while working on the project. So many other artists and practitioners merit inclusion, far more than the exhibition possibly could have reflected—and others will come. They will make art, write, and organize exhibitions that may support and advance, or for that matter counter or even dispute, aspects of what we have presented here. Like many thematic exhibitions, *When Home Won't Let You Stay* is an incomplete account; it has no ambition to be either the first or last word (as if that were even possible). We consider it an entry, signpost, bookmark, link, to the ongoing conversations that have preceded and will follow our endeavor.

- - - - - - - -

1. We are indebted to Anne Ring Petersen's account of art's role in the discourses of migration in *Migration into Art: Transcultural Identities and Art-Making in a Globalised World* (Manchester: Manchester University Press, 2017).

2. In its 2017 International Migration Report, the United Nations estimates that international migration has reached 258 million people, while the World Health Organization estimates internal migration reaching 763 million people. Together, these numbers are equivalent to roughly one in seven of the world's total population. See United Nations,

Department of Economic and Social Affairs, Population Division, *International Migration Report 2017: Highlights* (ST/ESA/SER.A/404). See also World Health Organization, "Refugee and migrant health," online at https://www.who.int/migrants/en/ (accessed March 6, 2019).

3. In the development of this exhibition, we thought carefully about our use of the words most frequently referenced in this book, including "migrant," "immigrant," or "refugee." We recognize the plurality of meaning of many of these terms, especially with the rise of xenophobic and racist connotations that often accompany their deployment in political and popular rhetoric. Throughout this book, we use "migrant" to encompass many experiences of movement—chosen or forced, historical or contemporary—to encapsulate many of the conditions that our exhibition's artists explore in their works. In addition, Peggy Levitt's contribution to this volume (pp. 212–19) tackles the shifting terminology around migration.

4. Many consider the exhibition *Magiciens de la terre*, at the Centre Georges Pompidou and the Grande Halle de la Villette, Paris, May 18–August 14, 1989, curated by Jean-Hubert Martin, one of the first to mark this global moment, and a precursor to later exhibitions on globalization. See Julia Friedel, "Exhibition Histories: Magiciens de la Terre," *Contemporary&*, August 12, 2016. Available online at https://www.contemporaryand.com/magazines/magiciens-de-la-terre/ (accessed March 6, 2019). Pamela M. Lee has written about the art world as both object and agent of globalization in *Forgetting the Art World* (Cambridge, MA: The MIT Press, 2012).

5. See, e.g., Michael D. Shear and Helene Cooper, "Trump Bars Refugees from 7 Muslim Countries," *New York Times*, January 27, 2017, available online at www.nytimes.com/2017/01/27/us/politics/trump-syrian-refugees.html; Julie Hirschfeld Davis, David E. Sanger, and Maggie Haberman, "Trump to Order Mexican Border Wall and Curtail Immigration," *New York Times*, January 24, 2017, available online at www.nytimes.com/2017/01/24/us/politics/wall-border-trump.html; Bill Chappell and Jessica Taylor, "Defiant Homeland Security Secretary Defends Family Separations," NPR, June 18, 2018, available online at www.npr.org/2018/06/18/620972542/we-do-not-have-a-policy-of-separating-families-dhs-secretary-nielsen-says; Maria Sacchetti, "ICE says it needs a $1 billion funding boost to meet Trump's aggressive deportation goals," *The Washington Post*, September 13, 2018, www.washingtonpost.com/local/immigration/ice-says-it-needs-a-1-billion-funding-boost-to-meet-trumps-aggressive-deportation-goals/2018/09/13/179819b2-b6c0-11e8-94eb-3bd52dfe917b_story.html?utm_term=.58c715c69878; and Davis and Thomas Gibbons-Neff, "Trump Considers Closing Southern Border to Migrants," *New York Times*, October 25, 2018, available online at www.nytimes.com/2018/10/25/us/politics/trump-army-border-mexico.html (all accessed March 6, 2019).

6. We convened an advisory board of Boston-based artists, curators, scholars, and others with experience and expertise on this topic. We wish to thank these individuals for their talents, time, and expertise, and for challenging us and indelibly shaping this project. Their names appear on page 237 of this volume.

7. For important and inspiring contributions see Petersen, *Migration into Art*; T. J. Demos, *The Migrant Image: The Art and Politics of Documentary during Global Crisis* (Durham, NC: Duke University Press, 2013); Saloni Mathur, *The Migrant's Time: Rethinking Art History and Diaspora* (New Haven: Yale University Press, 2011); Kobena Mercer, *Exiles, Diasporas, and Strangers* (London: Iniva, 2008); Sam Durrant and Catherine M. Lord, *Essays in Migratory Aesthetics: Cultural Practices between Migration and Art-Making* (Amsterdam: Rodopi, 2007); Judith Butler, *Precarious Life: The Politics of Mourning and Violence* (London: Verso, 2006); and Homi K. Bhabha, *The Location of Culture* (London: Routledge, 1993). For more references, see the bibliography in the present volume, p. 223.

8. See Tania Bruguera, "Introduction on Useful Art," available online at www.taniabruguera.com/cms/528-0-Introduction+on+Useful+Art.htm, and Anthony Romero, "Museum Resolution: Build Social Relations Over Property Relations," Walker Reader Soundboard, ed. Paul Schmelzer, January 8, 2019, available online at https://walkerart.org/magazine/soundboard-museum-resolutions-anthony- romero?fbclid=IwAR0ETF7YXk9j4Dh1X-14jC7VwpQLvW31U-3ZMjPUbaGQRsDIBRP1wudIBRY (both accessed March 6, 2019).

9. According to the City of Boston, over 50 percent of the households in East Boston since 2015 identify as Hispanic, suggesting Spanish as the largest language grouping in this neighborhood. See Boston Planning & Development Agency Research Division, "East Boston," May 2017. Available online at www.bostonplans.org/getattachment/28c2e99c-af11-47e0-b65e-b609fbdc44bd (accessed March 6, 2019). For more on Boston's Latinx population, see Boston Planning & Development Agency Research Division, "Profiles of Boston's Latinos," June 2017. Available online at www.bostonplans.org/getattachment/e0019487-138b-4c73-8fe5-fbbd849a7fba (accessed March 6, 2019).

10. See The Pluralism Project, Harvard University, "Native Peoples in Boston," 1997–2019. Available online at http://pluralism.org/timeline/native-peoples-in-boston/ (accessed March 6, 2019).

11. See Betsy Mason, "How Boston Made Itself Bigger," *National Geographic*, June 13, 2017. Available online at https://news.nationalgeographic.com/2017/06/Boston-landfill-maps-history/ (accessed March 6, 2019).

12. On Boston's history of European settlement and migration see Global Boston, Boston College, Department of History, "Eras of Migration," online at https://globalboston.bc.edu/index.php/home/eras-of-migration/ (accessed March 6, 2019).

13. Sara Ahmed, "Home and Away: Narratives of Migration and Estrangement," *International Journal of Cultural Studies* 2, no. 3 (December 1, 1999):340.

14. Hayv Kahraman, on p. 49 in the present volume.

15. See Tom Keenan's essay on maps and mapping on pp. 190–203 in this volume.

16. In 2018, the world's largest refugee camp was the Kutupalong Refugee Camp in Cox's Bazaar, Bangladesh, following escalated violence against the Rohingya Muslim community in Myanmar. There were camps holding more than 100,000 people each in Pakistan, Uganda, Kenya (which had two such camps), Tanzania, and the Gaza Strip. The last of these, the Jabalia camp, has existed since 1948. See Raptim Humanitarian Travel, "World's Largest Refugee Camps in 2018," June 7, 2018, online at www.raptim.org/largest-refugee-camps-in-2018/ (accessed March 6, 2019).

17. Okwui Enwezor, on p. 173 in this volume.

18. Romero, e-mail to the authors, January 22, 2019.

19. Romero, "Build Social Relations Over Property Relations."

Home

Warsan Shire

B. 1988, Kenya;
lives and works in London and Los Angeles

No one leaves home
unless home is the mouth of a shark.

You only run for the border
when you see the whole city
running as well.

Your neighbours running faster than you,
the boy you went to school with
who kissed you dizzy behind
the old tin factory
is holding a gun bigger than his body,
you only leave home
when home won't let you stay.

No one would leave home unless home
chased you, fire under feet,
hot blood in your belly.

It's not something you ever thought about
doing, and so when you did—
you carried the anthem under your breath,
waiting until the airport toilet
to tear up the passport and swallow—
each mouthful making it clear that
you would not be going back.

You must understand,
no one puts their children in a boat
unless the water is safer than the land.

Who would choose days and nights
in the stomach of a truck,
unless the miles travelled
meant something more than journey.

No one would choose to crawl under fences,
be beaten until your shadow leaves you
raped, then drowned, forced to the bottom of
a boat because you are darker, be sold,
starved, shot at the border like a sick animal,
be pitied, lose your name, lose your family,
make a refugee camp a home for a year or two or ten
stripped and searched, find prison everywhere
and if you survive
and you are greeted on the other side
go home blacks, refugees
dirty immigrants, asylum seekers
sucking our country dry of milk,
dark, with their hands out
smell strange, savage—
look what they've done to their own countries,
what will they do to ours?

The dirty looks in the street
feel softer than a limb torn off,
the indignity of everyday life more tender
than fourteen men who look like your father,
Between your legs. Insults easier to swallow
than rubble, than your child's body
in pieces—for now, forget about pride
your survival is more important.

I want to go home,
but home is the mouth of a shark
home is the barrel of the gun
and no one would leave home
unless home chased you to the shore
unless home tells you to
leave what you could not behind,
even if it's human.

No one leaves home until home
is a damp voice in your ear saying
leave, run now, I don't know what
I've become.

Artists and Artworks

Reenа Saini Kallat

B. 1973, New Delhi, India;
lives and works in Mumbai

Grounded in ideas of memory and national belonging, Mumbai-based artist Reena Saini Kallat crosses medium and material to express these thematic intersections. While trained in painting, she incorporates sculpture, drawing, textiles, photography, and sound, and questions the means by which national histories and ideologies shape individual relationships to the past. "What often occupies my mind," states Kallat, "is the fate of an individual and how s/he is susceptible to being reduced to an anonymous and forgotten statistic, in the vast ocean of humanity."[1] Foregrounding the personal, Kallat's oeuvre reflects a conception of history as a malleable narrative device, and one necessarily susceptible to unmaking.

Woven Chronicle (2011–16) [pp. 34–37] seeks new forms of history-making from within the everyday movements of peoples, goods, and cultures. The work comprises electric wire and auditory devices knitted together to form a map of the world. Kallat twists colored electrical wires to mimic the appearance of barbed wire, then weaves them over the outlines of countries and continents spread at a length of nearly forty feet. Her laborious process yields what appears from a distance as a threaded fabric or an illuminated atlas—an intentional confusion of media and perspective. For the artist, the play between line and territory already represents an important conflation. The imposed borders that delineate most maps connote division and reinforce exclusion; yet these lines are not natural entities but rather expressions of political ideology. By conducting this cartographic exercise with electrical wire instead of a penciled line, Kallat explores "the notion of the map as dynamic, ever changing, streaming and transferring data with the global flows of energies and people."[2]

Woven Chronicle reads as a legible representation of the known world, with countries and continents represented to scale. The crisscrossed network linking certain cities and regions, however, introduces an unknown language. These pathways describe the historical and contemporary movement of goods and peoples between major centers of export and development—and also that of refugees, asylum seekers, enslaved populations, and other migrants. The travel routes they represent vary in each of the work's installations.[3] Kallat selects routes based on ongoing research into historical and contemporary trade and industry, adding, with each installation, to a roster of migration patterns that includes Mumbai–New York, Amsterdam–Jakarta, and the West African coast throughout the Atlantic Basin. Her choice to map trajectories of peoples and products together emphasizes both the trafficking of goods and the geopolitical conflicts that perpetuate those movements, enveloping individual decisions within larger constitutive systems.

These relationships inspire the orchestrated hum of global activity that appears in the work's accompanying soundtrack. Kallat mixes electrical sounds with the ambient noise of global industrial movement, including ship horns, telephone tones, factory sirens, airborne drones, and bird calls. The atmospheric soundscape, and its evocation of psychic, social, and environmental energies, channels the powerful undercurrents that surround and connect us.

An interest in this volatile energy inspired Kallat's decision to use electrical wire for *Woven Chronicle*, as she has in other works. This speaks to her fascination with the material's symbolic contradictions: electrical wire may be seen as both conduit—the carrier of data or energy in electric cables—and obstacle, as in the electric fence or the barbed-wire barrier. Kallat incorporates electrical wire to explore the symbolism of borders and their violent histories. In *Half Oxygen* (2014) [fig. 1], for example, tightly wound electrical wire takes the shape of a pair of lungs divided as the national trees of India and Pakistan (the banyan and deodar trees, respectively), while built-in speakers rehearse the sound of a steady heartbeat and flowing water. These rhythms, coupled with the prickly wire, symbolize the experience of living after the violent Partition of India in 1947, in which millions of people were displaced, expelled, or killed when the present-day borders of India, Pakistan, and Bangladesh were enforced along colonial-era lines.

Indeed, much of Kallat's work exposes how national borders and territorial lines—such as those between India and Pakistan, Ireland and the United Kingdom, or the United States and Mexico—are as bureaucratically determined as they are ideologically reinforced. Her most recent projects, including *Garden of Forking Paths* (2017) [fig. 2], examine the prolific and restrictive ideations of national symbols. Made of gouache, charcoal, electrical wire, and ink on handmade paper, this work examines the national symbols of disputing nation-states—often those sharing geographic boundaries—and remake them as strange, mythical

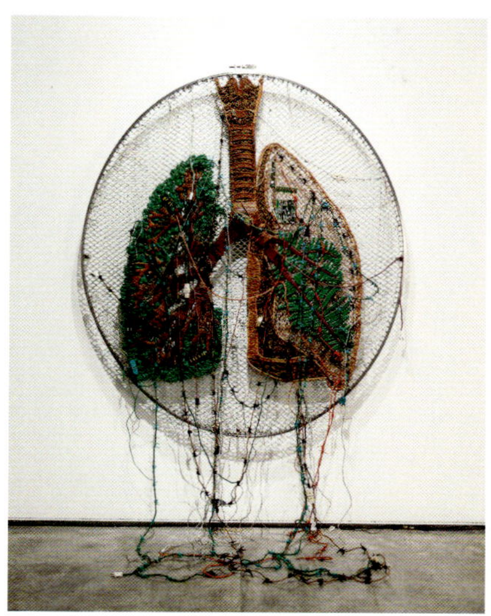

Fig. 1. Reena Saini Kallat, *Half Oxygen*, 2014. Electrical wire, metal ring, and speaker, 72 x 63 inches (182 x 160 cm)

hybrids. Motivated by the question of "what really transpires at the border," these works illustrate for Kallat how national heritage, and our fixation with its symbolic expressions, have made claims to political identity through associations that cannot manifest themselves naturally.[4] The resulting tableau, both fantastical and frightening, behaves like a false promise of the utopian, hybrid world whose presence Kallat sees on the surface of *Woven Chronicle*. Both depict the possibility of a cosmopolitan world, eliding difference in condition and circumstance even as they appeal to the promise of harmony.

The risk in such a utopian perspective is intentional and dangerously approaches what Kallat describes as "this idyllic vision of multiculturalism that we seem to have, even though there are flaws that are ingrained in the system that prevent it from being ideal."[5] If *Garden of Forking Paths* represents a fantastic impossibility, *Woven Chronicle* imagines another scene: in layering industrial and migratory pathways over a world map, the work appears to render a narrative of industry, power, and trade as produced by a robust global modern order. Modernity, however, masks the often inequitable and violent systems that built it, such as histories of imperialism, the forced displacement of peoples, and cheap and hazardous industrial centers. *Woven Chronicle*'s menacing soundscape and materiality evoke the violent inequity at the heart of global capitalism, an ominous undercurrent in myths of progress and peaceful exchange. At once a caution, a fantasy, and a reckoning, Kallat's work invites a vigilant critique of how political narratives shape perceptions of the present world, leaving open the possibility for their undoing. —AP

1. Reena Saini Kallat, in "Interview with Stina Edblom," *Pandemonium: Art in a Time of Creativity Fever* (Göteborg: Göteborg International Biennial for Contemporary Art, 2011). Available online at http://reenakallat.com/pandemonium (accessed January 27, 2019).

2. Ibid.

3. *Woven Chronicle* has been exhibited four times in addition to the iteration at the ICA/Boston. It was first developed as *Untitled (Map/Drawing)* for the 6th Göteborg International Biennial for Contemporary Art in 2011. Its most recent iteration prior to the ICA's installation involved an upside-down orientation of the world map, staged for the Art Gallery of New South Wales, Sydney, in 2018.

4. See "Jason Singh and Reena Kallat in conversation," Manchester Museum YouTube channel, November 13, 2017, online at www.youtube.com/watch?v=OOOPFe7CTNO (accessed January 27, 2019).

5. Kallat, in Nimritta Parmar, "Woven Chronicles: In Conversation with Artist Reena Saini Kallat, *Jugni Style*, June 15, 2015, online at https://jugnistyle.com/woven-chronicles-reena-saini-kallat/ (accessed January 27, 2019).

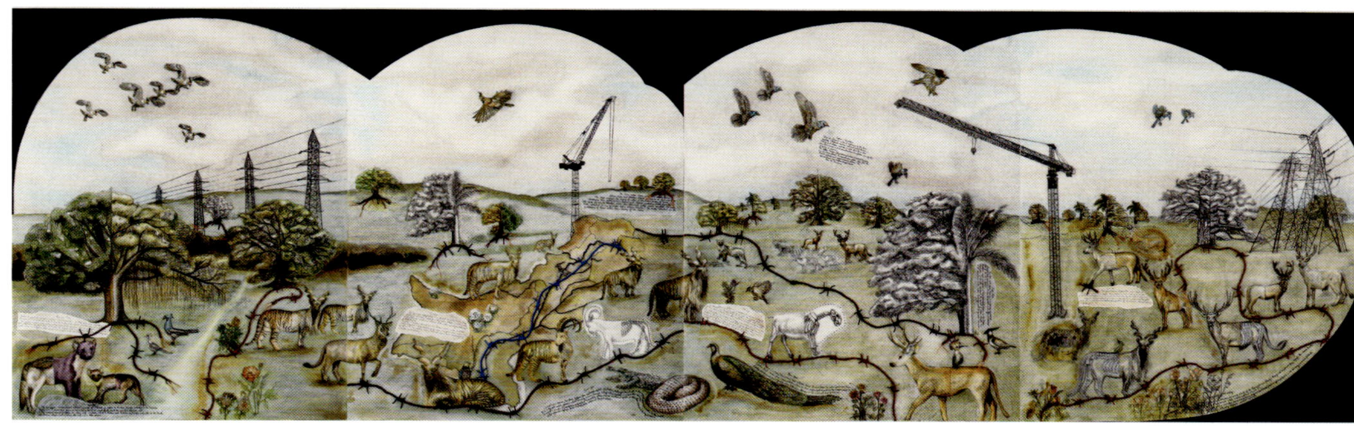

Fig. 2. Reena Saini Kallat, *Garden of Forking Paths*, 2017. Gouache, charcoal, ink, and electrical wire on handmade paper, four parts, each 55 inches x 15 feet (139.7 cm x 4 m 57.2 cm)

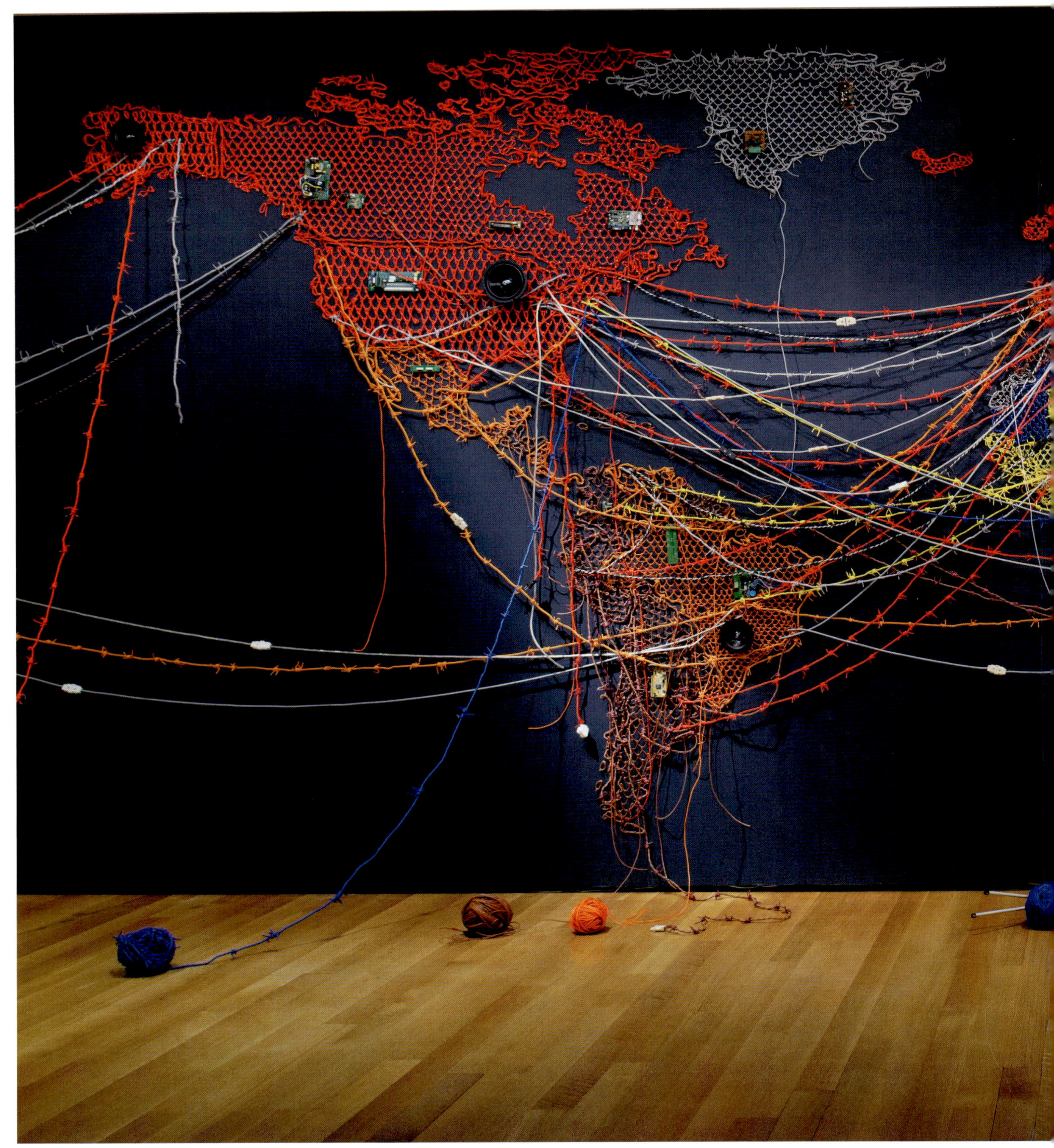

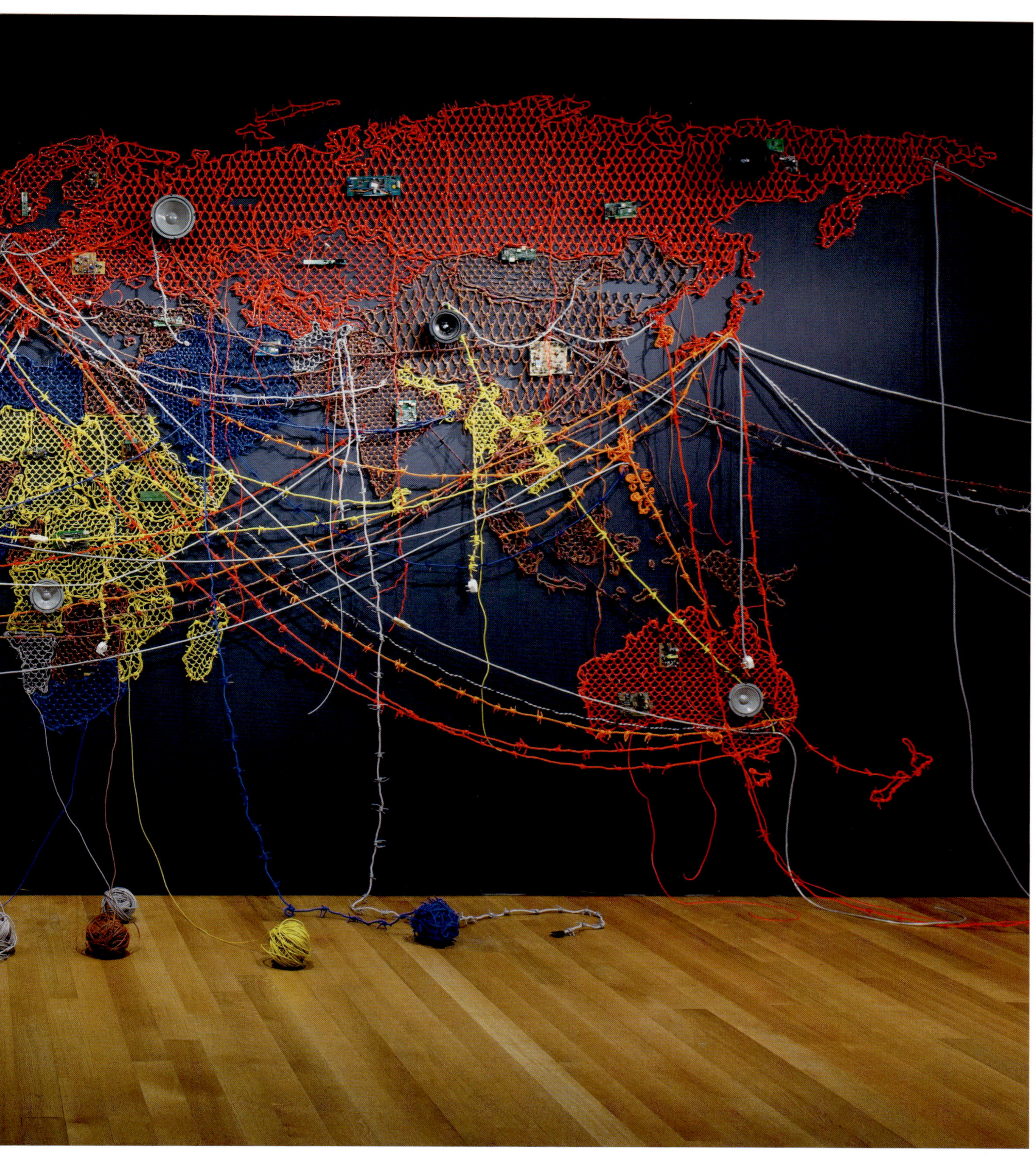

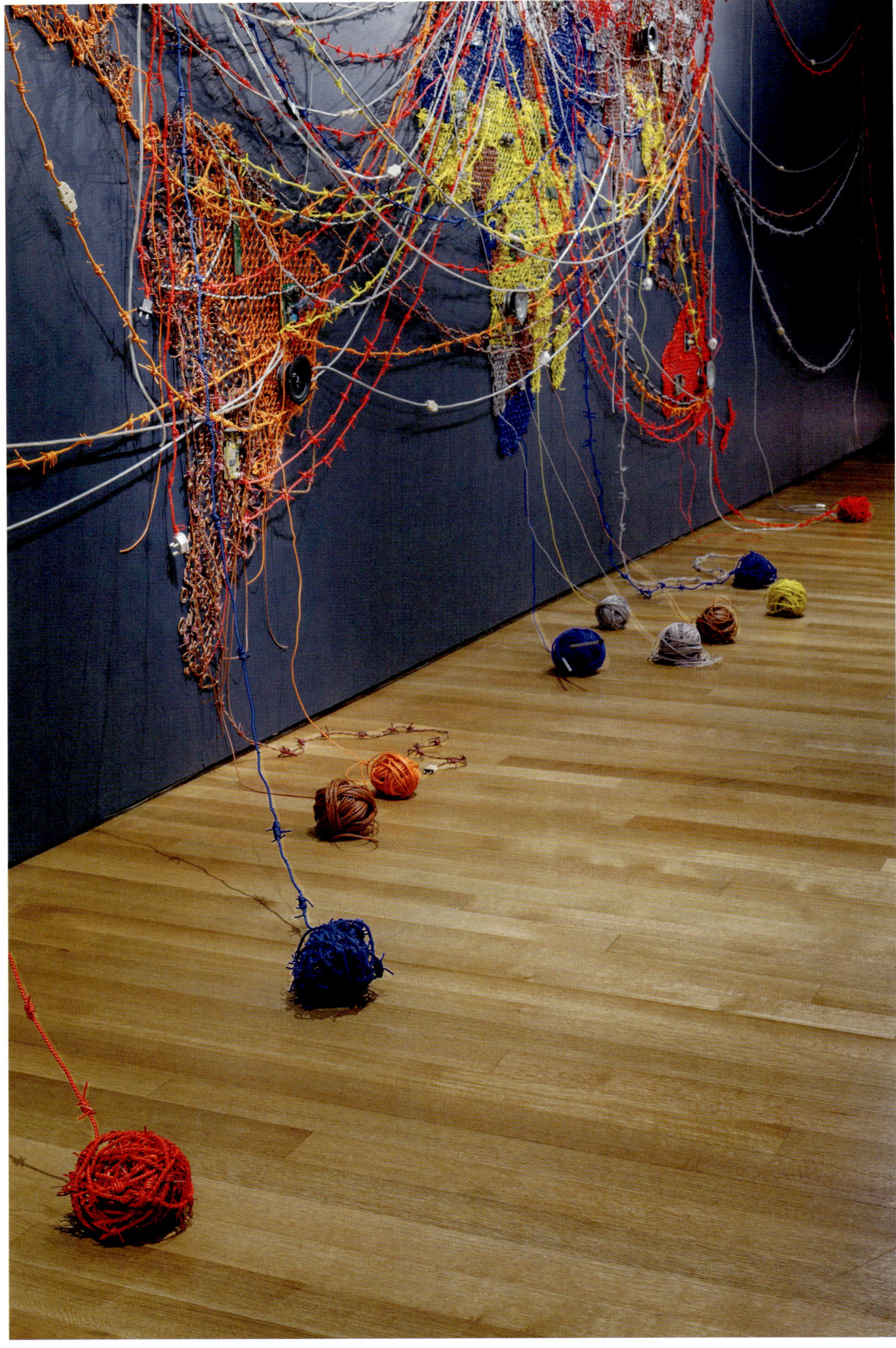

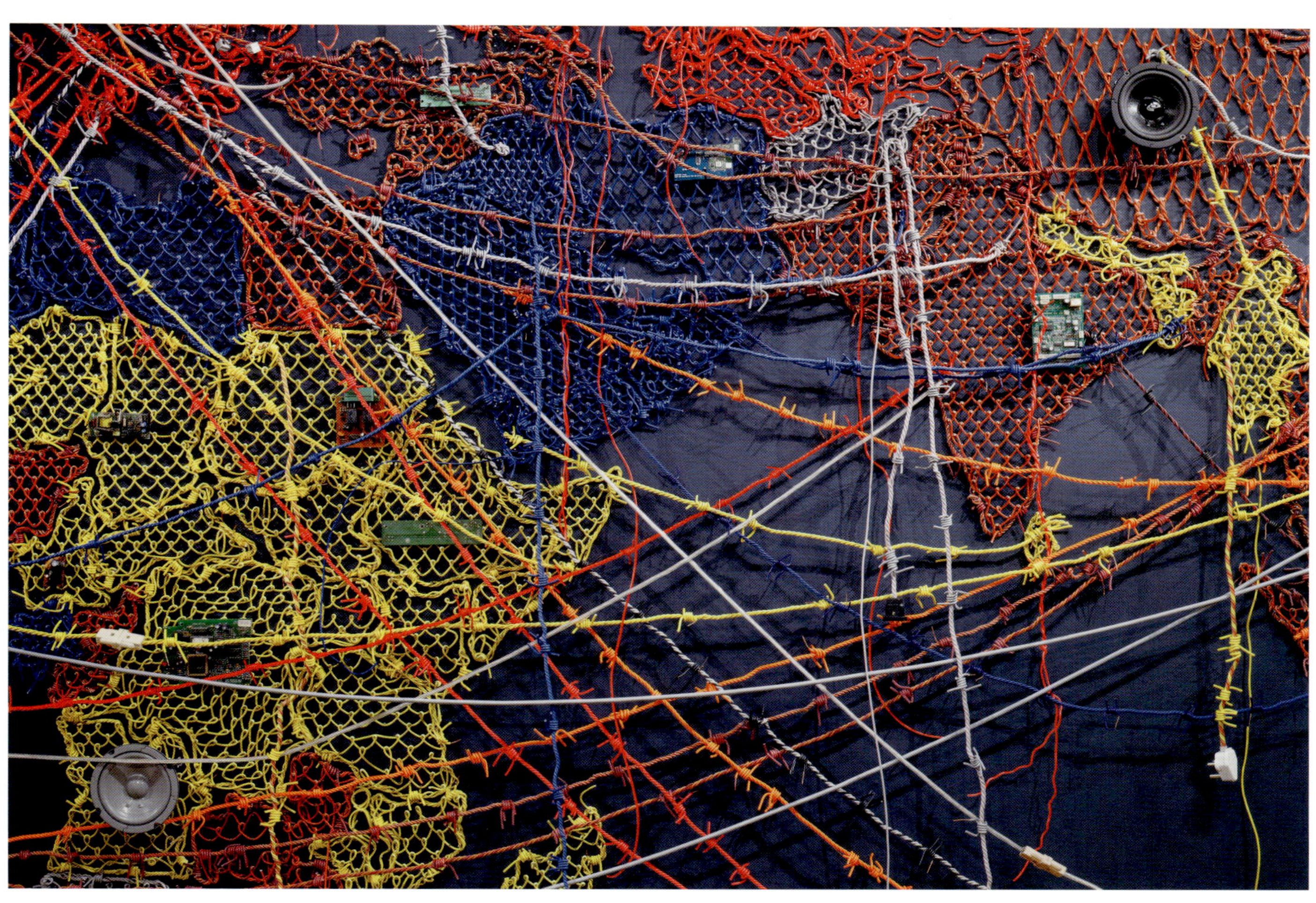

Previous spread, opposite (detail), and above (detail):
Reena Saini Kallat, *Woven Chronicle*, 2011–16.
Circuit boards, speakers, electrical wires, and fittings; single-channel audio sound (10:00 minutes).
Approximately 11 x 38 feet (335.3 x 1158.2 cm).
Installation view, *Insecurities: Tracing Displacement and Shelter*,
The Museum of Modern Art, New York, 2016–17

Adrian Piper

B. 1948, New York, United States;
lives and works in Berlin

Artist and philosopher Adrian Piper is an incisive voice in contemporary art, particularly for her engagement with the long legacy of Conceptual art since the late 1960s. Interrogating the fundamental tenets of ethics and rationalism in the visual art of that time, Piper's work and writings query how to reconcile the artistic idea as a form of intuition, the possibility of "objectivity" in the making of the artwork, and the reality of subjective attitudes held by individuals.[1] One such approach is her notion of "Meta-art," a form of self-consciousness within art practice that acknowledges the systems within which artworks and those who create them exist by identifying the social, psychological, political, metaphysical, and aesthetic conditions and presuppositions that shape artistic intuition.[2] Piper's thinking created possibilities for reading Conceptual art that explored the notion of aesthetic withdrawal (prioritizing the idea behind the art object over the object itself) in relation to the politics of race and gender, xenophobia, and social engagement.

The ongoing series Everything (2003–) telescopes between the philosophical and the everyday in a wide array of forms, each using the phrase "Everything will be taken away" as a multivalent mantra whose meaning shifts with its context.[3] Whether inscribed on school chalkboards, a pane of glass, a scratched-out photograph, or people's foreheads, the phrase implies something potentially transcendent in its premonition of loss. *Everything #4* (2004) [p. 41] centers the phrase in all-capital gold lettering on a small mahogany-framed mirror, whose reflection of ourselves and those around us creates an ambiguous viewing situation. On the one hand it might reassure us that despite the potential for the world we "know" to disappear, we—as in our bodies—are still here. On the other hand, the evanescence of the constantly shifting reflection suggests that the everything we know is simply an illusion.[4] The phrase "Everything will be taken away" relates to a passage from Aleksandr Solzhenitsyn's 1968 novel *In the First Circle*: "The man from whom you've taken everything is no longer in your power; he is free again."[5] But the textual intervention in the mirror's reflective surface can also produce a sense of alienation; indeed, the Everything series may be inspired in part by histories of disenfranchisement and racism in the United States and the increasingly divisive issue of immigration in Germany, where Piper has lived since 2005.

In 2006, Piper learned that she was listed as a "Suspicious Traveler" on the watch list of the federal government's Transportation Security Administration. Rather than returning to the United States, she remained in Germany, refusing to participate in—and thus sanction—a legal system that identified her as suspect. If *Everything #4* prompts individual reflection, the room-sized installation *Everything #21* (2010–13) [fig. 1] surfaces the friction between the potential for transcendence and our hard-edged contemporary reality, characterized as it is by an overwhelming loss of rights, life, and livelihood. Each of a range of chalkboards is covered with the work's signature phrase, handwritten in cursive and repeated twenty-five times in white chalk, invoking the collective disciplining of the body and mind.

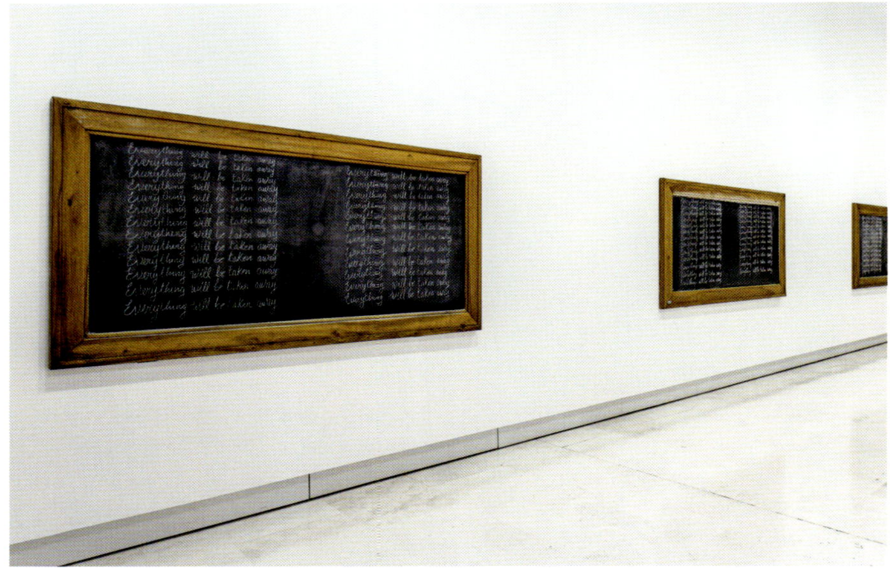

Fig. 1. Adrian Piper, *Everything #21*, 2010–13.
Rennie Collection, Vancouver. Installation view, *Empire State. Arte a New York oggi* (Empire state. New York art now), Palazzo delle Esposizioni, Rome, 2013

Dear Friend,
I am black.
I am sure you did not realize this when you made/laughed at/agreed with that racist remark. In the past, I have attempted to alert white people to my racial identity in advance. Unfortunately, this invariably causes them to react to me as pushy, manipulative, or socially inappropriate. Therefore, my policy is to assume that white people do not make these remarks, even when they believe there are no black people present, and to distribute this card when they do.
I regret any discomfort my presence is causing you, just as I am sure you regret the discomfort your racism is causing me.

Fig. 2. Adrian Piper, *My Calling (Card) #1 (for Dinners and Cocktail Parties)*, 1986– . Performance prop: brown business card with printed text on cardboard, 2 x 3½ inches (5.1 x 9 cm)

Piper's exploration of subjectivity has been motivated by her dedication to merging personhood and objecthood through both language and performance. She was active among the first generation of Conceptual artists, including Sol LeWitt, Hans Haacke, Yvonne Rainer, and others whom she met in 1968–69 through working at the Seth Siegelaub Gallery and exhibiting at the Dwan Gallery and the Paula Cooper Gallery, some of the very few spaces that showed Conceptual art at the time. In 1970 Piper was included in the groundbreaking exhibition *Information* at The Museum of Modern Art in the form of *Context #7*, a discursive situation centered on a comment book in the gallery that visitors were invited to populate. Reflecting on intensifying experiences of discrimination within the art world, in the 1970s she increasingly used her own body as an object in various documentary and performative situations, often drawing attention to the mutability of race and gender and to the social fears that arise when they are rendered ambiguous. In *Mythic Being* (1973–75) she inhabited an alter ego as an African-American man whose Afro hair, mustache, and bell-bottom jeans gave the appearance of both performed male bravado and white appropriation of "hipness" (Piper's light-skinned appearance is a significant topic of her art).[6] Piper's ambiguous identity was further mystified by her recitation of material from personal diaries as she navigated public space. In the 1980s she focused on participatory intersubjective dynamics in works such as *Funk Lessons* (1982–84), in which participants were invited to get down and party together, using popular music and dance as vehicles for overcoming inhibition and transcending racial and cultural boundaries. Between 1986 and 1990 Piper distributed pointed "calling cards" [fig. 2] at private social events when she felt the need to confront someone about his or her racism or rebuff an unwanted sexual advance.

Piper's work continues to comment on entrenched ideologies of otherness that fuel contemporary violence, paranoia, and xenophobia. In the 2008 installation *Here*, three adjoining white walls bear three lines of vertically stacked text reading "I was here/We were here/We are here" in three different languages: Arabic, English, and Hebrew. The work's optical subtlety and quiet linguistic assertion recall the sparse strategies of 1960s Conceptual work, which often employed language as a means to an end. The linguistic shifters "I" and "we" create a relay between the singular and the collective characteristic of Piper's exploration of the ethical and social dynamics of direct address, which have animated her artistic practice as a tool to "scrutinize the viewer's consciousness in the act of looking."[7] Like *Everything #4*, *Here* creates a looking environment in which the linguistic context of identifying language ("I" and "we") is radically transformed within a seemingly uniform spatial context. The mantralike recitation of the text sets up "here" not only as geographic in connotation but also as a site of social exchange across difference. As Piper explains, "I want my work to contribute to the creation of a society in which racism and racial stereotyping no longer exist. In such a society, the prevailing attitude to cultural and ethnic others would be one not of tolerance but of acceptance."[8]
—ET

1. See Adrian Piper, "A defense of the 'conceptual' process in art," 1967, in Piper, *Out of Order, Out of Sight*, vol. 2, *Selected Writings in Meta-Art 1968–1992* (Cambridge, MA: The MIT Press, 1996), pp. 3–4.

2. See Piper, "In support of meta-art," *Artforum* 12, no. 2 (October 1973):79–81, repr. in Alexander Alberro and Blake Stimson, eds., *Conceptual Art: A Critical Anthology* (Cambridge, MA: The MIT Press, 1999), pp. 298–301.

3. "The defining task that unites all of the work in all media that constitute this open-ended series is to situate the text, Everything will be taken away, in a wide variety of contexts, in a wide variety of media and in conjunction with a wide variety of images, in order to examine how these different visual contexts change its meaning." Sarah Jane Cervenak, "Dignity, the Sacred, and the Ends of Black Performance," *Spectator* 30, no. 2 (Fall 2010):23.

4. Returning to Piper's 1967 treatise "a defense of the 'conceptual process in art," one notes parallels between the mirror as writing surface and the sort of confrontation with the self that conceptual processes might engender: "It is only when one subordinates the original intuition to the subjective distillations and limitations of one's own personality that one need be finally confronted with a kind of mirror image of one's egotistical conflicts as an end product." Piper (1967), p.3

5. Aleksandr Solzhenitsyn, *In the First Circle*, 1955–58, trans. Harry T. Willetts (New York: Harper Perennial, 2009), p. 95. The translation of Solzhenitsyn's phrase as used by Piper in another work, *Black Box/White Box* (1992), is "Once you have taken everything away from a man, he is no longer in your power. He is free."

6. See John Bowles, "Acting Like a Man: Adrian Piper's Mythic Being and Black Feminism in the 1970s," *Signs: Journal of Women in Culture and Society* 32, no 3 (2007):621–47.

7. Cornelia Butler and David Platzker, "Adrian Piper: Reading the Work," in Butler and Platzker, eds., *Adrian Piper: A Reader* (New York: The Museum of Modern Art, 2018), p. 8.

8. Piper, "Xenophobia and the Indexical Present I: Essay," 1989, repr. in Piper, *Out of Order, Out of Sight*, vol. 1, p. 245.

Adrian Piper, *Everything #4*, 2004.
Oval mirror with gold-leaf-engraved text in traditional mahogany frame.
13 x 10 inches (33 x 25.4 cm)

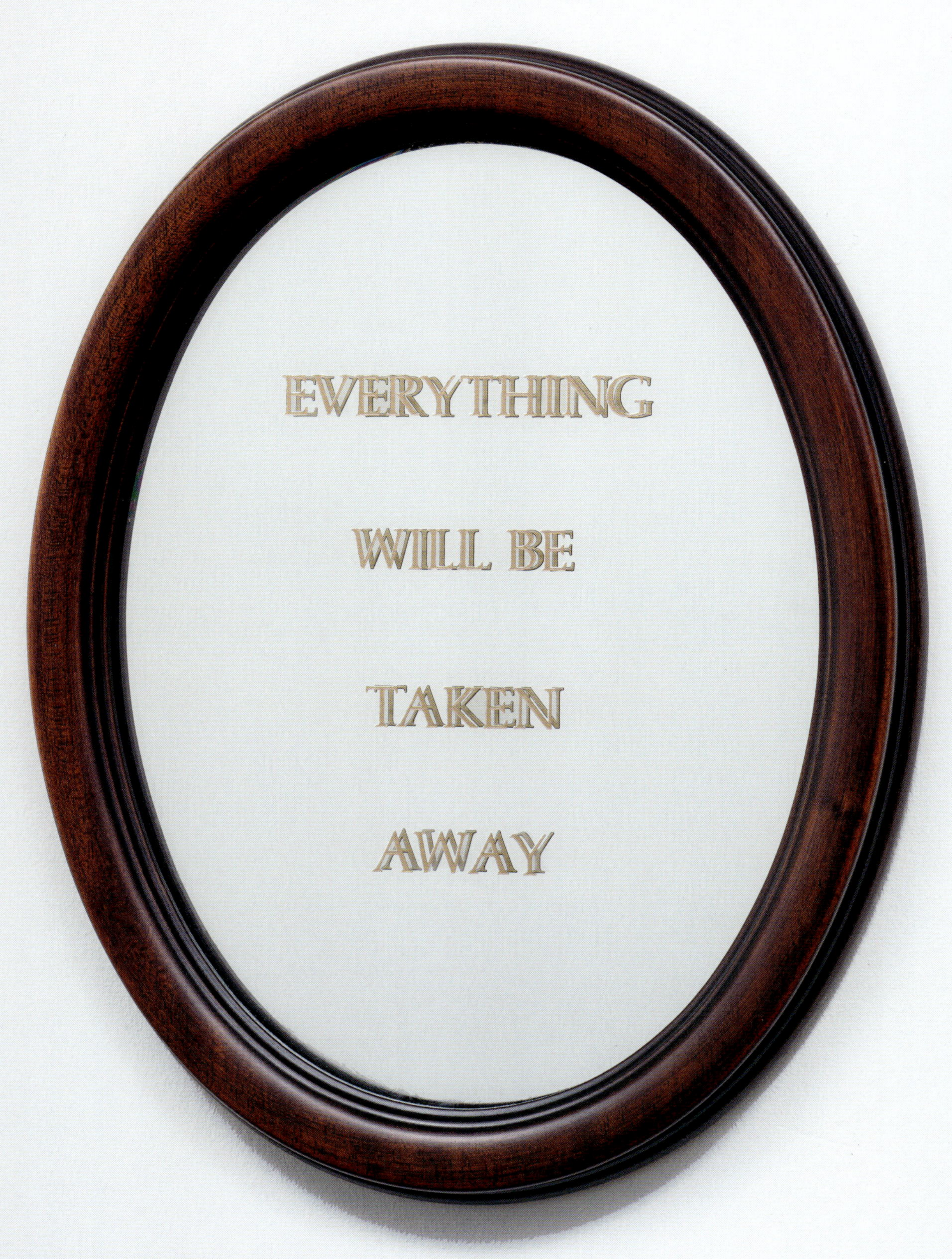
EVERYTHING
WILL BE
TAKEN
AWAY

Camilo Ontiveros

B. 1978, El Rosario, Sinaloa, Mexico;
lives and works in Los Angeles

Camilo Ontiveros's practice centers on collecting materials of migrant experiences and repurposing them into sculptures, installations, and performances. Conceptual in orientation yet often material and formal in completion, Ontiveros's projects have involved objects ranging from washing machines and mattresses to a cubic meter of soil; they mine issues of movement, value, and exchange, especially between the United States and Mexico. Attentive to both individual and collective experience, Ontiveros focuses on the systems engaged in dispossessing migrants as well as to those that migrants themselves create to survive. The artist first came to the United States from Mexico as a teenager and since 1993 has been based in Southern California, a crucial zone of interest in the complex contacts between the two nations.

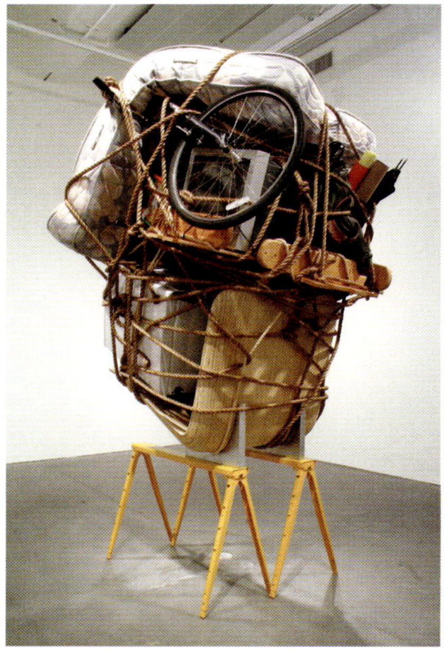

Fig. 1. Camilo Ontiveros, *Temporary Storage*, 2009. Found objects, dimensions variable

The bundled objects forming *Temporary Storage: The Belongings of Juan Manuel Montes* are all of the possessions that remained in the bedroom of Juan Manuel Montes after his deportation from the United States in 2017 [pp. 45–47].[1] Montes was the first person deported by the Donald Trump administration while protected under the Deferred Action for Childhood Arrivals (DACA) program. *Temporary Storage*... repeats a sculpture Ontiveros made in 2009 as a graduate student at the University of California, Los Angeles, in which he similarly stacked and tied his own belongings as a way to store them during a period of temporary homelessness [fig. 1]. Recalling what drew him to Montes's story, Ontiveros notes, "I see a reflection of me. I was here illegally. I went through the same kinds of fears growing up. I was a student. I went to college."[2] Upon learning of Montes's experience, Ontiveros contacted the young man's mother and proposed to gather his belongings into a sculpture. She agreed, lending her son's possessions.[3] Piled and bound with rope, Montes's bed, television, desk chair, books, suits, karate uniform, basketball, and tennis racket form a towering, tilting bundle balanced on two metal sawhorses, offering a portrait of Montes through his belongings and an instantiation of the uneven experience of belonging.

Recalling the haphazard loads one might see in the back of a pickup truck, *Temporary Storage*... evokes transit and, more symbolically, the precarity of Montes, Ontiveros, and other immigrants, documented and undocumented.[4] If the first sculpture emerged in reaction to Ontiveros's own impermanence, in repeating it he moved from his personal experience to Montes's. The reverberation points to both affinities and stark differences between the two, revealing their shared transience and the arbitrariness of the system that impinges on their attempts to live their lives. This act of repetition points to the American history of deportation, to the mercurial policy shifts that have guided the state's actions, and to the uncertainty and vulnerability felt by many immigrants under the Trump administration.

The mundane yet charged objects that Ontiveros combines in *Temporary Storage*..., and his method of binding them, connect to other works of his, and more broadly to his investigation of migration and its attendant effects. Knotted rope has both a functional and a symbolic value in his practice. For his series Deportables (2008) [fig. 2] he collected discarded mattresses from around Los Angeles, folding and tying the soft objects to create oddly shaped bundles that appear at once corporeal and objectlike. Having served as places for bodies to rest and sleep, the abandoned mattresses evoke itinerancy and society's neglect of those experiencing homelessness or even exile, as referenced in the title. The crisscrossing rope in both Deportables and *Temporary Storage*... holds the enlaced objects tightly together, forming a netlike skin over their irregular surfaces. And yet, as firm as this grip appears, it simultaneously underscores the potential—even the inevitability—of coming undone and falling apart. In both series the collected objects relate intimately to bodies, being close to them in life and sleep, and the

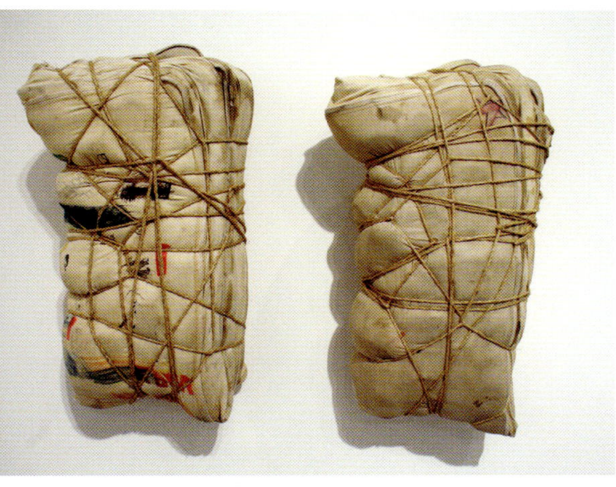

Fig. 2. Camilo Ontiveros, *Colchones 1* (Mattresses 1), 2008, from the series Deportables, 2008. Mattresses and rope, 48 x 48 inches (121.9 x 121.9 cm)

interwoven rope evokes the simultaneous resilience and instability of those bodies. Ontiveros's careful work in gathering, knotting, and binding evinces the care he takes with these deserted things, and the value he finds in their presence.

Another tactic of *Temporary Storage*..., and of Ontiveros's practice more broadly, is displacement. A number of his projects have involved the relocation of materials from one realm to another, a means to prod the borders and systems that demarcate existence. In *I Want Your Washing Machine* (2009) Ontiveros installed secondhand washing machines in a Los Angeles gallery. His unfinished piece *El Pedón*, initiated for the Hammer Museum's exhibition *Made in L.A.* (2012), hinged on the extraction of a cubic meter of soil from Nayarit, Mexico, for presentation in the museum, a proposal ultimately refused by the U.S. Department of Agriculture.[5] (*Pedón* is a technical term for the smallest volume of soil that contains all the soil layers of that region.) These "found" materials, which mimic Minimalist cubic forms, evidence the processes of exchange—both informal, such as the trade of used appliances among immigrant communities in L.A., and formal, such as those regulated by transnational laws and agreements such as NAFTA (the North American Free Trade Agreement). The literal displacement of goods or raw materials—as in that of Montes's belongings to the permanent collection of a museum—references the regimes of power that subtend movement, engender transience, and define the value of materials and people alike. The friction triggered by every relocation speaks to a general intolerance of movement beyond ascribed places and categories. Through his pointed displacements, Ontiveros rehearses the nation state's shifting tolerance for immigration and exposes a general antagonism toward such democratic promises as acceptance and hospitality.

It needs no repeating here that the Trump administration has issued dozens of executive orders banning the arrival of certain immigrants to the United States, removing protections for refugees seeking asylum, and enforcing the strictest interpretations of immigration laws, in addition to attempting mightily to erect a wall at the U.S.-Mexico border. The administration is, by its own statements, at war with immigration. *Temporary Storage*... is emblematic of our contemporary moment and of the particular perils facing migrants both inside and arriving in the United States, yet it is also a testament to the forces of migration and to the traces of displacement that mark human history. —RE

1. The circumstances of Juan Manuel Montes's deportation are disputed, with Montes claiming to have been forcibly deported by Border Protection agents on the night of February 17, 2017, and Homeland Security claiming to have deported him only once he tried to cross back into the United States, on February 18, 2017. See Alan Gomez and David Agren, "First Protected dreamer Is Deported under Trump," *USA Today*, April 18, 2017, available online at https://www.usatoday.com/story/news/world/2017/04/18/first-protected-dreamer-deported-under-trump/100583274/, and National Immigration Law Center, "New Evidence Proves Deported DACA Recipient Juan Manuel Montes Was Kicked Out of the U.S. by Immigration Officials against His Will," July 14, 2017, available online at https://www.nilc.org/2017/07/14/new-evidence-proves-deported-daca-recipient-juan-manuel-montes-was-kicked-out-of-the-u-s-by-immigration-officials-against-his-will/ (both accessed December 23, 2018).

2. Camilo Ontiveros, quoted in Carolina A. Miranda, "How Artist Camilo Ontiveros Acquired the Belongings of a DACA Deportee and What He Did with Them," *Los Angeles Times*, September 15, 2017. Available online at https://www.latimes.com/entertainment/arts/miranda/la-et-cam-camilo-ontiveros-lacma-20170915-htmlstory.html (accessed December 23, 2018).

3. Montes's mother also agreed to the 2018 sale of *Temporary Storage*... to the Museum of Fine Arts Houston, splitting the revenue evenly with Ontiveros. Conversation with the artist, October 4, 2018.

4. Conversation with the artist, January 12, 2018.

5. See Cesar Garcia, "Camilo Ontiveros," in *Made in L.A.*, exh. cat. (Los Angeles: Hammer Museum, University of California, 2012), pp. 47, 67–70.

Opposite and following spread (details):
Camilo Ontiveros, *Temporary Storage: The Belongings of Juan Manuel Montes*, 2017.
Personal belongings of Juan Manuel Montes, rope, metal sawhorse,
aluminum base, and wood. Approximately 72 x 72 x 18 inches (˙82.9 x 182.9 x 45.7 cm)

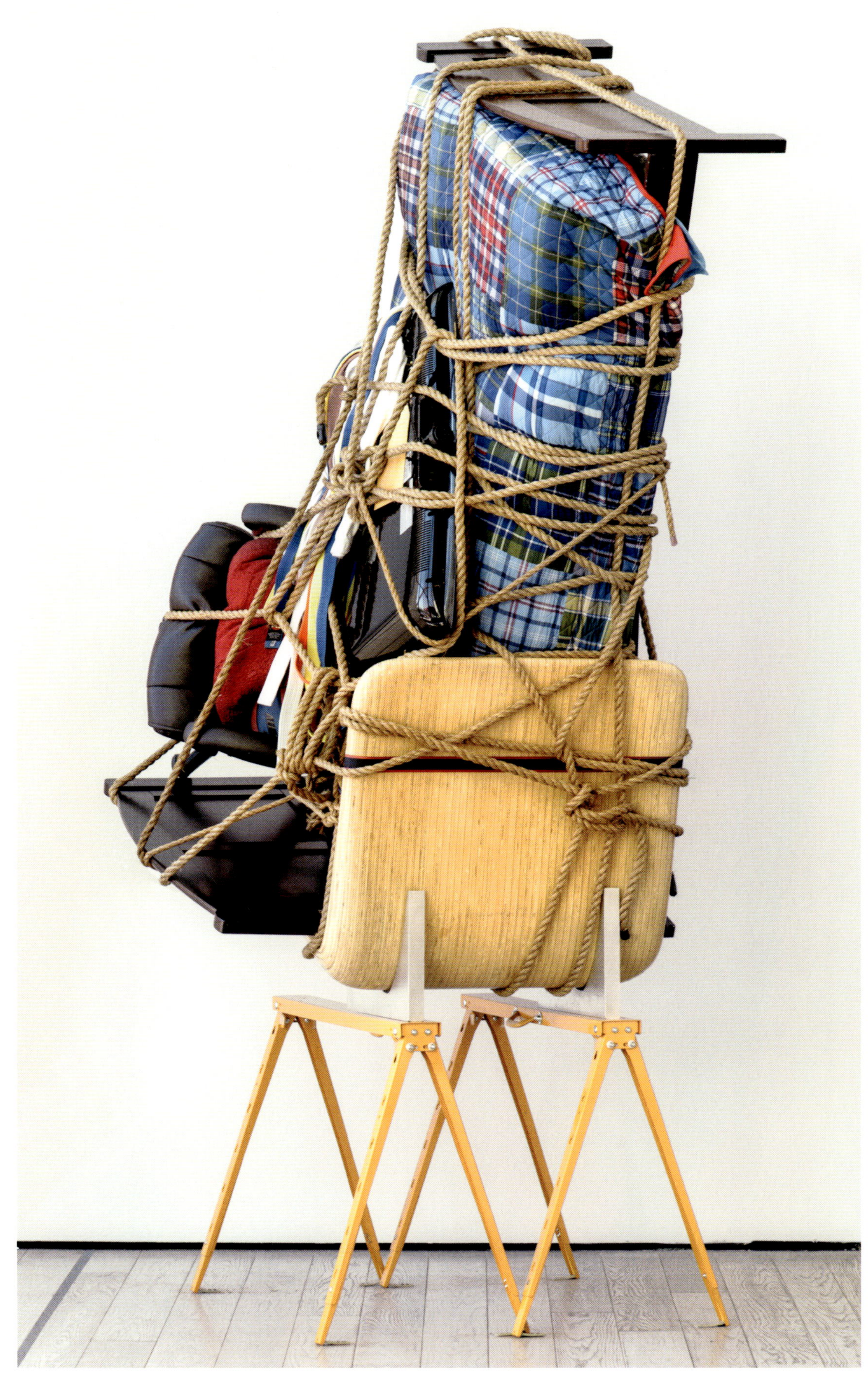

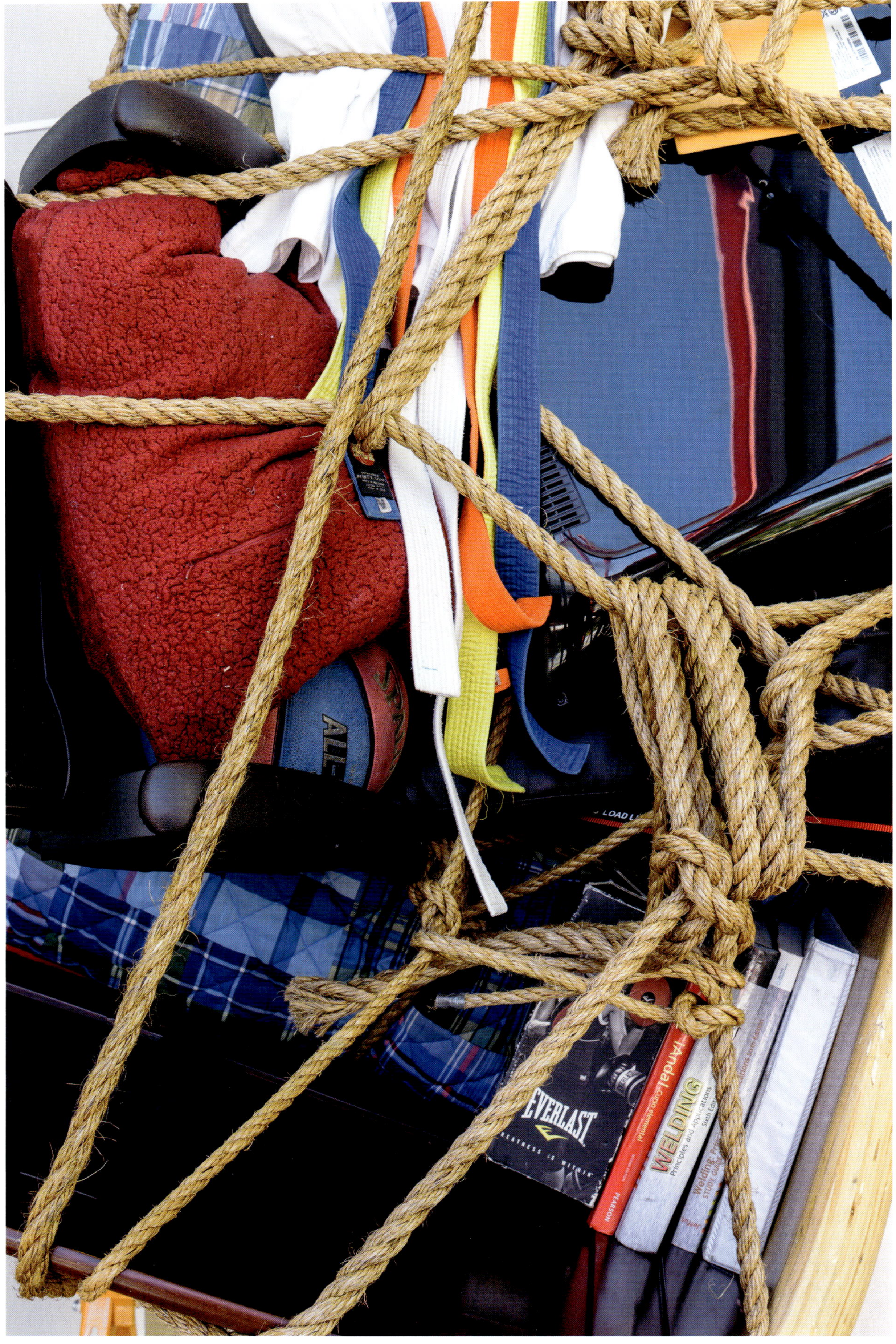
EVERLAST
WELDING
Principles and Applications
PEARSON

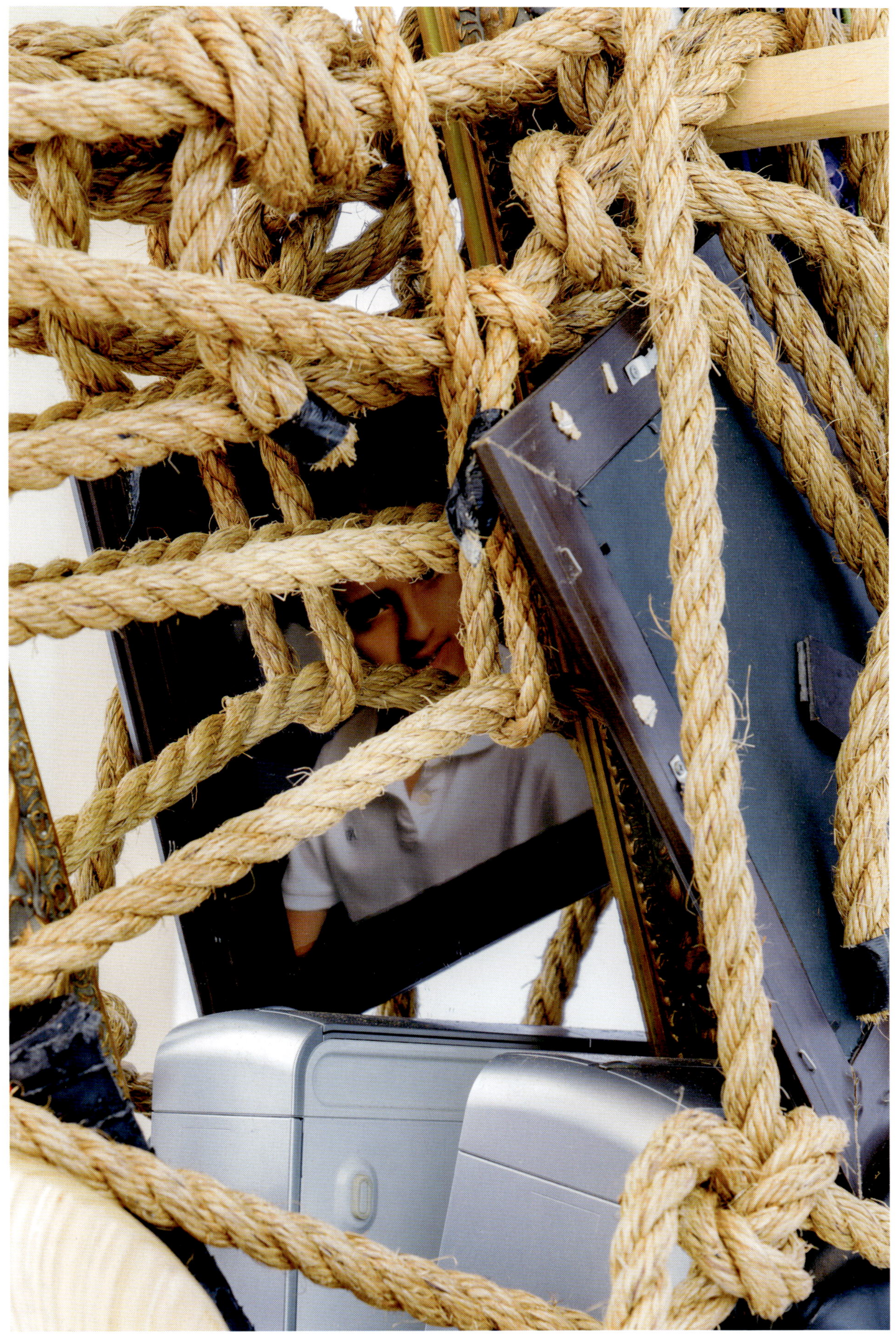

Conversation

Hayv Kahraman and Reena Saini Kallat

REENA SAINI KALLAT How would you see your training as an artist? I believe you left home at the age of eleven or twelve, right?

HAYV KAHRAMAN Yeah, I actually fled the war at the age of ten. It was the first Gulf War in Iraq, and I became a refugee at that point. I moved to the northern part of Sweden, to a small town with 30,000 inhabitants, and I was literally the only kid with black hair in my class. So I was clearly, distinctly, an other. It was like I was hypervisible through my skin, yet completely invisible with what I had to say.... Then I got a really great art teacher and he was very encouraging. Art class became a way for me to be me, or to be okay with being me—to have the ability to express myself in whatever way I wanted to. But I actually never went to art school. I studied graphic design in Italy for three years, but I've never taken an art-crit, I've never taken courses on painting or drawing or anything. I learned art more as a form of mimicry, which I'm very good at, I have to say. When you're a refugee, and you really have to survive this new environment, you become really good at mimicking people.

RSK Art is certainly a place to ask all the larger questions of life, about where we come from, what's our place in the world. I can see why you would choose to become an artist sort of naturally, because these are the larger questions of life that occupy artists more than other professions. But I'm wondering about your iconography, your imagery—how did that develop? Was it a conscious choice to go back and draw from your memories? To reconnect to your roots in some sense?

HK That's a good question. I think the iconography that you see in my work was born in Italy. I would go to all the museums and I would sit and copy old master paintings, and I was obsessed completely with the Renaissance aesthetic, to the point where I felt like my mind was colonized. I talk about "*Her*," this figure, as a colonized body because she was born in that context, you know? She was born of a place where that white European art history would override anything else, so that any other histories were wiped out. What about you?

RSK Well, I grew up in a convent school in Mumbai, a very diverse and rich landscape where you had so many cultures, religious identities, all living together. I was never very religiously minded, but I grew up in a climate that seemed very multicultural and cosmopolitan. Then came the destruction of the Babri Masjid mosque [in Ayodhya, Uttar Pradesh, in 1992], the 1993 Mumbai bombings, the 2002 [Gujarat] riots, and so on. They really put all of my ideas about India's multiculturalism into question.

I also lost my mother when I was really young, so I often think about loss and how that changes you and molds you as a person, how that impacts you psychologically, emotionally, at various levels. In my work, I almost always chose not to speak so directly about the personal, but I realized I kept returning to certain ideas, like this certain sense of longing, this shadow of absence. I wonder why I keep going back to the past, but perhaps it's to understand the present, to look for all those legacies of partitions of nations but still hold the sense of pain or loss in a shared, inclusive space. Does that make sense?

HK It makes complete sense, and I can see that in your work.

RSK I think I was always in denial of wanting to be an artist. I always felt it was something I was passionate about, yet I never saw it as a profession. I mean, I still don't see it as a profession, really [*laughter*]. It's more the need to try to continue to engage myself with these broader ideas of how we see the world, of how we access the world and our environment and so on.

HK I want to say something about loss, this sudden interruption that happened in your life—I can completely identify with that. With me it's not something that comes through the work subconsciously, it's something I choose to insert, maybe in a way as a healing process, a therapeutic act. Do you ever feel that there's an immense importance there for you?

RSK The one piece that's truly personal, *Walls of the Womb*, which I made in 2007, is these scrolls that are each cut to the length of a sari. I grew up looking at a lot of things that my mother left behind, her personal belongings—I sort of built a secret relationship with them where I would bring them out, try them on, put them back. It was my way of feeling a sense of closeness to her. Yet this was a kind of secret relationship that I would put away. When I came full circle with my own experience with motherhood, I kept going back to those early years, so I decided to make translations from her handwritten recipe books into braille. I wanted the viewer to face a kind of inaccessibility in this text, much like my own relationship with her, which was sort of built through inscrutable fragments of memory. I had great difficulty even talking about the loss of my mother, and I felt that creating this work made me come to terms with that. In a sense, it became a kind of—not a monument, but a kind of memorial, you know what I mean?

HK Yeah.

RSK I do see healing as an undercurrent in a lot of my work—there's an attempt to take recourse, to try to secure a fragmented terrain. I see the porosity of borders rather than the fissures—I want to see how we can transcend these spaces, how we can try to reconstruct through the act of deconstructing.

HK That's something else we can connect on, that idea of mending—a physical act of weaving or integrating various materials in whatever we're making as a form of healing. You also said something I really like about the inaccessibility of the connection to or the memories of your mother. That makes me think about inaccessibility in my own life in relation to a place that I used to call home that's not my home anymore, a place that I'm supposed to be completely a part of but that at this point in my life I don't understand.... When you're talking about loss, or when you're talking about memories, within the context of a diasporic people, for me this link to the past becomes so urgent that you cannot actually exist in your present or your future. You need to kind of go back to the past in order to form your present.

RSK Memory is a complex set of interactions among seeing, remembering, imagining. I find the space of the imagination, of the fictional, an interesting space. I mean, memory isn't always accurate. It's selective; it's what we choose to want to remember, or what continues to haunt us or trouble us, or a kind of imaginary utopia. I've never been displaced in the literal sense of having to move, but I have cultural memories of displacement through my family. My father was born in Lahore, which is now in Pakistan, but he moved before the partition [of India and Pakistan], while his brother moved during the partition. There was this sense of, "Okay, we need to move temporarily and we will go back." I grew up listening to how they left everything behind, not knowing they would never return.

To understand or to break the silence around so many people who have moved, I began to think of the lines that are drawn across territories, how they decide people's fate across these borders that don't really exist. These are imaginary borders, yet they impact people on both sides. My recent work has to do with these lines, whether it's the Durand Line between Afghanistan and Pakistan, the Radcliffe Line between India, Pakistan, and Bangladesh, or the Hindenburg Line and the Siegfried Line through France and Germany in World War I and World War II. These lines are part of colonial history, they're often named after a colonizer who just comes in, and they're drawn so randomly across territory. Yet these arbitrary lines are arbiters of meaning, and they're decisive in the lives of so many people who migrate.

I also began using rubber stamps as a metaphor for the bureaucratic parties that confirm and obscure identities. I think about this role of the state vis-à-vis the citizen, how everything needs the stamp of approval or disapproval, so I started to make works about those who are denied visas, about migration within cities, the disenfranchised who have no legal status in terms of being able to be part of the democratic process. There were these kind of informal settlements in the neighborhood where my studio was, and I'd often go and talk to people about why they'd chosen to come and live and work in the city of Mumbai.

HK There's something about your work that makes me think about visual analysis. They're infographs, especially *Woven Chronicle* [2011–16] [pp. 34–37], right?

RSK There are many ways in which your work just organically develops, and it's not as though you have all the answers, but you begin with a set of questions and then those sort of take you ahead. In this case I was thinking about how creativity emerges out of a state of chaos. I thought about the electric cable as a transmitter of energy, of exchange—it's a communication cable and yet it can morph into barbed wires and fences. It's a conduit, a carrier, and at the same time a barrier. I think a lot of that work really pulls at these inherent contradictions of crossing borders. It also became about cartography, about the fact that no rendition of the world is really complete, that each projection of the world is a distortion and no orientation is more correct than another.

HK For me, maps have become a reflection of power, the power of Western modernity.

RSK Right. Africa is fourteen times the size of Greenland, yet they look close in scale in the Mercator projection, which retains shape and form but distorts relative scale.

HK I guess it goes back to who is creating this knowledge within our institutions. I mean, growing up in Sweden, my education was very Eurocentric [*laughs*], and honestly, I didn't even notice that until much further on in my life. But I want to go back to your idea of highlighting these projections of power, right? That's so important, and it makes me think of being and coming from a different, other space. It's very important for us to bring our own history and our own memory into our new space—how else are we going to be able to survive it? So I have an extreme sense of urgency to speak about not only myself, but also how I feel I can pertain to a larger collective. My work has a lot to do with breaking those really rigid, systemic structures of power that we spoke of earlier, exploring what it means to be seen as a brown woman with black hair in this white environment.

I've also been thinking about whether my work is political. I used to be completely against that because I felt it was reductive [*laughs*]; now I feel the complete opposite. Now I'm very fueled—it's a catalyst to the work. I was listening to the [U.S. Supreme Court Justice Brett] Kavanaugh hearings and flipping out! Usually I come up with my ideas by reading academic texts; I read a lot of theory, and that's how I develop the concepts behind my work. But this time it was a very literal and direct relationship with current politics that fueled my work, you know?

RSK Right. And, of course, there's always the question of what art can do and what it cannot do. For me, it's about creating a space where there's a slippage of meaning, a space of self-reflection, of self-criticality. I think a lot about our prejudices, our vices, but I also try to then reimagine the world, through works where I think about our own inherent gaps in communication, between what is said and how it's often understood and interpreted, and where those gaps lie. I find that art, through its process of creation, provides a space for the transformative. Not only do you yourself feel a sense of transformation, but art allows its viewers to transcend their own views, to expand their horizons of thinking and to reimagine.

– – – – – – – –

Recorded via Skype on October 23, 2018.

Richard Mosse

B. 1980, Kilkenny, Ireland;
lives and works in New York

Richard Mosse is committed to making visible the complicated ethical terrain of contemporary art at the intersection of photojournalism and politics. His subjects are familiar to the field of photojournalism, from ruins in the former Yugoslavia to earthquake devastation in Iran, Pakistan, and Haiti. His film *Incoming* (2014–17) [pp. 54–59] focuses on refugees and migrants traveling into Europe. Through his use of unconventional photographic tools, however, such as military-grade imaging and surveillance technology, Mosse identifies the intangible contingencies that traditional documentary modes often fail to capture.[1] Thermographic surveillance technology, for example, yields an uncanny aesthetic, defamiliarizing the reality it captures. Mosse's most recent projects subvert such weaponized photographic technologies, challenging the capacity of the photograph to communicate tragedy in a public domain already saturated with—and thus indifferent to—such imagery.[2]

Military conflict poses a challenge to photography: it is durational, complicated, often fractured, and always changing. Mosse's photographic series Infra and his multichannel film installation *The Enclave* [fig. 1] emerged from travels in the Democratic Republic of the Congo in 2012–14.[3] The use of Kodak Aerochrome film, which captures infrared light—invisible to the human eye—and filters out chlorophyll in vegetation introduces fantastical colors into the documentary image. Developed for the U.S. military during World War II as a way of identifying camouflaged targets amid dense vegetation, Aerochrome renders the Congolese landscape's botanical palette of greens and browns in bright

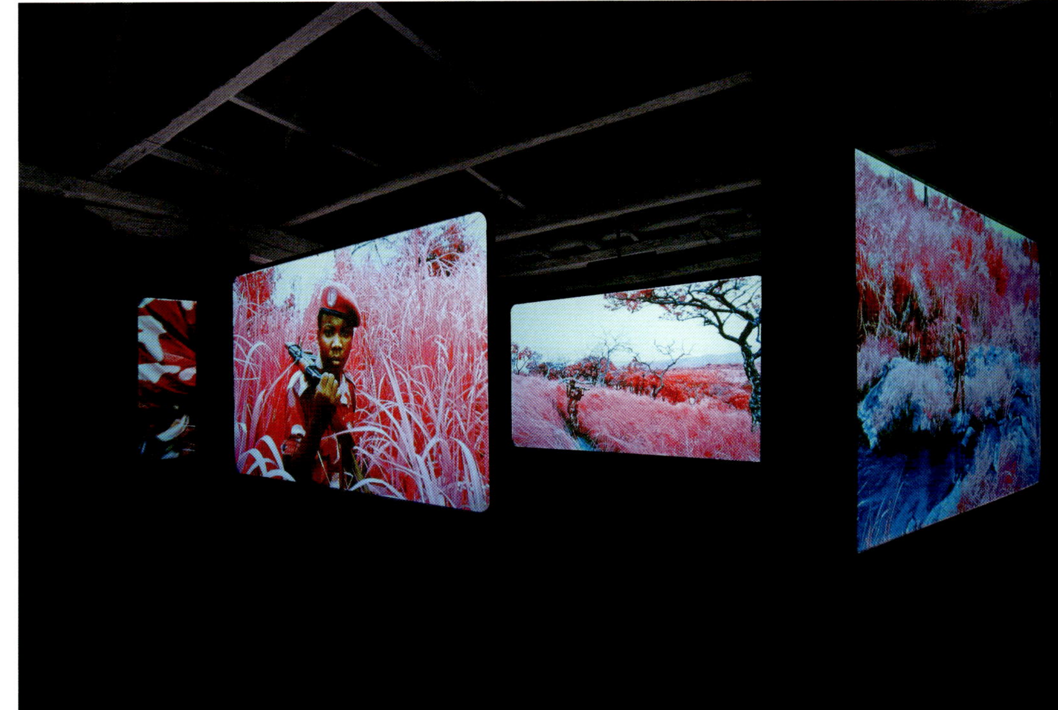

Fig. 1. Richard Mosse, *The Enclave*, 2013.
Installation view, 55th International Art Exhibition, La Biennale de Venezia, 2013

shades of hot pink, crimson, and purple. The works, Mosse explains, collide "art's potential to represent narratives so painful that they exist beyond language, and photography's capacity to document specific tragedies and communicate them to the world."[4]

In *Incoming*, Mosse's use of a thermal imaging camera—patented by the U.S. military and classified as an advanced weapons system—presents an unfamiliar image of surveillance. Rather than eliminating elements of the light spectrum, as Aerochrome film does, this camera registers only the contours of heat differences within a scene, rendering heat on an opalescent spectrum to create alien-looking bodies. "Using a part of a weapon to figure the refugee crisis," Mosse says, "is a deeply ambivalent and political task. And building a new language around that weapon—one of compassion and disorientation, one that allows the viewer to see these events through an unfamiliar and alienating technology—is a deeply political gesture."[5]

Incoming tracks two of the busiest and most dangerous routes into Europe: one from the east, with migrants from Syria, Iraq, and Afghanistan crossing Turkey and the Aegean islands and then passing north, and one from the south, across the Sahara Desert and then the Mediterranean to Italy. The three-channel film portrays refugees led by human traffickers at night in the hills of Turkey, volunteers warming people suffering from hypothermia, young servicemen and -women affixing weapons to fighter jets, children bored or at play in a camp, and other scenes. Recorded at sixty frames a second, the film has a slow pace to match its dirgelike score, in which ambient noise, muffled dialogue, and faded music recorded onsite signal the breakdown of information over distance and mediation.

Visualizing an otherwise invisible quality—radiant heat—the thermal camera generates a unique representational mode for the migrant's recognizable but unclassified identity, or what Giorgio Agamben calls "bare life."[6] Heat becomes a metaphor for physical states (many journeying migrants die of exposure to cold), and for public interest in a subject (once a "hot topic" fades from the news, people's attention and compassion cool). The camera's range—it can see a heat signature more than thirty miles away—enables a view of a subject who is unknowingly surveilled and whose face cannot be recognized, while the camera's operator is displaced from his or her target behind an array of computer monitors. In Mosse's hands the technology becomes more than a means to an aesthetic end: by defamiliarizing individual migrants through the camera's estranging vision, he draws attention to the rhetoric of dehumanization that resists their movement. —ET

1. "Documentary photography is as constructed a way of seeing the world as anything else." Richard Mosse, quoted in Tom Seymour, "Incoming," *British Journal of Photography*, February 15, 2017. Available online at www.bjp-online.com/2017/02/mosse/ (accessed March 6, 2019).

2. See Cathy Haenlein, "Richard Mosse's *The Enclave*: Mediating Conflict in the Democratic Republic of the Congo," *The RUSI Journal* 159, no. 1 (February/March 2014):107.

3. Of his time in the Democratic Republic of the Congo, Mosse notes, "By the time photographers arrive there is nothing left to see. It was this lack of trace that interested me and ultimately the failure of documentary photography. Conflict is complicated and unresolvable and it's not always easy to find the concrete subject, the issue, and put it in front of the lens." Quoted in Seymour, "Incoming."

4. Mosse, quoted in Teo Kermeliotis, "Stunning Congo artwork shows conflict in a different light," *Inside Africa*, CNN, June 5, 2013. Available online at www.cnn.com/2013/06/05/world/africa/congo-richard-mosse-the-enclave/index.html (accessed January 27, 2019).

5. Mosse, in Seymour, "Incoming."

6. In "Biopolitics and the Life of Man," the primary essay in *Incoming*, Giorgio Agamben argues that the refugee—a person with no sovereignty but only "bare life"—should be considered not beyond human rights but rather the ideal of twenty-first-century civilization. This text was originally published in Agamben, *Homo Sacer: Sovereign Power and Bare Life* (Stanford, CA: Stanford University Press, 1998). See also Christy Lange, "One Take: Incoming." *Frieze*, March 4, 2017. Available online at https://frieze.com/article/one-take-incoming (accessed January 27, 2019).

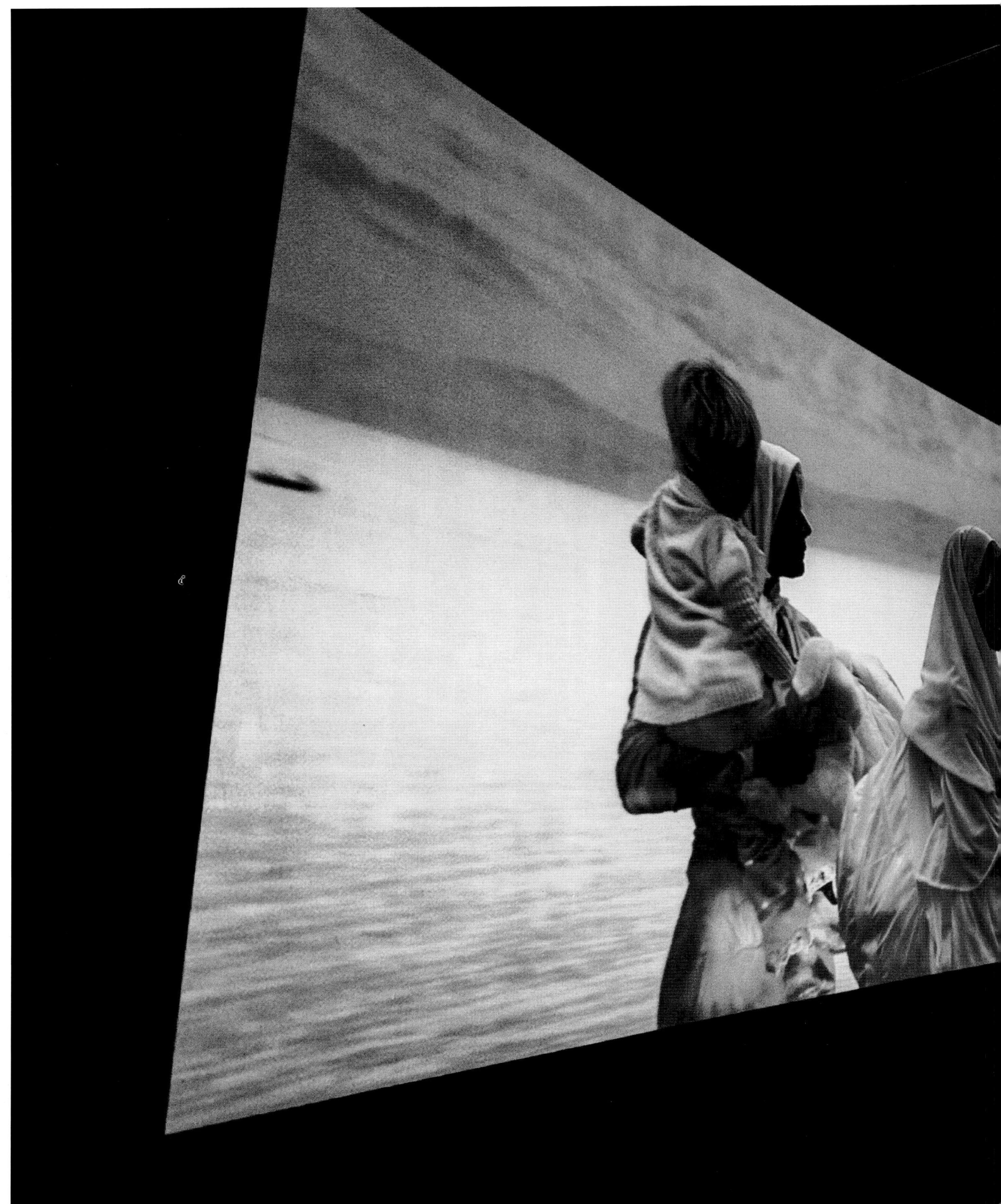

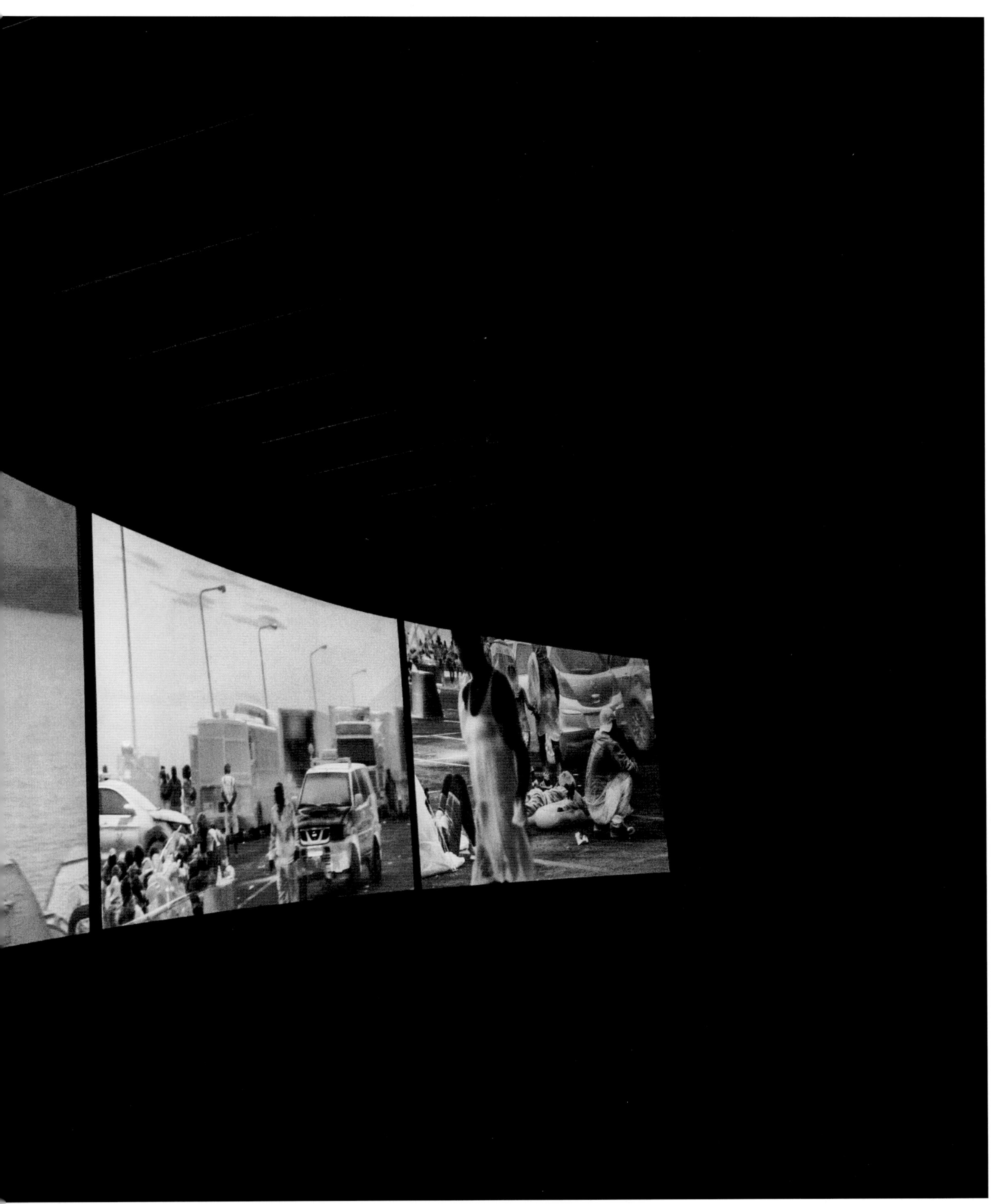

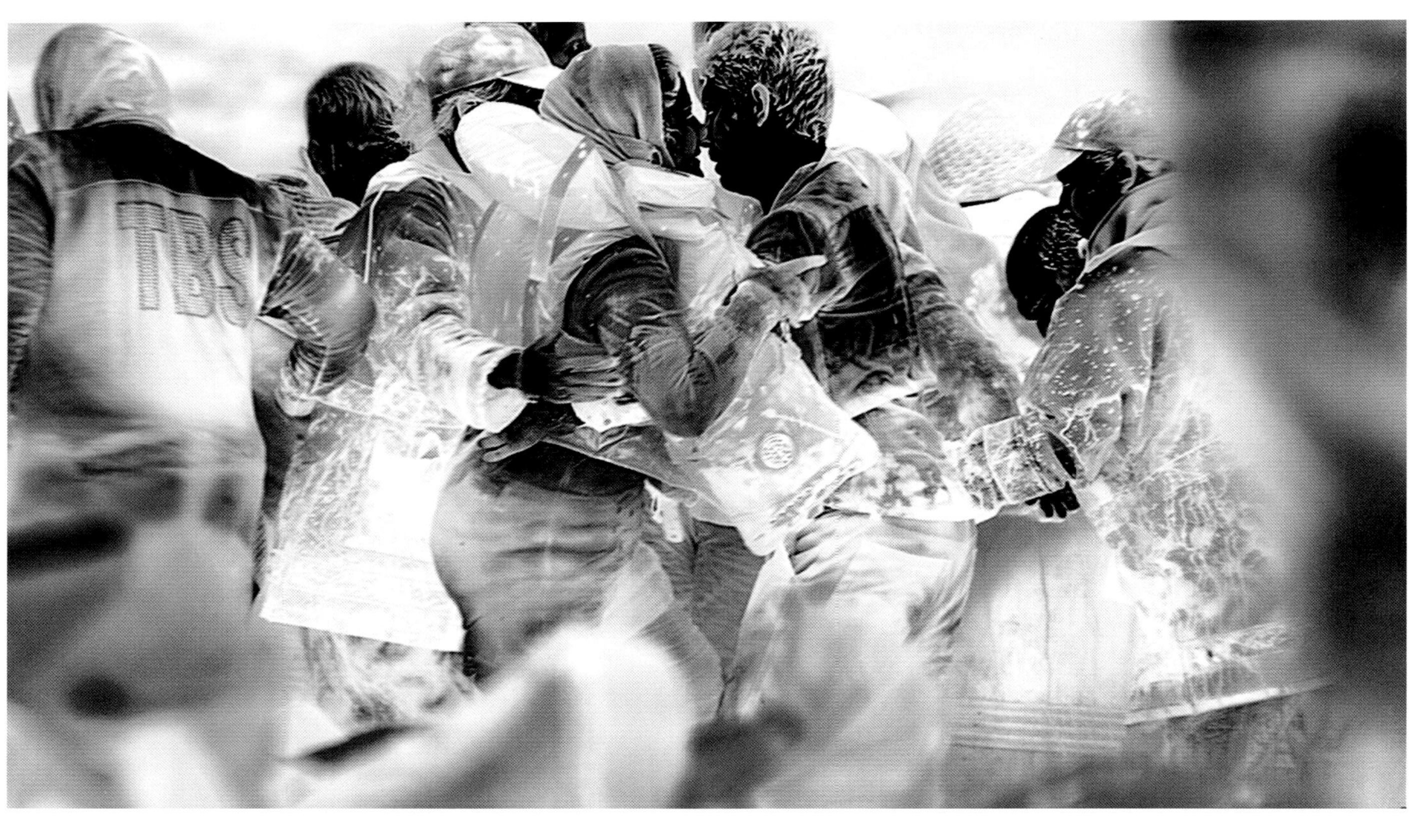

Previous spread:
Richard Mosse, *Incoming*, 2014–17.
Three-channel HD video installation (black-and-white, 7.3 surround sound; 52:10 minutes). Dimensions variable. Installation view, *Richard Mosse: Incoming*, The Curve, Barbican Centre, London, 2017

Above, opposite, and following spread:
Richard Mosse, *Incoming* (stills), 2014–17

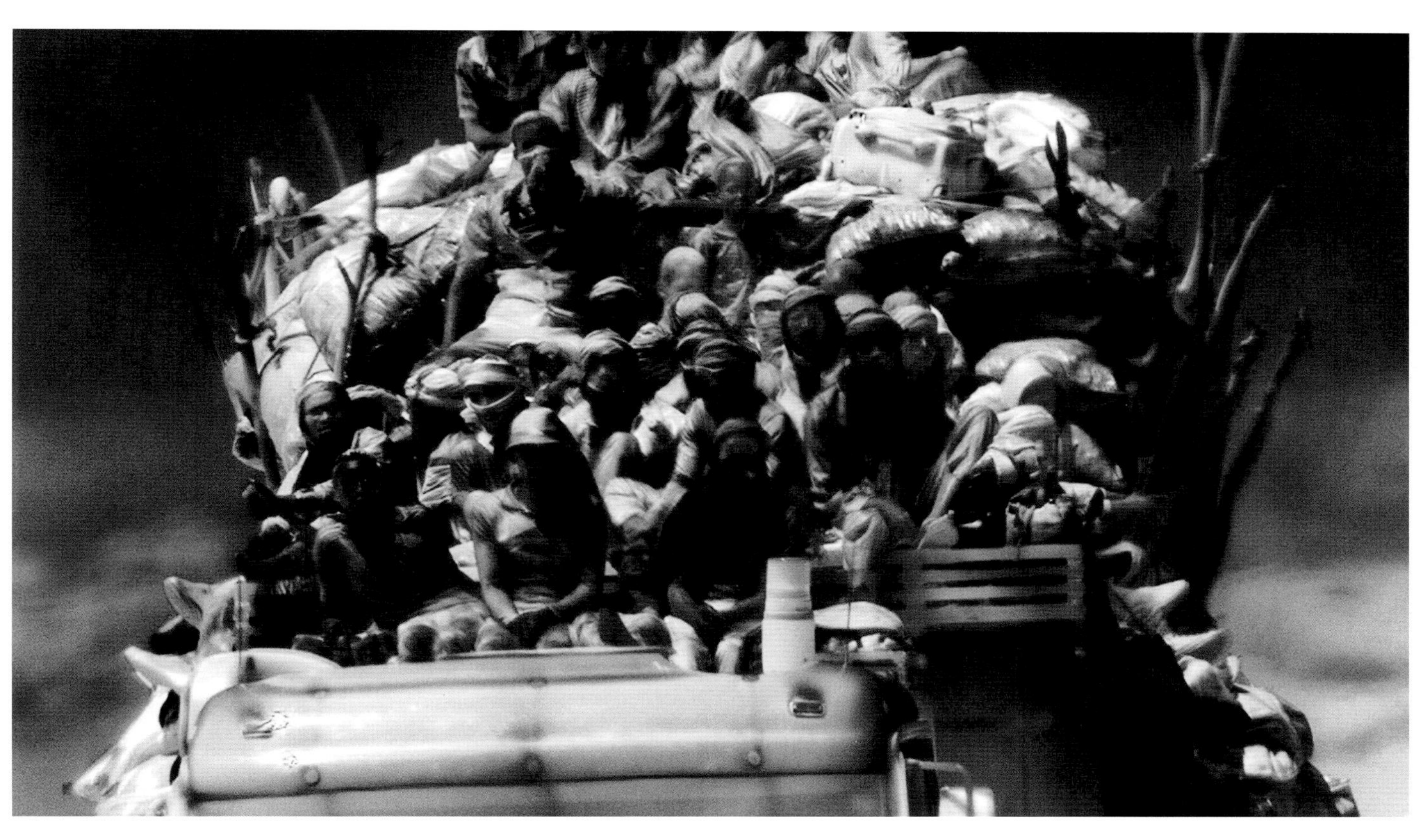

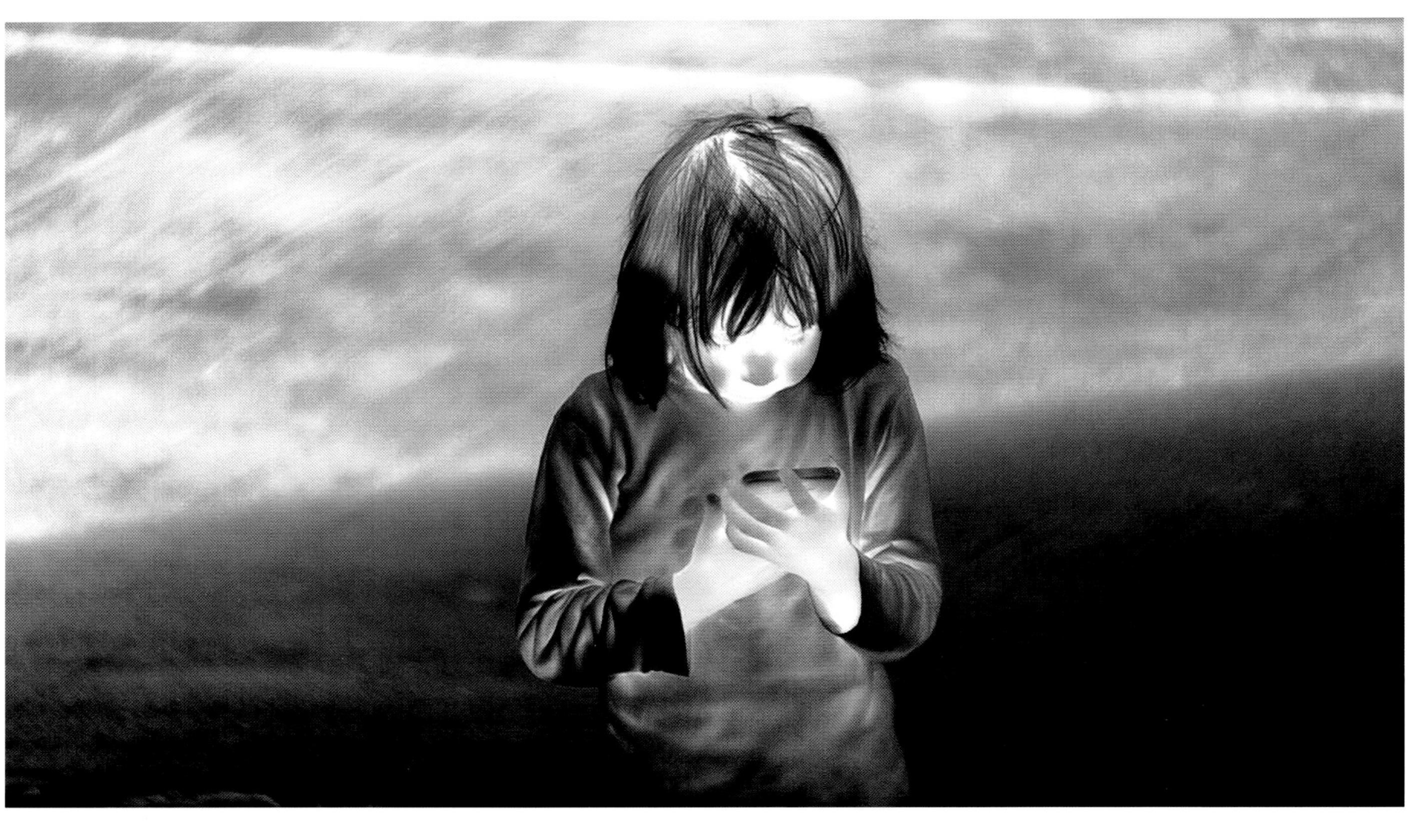

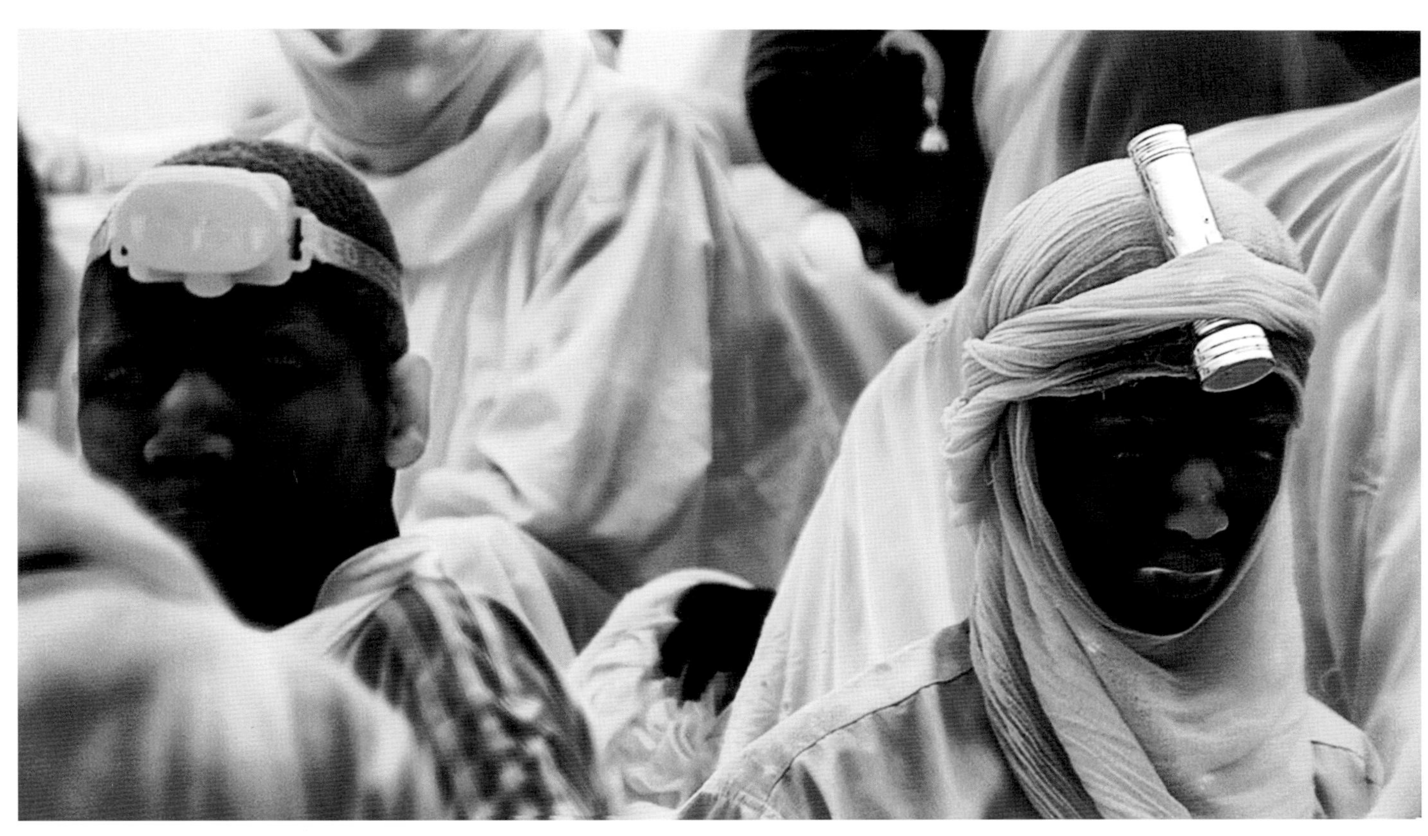

Hayv Kahraman

B. 1981, Baghdad, Iraq;
lives and works in Los Angeles

Born in Baghdad, Hayv Kahraman became a refugee at the age of ten, when she and her family sought asylum in Sweden during the 1990–91 Gulf War. Feeling visibly "other" compared with her blond and blue-eyed peers, Kahraman turned to art to cope with her difficult personal experiences, finding in her artistic practice "some sort of survival mechanism," in her words.[1] She continued her training at Umeå University in Sweden and the Cappiello-Accademia di Design e Comunicazione in Florence, Italy, before establishing a studio practice in the United States. Now based in Los Angeles, Kahraman continues to work primarily in painting and fabric arts, with a recent interest in sculpture, installation, and performance.

For Kahraman, the body, like the home, is a shifting specter of refuge. Her paintings of women, often with thick black hair and translucent skin, are at once self-referential and open-ended: "Since my work is semi-autobiographical, using my body was a clear decision.... But the body is also our common denominator; it's a language that we all possess."[2] That this language possesses bodies differently, however, is key for Kahraman: "I prefer to stay away from any statements that universalize us. I understand that we have commonalities but I can't state that we are all the same, universally. I feel that there's a danger there in erasing the localities of peoples."[3]

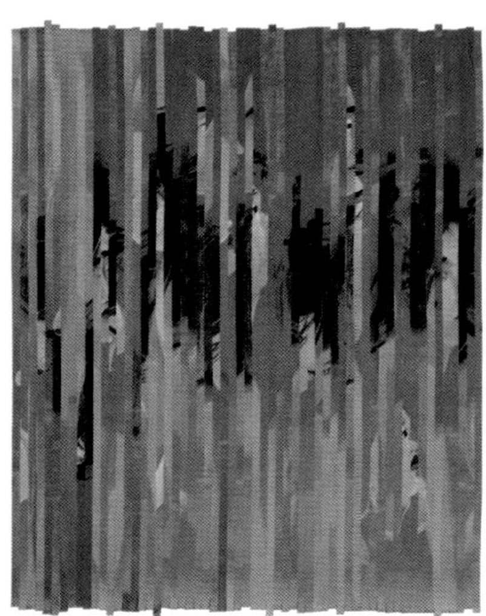

Fig. 1. Hayv Kahraman, *Strip 1*, 2017.
Oil on linen, 39 x 32 inches (99 x 81.3 cm)

The characters in her large-scale oil paintings hold their bodies in suspension, listless yet intensely physical. In *Bab el Sheikh* (2013) [pp. 62–63], life-or-near-life-size female-presenting figures reach for one another with subtle boldness and lethargic elasticity. Rendering faces in opaque white paint with dark haloes of black hair, Kahraman gives her characters' skin an almost transparent sheen. The figures circle over a schematic domestic floor plan, gazing through rooms and doorways. These subjects—the collective "*She*" that so often appears in Kahraman's paintings—are at once familiar and fleeting, existing not in the real of our experience but somewhere in the margins.[4]

In thinking with this "*She*," Kahraman troubles categorical ideas of who is included in "we" and "I." Her painting models in some ways a formal inquiry into how traditional notions of identity, community, and the human reify exclusionary structures and other oppressive systems, such as discrimination based on race, sex, or nationality. Her art examines identity as something that is practiced and constantly shifting, rather than fixed.[5] As Kahraman explains, "I am concerned with the multitude not the self. This is not only my story. It can be the story of more than 5 million people within the Iraqi diaspora or any diaspora."[6] Overall, her work represents what risks being lost in the reduction to a singular definition or perspective, whether by the myth of the universal or the overdetermined idea of the self.

Inspired by figurative and miniature paintings, Kahraman pays intense attention to details of face, posture, and costume, while her usually muted backgrounds incorporate architectures gleaned from memories of Iraq and other places she has lived. Regardless of medium, her practice seeks to evoke and mirror the ways in which identities, stories, and memories take hold of our psychic and social relationships. *Bab el Sheikh*, for example, models a subversive return of the gaze in which the figures avoid our own even as they search, instead, for each others'. This coy disinterest in any other authority but their own feels at odds with how the brown female subject has been depicted in popular media and cultural mores, in stereotypes of the submissive or the sequestered; here, the domestic space is commanded by figures who hover imposingly at its margins, always present but still out of reach. An artist's text accompanying the installation declares, "The house is my domain.... I am behind these walls. Tamed and constrained. Yet this is my domain."[7]

Seeing the body as "a language that we all possess," Kahraman creates characters that challenge assumptions of how identities form and attach to racialized subjects, especially those perceived as "other."[8] She explains, "My work confronts those notions of the exotic other seen and perceived in the

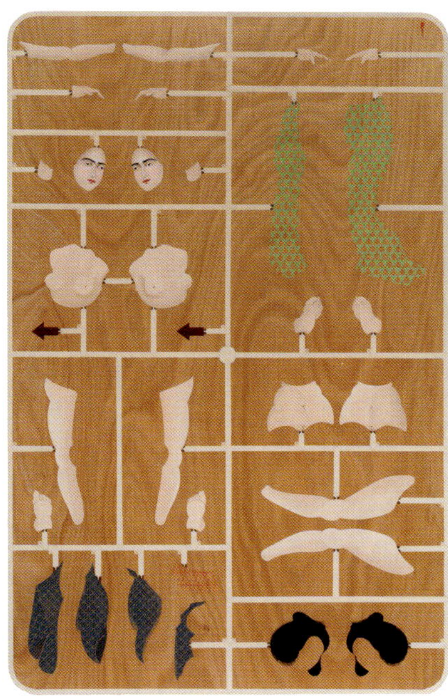

Fig. 2. Hayv Kahraman, *Iraqi Kit*, 2016. Oil on panel, 74 x 48 inches (188 x 121.9 cm)

west. . . . And I do so via a reverse logic, by painting what the western eye is so accustomed to seeing, the figure of the Renaissance."[9] We may see Renaissance ideas in the contrapposto postures of her characters, such as the figure who stretches her raised arm in the bottom-right panel of *Bab el Sheikh*. At the same time, Kahraman is highly conscious of her art-historical references, describing this reliance on the Western eye—even to upend or confuse it—as a marker of her own colonization.[10] In an effort to grapple with these associations, she often introduces disorienting strategies and perspectives that belie the tranquility of her compositions, such as the disintegrating faces that lurk between planes in *Strip 1* (2017) [fig. 1], or the "other" body easily broken into pieces in *Iraqi Kit* (2016) [fig. 2]. As Kahraman explains, the sense of nonchalant violence that haunts her works mirrors the psychic qualities of rootlessness, "a subdued state of mind; of being and existing as a refugee. These women are left fragmented and abnormal, sort of like cyborgs or hybrid identities that are the outcome of colonialism and war."[11] This notion of fragmentation, as well as the desire to surmount or evade it, is palpable in *Bab el Sheikh*, whose figures are separated from each other and from the home they encircle, even as they lie close and outstretched toward it.

Kahraman's practice reckons with an inescapable sense of unknowability among diasporic communities, something also explored in her projects documenting the architecture of her childhood home in Iraq. In *Bab el Sheikh*, the absent home is rendered only as blueprint, unrealizable in physical form, just as the translucent figures who hover over the space appear to exist in some third, other dimension. The feeling of imminence, whether of departure, arrival, belonging, or materiality, hovers over the work, and through much of the artist's practice. Kahraman explains, "When you work so hard to shed that brown skin and black hair in order to fit into a western context, eventually you grow tired. So where do you go after that? Back to the past."[12] —AP

1. Hayv Kahraman, in e-mail correspondence with the author, August 22, 2018.

2, Kahraman, in Olivia Parkes, "The Artist Painting Memories of Iraq," *Broadly*, July 9, 2016. Available online at www.hayvkahraman.com/2017/01/23/the-artist-painting-memories-of-iraq-broadly-vice/ (accessed December 25, 2018).

3, Kahraman, in e-mail correspondence with the author, January 29, 2019.

4. Kahraman, "The Art of Mending," in *Hayv Kahraman: Acts of Reparation*, exh. cat. (St. Louis: Contemporary Art Museum St. Louis, 2017), p. 15.

5. Kahraman has often referenced the work of postcolonial theorist Trinh T. Minh-ha, whose work on postcolonial and diasporic identity continues to influence the artist's conception of time, history, and the self. See Trinh, *Woman, Native, Other: Writing Postcoloniality and Feminism* (Bloomington and Indianapolis: Indiana University Press, 1986).

6. Kahraman, in "Ladies in Waiting: Glass meets seminal Iraqi artist Hayv Kahraman," *Glass Magazine* no. 28 (Winter 2016). Available online at www.hayvkahraman.com/2017/01/22/ladies-in-waiting-glass-magazine-2016/ (accessed December 25, 2018).

7. Kahraman, quoted in Walter D. Mignolo, "Let the guest be the master: Border thinking and the Aesthetic Potential of Migrant Consciousness," 2013. Available online at http://www.hayvkahraman.com/2017/01/22/let-the-guest-be-the-master-border-thinking-and-the-aesthetic-potential-of-migrant-consciousness-walter-d-mignolo/ (accessed December 25, 2018).

8. Kahraman, in Parkes, "The Artist Painting Memories of Iraq."

9. Kahraman, in Anna Adell, "Hayv Kahraman, body as a container of diasporic memories," *le bastart*, March 2018. Available online at http://lebastart.com/en/2018/03/hayv-kahraman-body-container-diasporic-memories/ (accessed December 25, 2018).

10. Kahraman, in Parkes, "The Artist Painting Memories of Iraq."

11. Kahraman, in Myrna Ayad, "Extimacy," 2012. Available online at www.hayvkahraman.com/2017/01/22/extimacy-myrna-ayad/ (accessed December 25, 2018).

12. Kahraman, in "Ladies in Waiting: Glass meets seminal Iraqi artist Hayv Kahraman."

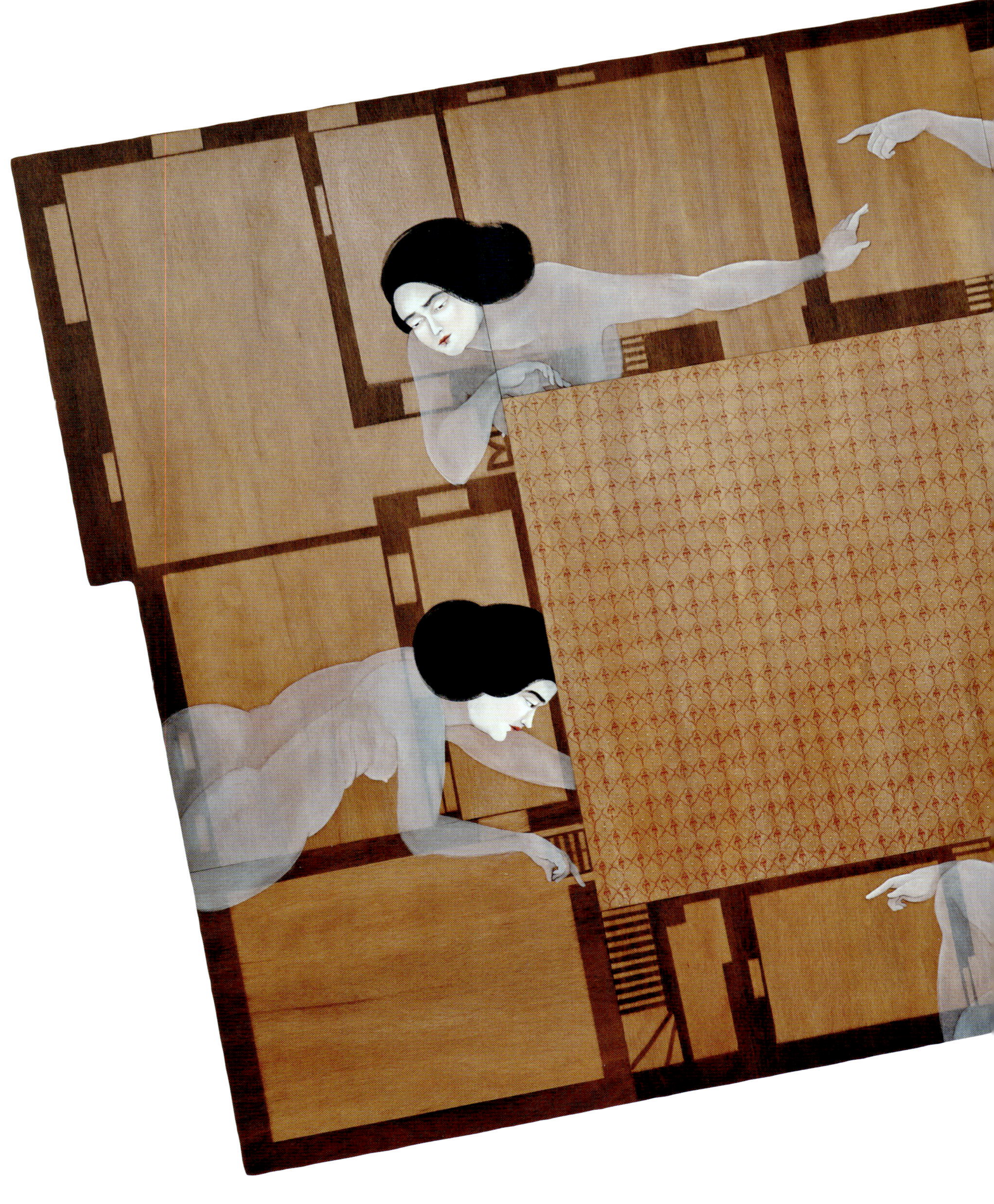

Hayv Kahraman, *Bab el Sheikh*, 2013.
Oil on wood. 9 feet 3 inches x 11 feet 10 inches (281.9 x 360.7 cm)

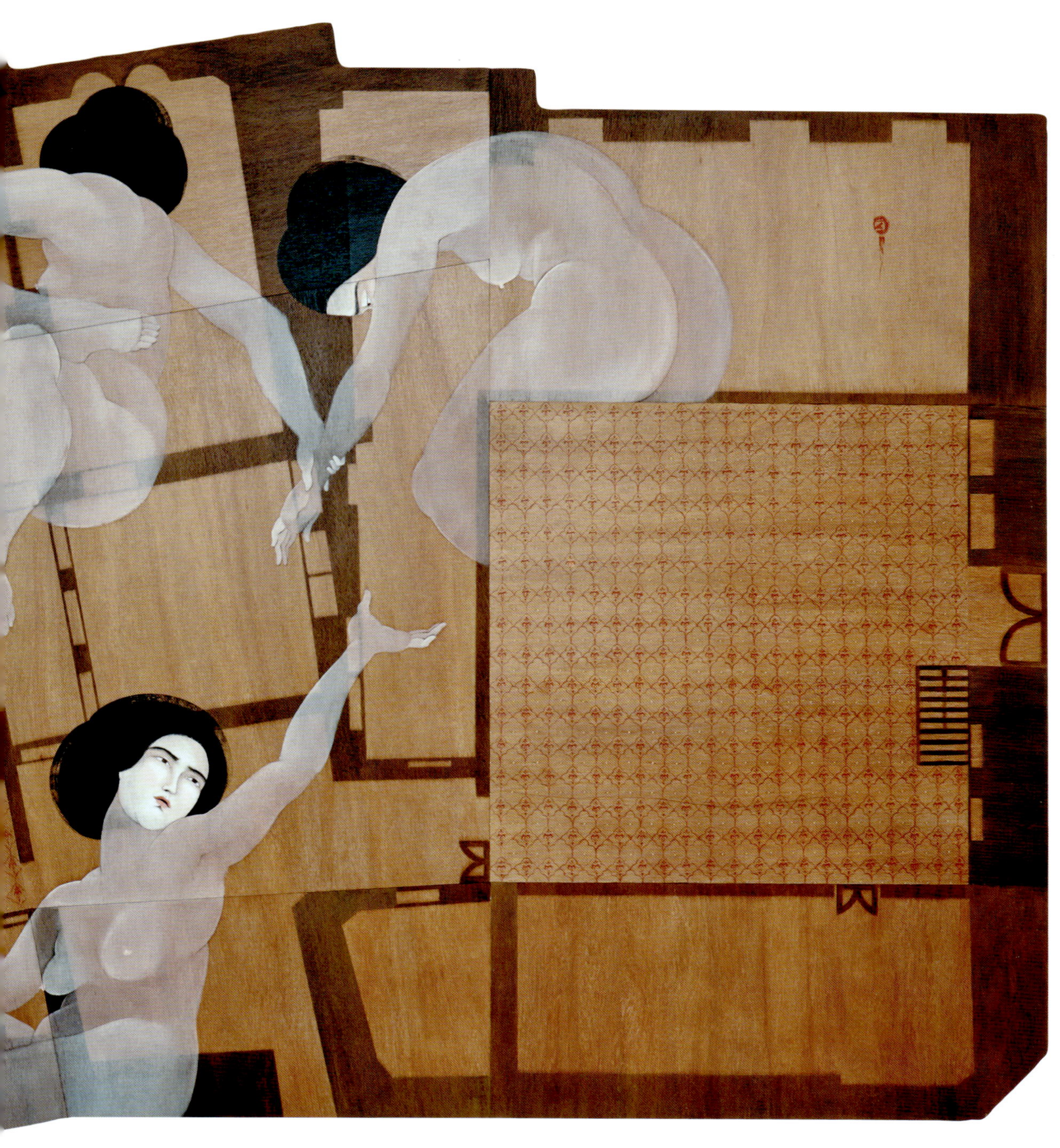

Rineke Dijkstra

B. 1959, Sittard, the Netherlands;
lives and works in Amsterdam

Rineke Dijkstra's photographic portraits present a rare glimpse into the psychology of her subjects. Before being admitted to the Gerrit Rietveld Academie in Amsterdam, Dijkstra studied at the city's De Moor photography center (now the Amsterdams Centrum voor Fotografie). She came to appreciate photography for its ability to toy with its own aesthetic conditions: according to the artist, a person's portrait enables "a relationship with the *picture*, not necessarily with them."[1] The portraits she has produced since then depart from objective orchestration while maintaining a concentrated composition. The rich detail of her large-format prints offers viewers an unadorned look at her sitters, who are often photographed during vulnerable moments in their lives—as teenagers on the cusp of change, say, or as young mothers.

Dijkstra creates her photographs using an analogue 4-by-5-inch camera, a cumbersome mechanical device that requires the use of a tripod, an outdoor flash, and an exacting, intuitive expertise. "People get nervous" when they see such a sizeable device, according to Dijkstra, who has described herself as a shy person who sympathizes with the difficulty of being before the camera.[2] In her portrait sessions, she often coaches her subjects through this self-conscious performance, inviting them to try their own poses at their own pace. "I try and look for an uninhibited moment," she explains, "where people forget about trying to control the image of themselves."[3] To achieve this, Dijkstra works to put her subjects at ease before the camera, until, at last, "a pose arises sort of unconsciously or naturally."[4]

It was during one such portraiture session that Dijkstra first met Almerisa, then a six-year-old Bosnian refugee living in the Netherlands. In 1994, the artist included the young girl in a commissioned project to document the children of refugees in Leiden and Amsterdam; she later chose to stay in touch with the family. Dijkstra has made portraits of Almerisa roughly every two years since, developing a visual archive of her transition from childhood to puberty to early adulthood, encompassing all the imprecise emotional and social changes that affect her body language, expression, and gaze as the series progresses [pp. 66–69; as of 2019 there are fifteen portraits in total]. In the first portrait, from March 1994, a young Almerisa sits demurely on a chair too high for her young legs to reach the ground. Curiously, it is the red chair that centers the photograph's formal composition, while Almerisa sits just off-center, turned at an angle, hands on her knees. This posture shifts in each subsequent portrait, from the slouch of a self-conscious adolescent to the protective embrace of a young mother, charting both physical and emotional transformations over time.

Dijkstra describes her choice to focus the camera only on Almerisa, rather than on her broader domestic surroundings, as part of an aesthetic decision she made early on with her portrait work: "If you show too much of a subject's personal life, the viewer will immediately make assumptions. If you leave out details the viewer has to look for much subtler hints."[5] Thus, throughout the series, the viewer is compelled to engage only with what Almerisa allows; she commands the images through gesture and gaze, as though she had authored them herself. In another sequential portrait series, titled Olivier (2000–03) [figs. 1–3], Dijkstra photographed a young Israeli enlistee in the French Foreign Legion over the course of three years. As the man's training and time in the army lengthen, his countenance, posture, and uniform change. Dijkstra notes, "When I was photographing Olivier Silva, every time I went to see him I thought he hadn't changed at all. But in the picture you can see the change in his eyes, in his expression."[6] Dijkstra is drawn to such intimate familiarity, casting attention to the face as a mask that, if examined closely enough, might reveal and invite another sense of self.

Dijkstra's compositional choices and exacting practice demonstrate her visual training, as well as how she has trained herself to be ready, always, for the moment when a subject has "dropped all pretense of a pose."[7] Inspired by photographers such as Diane Arbus and August Sander, Dutch masters such as Rembrandt van Rijn and Johannes Vermeer, and Impressionist painters such as Édouard Manet, Dijkstra also explains that her primary interest is in the emotional and psychological underpinnings of body, posture, and wordless behaviors. Her studied portraits suggest this visual lineage, but rather than follow fixed ideas of how ideal form reveals ideal interiority, they evoke instead a deliberate and almost painful rawness. In New Mothers (1994), for example, Dijkstra photographed three women who had just given birth to their first child, rendering images awash with the emotional arrival of new, and changed, life. Apart from the title of the work and the subjects depicted, no other narrative details are offered, lending the portrait an intense concentration. This focused, simple singularity is also what makes Almerisa's

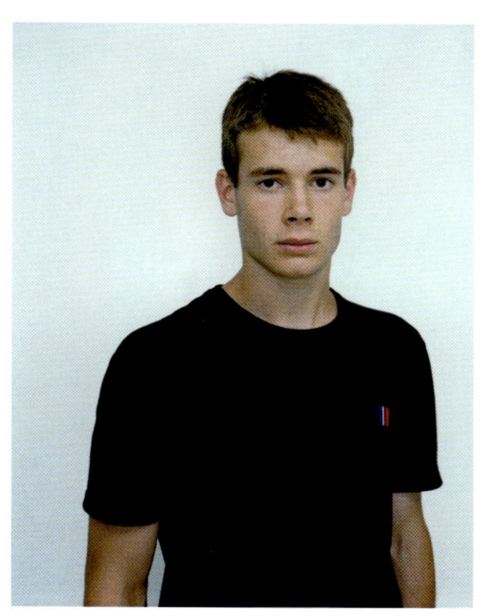

Olivier, Quartier Viénot, Marseille, July 21, 2000, 2000

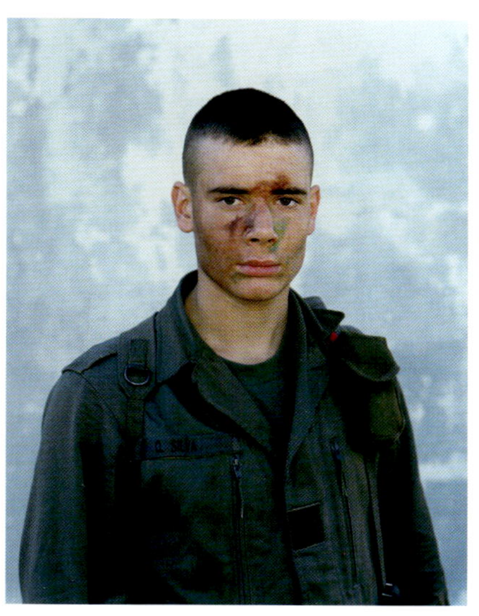

Olivier, Les Guerses, France, November 1, 2000, 2000

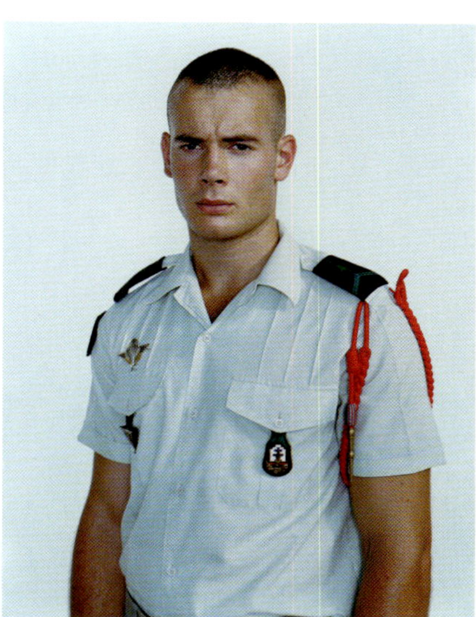

Olivier, Quartier Monclar, Djibouti, July 13, 2003, 2003

Figs. 1–3. Rineke Dijkstra, from the series Olivier, 2000–03.
All chromogenic color prints, 49 13⁄16 x 42 11⁄16 inches (126.5 x 108.5 cm)

portraits so striking, even as they elide much of her personal circumstances beyond what she (like all of Dijkstra's subjects) chooses to share with the gaze of the camera.

Dijkstra's photographs demonstrate her mastery in eliciting not what only the camera can see, but what lies behind how we wish to be seen by others, and sometimes even by ourselves. As she explains, in photography "I think I found a language, how to show things, that can make you look at things in a slightly different way than what you're used to."[8] With entrancing effect, Dijkstra's portraits question how the assumptions we make from what we see of others affect our judgments about them. Although Almerisa's portraits chart the transition of a child into an adult, they offer little else about the specific kinds of challenges that a refugee and woman might experience in a new country. Less a documentation of a single life than a steady meditation on life's pace, the series manages to evoke an individual experience of migration while retaining the subject's agency in how—and how much of—this experience is shared with viewers. —AP

1. Rineke Dijkstra, in Sabine Mirlesse, "The Vulnerables: Interview with Rineke Dijkstra," *Art in America*, June 25, 2012. Available online at www.artinamericamagazine.com/news-features/interviews/rineke-dijkstra-guggenheim-sfmoma/ (accessed January 28, 2019).

2. Dijkstra, quoted in Conor Risch, "Rineke Dijkstra: Seeing Is Believing," *PDN*, January 23, 2012. Available online at www.pdnonline.com/features/photographer-interviews/rineke-dijkstra-seeing-is-believing/ (accessed January 28, 2019).

3. Dijkstra, in Anne-Celine Jaeger, "A Conversation with Rineke Dijkstra," *Popular Photography*, December 16, 2008. Available online at www.popphoto.com/how-to/2008/12/conversation-rineke-dijkstra (accessed January 28, 2019).

4. Dijkstra, quoted in Grace Banks, "One for all: Rineke Dijkstra's portraits go on show at Louisiana Museum of Modern Art," *Wallpaper**, November 30, 2017. Available online at https://www.wallpaper.com/art/rineke-dijkstra-louisiana-museum-of-modern-art (accessed January 28, 2019).

5. Dijkstra, quoted in Alissa Guzman, "Rineke Dijkstra: Contemporary Photographer or Old Master?," *Hyperallergic*, October 2, 2012. Available online at https://hyperallergic.com/57764/rineke-dijkstra-retrospective-guggenheim/ (accessed January 28, 2019).

6. Ibid.

7. Ibid.

8. Dijkstra, quoted in Risch, "Rineke Dijkstra: Seeing Is Believing."

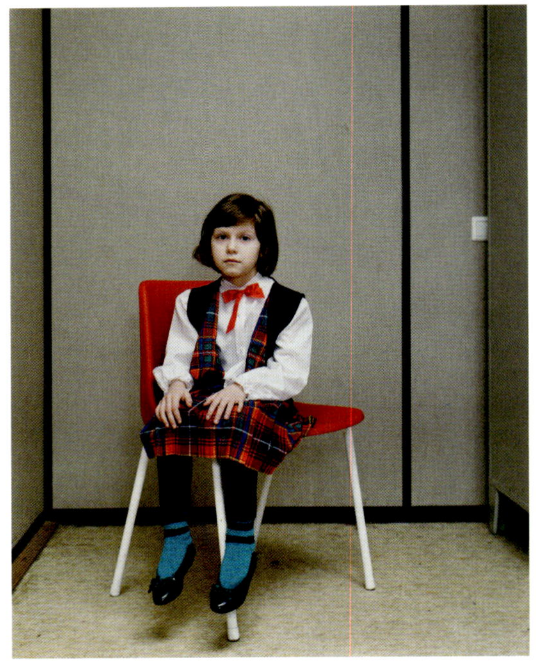

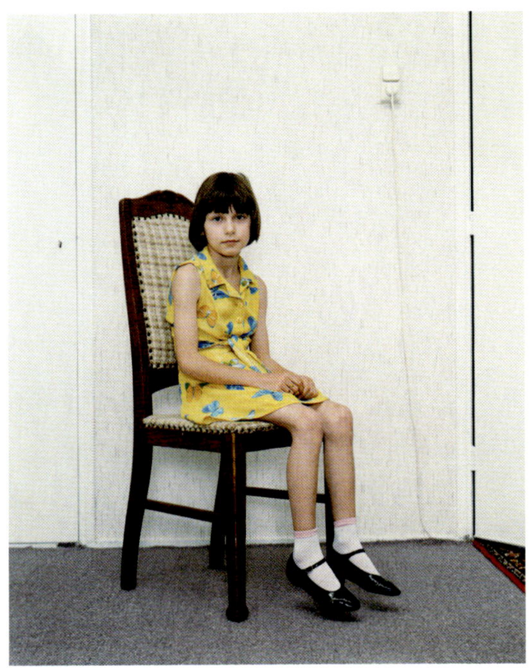

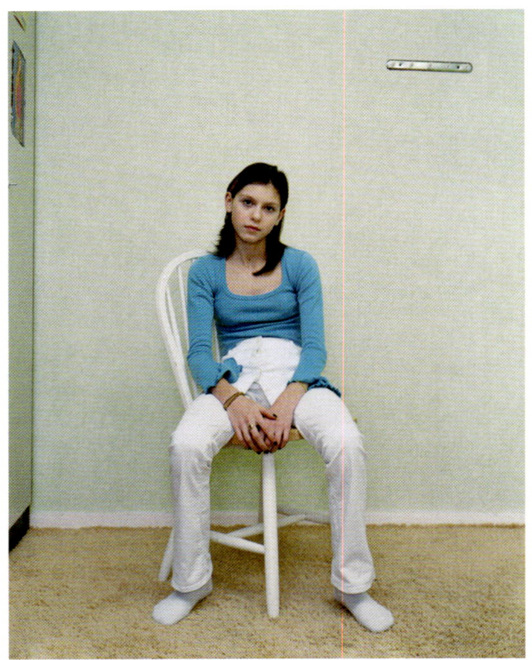

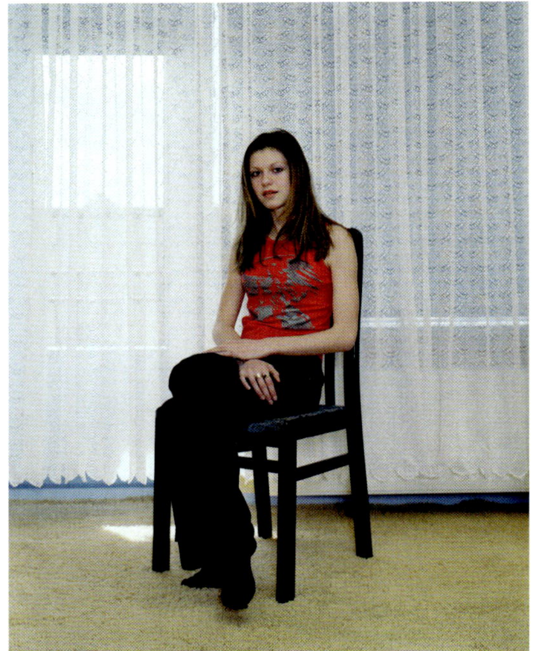

Above, opposite, and following spread:
Rineke Dijkstra. Chromogenic color prints.
14 15⁄16 x 11 13⁄16 inches (38 x 30 cm)

Almerisa, Asylum Seekers' Center, Leiden, the Netherlands, March 14, 1994, 1994

Almerisa, Wormer, the Netherlands, June 23, 1996, 1996

Almerisa, Leidschendam, the Netherlands, December 9, 2000, 2000

Almerisa, Leidschendam, the Netherlands, April 13, 2002, 2002

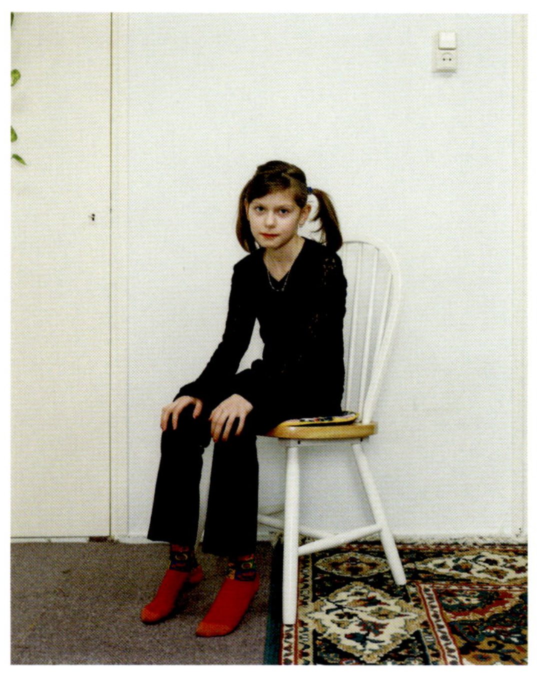

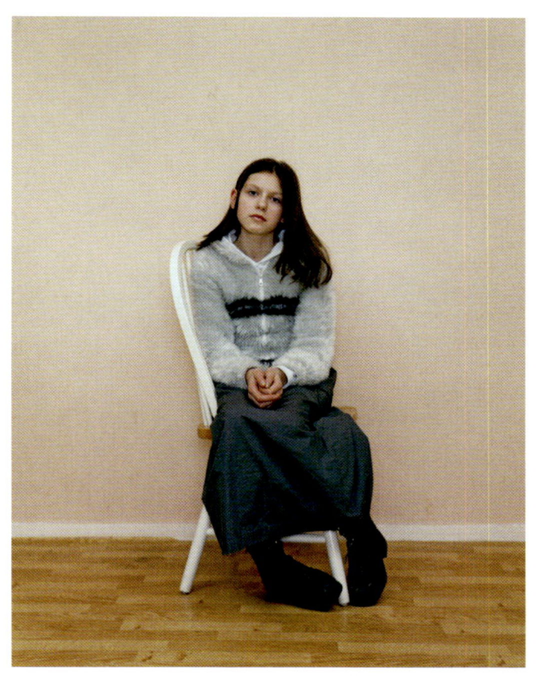

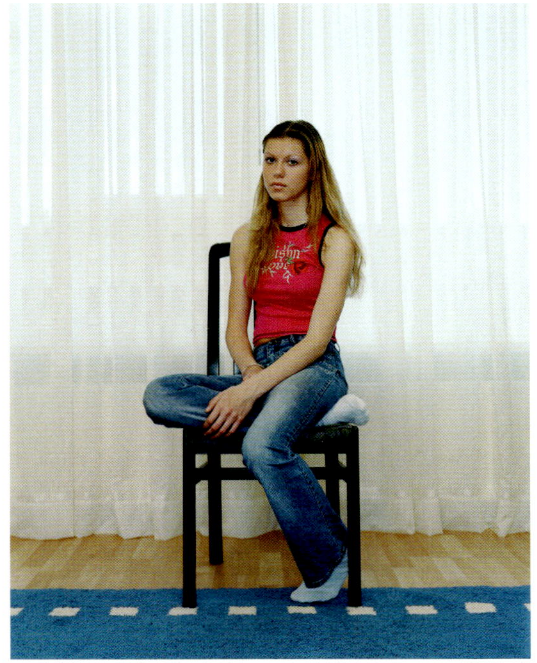

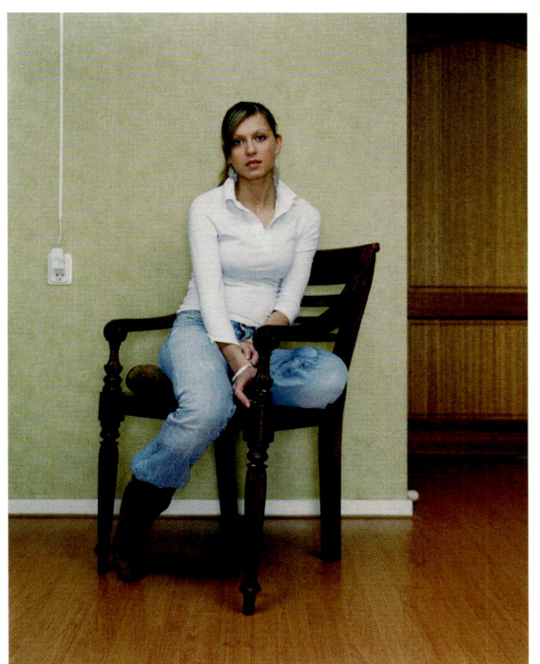

Almerisa, Wormer, the Netherlands, February 21, 1998, 1998

Almerisa, Leidschendam, the Netherlands, March 19, 2000, 2000

Almerisa, Leidschendam, the Netherlands, June 25, 2003, 2003

Almerisa, Leidschendam, the Netherlands, March 29, 2005, 2005

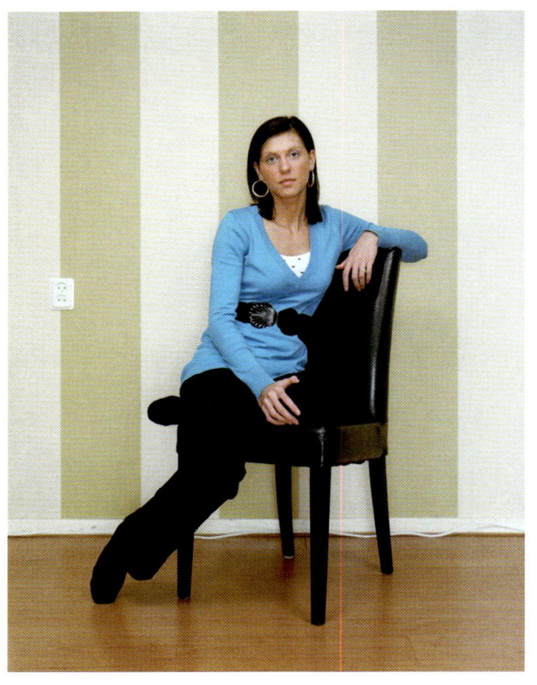

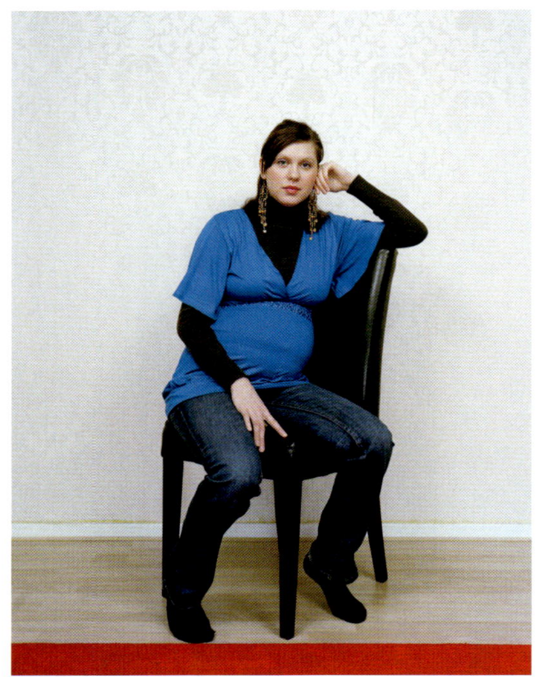

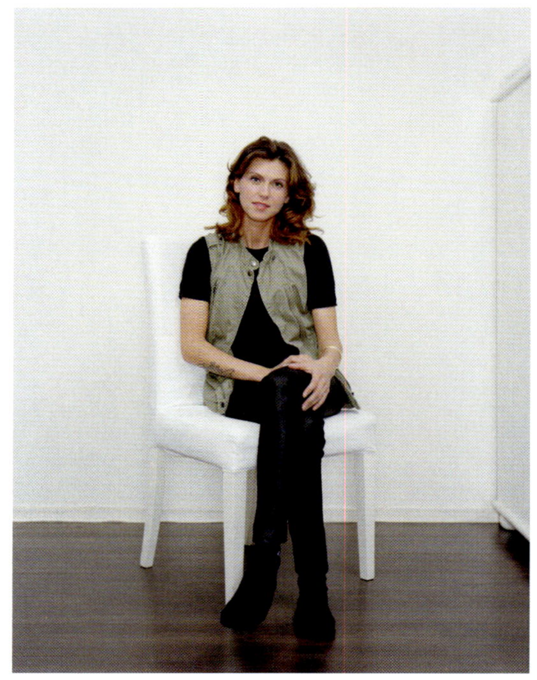

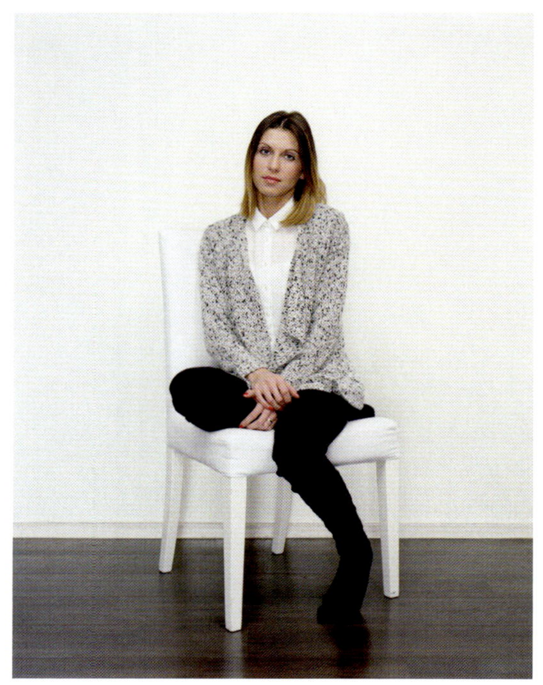

Almerisa, Zoetermeer, the Netherlands, March 24, 2007, 2007

Almerisa. Zoetermeer, the Netherlands, January 4, 2008, 2008

Almerisa, Rotterdam, the Netherlands, August 8, 2013, 2013

Almerisa. Rotterdam, the Netherlands, February 8, 2015, 2015

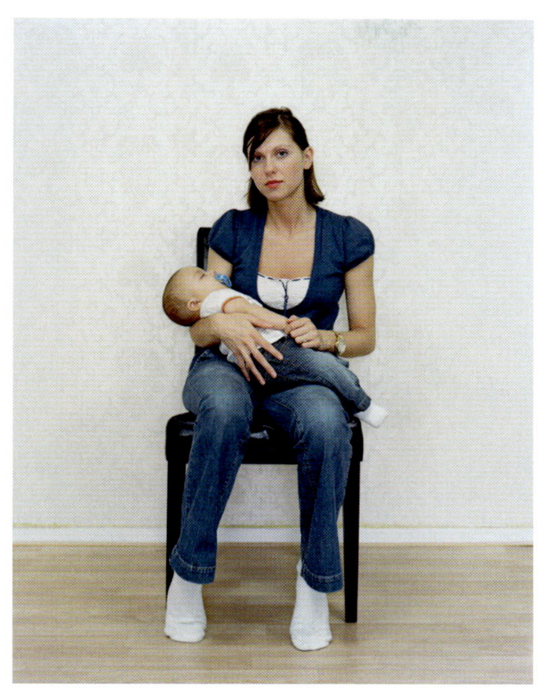

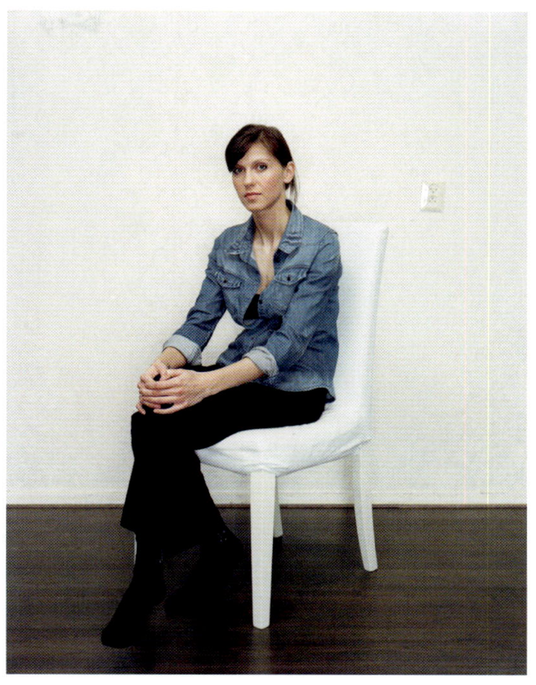

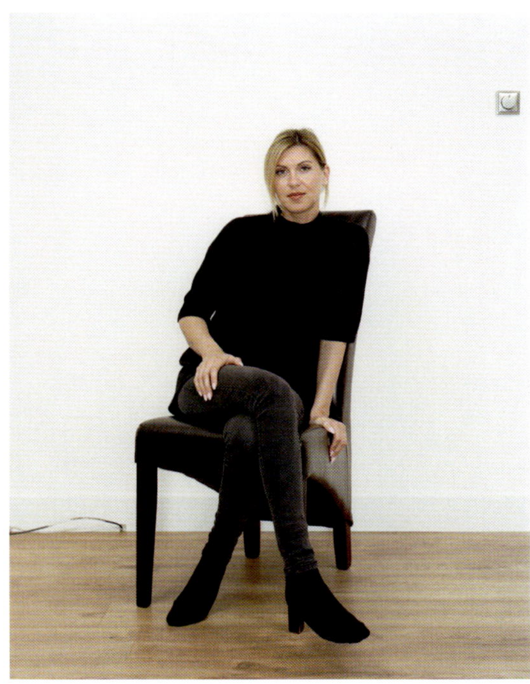

Almerisa, Zoetermeer, the Netherlands, June 19, 2008, 2008

Almerisa, Rotterdam, the Netherlands, December 27, 2011, 2011

Almerisa, Rotterdam, the Netherlands, May 26, 2017, 2017

Do Ho Suh

B. 1962, Seoul, Korea;
lives and works in London, New York, and Seoul

Whether through immense sculptures dealing with the figure of home or the body, or small-scale fabric works that tease at the intimacies of memory and time, Do Ho Suh engages the relationship between the individual and the collective. Born in South Korea, Suh studied painting and sculpture at Seoul National University, the Rhode Island School of Design, and Yale University before establishing a small studio in his rented New York basement apartment in the early 1990s. Here he began to explore the attachment of memories to physical space, or how, as he has remarked, "your house gets inside of you."[1] Finding a language of memory in the materiality of place, Suh's work traverses media, scales, and sites to negotiate the personal associations and social relationships that regenerate as people move from place to place.

Suh is perhaps best known for fabric sculptures that are one-to-one-scale replicas of the various rooms, corridors, and thresholds of the many places he has called home. For Suh, the life of a home is layered—many people may pass through a given place, leaving innumerable traces behind—and as such, home is a mutable condition: "As we all move around from one country to another, from one city to another and from one space to another, we are always crossing boundaries of all sorts.... And with this constant passing through spaces, I wonder how much of one's own space one carries along with oneself."[2] Interpreting one's longing for home as a kind of second skin, the artist endeavors to give these sensations a material form, evoking the fragility of memory itself. Translucent fabrics such as silk or polyester are a natural choice for rendering the precarity of memory, a concept that Suh has addressed throughout his prolific career.

His first fabric sculpture, *Seoul Home/L.A. Home/New York Home/Baltimore Home/London Home/Seattle Home/L.A. Home* (1999), was developed as a portable version of his family's home in South Korea, to which he began attaching recreations of his other dwellings, including (as the title indicates) his homes in New York, Baltimore, London, Seattle, and Los Angeles.[3] For each addition, Suh takes precise measurements of a physical space such as a stairwell, room, or corridor (sometimes with the aid of computer modeling software), including not only the architectural design but also everyday fixtures such as a toilet, sink, or kitchen equipment. Everything from a staircase to a radiator is reproduced in thin colored polyester fabrics or silk, hand stitched using a traditional Korean sewing method, and supported by a structure of thin metal rods. The result is a delicate rendering of a given home's skeletal residue, one that viewers are invited to traverse and share, despite the autobiographical tone of the installation's production and content.

Experiential entanglement is an important feature of these fabric works, which are more sculptural than architectural. The fabric's translucency is haunting, as though this physical manifestation could fade as much as Suh's own memories of his various homes. Indeed, the artist avoids suggesting that the homes are exact representations; rather, for Suh, "it's more about capturing enough visual and physical information to evoke a sense of the space as I experienced it."[4] He appears interested less in reproducing a tangible artifact of his lived experiences than in preserving the feeling of traversing again once-familiar spaces.

Suh's fabric structures are often installed next to one another, like parts of a single home. Each is a sculptural imitation of the different spaces Suh has inhabited in the course of his life, usually constructed in part rather than in full. Among his most recent productions, *Hub-2, Breakfast Corner, 260-7, Sungbook-Dong, Sungboo-Ku, Seoul, Korea* (2018) [p. 76] and *Hub-1, Entrance, 260-7, Sungbook-Dong, Sungboo-Ku, Seoul, Korea* (2018) [p. 77] respectively depict an eating area and the threshold to his childhood home in South Korea; *Wieland-str. 18, 12159 Berlin—3 Corridors* (2011) [pp. 4–5], meanwhile, shows the hallways in his German apartment. Produced in different colors (pink, yellow, and green, respectively), the passageways between the rooms are connective threads, inviting an interspatial movement rooted in memory, nostalgia, and imagination. This wistfulness is a central motivation for Suh:

> At some point in your life, you have to leave your home. And whenever you go back, it's just not the same home anymore.... I didn't want to sit down and cry for home. I wanted to more actively deal with these issues of longing. I decided not to be sad about it. I just want to go with it. I just want to carry that with me, you know, all the time.[5]

By centering experience, Suh's works isolate highly individual associations and confront assumptions of how we inhabit the world as social beings. He explains, "I am interested in the space that moves

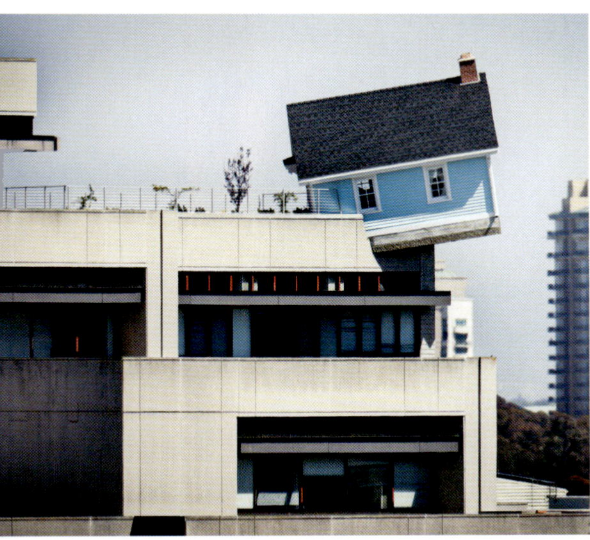

Fig. 1. Do Ho Suh, *Fallen Star*, 2012. Steel-frame house, concrete foundation, brick, chimney, garden, lawn chairs, table, hibachi-style grill, bird bath and bird house, 15 x 18 feet (457.2 x 548.6 cm). The Stuart Collection, University of California San Diego

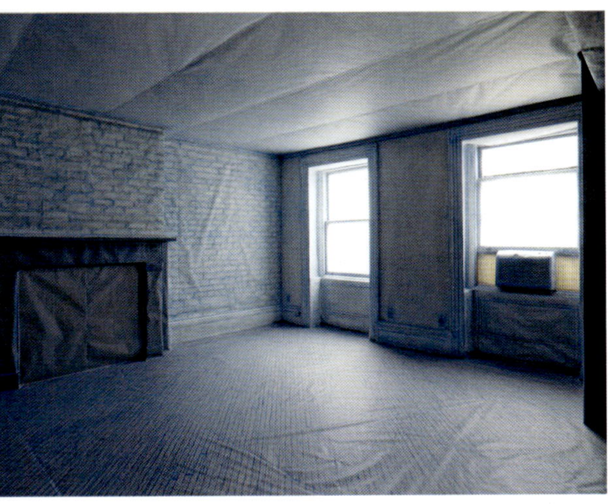

Fig. 2. Do Ho Suh, *Rubbing/Loving Project: Apartment A, 348 West 22nd Street, New York, NY 10011, USA*, 2014. Rubbing paper on wooden panels, dimensions variable

along with me, or that I move with me . . . the space in/through which I feel good, protected, comfortable, liberated, and the space that is imposed on me and therefore oppresses, confines, and alienates me."[6] This anxious attention to confinement and alienation also manifests in *Fallen Star* (2012) [fig. 1], a fully furnished cottage suspended at a precarious angle off the top of the Jacobs School of Engineering on the La Jolla campus of the University of California, San Diego. Recalling the disorientation he experienced upon arrival in the United States, Suh associates the work's literal instability with the discomfort of being in an unfamiliar and sometimes hostile land. Like the fabric works, *Fallen Star* asks the viewer to see place not merely as rooted in a particular location but equally as centered on the intangible and immaterial qualities of one's environment.

In 2012, Suh began a project he calls "rubbings," in which he applies crushed colored pastel to his fingers and laboriously rubs them over thin paper affixed to every inch of a living space. In 2016, he returned to his New York apartment soon after his former landlord had passed away, and began what would be his last project dealing with this space, as both a coping mechanism and a practice of letting go of his attachment to the apartment [fig. 2]. In taking his hands to each corner of the home, Suh hopes to "show the layers of time" that have marked his and others' relationships to the townhouse, tasking his concentration with the active and deliberate work of recollection.[7] Suh remarks, "I see life as a passageway, with no fixed beginning or destination."[8] His works dwell in this transient imminence of the in-between, framing the conditions by which we may see our past and present as intimately enfolded. —AP

1. Do Ho Suh, in Julian Rose, "Interviews: Do Ho Suh," Artforum.com, January 19, 2017. Available online at www.artforum.com/interviews/do-ho-suh-discusses-rubbing-loving-66014 (accessed December 23, 2018).

2. Suh, quoted in Hau Chu, "Colorful Fabric Structures at Smithsonian Explore What Home Means," *Washington Post*, March 27, 2018. Available online at www.washingtonpost.com/lifestyle/kidspost/colorful-fabric-structures-at-smithsonian-explore-what-home-means/2018/03/27/d02983fe-2dda-11e8-b0b0-f706877db618_story.html?utm_term=.46abcccf2195 (accessed December 23, 2018).

3. See Jennifer Johung, *Replacing Home: From Primordial Hut to Digital Network in Contemporary Art* (Minneapolis: University of Minnesota Press, 2011), p. 166.

4. Suh, in Rose, "Interviews: Do Ho Suh."

5. Suh, in Art21, "Seoul Home/L.A. Home"—Korea and Displacement. Do Ho Suh," November 2011. Available online at https://art21.org/read/do-ho-suh-seoul-home-la-home-korea-and-displacement/ (accessed December 23, 2018). Originally published on pbs.org in September 2003.

6. Suh, quoted in Sunjin Kim, *lightregularbold*, available online at www.lightregularbold.com/p/do-ho-suh/ (accessed December 23, 2018).

7. Suh, quoted in Art21, "Rubbing/Loving: Do Ho Suh," December 9, 2016. Available online at https://art21.org/watch/extended-play/do-ho-suh-rubbing-loving-short/ (accessed December 23, 2018).

8. Suh, quoted in Jim Biddulph, "Do Ho Such: Passage/s," Material Lab, March 3, 2017. Available online at https://www.material-lab.co.uk/journal/do-ho-such-passage-s/ (accessed December 23, 2018).

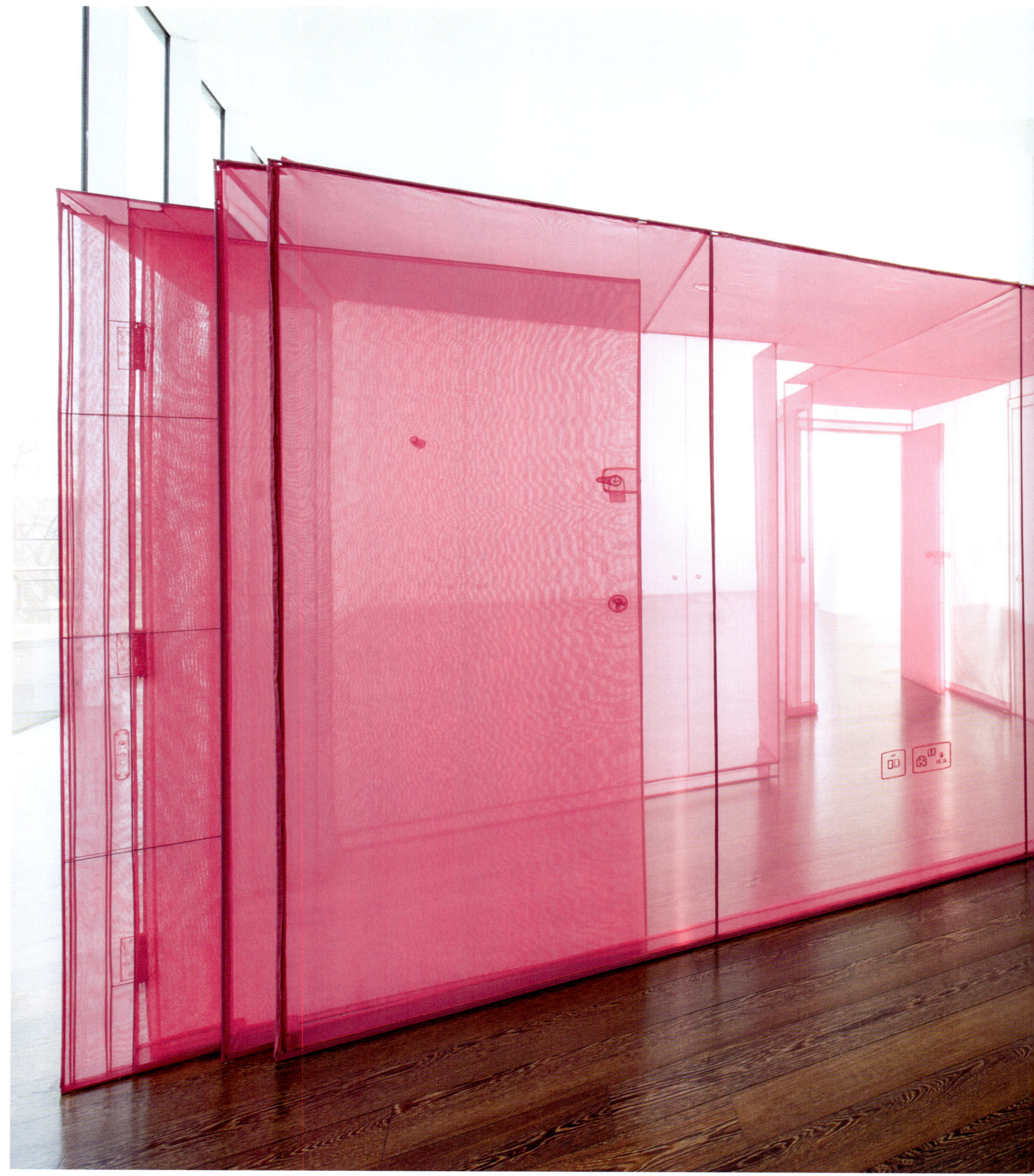

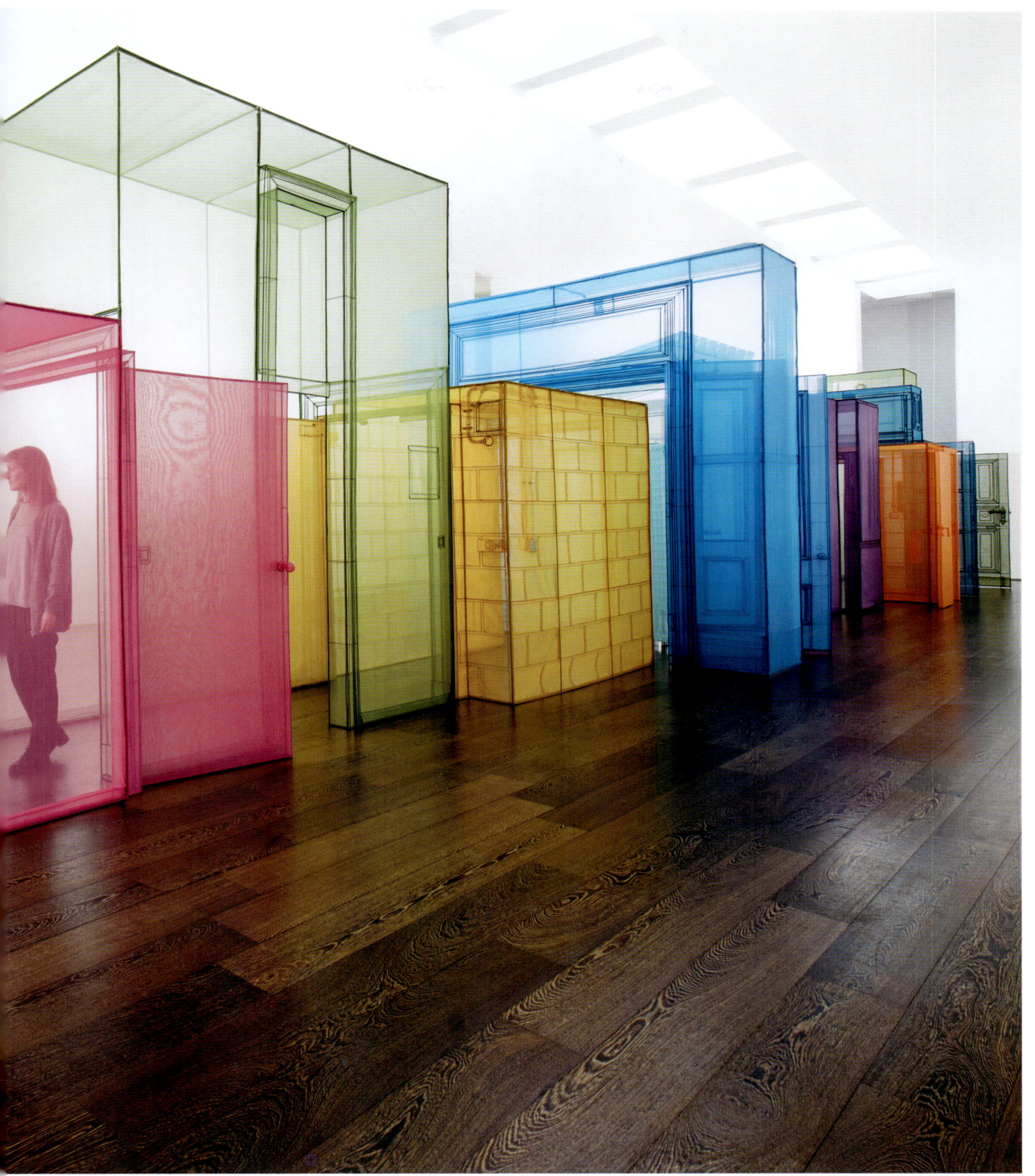

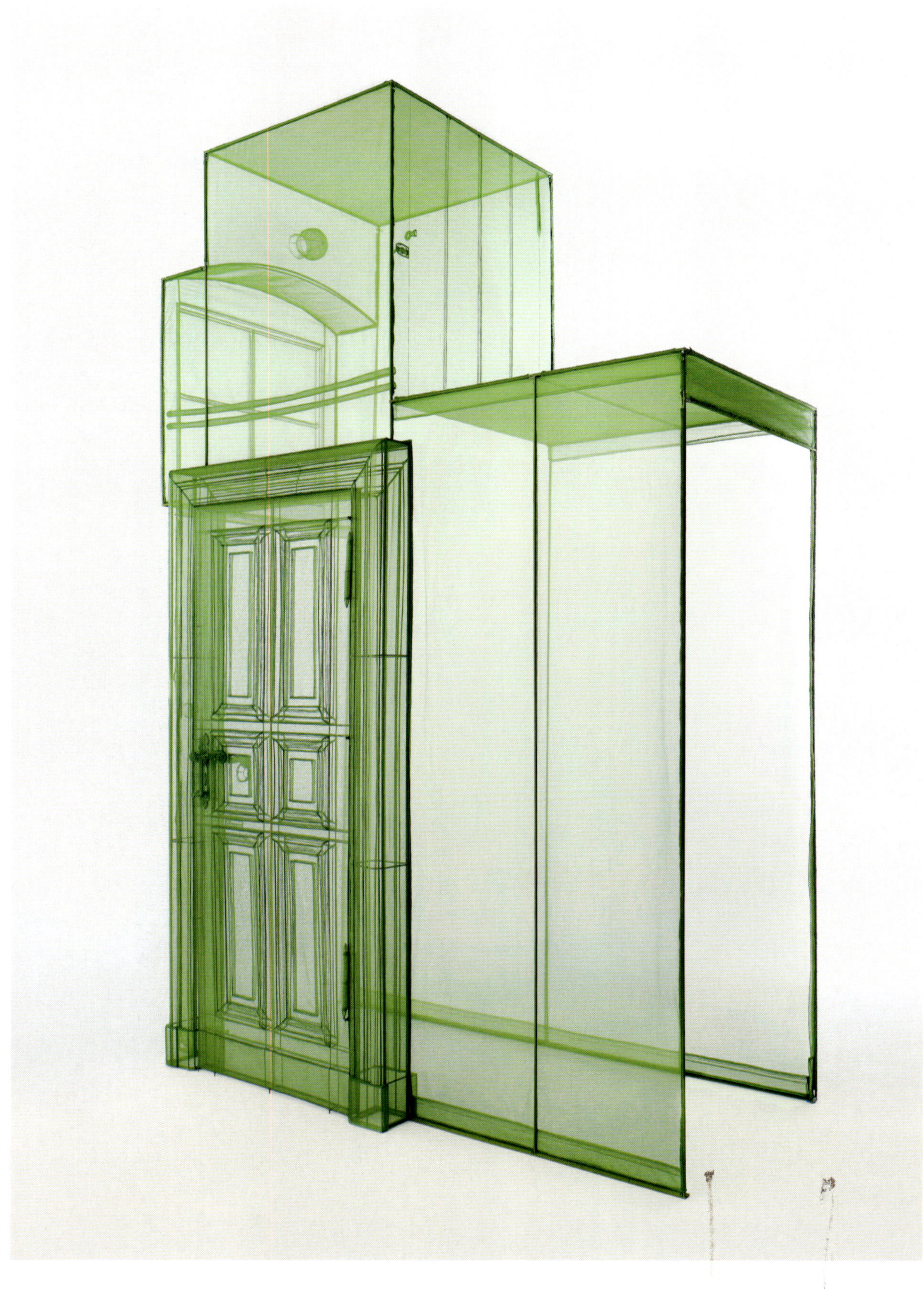

Previous spread:
Installation view, *Do Ho Suh: Passage/s*, Victoria Miro Gallery, London, 2017

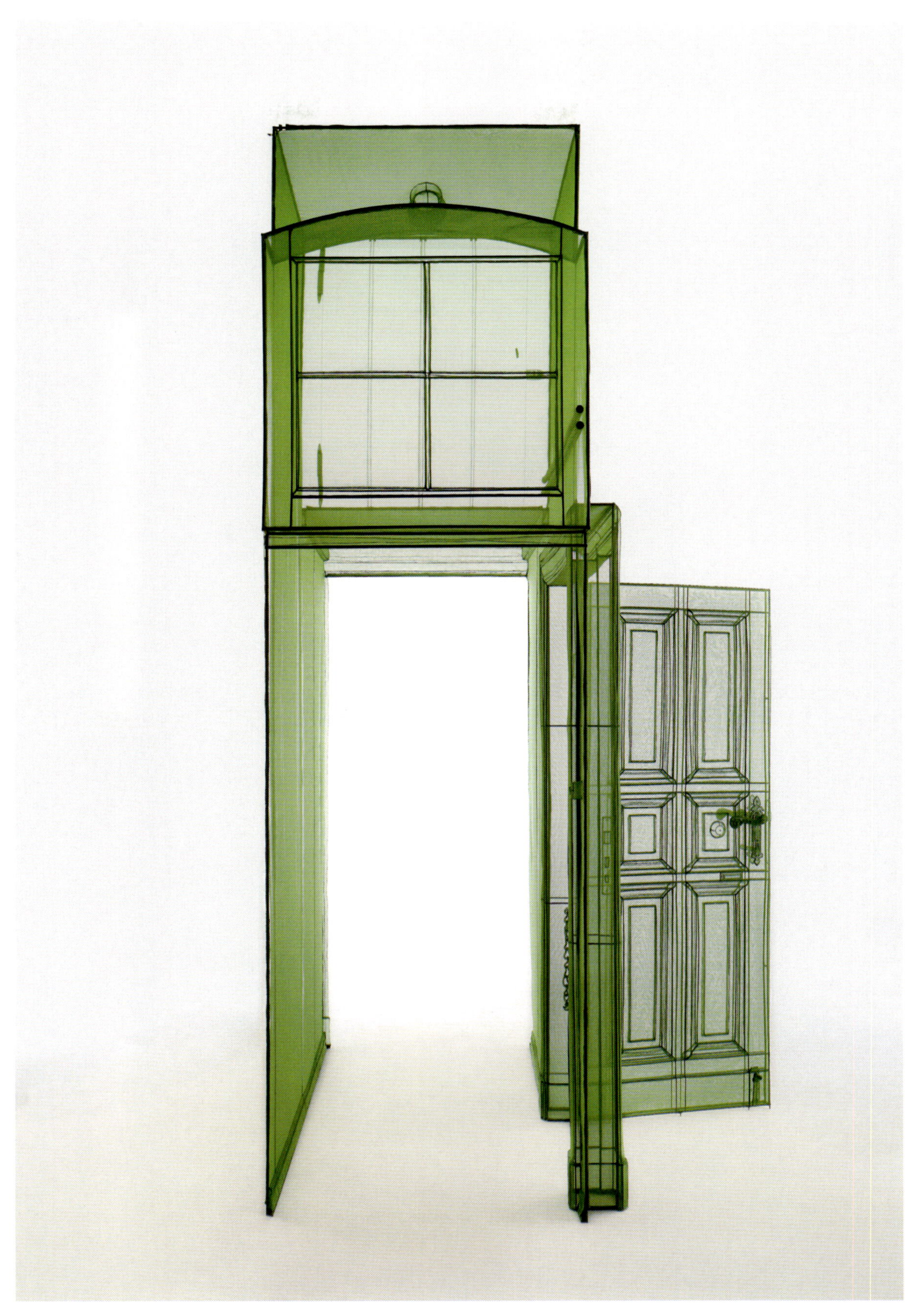

Opposite and above:
Do Ho Suh, *Corridor-4, Wielandstr. 18, 12159 Berlin, Germany*, 2015.
Polyester fabric and stainless steel.
11 feet 4 ¾ inches x 92 ⅜ inches x 48 ⅛ inches (347.3 x 234.5 x 122.1 cm)

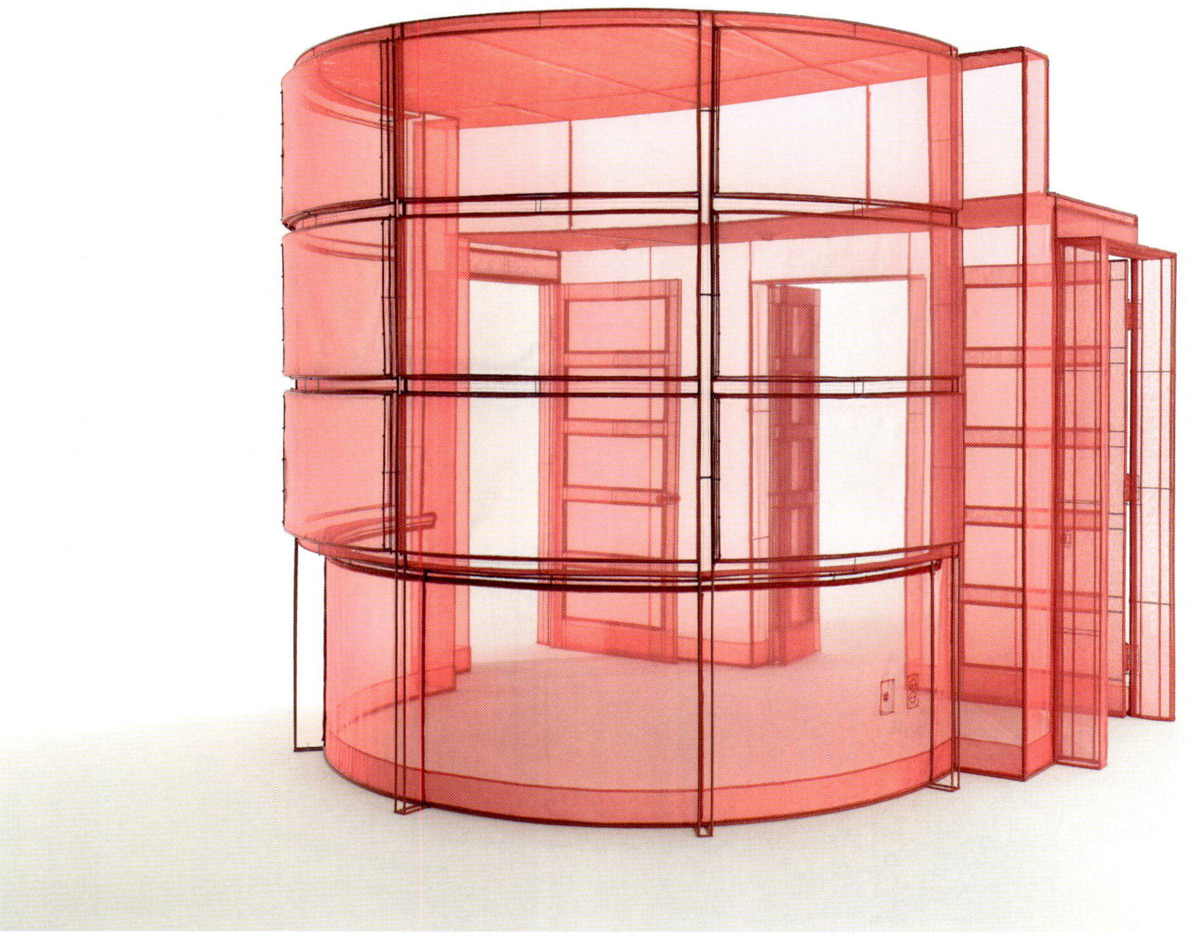

Do Ho Suh, *Hub-2, Breakfast Corner, 260-7, Sungbook-Dong, Sungboo-Ku, Seoul, Korea*, 2018.
Polyester fabric and stainless steel.
8 feet 10½ inches x 10 feet 8⅜ inches x 11 feet 8½ inches (271 x 326 x 357 cm)

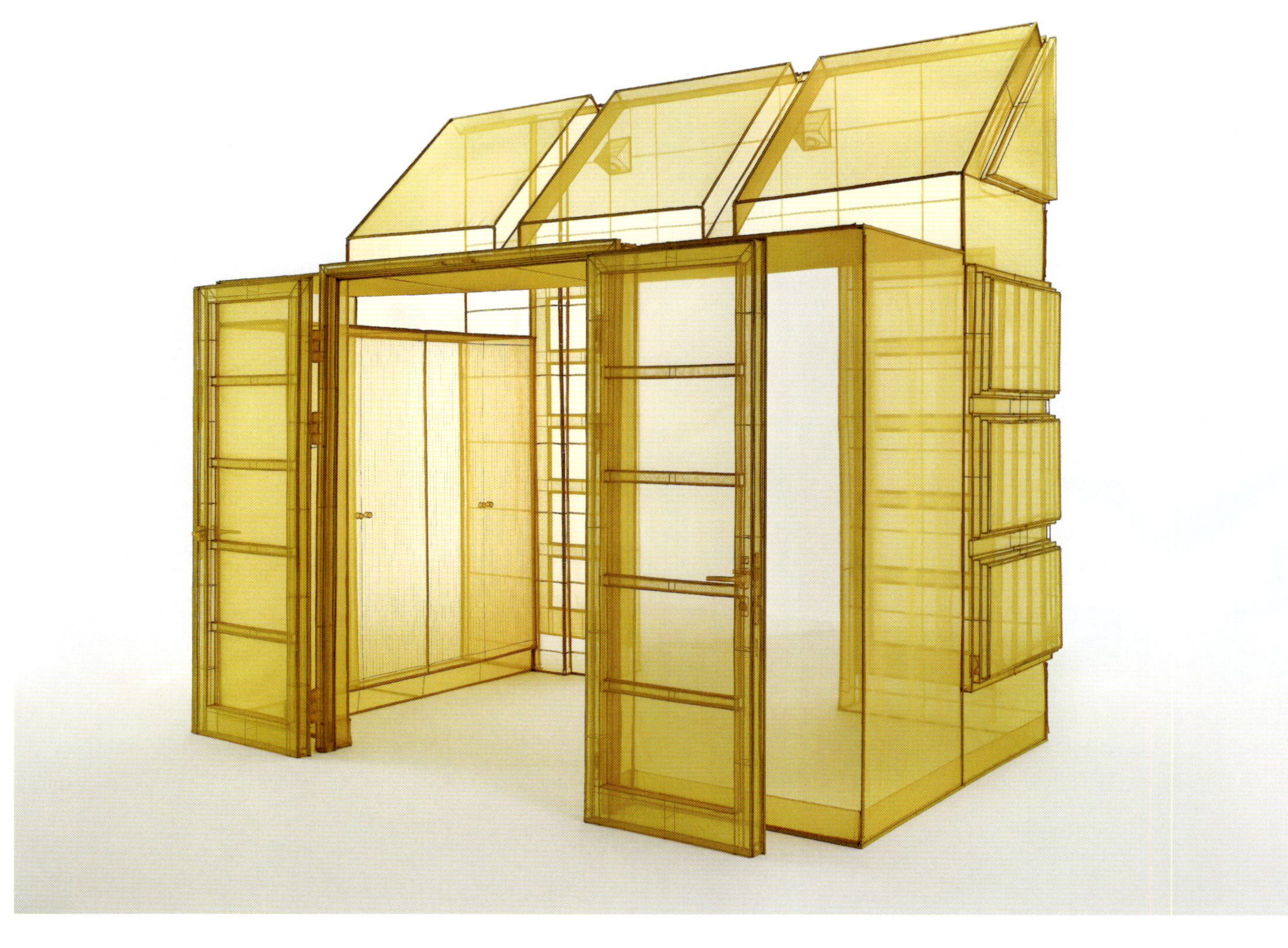

Do Ho Suh, *Hub-1, Entrance, 260-7, Sungbook-Dong, Sungboo-Ku, Seoul, Korea*, 2018.
Polyester fabric and stainless steel.
11 feet ¼ inch x 12 feet 6 inches x 8 feet 1¼ inches (336 x 381 x 247 cm)

Mona Hatoum

B. 1952, Beirut, Lebanon;
lives and works in London

Throughout her career, Mona Hatoum has advanced an understanding of identity as a moving, dynamic process of becoming rather than a fixed quality of personhood. A British Palestinian born in Lebanon, she unexpectedly became doubly an exile when Lebanon's civil war of 1975–90 broke out while she was away from the country, visiting London, and she was unable to return. Hatoum has often referred to the "sense of dislocation" that comes with her family history, but is cautious of subscribing to any unified notion of identity, even her own.[1] This resistance to fixed categorical thinking extends to her art, in which she incorporates everyday or found objects to invite and inspire unusual and sometimes uncomfortable readings. Resisting institutional attempts "to fix the meaning in [her] work by wanting to include it in very narrowly defined theme shows," Hatoum stages opportunities for the viewer to "question the solidity of the ground you walk on, which is also the basis on which your attitudes and beliefs lie."[2]

Hatoum's multimedia installations often conjure Surrealist or Minimalist aesthetics, in which the immediate, formal presence of the work confronts the viewer phenomenologically and emotionally. "We relate to the world through our senses," Hatoum explains. "You first experience an artwork physically.... Meanings, connotations, and associations come after the initial physical experience as your imagination, intellect, psyche are fired off by what you've seen."[3] *Exodus II* (2002) [p. 81] is one such work, in which two leather suitcases, set side by side, are linked together by strands of human hair. The hair appears entangled and unwieldy while the suitcases suggest departure, whether imminent or historical. Indeed, the title of the work finds its origins in the Abrahamic story of Exodus, in which the prophet Moses delivers the Israelites from slavery in Egypt.

Hair combines with wire, leather, and metal in this work, with deliberate unease. Hatoum, who often chooses her materials based on what moves her viscerally, has long been intrigued by hair and the gaze as intimate symbols of the body. In emphasizing these bodily features in her work, Hatoum caters to what she describes as a fascination with what might repulse us: "There is a moment of uncertainty as we approach the object because we are not sure if we can trust the information our eyes are conveying about it." It is only upon closer inspection of her works that we discover what disturbs us, such as the hair emerging between the two leather suitcases in *Exodus II*. Their potential separation is another source of discomfort: we can liken the painful work of disentangling the hairs to the nostalgic difficulty of departing for an unknown journey, noting that, in *Exodus II*, one cannot happen without the other.

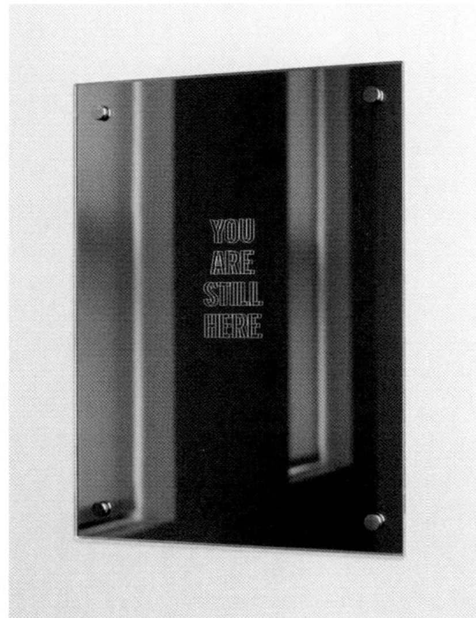

Fig. 1. Mona Hatoum, *YOU ARE STILL HERE*, 2013. Sandblasted mirrored glass and metal fixtures, 14 ¹⁵⁄₁₆ x 11 ½ inches (38 x 29.2 cm)

A looming sense of movement, exile, and departure appears throughout Hatoum's practice. There are moments in her repertoire where feelings of division, separation, and paradoxical longing confront our impulse to find order amid loss: in *YOU ARE STILL HERE* (2013) [fig. 1], for example, Hatoum inscribes the work's title on a mirror installed in such a way that it is impossible to detach the "you" from the "here." Instead, images, ideas, and memories of both conditions shift in and out of the mirror's frame, and indeed one's own visual field, questioning the very consolidation of consciousness at any given moment.

These examinations of what is here, what can remain, are found also in Hatoum's performances, which often concern questions of displacement within the private sphere. Positing the human body as the boundary between one's self and the external world, Hatoum seeks strategies for navigating the territory where ideas of refuge and attitudes toward the body intersect. Her famous video works, including *Corps étranger* (1994), approach the paradox of the body as both foreign (in that it contains landscapes we cannot see for ourselves) and territorialized, whether by disease or by social and systemic oppression. Hatoum explains, "I wanted the work to be about the body probed, invaded, violated, deconstructed, by the scientific eye."[4]

The foreboding undercurrent of violence, for Hatoum, is inseparable from the body, private space, and other conditions of home. *Home* (1999) and *Homebound* (2000) [fig. 2] are installations of common domestic objects, such as kitchen utensils, light bulbs, and furniture, set behind a room-length steel-wire fence. In both, electrical wire, flickering light fixtures, and speakers that emit a low hum of energy pulsate with restrained threat. Here, the boundary of home carries a tinge of danger, even as the source of harm is difficult to ascertain: "I'm working with feelings of displacement, disorientation, estrangement—when the familiar turns into something foreign or even threatening. It's about shattering the familiar to create uncertainty and make you question things that you normally take for granted."[5]

The familiar note of anxious departure in *Exodus II* leaves unanswered the question of arrival, or even the conditions of the journey. We are left instead with the twinning accompaniment of body and movement, as suggested by the human hairs and the symbol of the suitcase. Yet even the luggage motif is itself a promise of movement, a vessel within which an entire life may be contained; it calls to mind what we carry when we move temporarily by choice, or what is left behind when people undergo a forced or permanent migration. Hatoum's use of the suitcase in *Exodus II* speaks to this duality in purpose and symbol: "We usually expect furniture to be about giving support and comfort to the body. If these objects become either unstable or threatening, they become a reference to our fragility."[6] Invoking myriad associations of the body and movement, *Exodus II* draws on a discourse at odds with assumptions of safety and freedom, a visual poem on the fissures of home.
—AP

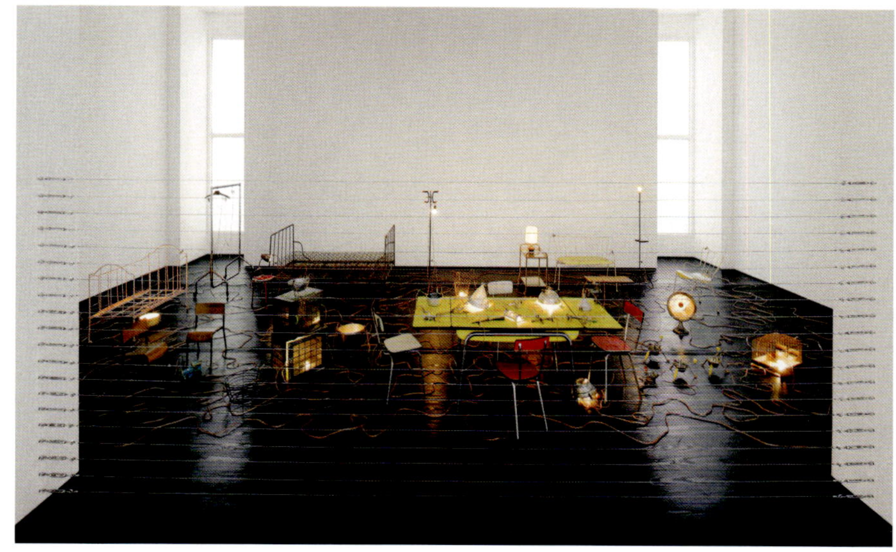

Fig. 2. Mona Hatoum, *Homebound*, 2000.
Rennie Collection, Vancouver. Installation view, The Menil Collection, Houston, 2000

1. Mona Hatoum, in "Mona Hatoum by Janine Antoni," *Bomb*, April 1, 1998. Available online at https://bombmagazine.org/articles/mona-hatoum/ (accessed January 22, 2019).

2. Ibid.

3. Hatoum, in "Using the Body against the Body Politic: Mona Hatoum on How Art Can Be a Form of Resistance," *Artspace*, November 11, 2016. Available online at www.artspace.com/magazine/art_101/book_report/using-the-body-against-the-body-politicmona-hatoum-on-lessons-in-art-as-resistance-54354 (accessed January 21, 2019). First published in Michael Archer, *Mona Hatoum* (London: Phaidon, 1997).

4. Hatoum, in "Mona Hatoum by Janine Antoni."

5. Hatoum, quoted in Emma Robertson, "Mona Hatoum: 'It's about Shattering the Familiar,'" *The Talks*, October 19, 2016. Available online at http://the-talks.com/interview/mona-hatoum/ (accessed January 21, 2019).

6. Hatoum, in "Mona Hatoum by Janine Antoni."

Mona Hatoum, *Exodus II*, 2002.
Compressed card, leather, metal, human hair, and beeswax.
19¾ x 26 x 26 inches (50 x 66 x 66 cm)

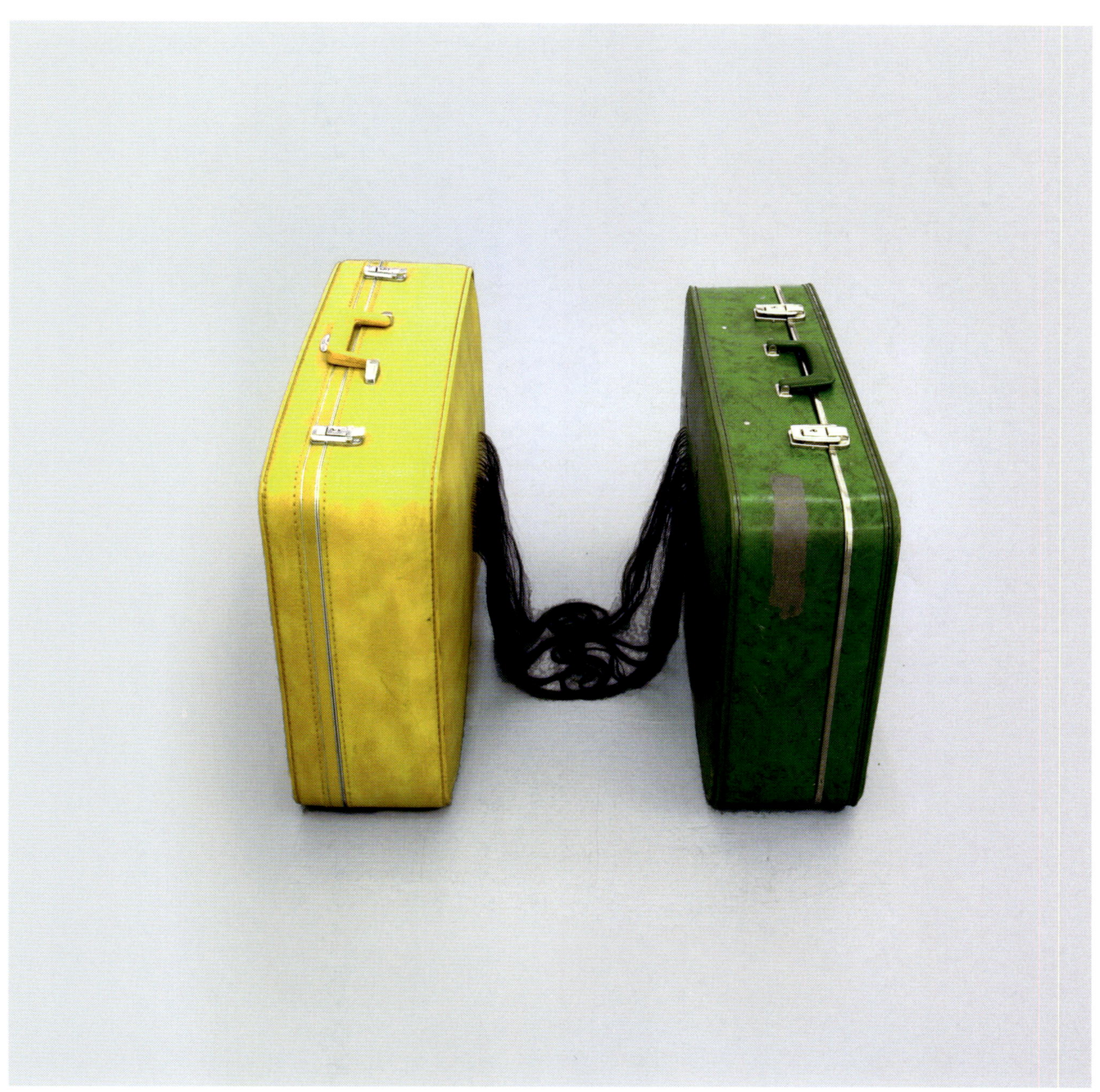

Xaviera Simmons

B. 1974, New York, United States;
lives and works in New York

Using photography, painting, mixed media, sound, and installation art, Xaviera Simmons has developed a visual language to question and attend to the work of historical memory in contemporary life. After receiving a B.F.A. in photography at Bard College in 2004, she trained as an actor, exploring various artistic mediums as "anchors" that have helped develop her current interdisciplinary approach to the creative process. She describes her overall practice as "engaged with in-between spaces, with nonlinear narratives, with narratives that drop off and then continue."[1]

Her most recent work, including the series Sundown (2018–) [pp. 84–87], offers a visual account of the ways in which anti-Black racism continues to permeate ideas of race, whiteness, and the myth of the nation in the United States. Simmons explains,

> New immigrants face different fights and also have a different set of references to homeland than Black Americans; be it conflictual, nostalgic, comfortable or comforting. Black American descendants of slavery as a group are a construction of the American landscape, meaning we would not exist had America not been constructed.... For the bulk of us, we have no idea which country or tribe we come from in Africa. Our lineage is Africa and Europe and Indigenous America. I would posit that Black Americans have been in exile and have been migrants in the country of their construct, the country of their origin, continuously for 400 years. That's why I started to produce the images in Sundown.[2]

Sundown mixes found archival images and texts with brightly patterned floral wallpaper and fabric backdrops. The photographic works also introduce a protagonist—a Black woman—whose face is always obscured, and who holds, carries, or displays an enlarged printed and framed archival image or text. In some, the figure (as performed by Simmons, who identifies as a Black American descendant of slaves, in her words "a mixed race group") wears various block-patterned dresses, blouses, or skirts; in others, the figure dons any number of West African-style masks, the type commonly collected in European imperial expeditions.[3] This visual and cultural appropriation of African cultures echoes for Simmons an entrenched history of theft, violence, and loss across the continent and for those of African descent today, reminiscent, as she points out, of a complex lineage of peoples "who sold, helped to capture, and benefited from selling or trading their fellow men into American slavery."[4]

The Sundown series is named for "sundown towns," a nickname for cities where it was (and still is) considered unsafe for Black Americans to traverse after dark, for fear of being terrorized, brutalized, killed, or lynched by any type

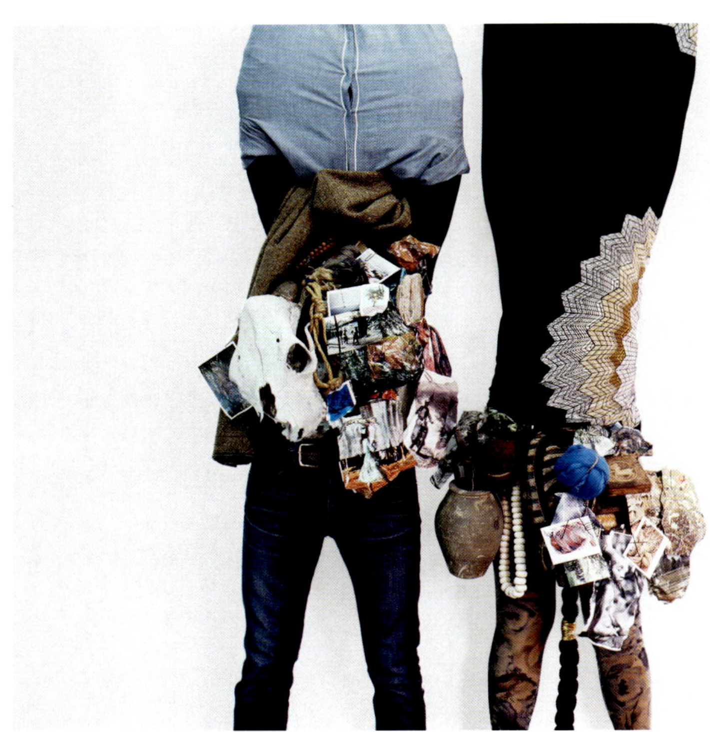

Fig. 1. Xaviera Simmons, *Index Six, Composition One*, 2013. Chromogenic color print, 50 x 62½ inches (127 x 161.3 cm)

of white individual or group. By incorporating references to such conditional experiences, as well as to the history of whiteness and systemic racism as foundational to the American democratic experiment, the series traces a visual lineage of twentieth-century American life in the United States, chronicling over four centuries of white-supremacist, settler colonial violence, especially as enacted toward Black Americans: "Black people are some of the most vulnerable people in this country. We're continuously migrating. [Yet we still] can't take [this history] in as a country, because what would that mean?"[5] Sundown aims to resite these histories through deftly woven visual and textual links, producing a powerful resonance between the figures Simmons depicts and our present times.

Sundown also includes text paintings in which Simmons extracts quotations from Christopher Columbus's diaries, which she paints in white hand-lettering against a black background. The text is compressed as a running excerpt that begins and ends in the middle of sentences. Described as "cinematic images," these paintings interweave with photographic prints, organizing the series in a long march of action and reaction, encounter and reencounter, that brings history into the present space of the viewer. Says Simmons, "I'm just as interested in the structure as I am in the politics. I really want to make images that are beautifully engaged and politically stimulating."[6]

Simmons's other collage-based works also reference multiple historical legacies in a singular accumulation. *Index Six, Composition One* (2013) [fig. 1] involves an undifferentiated assortment of objects, such as trinkets, fabric swatches, or jewelry, as well as images cut or torn from newspapers, magazines, or printouts featuring popular media figures or historical and ethnographic photography. These objects are attached—paperclipped, tied, clothespinned—to a faceless and sometimes headless torso or pair of legs, covering the abstracted body so that only a limb or two is visible under the assemblage. Though inviting close looking, they remain reticent: much like Sundown, the collages do not resolve themselves, nor is it possible to isolate any one context from another.

Shifting temporalities, seen in the conflated time and space in her photographic work, are an important conceptual strategy for the work overall. Sundown is as much about "understanding [the] policies and practices that the country has sustained for centuries" as it as about how these histories continue to impact Black Americans today.[7] Simmons explains that she always works with "a deep awareness of NOW, [of] the mental assault [that] particularly Black American descendants of slavery continue to face."[8] Perhaps to account for or cope with these constant activations, Simmons poses in her photographs as though performing a role rather than in a mode of self-portraiture: "I come to my photographs prepared to develop a character, to evoke a certain feeling in the works, but in the moment of making a work, the gestures and movements in an image come from the moment and may change or shift my original intentions, even if slightly."[9]

Archival research sustains Simmons's practice, a method of preparation she has likened to that of an actor preparing for all possible emotions or motivations.[10] For Sundown, these preparation efforts involved numerous studies of local and national archives of American life, including local historical museums from Virginia to New York [fig. 2]. She describes the value of this work as being able to trace visual lineages between enslaved peoples standing amongst cotton fields to white mobs witnessing a lynching; from sharecropper towns in the American South to family photographs of the Great Migration; from the blaring headlines of white violence on Black bodies to the persistent presence of anti-Black rhetoric today. Sundown's citations move not temporally between these references but among them, weaving an encounter rather than a narrative, and suggesting the ever present nature of those systems of inequality and oppression that enabled the institution of slavery, the policies of Jim Crow, and the continued disenfranchisement of Black Americans by a white-majority population today. —AP, with Xaviera Simmons

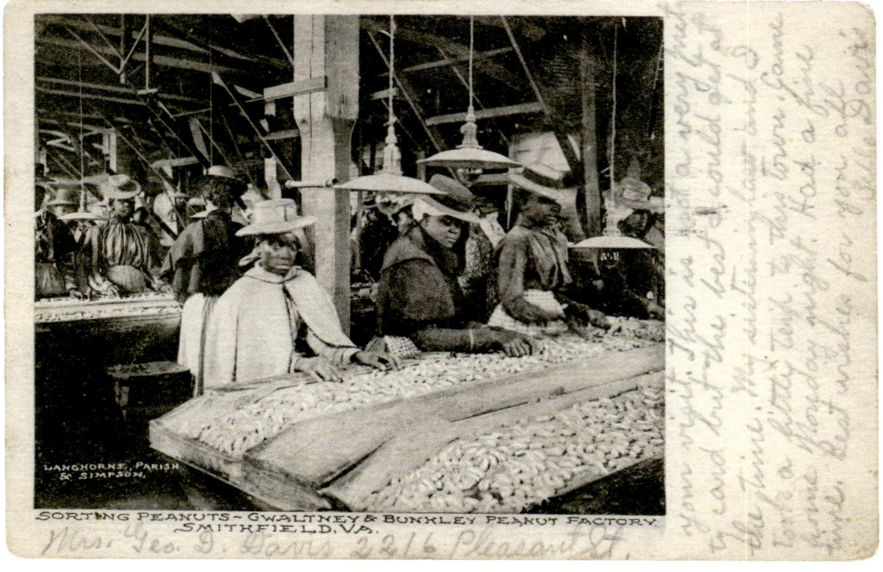

Fig. 2. Langhorne, Parish & Simpson, *Sorting Peanuts—Gwaltney & Bunkley Peanut Factory, Smithfield, Va.*, c. 1913. Postcard, dimensions unknown. Virginia Museum of History & Culture, Richmond, 2000.92.432

1. Xaviera Simmons, in Cara Despain, "Surveyor: An Interview with Xaviera Simmons," *Artpulse*, April 19, 2012. Available online at http://artpulsemagazine.com/surveyor-an-interview-with-xaviera-simmons (accessed January 29, 2019).

2. Simmons, e-mail to the author, January 15, 2019.

3. Simmons, e-mail to the author, January 14, 2019.

4. Ibid.

5. Simmons, e-mail to the author, January 16, 2019.

6. Ibid.

7. Ibid.

8. Simmons, e-mail to the author, January 14, 2019.

9. Simmons, in Despain, "Surveyor."

10. Simmons, quoted in Emily McDermott, "Xaviera Simmons, All Over the Place," *Interview*, December 4, 2013. Available online at www.interviewmagazine.com/art/xaviera-simmons-open (accessed March 28, 2019).

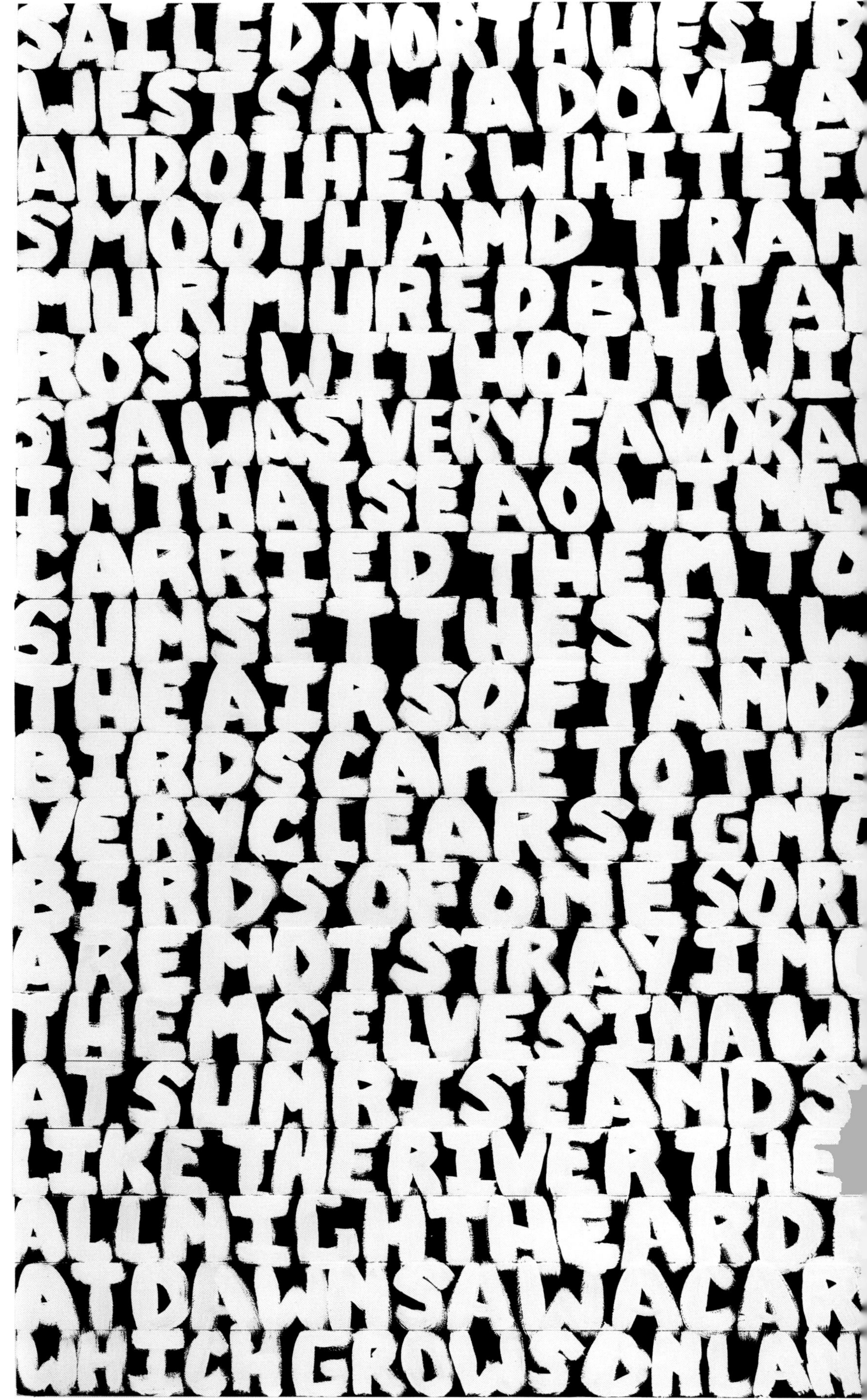
SAILEDNORTHWEST
WESTSAWADOVE
ANDOTHERWHITE
SMOOTHANDTRA
MURMUREDBUT
ROSEWITHOUTW
SEAWASVERYFAVOR
INTHATSEAOWIN
CARRIEDTHEMT
SUNSETTHESEA
THEAIRSOFTAN
BIRDSCAMETOTH
VERYCLEARSIG
BIRDSOFONESO
ARENOTSTRAYI
THEMSELVESINA
ATSUNRISEAND
LIKETHERIVERTH
ALLNIGHTHEAR
ATDAWNSAWACA
WHICHGROWSONLA

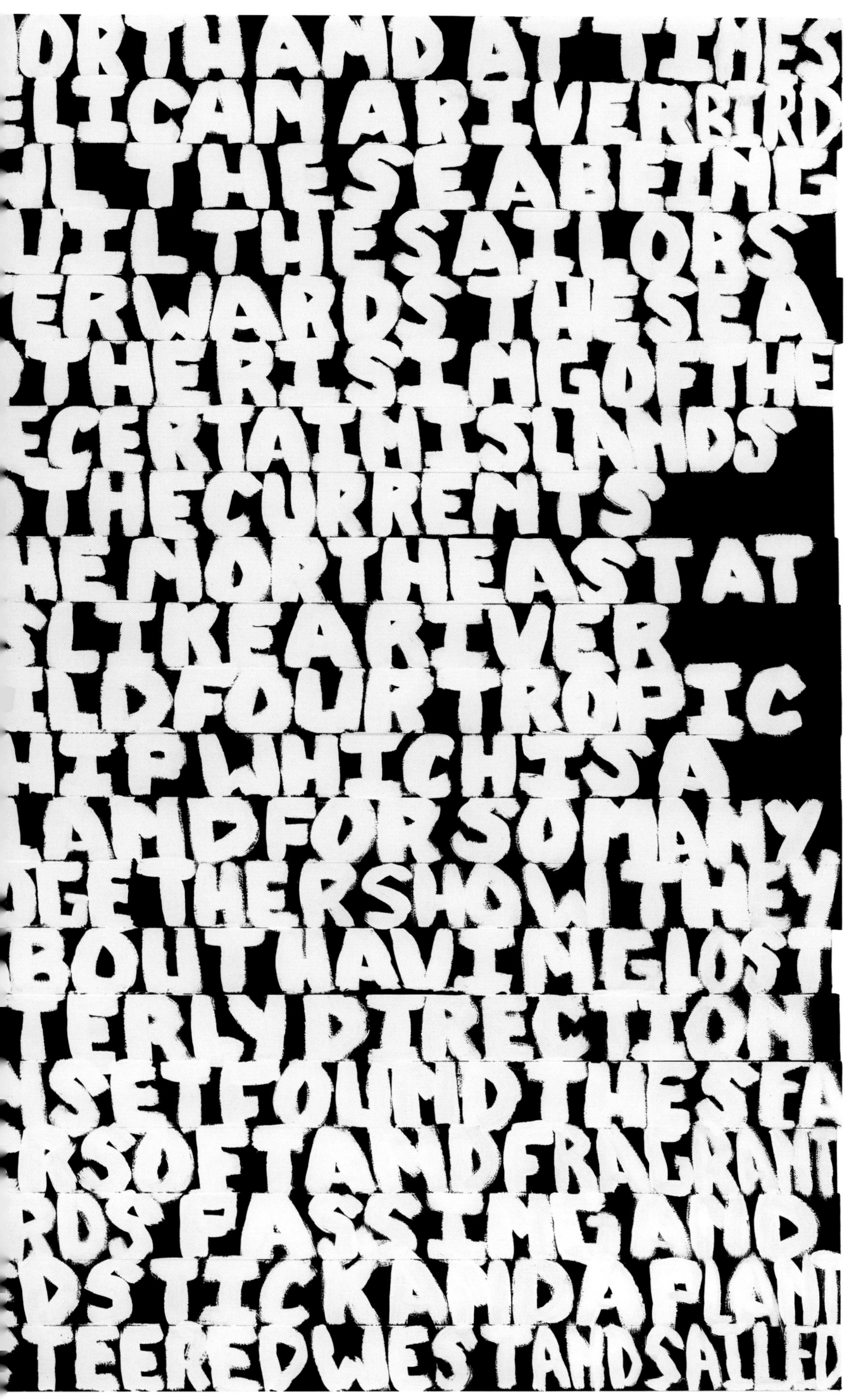
ORTHANDATTIMES
ELICANARIVERBIRD
LTHESEABEING
UILTHESAILORS
ERWARDSTHESEA
THERISINGOFTHE
ECERTAINISLANDS
THECURRENTS
HENORTHEASTAT
LIKEARIVER
ILDFOURTROPIC
HIPWHICHISA
LANDFORSOMANY
OGETHERSHOWTHEY
BOUTHAVINGLOST
TERLYDIRECTION
NSETFOUNDTHESEA
RSOFTANDFRAGRANT
RDSPASSINGAND
DSTICKANDAPLANT
TEEREDWESTANDSAILED

Previous spread:
Xaviera Simmons, *Found the Sea like the River*, 2018, from the series Sundown, 2018– .
Acrylic on wood panel. 72 x 96 inches (182.9 x 243.8 cm)

Opposite:
Xaviera Simmons, *Sundown (Number Twelve)*, 2018, from the series Sundown, 2018– .
Chromogenic color print. 60 x 45 inches (152.4 x 114.3 cm)

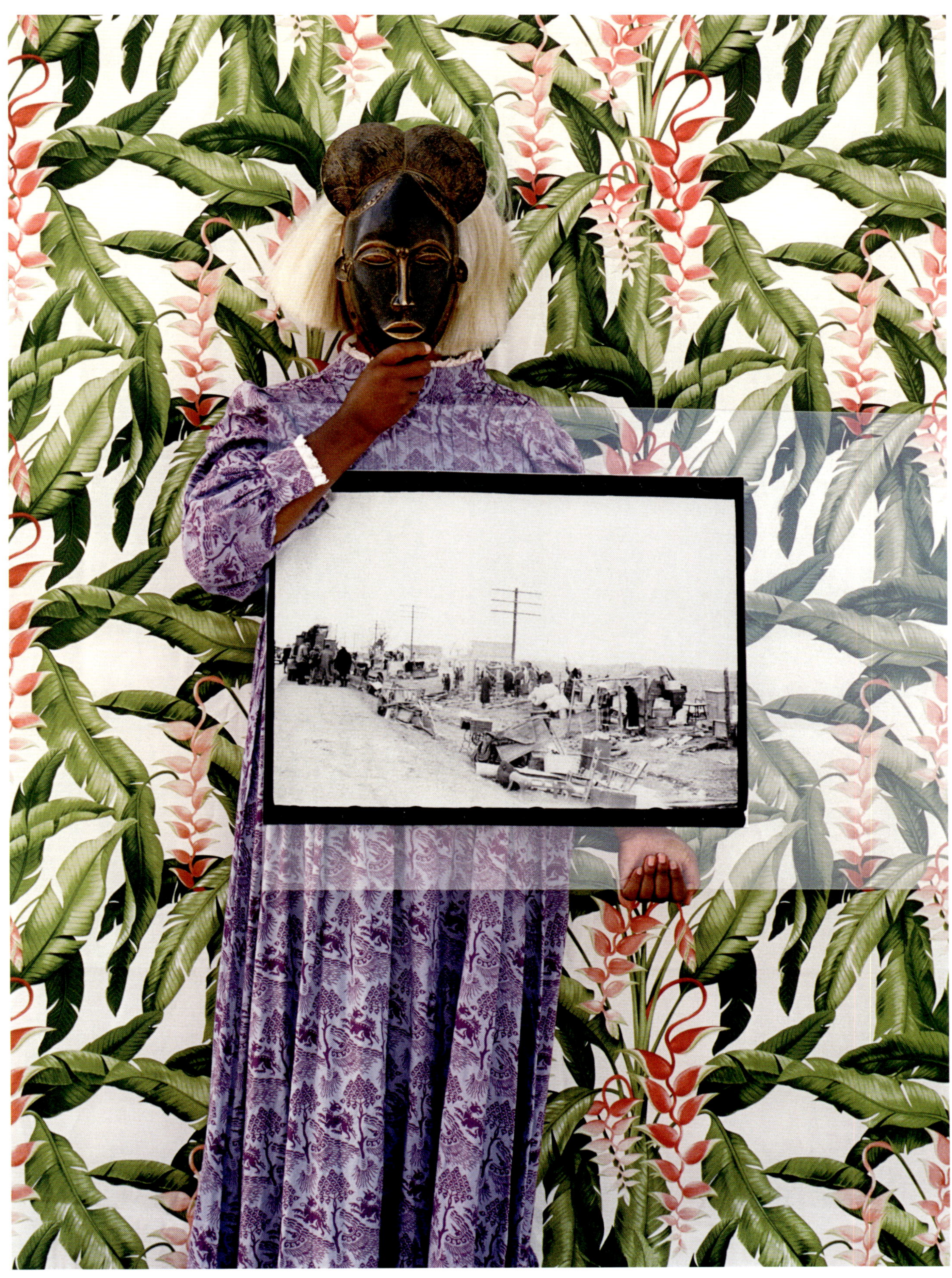

Yto Barrada

B. 1971, Paris, France;
lives and works in Tangier, Morocco, and New York

Born in France and raised between Tangier and Paris, photographer and filmmaker Yto Barrada has developed a practice that she describes as located in the space between poetry and politics. It focuses geographically on the city of Tangier, on the south side of the Strait of Gibraltar, that highly contested passage between Africa and Europe where mobility is strictly regulated. Politically, culturally, and historically, however, Barrada's interest lies in the intertwined histories of colonialism and global migration. The Gibraltar region anchors the artist's series A Life Full of Holes: The Strait Project (1998–2003), which captures life south of the Strait through color photographs that depict fragmented views of architecture, natural landscapes, and urban life.[1]

After studying history and political theory at the Sorbonne, Paris, Barrada studied in both Palestine and New York. In 2003 she returned to Tangier, where centuries of political contestation have shaped a palimpsestic history. "The 'scramble for Africa' is still a reality here," she says. "We still can't impose our own agenda, sixty years after independence.... It's important to map the mechanisms of the organization of domination; the reality of power as well as its symbolic support."[2] Barrada's work obliquely addresses the role of photography in Tangier's history, from the introduction of the medium in the colonial era as a tool of anthropological research to local family albums that imply genealogical maps of relations. Both of these image-based topographies erase the complex dynamics of the families that, in her parents' generation, were torn apart by war.

Morocco's history is one of human movement induced by power shifts: seventh-century Islamic conquests attracted Arabic-speaking migrants, Muslims and Jews fled there from Spain during the *Reconquista* of the Iberian peninsula from the eighth to the fifteenth centuries, and the trans-Saharan and transatlantic slave trades entailed forced migration in and out of Morocco from the sixteenth to the mid-eighteenth century. French-colonial presence in the mid-twentieth century launched another period of restructuring and made Tangier an international demilitarized zone; the city's cosmopolitan allure famously attracted expatriate artists, writers, spies, adventurers, criminals, and businessmen. Moroccan independence from French and Spanish rule in 1956 significantly foreclosed free movement, a shift accelerated by the Schengen agreements of 1995, which abolished internal border checks between Germany, France, and the Benelux countries (Belgium, the Netherlands and Luxembourg) while heightening security measures at external borders. This legal precedent has informed decades of EU policies and laws, both enhancing EU cooperation on immigration and expanding securitization of external borders, especially in southern Europe and even the sea—a key focus of Frontex (*Frontières extérieures*, or the European Border and Coast Guard Agency, established in 2004).[3] As such, the Strait of Gibraltar has become effectively traversable for Europeans but not for Africans without a visa.[4]

Barrada understands the map as a powerful instrument of the political control of space, codifying boundaries and territories as tools in the economic and political distribution of power. Terms such as "global South," "First World," and "East v. West" invoke this grammar to either reassure or oppress those identifying their place in it. In *Tectonic Plate* (2010) [fig. 1], a wooden model of the world with movable contents, the map is both a teaching tool and a mode of picturing alternative configurations of power.

If maps are ways of knowing the distant and displaced, the family tree or album is a nongeographic map, assembling personal relations over both distance and time.[5] *Arbre généalogique [Family Tree]* (2005) [p. 91] references Barrada's genealogical map, a framework that elides the conflicting political alliances and absent narratives that have shaped her family's history. The flesh-toned photograph documents dark silhouettes left behind by family photographs taken off the wall—as if they'd been burned into its surface—during a cleaning of the artist's mother's house. They allude at once to the significance of the family in Morocco, the photographic as an inscription of light, and the power of the map to orient or disorient one's sense of place in the world.

Barrada is intrigued by covert strategies of resistance, in her words "the 'hidden transcripts' of people who are faced with superior power."[6] *Autocar—Tangier* (2004) [fig. 2] invokes codes of mobility learned by illiterate migrants. Four brightly colored, seemingly abstract designs are in fact photographs of the logos printed on the sides of buses from Tangier to various European destinations, vehicles on which those immigrating illegally may try to ride unnoticed. They represent just one code of communication among the migrants who move through Tangier, successfully or unsuccessfully.

Inspired by but also resistant to documentary photography's implied logic of objectivity, the photos in A Life Full of Holes have a poetic, often unresolved quality that reflects what Anthony Downey calls the "purgatorial state" of a people caught in paradoxical conditions of escape and confinement, passage and stagnation, and one-way passage into a borderless European Union.[7] Refusing such representations of migration as refugees behind barbed wire or on boats, her photographs channel, in Barrada's words, "the suspense at the intersection of the same and the other: of physical and symbolic, of history and geography, of desire and the forbidden, of the promised life and exile."[8] Some index the contradictions between a tourist and a migrant economy through abstract details of urban surfaces; others speak metaphorically of the language of impassability confronting migrants through views of physical barriers, figures turned away, or the continent visible across the water from Tangier. Together they encode the life governed by the Strait, a word whose connotations in English and Arabic are aligned, Barrada notes, as narrowness (*dayq*) and distress (*mutadayeq*).[9]

Picturing the porosity of borders despite efforts to regulate them, Barrada's images observe the existential state of migrants, united by their longing to be elsewhere, the suspicion they attract, and their wait—often years long, and often unfulfilled—to cross over to where they want to be. "I try to expose the metaphorical character of the strait through a series of images that reveal the tension ... between its allegorical nature and immediate, harsh reality," writes the artist. "My work attempts in part to exorcise the unspoken violence of other people's departures. I too left Tangier for more than ten years. By moving back, I have placed myself amidst the violence of homecoming. There are no flaneurs here, and no innocent bystanders."[10] —ET

1. The project's title refers to Driss ben Hamed Charhadi's book *A Life Full of Holes* (New York: Grove Press, 1964). Charhadi was an illiterate North African servant and street vendor whose chronicles of daily life in 1930s Morocco were transcribed and translated from the Arabic dialect Moghrabi by the American author Paul Bowles. The novel was the first ever written in Moghrabi.

2. Yto Barrada, "A Grammar of Tangier: A Conversation between Yto Barrada and Sina Najafi," in Lionel Bovier and Clément Dirié, eds., *Yto Barrada* (Zurich: JRP Ringier, 2013), p. 147.

3. The Schengen Agreement was first established in 1985 between France, Germany, and the Benelux countries (Belgium, Netherlands, Luxembourg), dismantling intra-European border security and fostering greater EU cooperation around migration. As precedent for EU cooperation around immigration, it influenced a range of policies later incorporated into EU law, now known as the "Schengen acquis." A consolidated immigration policy, implemented in 1995, increased the securitization of the EU's external borders, communication over immigration "threats," and inequality between Europe and Africa. The 1990 Dublin Convention mandated that all asylum seekers access the EU through its southern countries. In 2004, to address the intensification of illegal southern-border crossings, the EU developed Frontex as an agency to monitor areas of maritime crossings to reduce migrant deaths at sea and, some argue, amplify the surveillance capacities and public face of EU border security.

4. For a more detailed study of the impact of EU immigration policies on migrants from West African countries, see Hannah M. Cross, "The EU Migration Regime and West African Clandestine Migrants," *Journal of Contemporary European Research* 5, no. 2 (2009):171–87. Available online at http://jcer.net/index.php/jcer/article/view/175/148 (accessed March 6, 2019).

5. "The retractable and extendable character of photography furnished a language of displacement and change of scale—modulating the private to the collective, the interior to the outside world, capable of overcoming time and distance, and apparently more 'faithful' than words." Marie Muracciole, "Something New about Plants (Biographical Sketch)," in Bovier and Dirié, eds., *Yto Barrada*, p. 28.

6. Barrada, quoted in Jennifer Higgie, "Talking Pictures," *Frieze* no. 142 (October 2011). Available online at https://frieze.com/article/talking-pictures-0 (accessed December 6, 2018).

7. Anthony Downey, "A Life Full of Holes," *Third Text* 20, no. 5 (September 2006):621.

8. Barrada, trans. in Mary Vogl, "Closed Encounters: Tangier, the Arts, and the North-South Divide," in Michela Ardizzoni and Valerio Ferme, eds., *Mediterranean Encounters in the City: Frameworks of Mediation between East and West, North and South* (Lanham, Md.: Lexington Books, 2015), p. 45. Barrada's original description is "le suspens au croisement du même et de l'autre: du physique et du symbolique, de l'histoire et de la géographie, du désir et de l'interdit, de la vie promise et de l'exil." In Barrada, *A Life Full of Holes: The Strait Project* (London: Autograph ABP, 2005), p. 63.

9. Barrada, artist's statement, *Yto Barrada: A Life Full of Holes—The Strait Project*, 2005. Available online at www.warwickartscentre.co.uk/mead-gallery/previous-exhibitions/2005/yto-barrada-a-life-full-of-holes-the-strait-project/ (accessed December 6, 2018).

10. Barrada, "Artist Project: A Life Full of Holes." *Cabinet* no. 16: *The Sea* (Winter 2004/2005). Available online at www.cabinetmagazine.org/issues/16/barrada.php (accessed December 6, 2018).

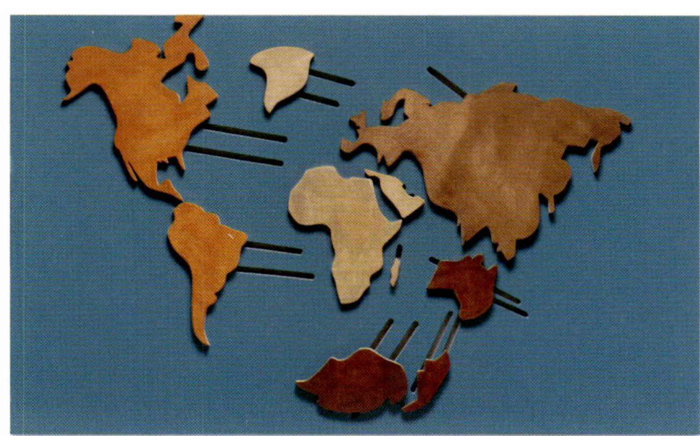

Fig. 1. Yto Barrada, *Tectonic Plate*, 2010.
Paint on wood, 48 1/16 x 78 3/4 x 1 3/16 inches (122 x 200 x 3 cm)

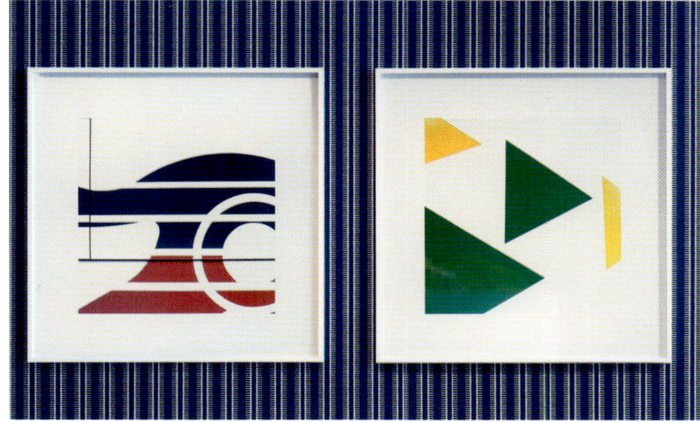

Fig. 2. Yto Barrada, *Autocar—Tangier, Figs. 2 and 1*, 2004.
Installation view, *Yto Barrada: Mobilier Urbain*, Pace London, 2012

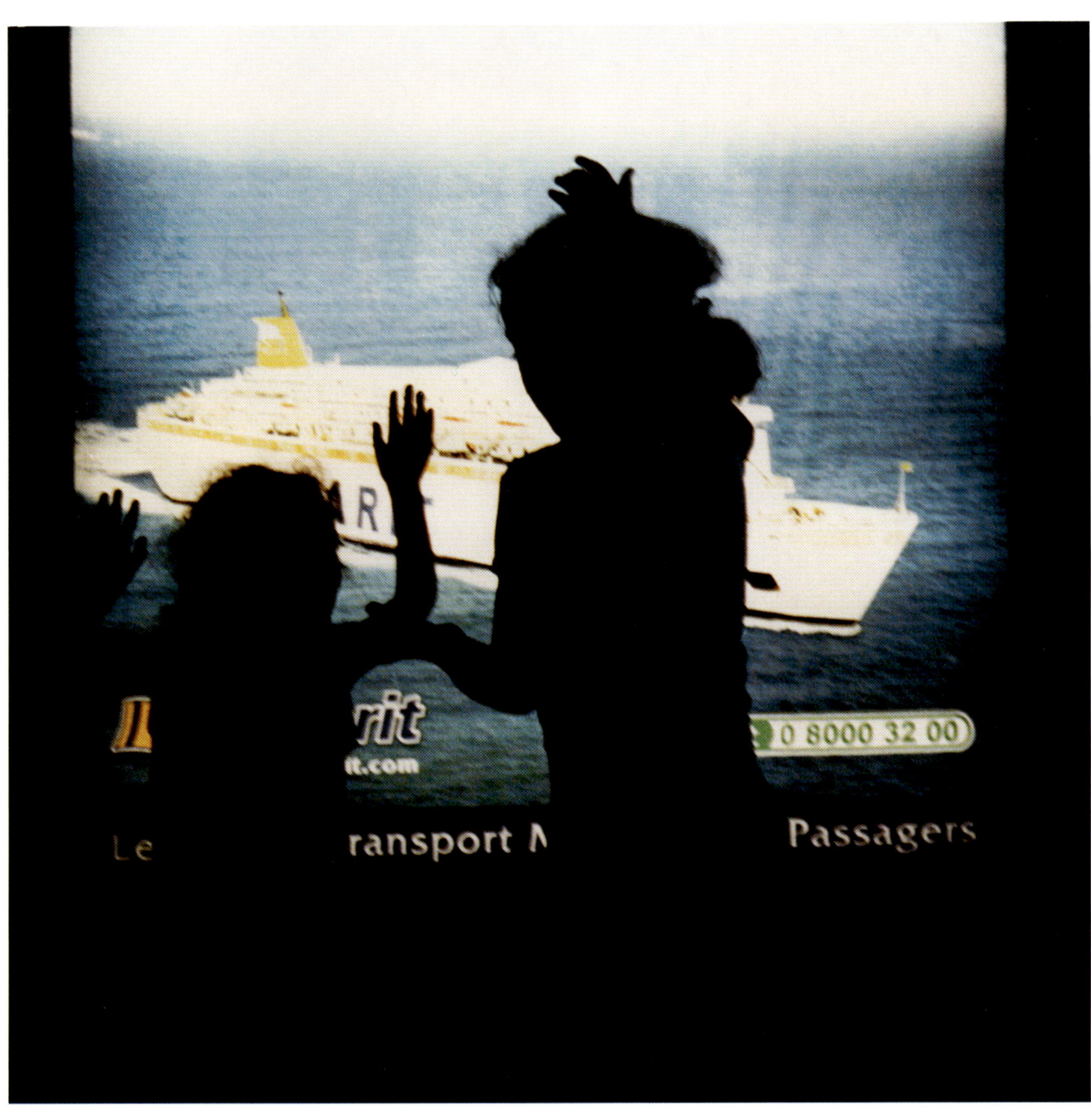

Yto Barrada, *Caisson lumineux—Lieu de transit—Tanger 2003 [Advertisement light box—Ferry port transit area—Tangier 2003]*, 2003, from the series A Life Full of Holes: The Strait Project, 1998–2003. Chromogenic color print. 23⅝ x 23⅝ inches (60 x 60 cm)

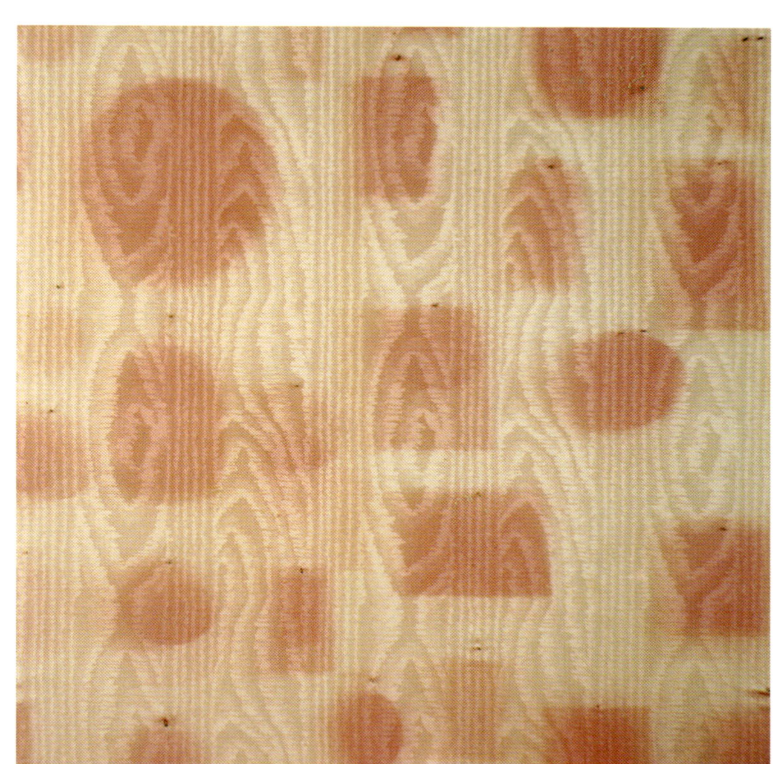

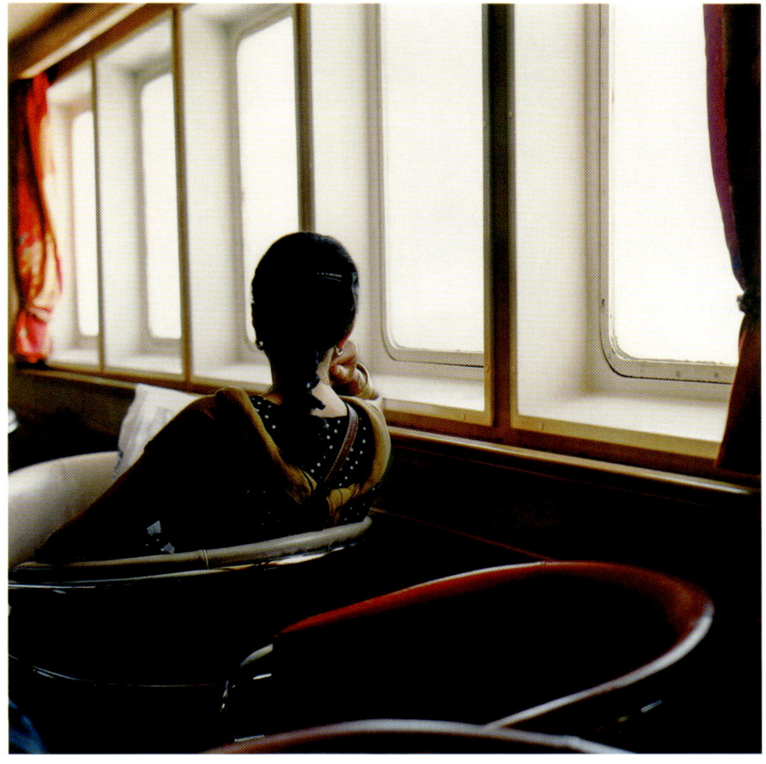

Yto Barrada, *Arbre généalogique [Family Tree]*, 2005.
Chromogenic color print. 59 x 59 inches (149.9 x 149.9 cm)

Yto Barrada, *Salon de première—Ferry de Tanger à Algesiras, Espagne—2002 [First class lounge—Ferry from Tangier to Algeciras, Spain—2002]*, 2002, from the series A Life Full of Holes: The Strait Project, 1998-2003.
Chromogenic color print. 33 x 33 inches (83.8 x 83.8 cm)

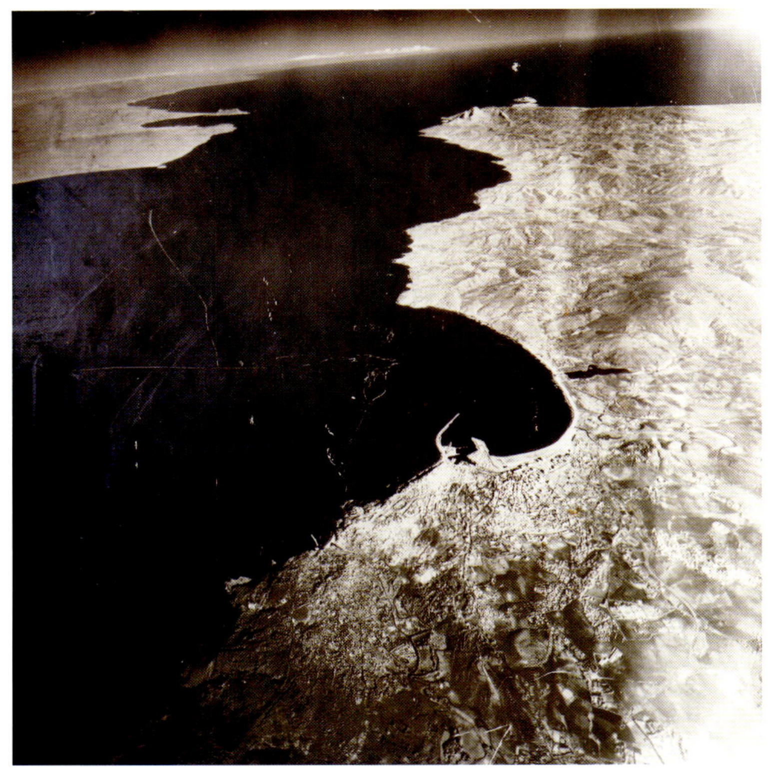

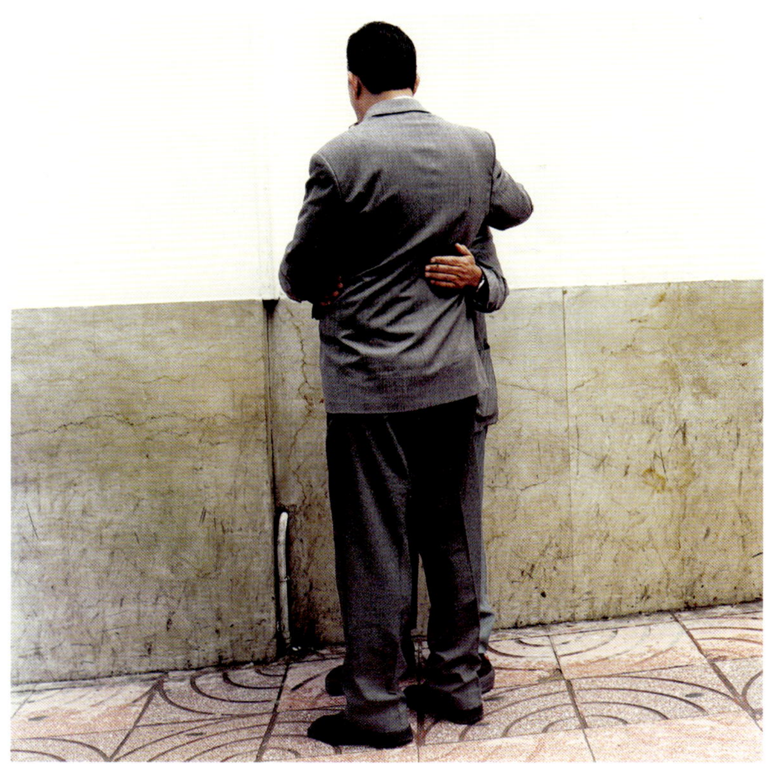

Yto Barrada, *Le Détroit de Gibraltar—Reproduction d'une photographie aérienne—Tanger 2003 [The Strait of Gibraltar—reproduction of an aerial photograph—Tangier 2003]*, 2003, from the series A Life Full of Holes: The Strait Project, 1998–2003. Chromogenic color print. 23 5/8 x 23 5/8 inches (60 x 60 cm)

Yto Barrada, *Rue de la Liberté, Tanger 2000*, 2000, from the series A Life Full of Holes: The Strait Project, 1998–2003. Chromogenic color print. 49 3/16 x 49 3/16 inches (125 x 125 cm)

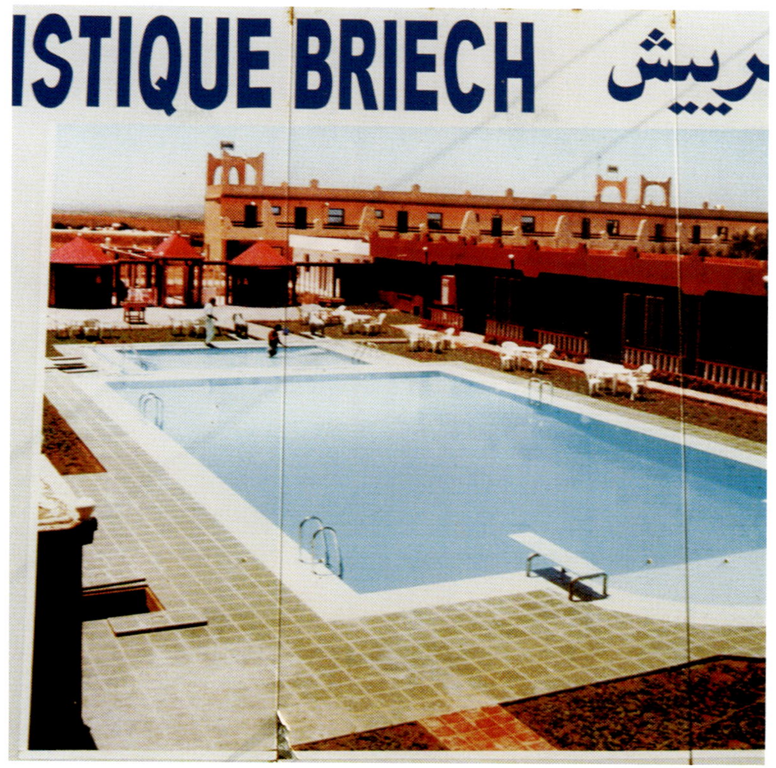

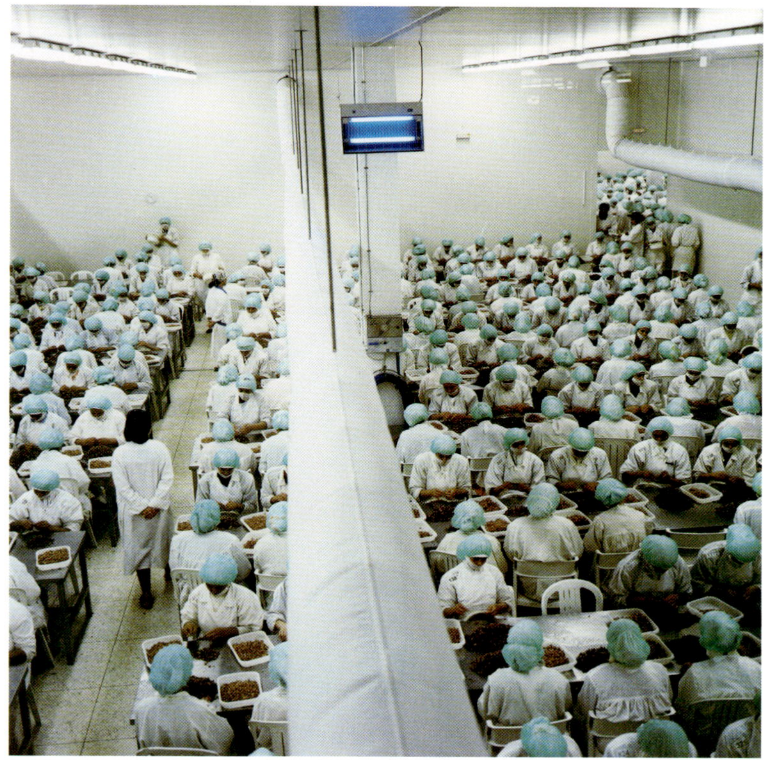

Yto Barrada, *Panneau—Publicité de lotissement touristique—Briech 2002 [Hoarding—advertising for a tourist development—Briech 2002]*, 2002, from the series A Life Full of Holes: The Strait Project, 1998–2003. Chromogenic color print. 31 ½ x 31 ½ inches (80 x 80 cm)

Yto Barrada, *Usine 1—Conditionnement de crevettes dans la zone franche, Tanger 1998 [Factory 1—Prawn Processing Plant in the Free Trade Zone, Tangier 1998]*, 1998, from the series A Life Full of Holes: The Strait Project, 1998–2003. Chromogenic color print. 40 9/16 x 40 9/16 inches (103 x 103 cm)

Kader Attia

B. 1970, Dugny, France;
lives and works in Berlin and Paris

As a visual artist and filmmaker, Kader Attia explores the possibility for freedom and reparation after postcolonialism. Born and raised outside Paris to Algerian Muslims, Attia has developed a practice concerned with questions of religion, representation, and the vulnerability of diasporic communities under state and police authority. Much of his work examines how ideas of the migrant, the refugee, and the immigrant circulate, often sensationally, in media and popular culture. Since 2015, for example, the so-called "migrant crisis" in Western Europe, where Attia lives and works, has been depicted as an uncontrollable "wave" or "mass" with which Mediterranean nations such as Spain, Greece, and Italy must "cope."[1] Attia's works unravel and expose the alarmist language directed toward these migrant populations, challenging viewers to reckon with the factual realities of migrant communities rather their fictive representations.

La Mer Morte (The Dead Sea) [pp. 96–97] was first staged in 2015 for the Deichtorhallen in Hamburg as part of the exhibition *Streamlines—Oceans, Global Trade and Migration*. Comprising variously blue-colored clothes such as jeans, denim jackets, trousers, and T-shirts, the installation covers the gallery floor in a seemingly haphazard spill, reminiscent of water or floating debris. This allusion, as the title might indicate, is intentional as well as timely. The International Organization for Migration, an agency of the United Nations, reports that over 100,000 migrants and refugees crossed the Mediterranean into Europe in 2018, with nearly 2,000 known deaths by drowning, numbers consistent with migratory patterns in the region since 2013.[2] *La Mer Morte* attempts to represent this loss with the symbolic power of strewn and discarded clothes that seem washed ashore or left behind.

These visual allusions have a significant resonance in today's mass media. *La Mer Morte*'s spewed clothes may recall the image of Alan Kurdi, a Syrian three-year-old who drowned while attempting to cross the Mediterranean from Turkey to one of the Greek islands in September 2015. The photograph, taken by journalist Nilüfer Demir, prompted a global outcry about the conditions of migration in the Mediterranean, as well as the circumstances governing the necessity of flight. (Kurdi's family had been trying to seek asylum from the Syrian Civil War.)[3] Such images have become increasingly commonplace, deployed almost sensationally in denoting the trauma of forced migration. They have become a consumable trope, desensitizing viewers to the realities of violence. *La Mer Morte*, which alludes to the figure through its use of clothes, nonetheless abstracts the figure into anonymous subjects: a sea of blue denim stands in for named persons, even as it names the loss of life in migrant crossings. The work's allegorical quality points to the discourses surrounding migration that abstract the private into the public "crisis."

Early in his career, Attia pursued a less poetic, more ethnographic approach to the representation of new and long-standing immigrant communities, groups who are often conflated in Western Europe based on their nonwhite identities. Many of these works are installations organized as critiques of taxonomy and categorization, principles generally seen as critical to museum practice: "I'm trying to illustrate that there's nothing more complex than the unbalanced relation between tradition and modernity—that traditionally the notion of categorising does not exist."[4] In *The Culture of Fear: An Invention of Evil* (2013) [fig. 1], for example, stereotypical images of France's former colonial subjects are affixed to twenty-one metal shelves, organizing the visual tropes by which the postcolonial other (specifically, the black or brown subject) is classified as "dangerous." The work draws from the language of the museum to question how cultural institutions participate in the rhetoric of "us" and "them," a meditation also present in the anonymous abstraction of *La Mer Morte*, where visitors may view the discarded blue-fabric mass as though it were itself an enclosure, a barricade that viewers cannot traverse. This echoes the boundary of the shoreline, a naturally occurring border that has become politicized in the age of the nation state, maritime law, and migration politics.

At the same time, Attia is not content to leave his work with only an affect of loss. His practice over the last decade has been particularly concerned with questions of repair, a concept he has found useful for articulating the real experiences of immigrant and diasporic communities: "Repair and hybridization are the terrain where many cultures begin to take back their liberty."[5] What might it mean to bring together what is still recoverable from a fractured world? *Repaired Broken Mirror* (2017) [fig. 2] returns to an earlier installation Attia had staged with broken mirrors pieced back together with metal staples. In this first iteration, the sharp glass

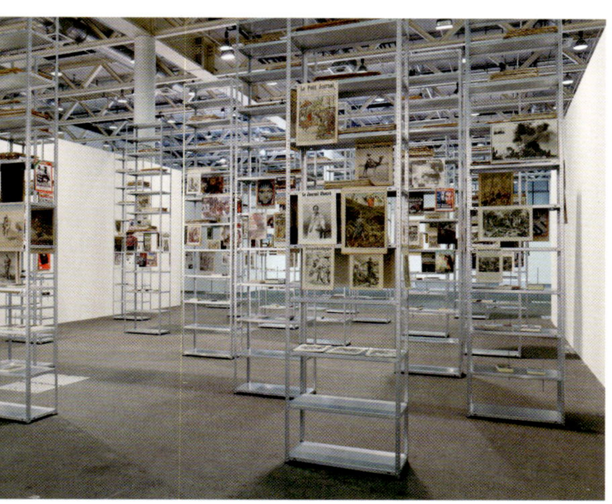

Fig. 1. Kader Attia, *The Culture of Fear: An Invention of Evil #1*, 2013. Installation view, Art Basel, Switzerland, 2016

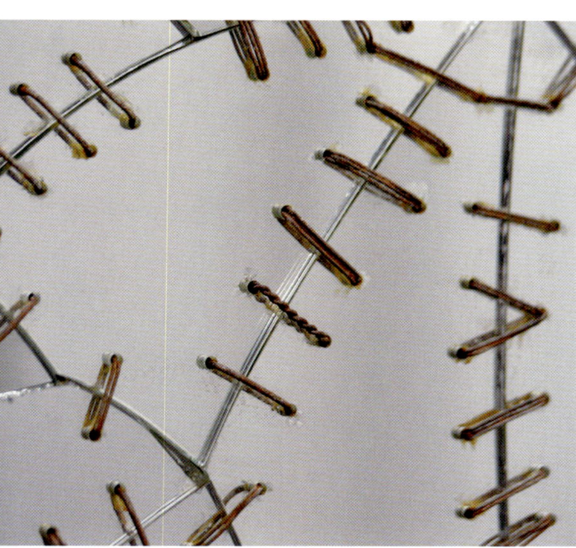

Fig. 2. Kader Attia, *Repaired Broken Mirror* (detail), 2017. Mirror and wire, dimensions variable

edges and threaded metal stitches appear strangely tender and full of care, even as they confront the viewer with a deeply internal reflection: "In the mended mirrors, the visitor will see his own face as if scarred by the metal wire."[6] The second version, completed in 2018, attempts to stitch together concrete slabs, to mend cracked pavement. The association is a hopeful one, suggesting an unavoidable wearing out but not an inevitable loss.

These installations leave us with the question of what may be recovered, or indeed repaired, from the overwhelming confrontation with *La Mer Morte*. In some iterations of the piece, Attia includes light boxes containing photographs of a shoreline with the sea beyond it, an oddly reversed backdrop for the sea of clothes strewn on the gallery floor. From this angle the viewer locates the mirrored waters—one evoked by the blue-fabric mass, the other imaged in the photographs—as an impossible crossing. For Attia, the reality of migration, of diaspora, and of exile are located in the contradictory impulses of the physical and the representational: he explains, "Exile is a geographical notion, but it is also psychological."[7] Even so, like the mended mirrors or the museo-taxonomical installation, the artist gestures to these fissures as sites for creative redress, where trauma might direct us to contend, meaningfully, with our political reality. Attia's practice of mending what comes together through force, violence, and loss presents us with the opportunity to consider these very places of exile, rupture, and fracture as sites for imagining what else might be possible in a more free world. —AP

1. Kader Attia describes how this language of "crisis" is embedded in the media: "mass media uses this terminology constantly, but migration is a norm in nature and culture evolution." See "Counter Knowledges and Permissions: Irit Rogoff in conversation with Kader Attia, 2016," available on Attia's website, online at http://kaderattia.de/counter-knowledges-and-permissions-irit-rogoff-in-conversation-with-kader-attia/ (accessed January 20, 2019).

2. See IOM UN Migration, "Mediterranean Migrant Arrivals Reach 100,630 in 2018; Deaths Reach 1,989," November 6, 2018. Available online at www.iom.int/news/mediterranean-migrant-arrivals-reach-100630-2018-deaths-reach-1989 (accessed January 20, 2019).

3. See, e.g., Hannah Bloch, "That Little Syrian Boy: Here's Who He Was," September 3, 2015. Available online at www.npr.org/sections/parallels/2015/09/03/437132793/photo-of-dead-3-year-old-syrian-refugee-breaks-hearts-around-the-world (accessed January 20, 2019).

4. Attia, in Hannah Gregory, "Archival Impulse: An Interview with Kader Attia," *Apollo*, April 10, 2015. Available online at www.apollo-magazine.com/archival-impulse-an-interview-with-kader-attia/ (accessed January 20, 2019).

5. Attia, quoted in Nazanin Lankarani, "French-Algerian Artist Explores Identity and Repair," *New York Times*, June 11, 2013. Available online at www.nytimes.com/2013/06/12/arts/French-Algerian-artist-Explores-Identity-and-Repair.html (accessed January 20, 2019).

6. Ibid.

7. Attia, in "Exiles: Interviews by Kader Attia," *EuropeNow Daily*, October 2, 2017. Available online at https://www.europenowjournal.org/2017/09/30/exiles-interviews-by-kader-attia/ (accessed January 20, 2019).

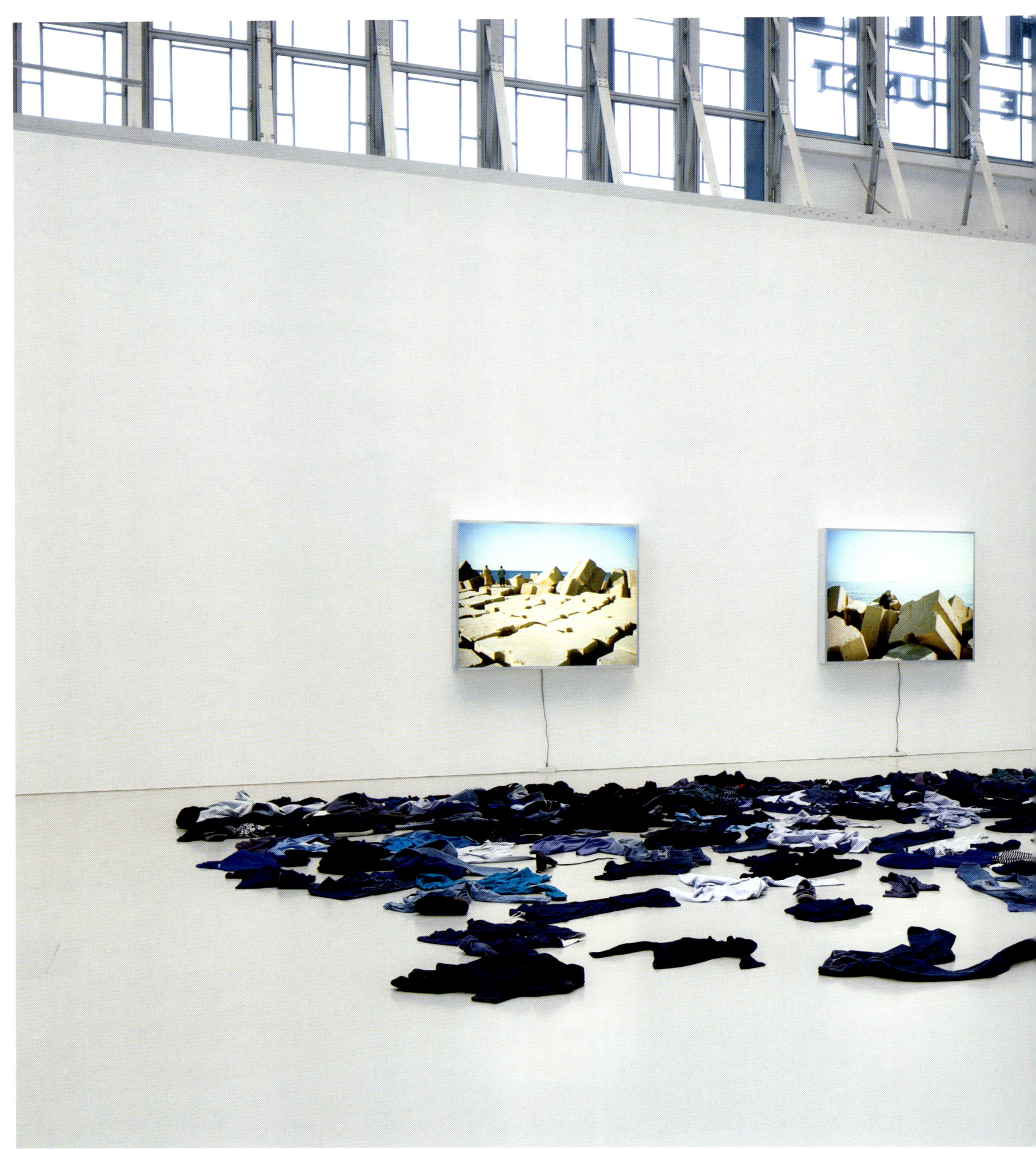

Kader Attia, *La Mer Morte* (The Dead Sea), 2015.
Clothes and light boxes. Each light box: 52 x 63 x 7 inches (130 x 160 x 18 cm);
overall dimensions variable.
Installation view, *Streamlines—Oceans, Global Trade and Migration*,
Halle für aktuelle Kunst/Deichtorhallen Hamburg, Germany, 2015–16

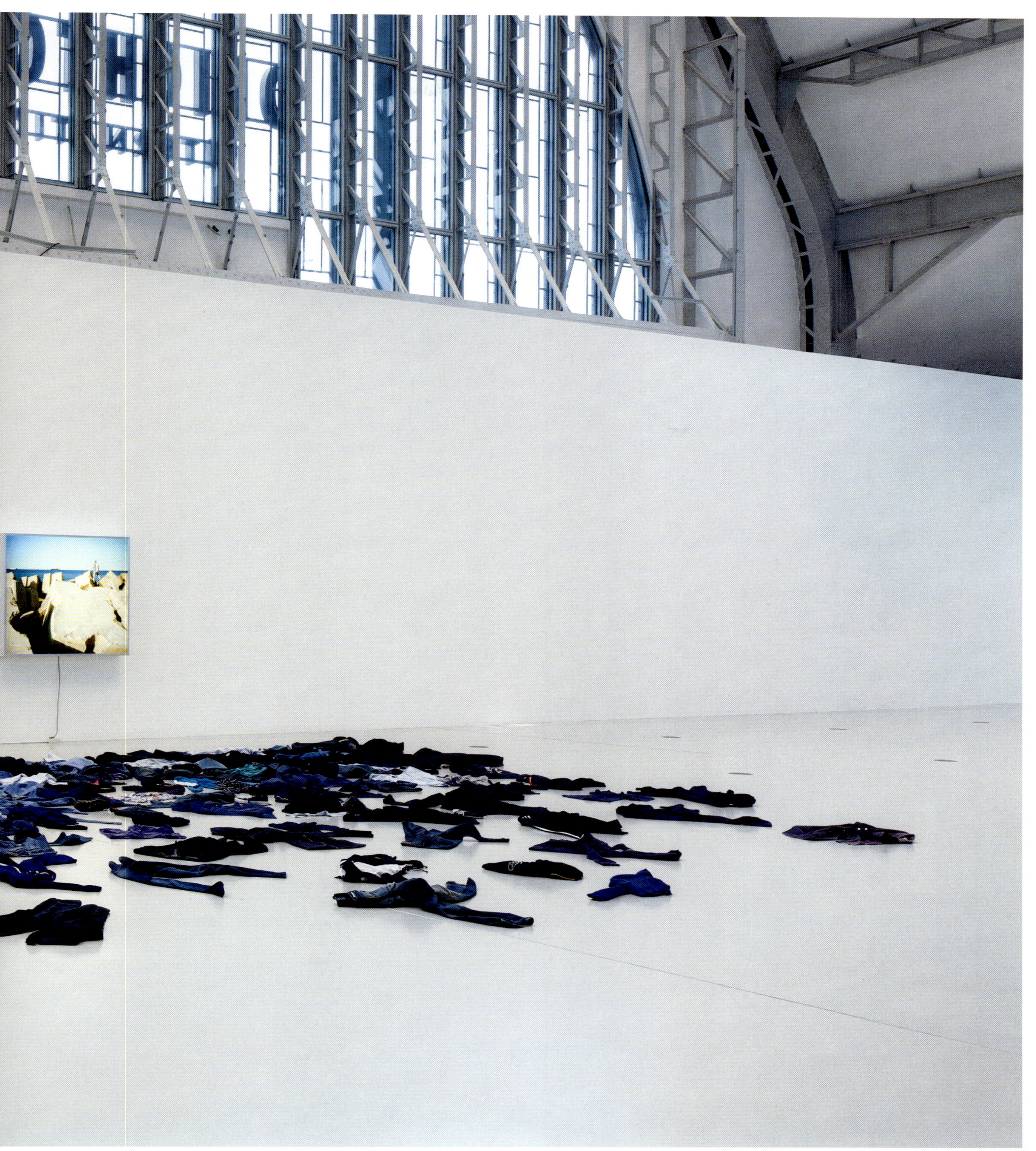

Isaac Julien

B. 1960, London, United Kingdom;
lives and works in London

Artist and filmmaker Isaac Julien is widely acclaimed for his interdisciplinary explorations of film form through immersive multichannel installations. In invoking the history of cinema, he manipulates the architectural setting of film spectatorship to explore the poetic intersections of documentary and fiction, memory and desire. Julien rose to prominence in the film world with the 1989 drama-documentary *Looking for Langston*, an intimate study of the writer Langston Hughes and the Harlem Renaissance. While that work can be screened conventionally in a cinema, Julien has since expanded into multiscreen installations that envelop the viewer in lyrical and often ambiguous conversations among the images on each screen. In these works, which often include large-scale photographs exhibited separately, he depicts figures at life scale or greater within physically encompassing environments. The effect, as art historian Jennifer González writes, "is to displace the viewer from a comfortable position of omniscience to one of immersion and identification."[1] The environmental scale of Julien's work transports the viewer to another visual realm, while the syncopated soundscapes of the films channel the dreamlike fragmentation of memory and the unconscious.

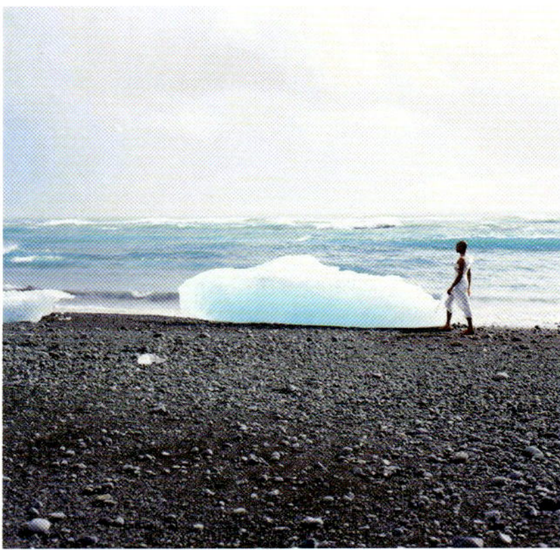

Fig. 1. Isaac Julien, *True North*, 2004. Digital print on Epson Premium Photo Glossy Paper, 39⅜ x 39⅜ inches (100 x 100 cm)

In 2004, Julien began the Expedition series, a trilogy of audiovisual installations that explore geographic and cultural displacement on a local and global scale. Deeply moved by documentary photographs of migrant corpses washed ashore on Spanish beaches, Julien began a lengthy research process that took him to various locations. The first work in the trilogy, *True North* (2004) [fig. 1], conjures a fragmented narrative linked by metaphors of endless traverse over the rugged landscape of Iceland, which serves as a metonym for the North Pole, its browned edges suggesting evidence of global warming. The film is loosely inspired by the story of Matthew Henson, the African-American explorer who accompanied Robert Peary on what many believe was the first successful expedition to the North Pole (1908–9).[2] The film's voice-over, sound, rapid montage, and epic shots of dramatic landscape emphasize the excitement and peril of the journey.

Fantôme Afrique (2005), the second in the trilogy, moves through both the rural landscape of Burkina Faso and the dense architecture of urban Ouagadougou, the country's capital and a site of tremendous growth in the contemporary African film industry.[3] Punctuated by archival footage of early colonial expeditions and of landmark moments in African history, the film features dancers who animate the film's meditation on the unique spaces that emerge, denationalized and deterritorialized, out of conflict.

The third film, *Western Union: small boats* (2007) [pp. 100–05], was shot on the Mediterranean island of Lampedusa—a popular entry point for African migration into Europe—and in nearby Sicily's Palazzo Valguarnera-Gangi, an eighteenth-century baroque mansion in Palermo that housed generations of aristocrats known as "leopards" for their extravagant lifestyles.[4] The aesthetic of *Western Union: small boats* fuses the opulent scenography of Luchino Visconti's 1963 film *The Leopard*—an epic period drama about the collapse of Italian aristocracy—with Lampedusa's more recent history as a primary transit point for migrants from Africa, the Middle East, and Asia who try to reach Europe by crossing the Mediterranean via Libya and Tunisia. In Julien's film, a man lying in the sun on the shore of the island drifts off into sleep and enters a dream phase: a dancer tumbles down, writhes, and is carried up a marble staircase in an opulent Baroque palazzo. In another scene, a different dancer flails underwater to a turbulent, gurgling soundscape [p. 103]. Throughout the film, metaphors of perilous water travel abound, whether in long shots of drowned bodies draped in cloth on the beach or in views of piled small boats, vessels that have become synonymous with the precarity and danger of contemporary migration across the waters off southern Europe. These sights also stand as metaphors or echoes of the Middle Passage, the transatlantic voyage that brought enslaved people to the Americas during the centuries of the slave trade, a history that resonates in the highly racialized discourse around migration in the Mediterranean.

Some have questioned the ethics of creating sensual, aestheticized works out of the real-life tragedies experienced by migrants.[5] But Julien's response acknowledges the broad crisis of representation with regard to migration—namely, that documentary approaches often fail to move people. Migration raises very serious questions, writes the artist, "and the usual method of exploring them in film is through documentary, a genre that conveniently helps us to keep them separate from life.... The question becomes: why is it we want these images separated from us? Why do we feel more comfortable when they're at a distance?"[6] As art historian Emma Chubb writes in her thoughtful analysis of *Western Union: small boats*, the film stands alone in the mediated representations of migration in the news, and more widely in the culture, in its insistence on the fictions and tropes that govern its representation and in its avoidance of a kind of "representational violence" that would visually echo the dehumanizing rhetoric too often used to characterize migrants.[7]

Made several years later, the ambitious nine-channel film installation *Ten Thousand Waves* (2010) [fig. 2] interweaves three stories linking China's ancient past with the present: the Morecambe Bay tragedy of 2004, in which twenty-three Chinese immigrants were drowned while at work gathering cockles; the Chinese legend of the sea goddess Mazu, protector of fishermen and sailors; and an exploration of the silent film *The Goddess* (dir. Wu Yonggang, 1934), shot in Shanghai during China's early cinematic golden age and portraying the tragic life of a woman who enters into prostitution in order to support herself and her son.[8] The film's rich imagery moves between the cold northwest coast of England, the buzzing rush hour of Shanghai, and a lush landscape of bamboo forest and stony mountains. An innovation in filmic storytelling across multiple screens, *Ten Thousand Waves* addresses the flow of global capital and the bodies it pulls along with it, enfolding themes of labor and itinerancy into the narrative of transcontinental journeys central also to Julien's Expedition series. —ET

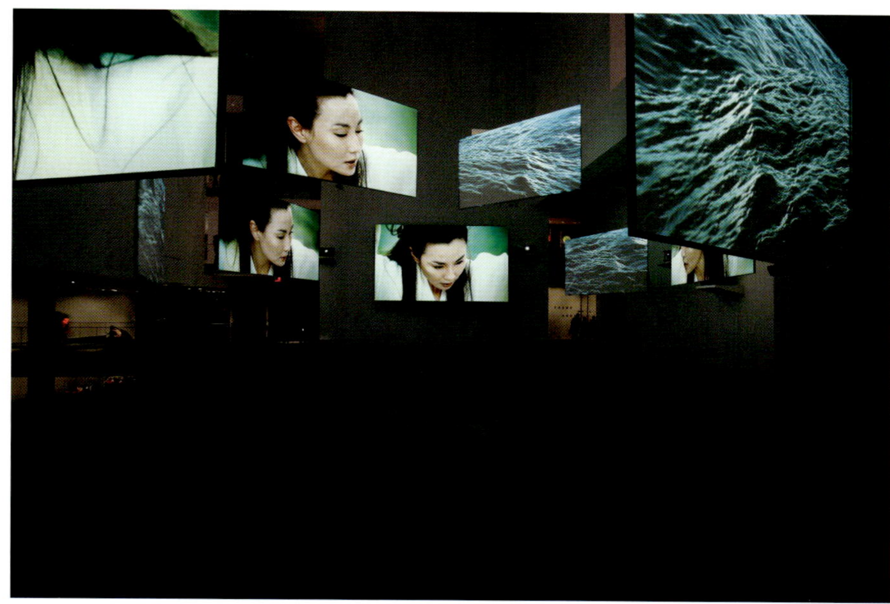

Fig. 2. Isaac Julien, *Ten Thousand Waves*, 2010. Installation view, *Isaac Julien: Ten Thousand Waves*, The Museum of Modern Art, New York, 2013–14

1. Jennifer A. González, "Sea Dreams: Isaac Julien's *Western Union: Small Boats*," in Saloni Mathur, ed., *The Migrant's Time: Rethinking Art History and Diaspora*, Clark Studies in the Visual Arts (Williamstown, MA: Sterling and Francine Clark Art Institute, 2011), p. 116.

2. Whether Matthew Henson and Robert Peary reached the North Pole is open to question. If they did, however, Henson rather than Peary may have been the first one there. See, e.g., Bill Norrington, "Who Was the First Person to Reach the North Pole?" University of California, Santa Barbara Department of Geography. Available online at: https://geog.ucsb.edu/who-was-the-first-person-to-reach-the-north-pole/ (accessed December 25, 2018).

3. Burkina Faso, among other former French-colonial nations in sub-Saharan Africa, has experienced this growth in its film industry, including a structurally formalized system of production and distribution, through foreign aid tied to economic development, but also as a representative of postcolonial efforts to strengthen national identity. In 1969 it established fespaco (Festival Panafricain du Cinéma et de la Télévision de Ouagadougou), the largest film venue in sub-Sarahan Africa. While Burkina Faso became a prominent site of feature-film production in the late 1990s, it has not yielded a profitable film industry. Nigeria has the oldest, most profitable and best-known film industry in African cinema. See Teresa Höfert de Turégano, "Film culture and industry in Burkina Faso," in Diana Barrowclough and Zeljka Kozul-Wright, eds., *Creative Industries and Developing Countries: Voice, Choice and Economic Growth* (London and New York: Routledge, 2008), pp. 111–29.

4. The aristocrat and author Giuseppe Tomasi di Lampedusa (1896–1957) inherited a mansion in Palermo. His posthumously published book *The Leopard* (1958) chronicles the decline of a noble Sicilian family in the mid-nineteenth century; it served as the inspiration for Luchino Visconti's eponymous film from 1963.

5. González sees the introduction of dancers as productively unsettling for viewers: "the audience may feel uneasily caught between theater and reality, experiencing a cognitive tension that brings into question familiar strategies and politics of spectatorship." González, "Sea Dreams," p. 124. Emma Chubb writes of the film's tension between atrocity and beauty: "In choosing this aesthetic approach, Julien sets himself apart from his peers and courts the danger of rendering beautiful the suffering, violence, exploitation, and, in many cases, deaths of contemporary migrants; he risks abstracting the migrants into sources of visual pleasure for an audience largely composed of the global, contemporary art biennial-visiting elite." Chubb, "Small Boats, Slave Ship; or, Isaac Julien and the Beauty of Implied Catastrophe." *Art Journal* 75, no. 1 (2016):24–43. Available online at http://artjournal.collegeart.org/?p=7197 (accessed December 26, 2018).

6. Isaac Julien, "Planet," in *Isaac Julien: Riot*, exh. cat. (New York: The Museum of Modern Art, 2014), p. 176.

7. Chubb, "Small Boats, Slave Ship."

8. The ICA/Boston presented *Ten Thousand Waves* in 2012. The film features well-known actresses Maggie Cheung and Zhao Tao, video artist Yang Fudong, poet Wang Ping, and venerable Chinese calligrapher Gong Fagen.

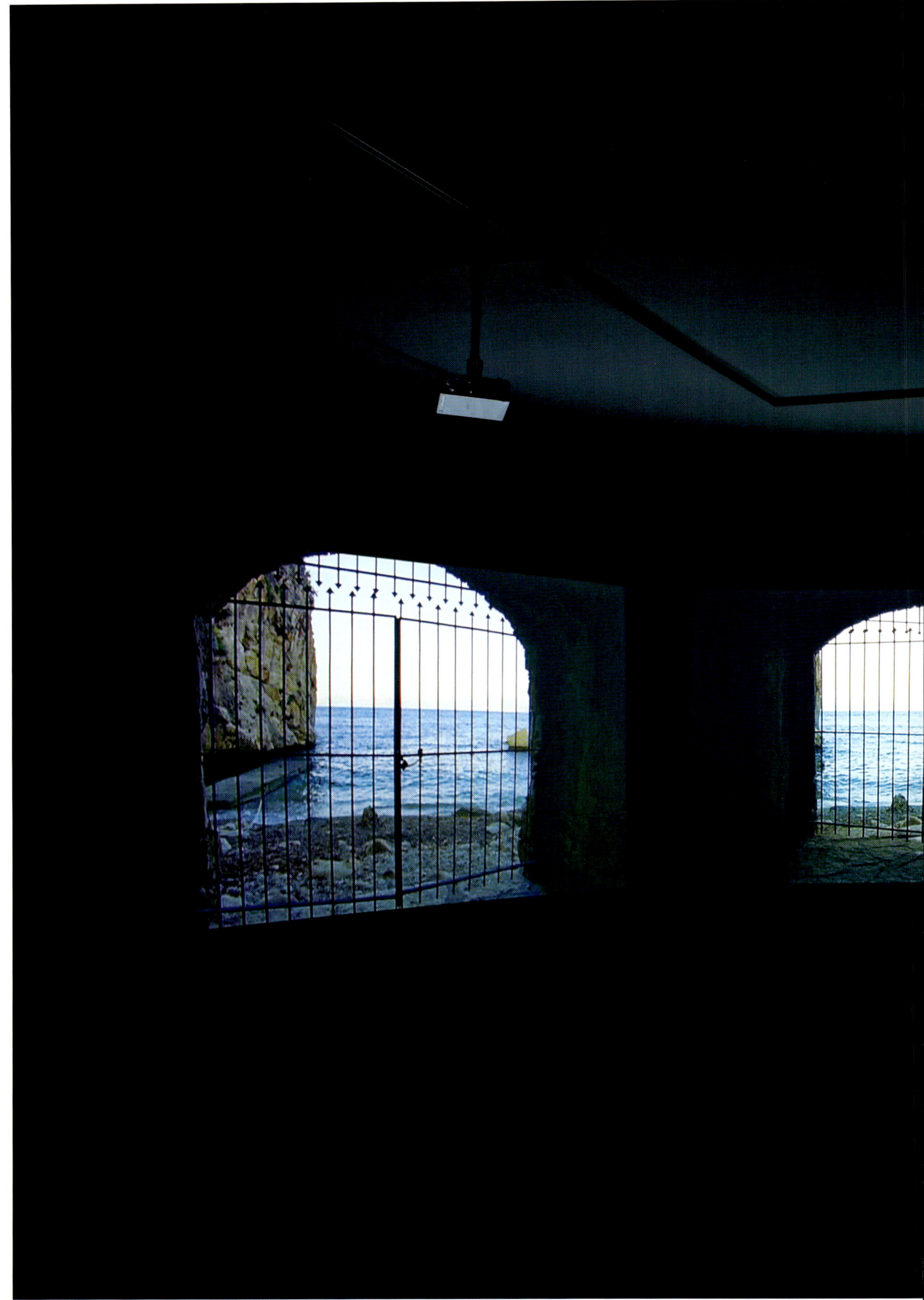

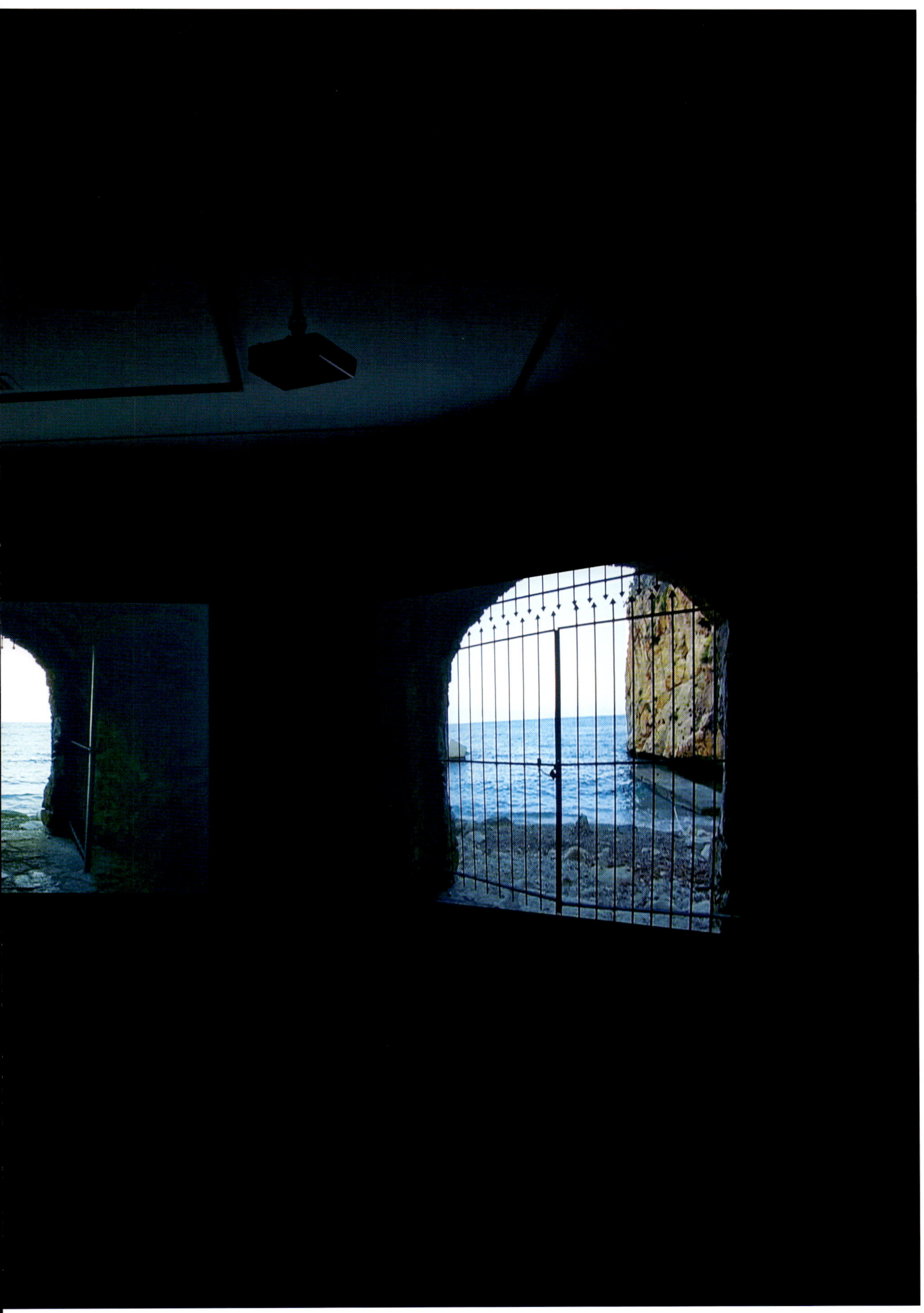

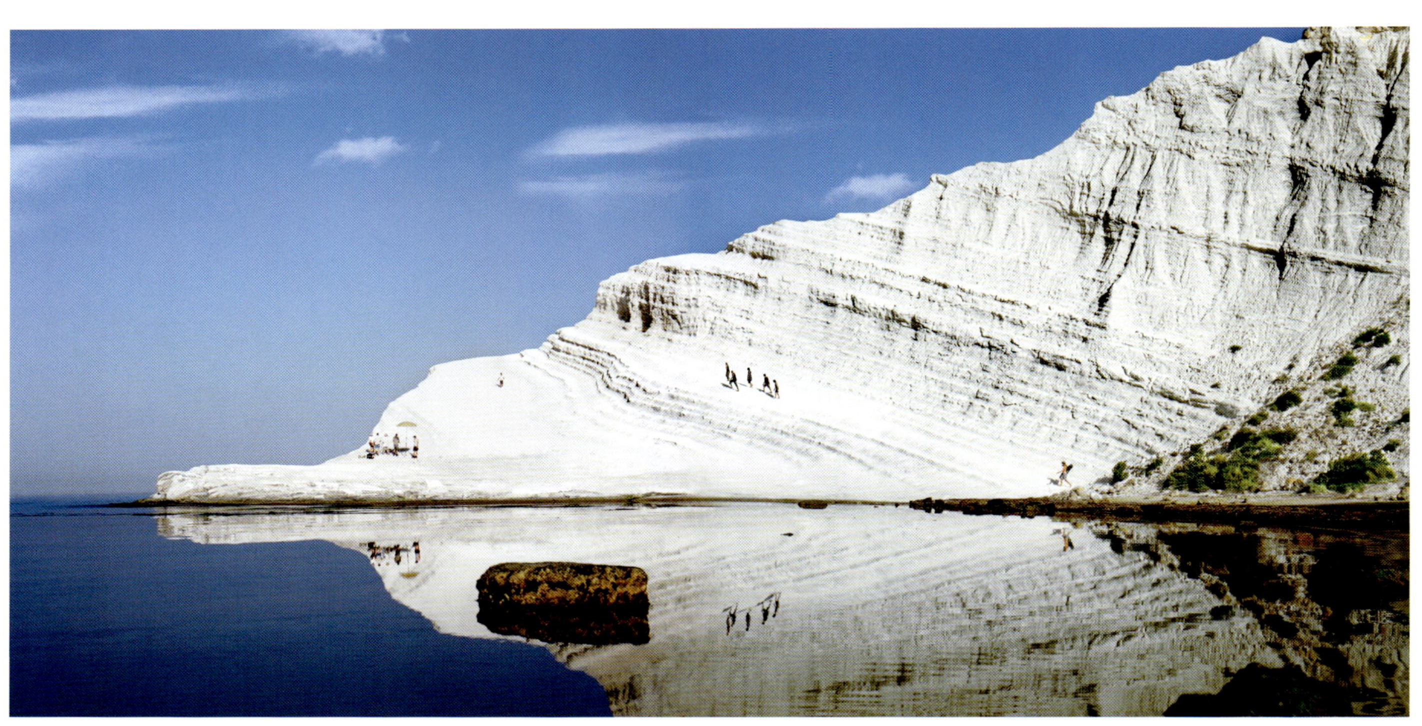

Previous spread and opposite (still):
Isaac Julien, *Western Union: small boats*, 2007.
Three-channel video installation, 35mm film transferred to DVD/HD
(color, 5.1 surround sound; 18:22 minutes). Dimensions variable.
Installation view, Galería Helga de Alvear, Madrid, 2008

Above: Isaac Julien, *Western Union: small boats No. 2*
(Flight Towards Other Destinies 1), 2007.
Duratrans image in light box. 47 ¼ x 96 ⅛ inches (120 x 244 cm)

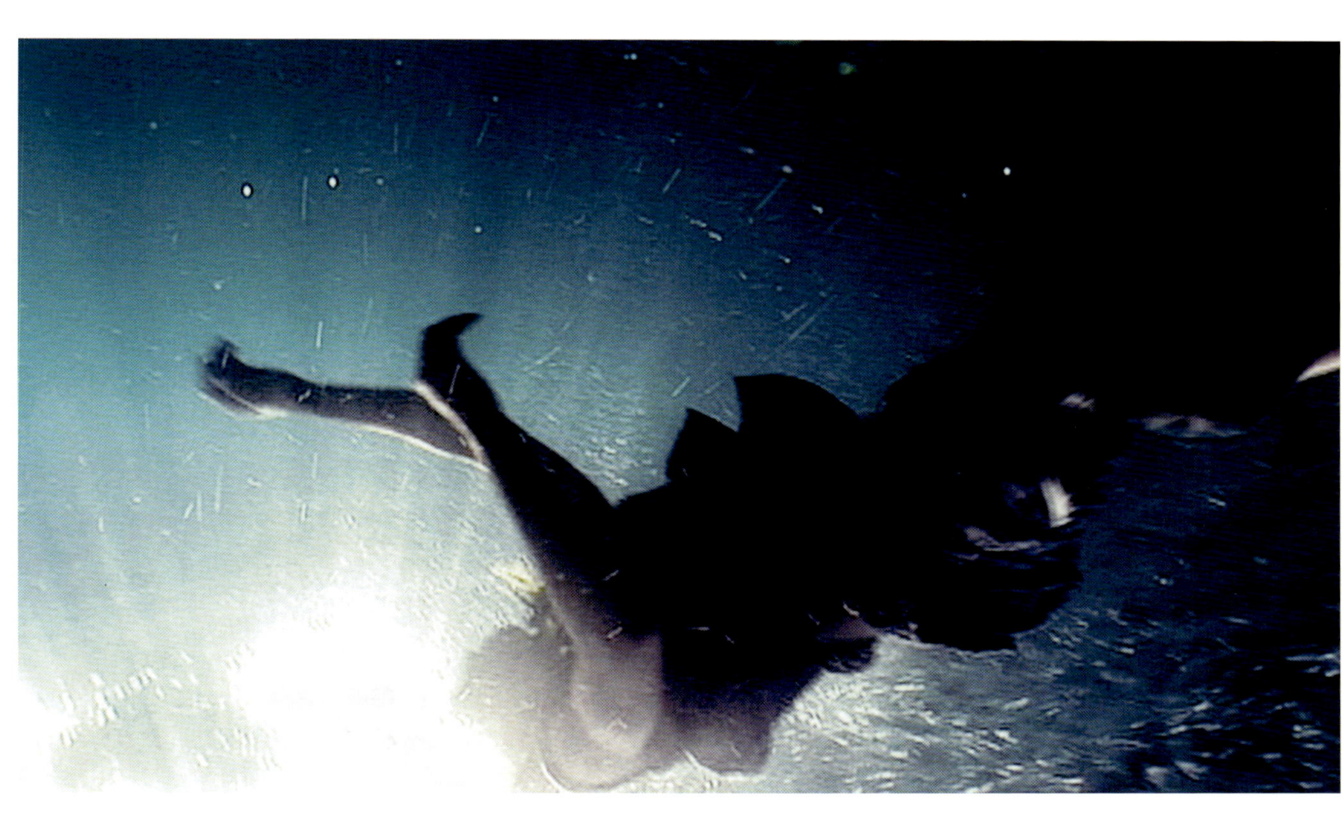

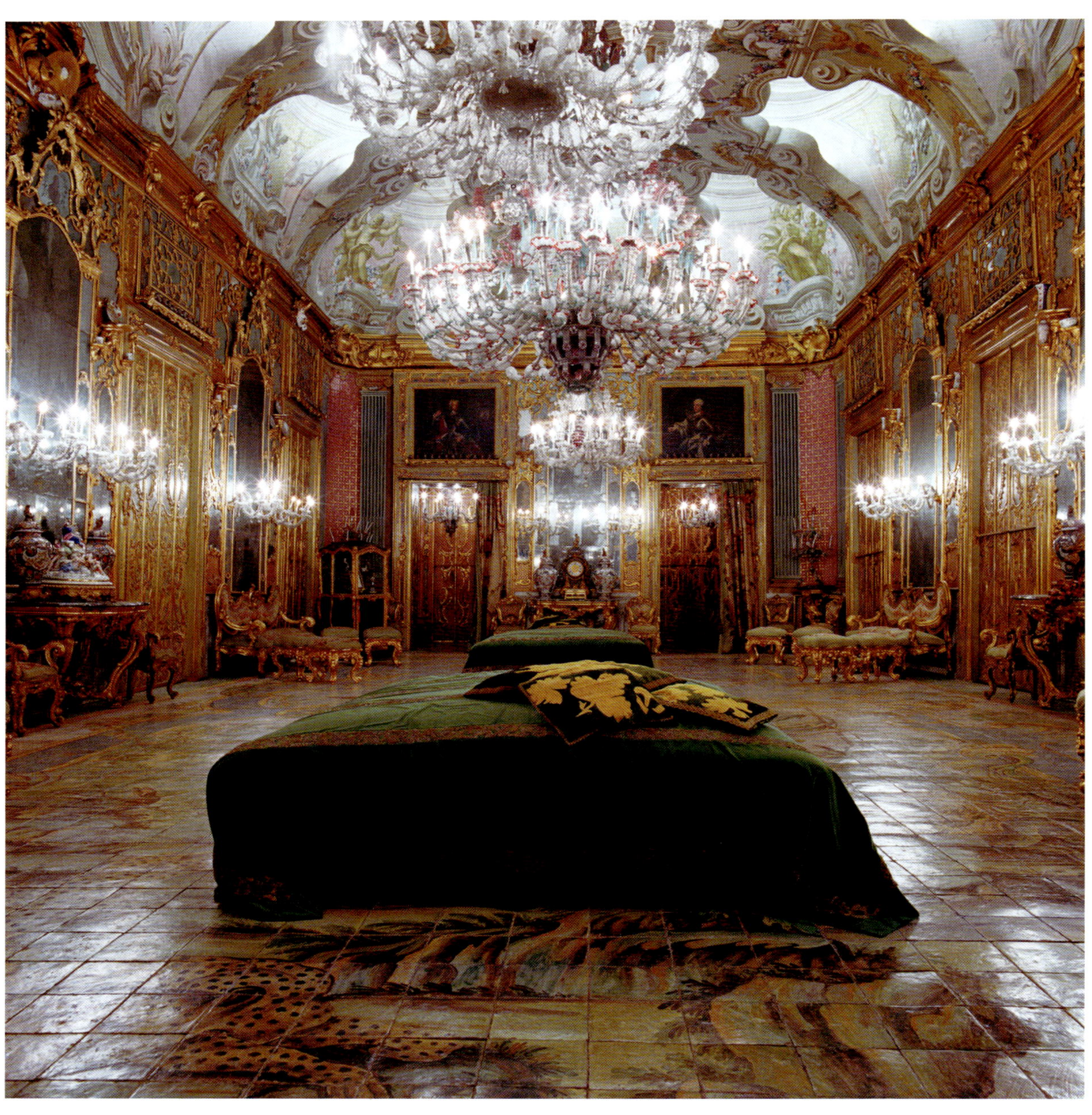

Isaac Julien, *Western Union Series No. 7 (The Leopard)*, 2007.
Duratrans image in light box.
48⅛ x 48⅛ inches (122 x 122 cm)

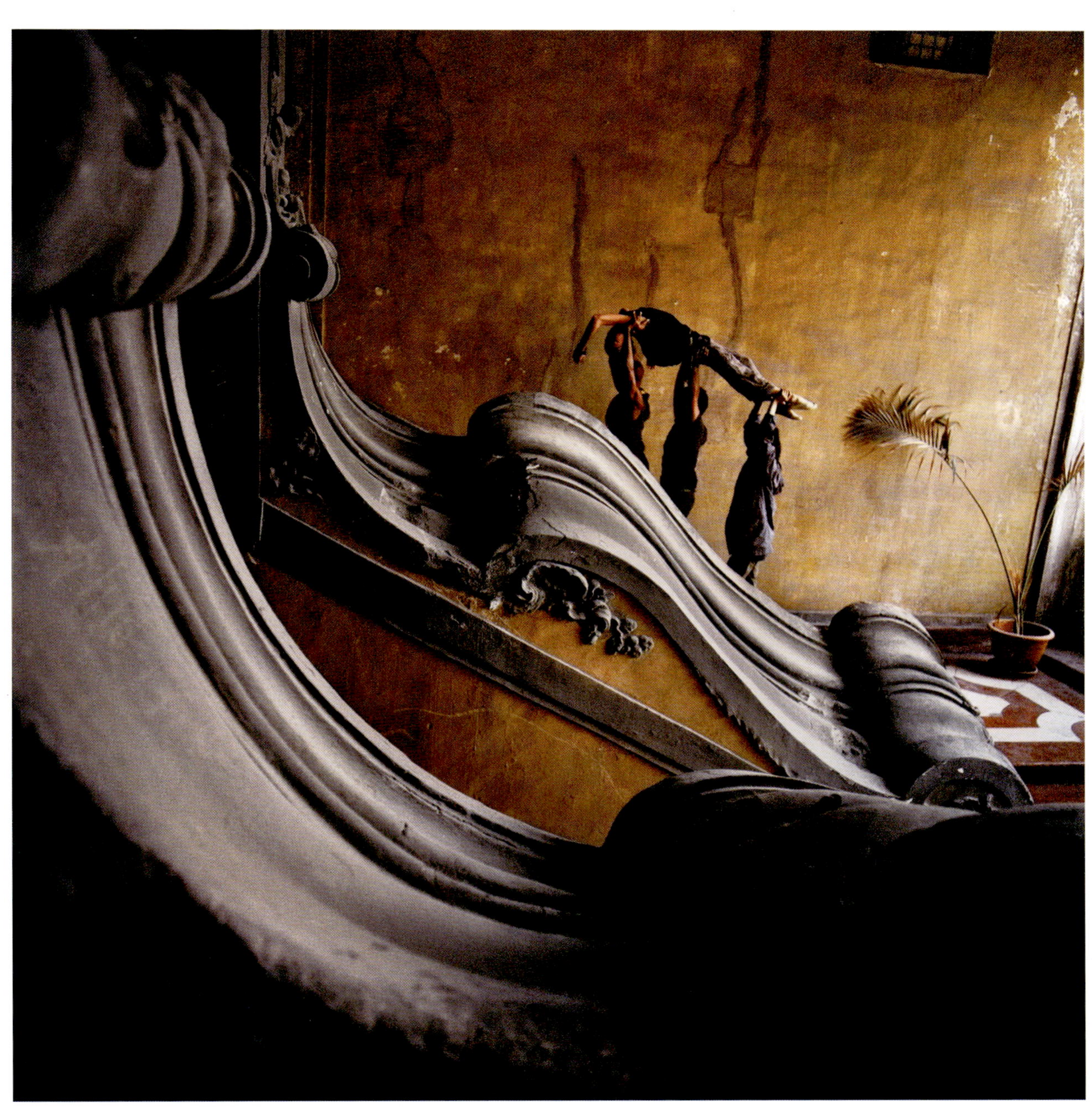

Isaac Julien, *Western Union Series No. 12 (Balustrade)*, 2007.
Duratrans image in light box.
47¼ x 47¼ inches (120 x 120 cm)

Conversation

Guillermo Galindo and Josh Kun

JOSH KUN Let's start with the state of thinking about and through sound. As many have argued, Western knowledge since the Enlightenment has been heavily rooted in the visual. Western writing and philosophy have rarely granted sound the central role in creating knowledge that we know it actually plays. At the same time, we must reckon with what Jonathan Sterne calls the "Ensoniment," the period 1750–1925 when the world became audible in new ways, when new listening practices and sonic epistemes were born through massive transformations of society, technology, and culture.

GUILLERMO GALINDO I agree. Unlike visual art, sound is a volatile, time-based medium, and there has always been the desire to materialize or preserve the experience of sound in physical formats. It is believed that the first music scores printed in the Middle Ages were not really meant for musicians but for royalty, so that they could preserve a physical memory of the performance. Later on we have analogue recording technology, which, aside from making sound "physical," suggested a completely different way of listening.

JK I think back to Thomas Edison's phonograph, of 1877, which was originally intended not for entertainment but for things like business dictation and recording family memories. One of the shocks about the phonograph was that it was a spiritual medium: somebody could die and their voice could live. What do you make of ideas about listening to the dead, or, in your work, of bringing back the voices of those who've gone missing?

GG The ability to hear the voice of a loved one who has passed plays with our perceptions of life. This is a psychological phenomenon: anything that makes sound moves; therefore, it's alive. So to hear a person's voice is not only about memory but more about the illusion that that person is alive. There's also the unconscious factor: I was in Lesbos at a time when Turkey had a deal with the European Union to halt the flow of refugees. The Lesbos beaches were practically abandoned and filled with all sorts of things that migrants had left scattered around. The sea, my breath, the breeze and the sounds the objects made were telling the story.... The objects were later turned into sonic devices. What I describe as silence was in fact the absence of human activity ("antrophony"), which wasn't really silence. Sound has a subjective part related to cognition and memory.

JK This is linked to the argument about what the first sounds of human existence are. Many have said, "Well, it's the heartbeat, the breath."

GG It's interesting that when we assume we're in silence, we can still hear our own bodily sounds. This is a primordial experience, reminding us of our existence through the experience of the "audible self." I became aware of the cultural body of sound through the work of the French composer Pierre Schaeffer, who suggested that the listener detaches the recorded sound from the object that produces it, thus isolating it from the physical world. He calls this "acousmatics," based on Pythagoras's requirement to have his students sit in silence while they listened to him lecture from behind a veil or screen. This connects to your question about hearing the recorded voice of someone who has died. It's almost a sonic photograph: you're not hearing or seeing the person or object that produces the sound; it's an illusion, a simulation that fools around with our memory.

JK You're reminding me of the trip you and I took to the Musical Instrument Museum in Phoenix. Looking at those skins, those bellies, those bones, I remember thinking there'd be no music as we know it without dead animals—that dead animals and their remains are really the foundation for the musical life that we speak of so casually.

GG In pre-Columbian cultures, the conception and purpose of music were very different from in Western cultures. If you made a flute out of a tree where a bird nested, or an instrument out of a person's bones, the music you produced with that instrument would be related to a particular symbolic meaning and physical presence. It wasn't about appreciating the beauty of sound itself, but about the *purpose* of the sound and the instrument as mediators connecting us to the physical world. The purpose of sound and music in Western cultures has always been more about the experience of sound, and about producing the perfect instrument in order to produce exactly the sound we want.

JK These are crucial, long-standing questions: where does the meaning of sound lie? Is its value in the instruments that shape it? The contexts and events that produce it? Its reception by a listener? The Nigerian musician Fela Kuti believed that once you recorded a song, the song was dead. So after he recorded a particular piece, he would never perform it live again.

GG Oh, that's good. I like that.... I think we're getting into something interesting: life and death in relation to sound. If anything is alive, it vibrates and produces sound—it vibrates, therefore it's alive. The record player is alive because electricity is part of the physicality of life, but a recording is just a representation of a performance, not the experience of the performance itself.

JK The conductor Daniel Barenboim wrote an interesting essay about music's relationship to silence. To talk about music, he says, is to talk about the human condition, which is to talk about the balance between life and death—let's say, a politics of life and death. Music emerges from silence, and it's always on the verge of becoming silent.[1]

GG The language of music depends on silence. Silence doesn't exist without music and vice versa. In music, what we call silence is the interval of time between producing and not producing sound. It's where music breaths.

JK But Guillermo, how do you feel about that—the idea that when you play, you're also facing an inevitable end that will soon come?

GG To produce sound, and to produce music, you need energy, life. Literally physical energy. To produce sound forever, you would need to produce energy forever. That's humanly impossible. When playing music, we know it will eventually and inevitably end. Sound exists as long as life exists. Performance depends on the limitations of life, time, and circumstances.

JK Does that interest you, the possibility of sound forever?

GG The universe is a perfect analogy for a sound continuum. I assume that's what Pythagoras called the "music of the spheres." We don't know when the planet's cycle started and we don't know when it's going to end, but everything in the universe, everything moving, is producing some kind of sound. The idea of something that can create sound forever has always fascinated composers and philosophers.... I dare to include myself.

JK Your Border Cantos instruments and scores [pp. 124, 126–27] make me think about the extent to which the material of the border wall contains sonic traces of the lives that have moved back and forth across it. As someone who both is a philosopher of sound and works with sound, is that a fair assessment?

GG I'm not sure. That raises the question, where does sound go? Does it really die? Or do the molecules of a sound just transform ... do they get trapped in physical objects, including the atmosphere, forever? Then we're dealing not just with sound but with the action that produces it. It's like karma: whatever you put out in the world will be out there forever and will eventually return to you. The energy that we put out there, including sound, may integrate into the objects around us and perhaps, just like a permanent footprint, stay there forever.

JK I've always had a fantasy about being able to release all the sounds stored in all the physical objects of the world.

GG [*laughs*] There's a theory of sounds lost in space. Nicolas Collins, in his book *Handmade Electronic Music*, talks about fans of VLF (Very Low Frequency) radio using homemade coils to try to pick up the sounds of the Aurora Borealis, meteorites entering the atmosphere, GPS satellites, and submarine communications.[2] Perhaps extraterrestrial sounds, or sounds from distant civilizations that ended thousands of years ago, are left wandering in the universe forever. At some point I also made an installation at the Bellas Artes Opera House esplanade in Mexico City. I had in mind the illusion of, somehow, extracting the particles of all the opera voices from the building and combining the fragments.

JK I love it. One of the things that music can do is remind us of our relationship to an encroaching silence. Being in the world is not a given. I was thinking about a scene at the beginning of Isaac Julien's *Western Union: small boats* [2007] [pp. 100–01]: a woman emerges from darkness, looking out at the Mediterranean through what seems to be a cave or an archway or tunnel, and we hear the voice of the Malian singer Oumou Sangaré, and we don't know what's happening in that moment. We don't know what we're supposed to be feeling. Music can be like echolocation; it can be a means of trying to find your place, or to find your way home, or to find your way to a new home. It's a way not of being in the world but of wanting to be in the world, or mapping one's way into the world.

GG Music can also become just a fraction of a whole soundscape, perhaps the signature of a particular place and time, a means of location. A piece of music doesn't exist on its own; it's experienced together with other things, such as environmental sounds. Imagine the sounds of a scene of the immigrant's journey. We're in the Sonoran Desert, norteño music coming from a transistor radio, insect sounds, the wind; cars, helicopters, the Border Patrol; laughs, coughs, engines. And then the imagined sounds. Music in this case doesn't exist on its own—it's part of the sonic universe of a particular moment. It blends with the whole audiovisual complexity of the experience. That's the space I like exploring. I don't see music as an isolated construct; instead, I try to incorporate it into the textures of a particular soundscape. I try to encompass the whole experience. This is not only about composing a piece of music but about recreating the situation in which the music exists, being a component of an immersive sonic experience. The experience of life.

JK Among the many things I love about your work is that to be in the presence of *Zapatello* [2014] [p. 127] or *Exterminating Angel* [2015] [p. 126] is to experience their materiality and its origins in a particular environment—to say, not, "Oh, that's a clarinet," or, "Oh, that's a drum," but, "Oh, those are water bottles from the desert." It's a reminder that what we call music is a construct. There's this whole elaborate ecology that has already gone into making what we casually call sound or music.

GG Exactly. I do everything I can to avoid conventionalism. I enjoy wandering within the forbidden limits between sound, visuals, time, experience, and imagination and the intersections between social justice and spirituality. In order to evolve, the construct we call music must remain open to change and transformation.

No matter how much I explain my "instruments" to the airport officers, every time I go through TSA or customs I always end up being searched and questioned. "They don't look like instruments to me." ... Yes, they say ... "They are not guitars, clarinets, violins or drums." ... Neither are they *recycled* items, and that's why I call my pieces "cyber totemic sonic devices."

About the experience itself, it is important for me to re-create sonic circumstances. This is my way of immersing the audience inside the actual experience. I'd like to quote Luís Alberto Urrea's book *The Devil's Highway* [2004]: "The FM keeps morale elevated. Radio calls to base often have a classic rock soundtrack—Van Halen and Led Zeppelin bleed through the call-ins. Sometimes, newbies will be blasting the radio so loud that they can't hear calls from the dispatch. 'Ten, Base, Ten. I'm twentied at the Pinacate Lava Flow. I'm going to give you every inch of my love! Over.'" [*laughter*] What's ironic here is the dissonance—a piece of music that was never written to be part of the drama and intensity of the situation.

JK I've always thought about a similar idea: when crossing the U.S.-to-Mexico border, you're sitting in that line for hours, and if you roll your window down you hear an incredible soundscape of car radios, engines, news broadcasts and ads, Border Patrol agents, people selling *chicle* or coffee or *elote*. There is this soundscape that most people don't think about, but it reveals the complexities and nuances of a given social situation.

GG Pauline Oliveros, one of my mentors, taught me to take sound as an act of consciousness. If you listen to the metadata of a piece of music within its environment, listening becomes another level of consciousness. She called this "deep listening." To that experience we can add what happens at the subconscious level, and the thoughts that each element triggers in our memory. Any song can be redefined by the context in which it is listened to.

JK Music is always contingent. It's contingent on the space it's in, the transmitter, the receiver, one's state of mind when that music is made and/or received—it's always relational. It's very difficult to talk about music and sound without talking about one's self in relationship to it, and to some other, an other, another being, another object. It still moves me, thrills me, to think about how the music that we all love so much, that matters to us the most, that lives inside our bodies, that enters our bodies through our ears and our bones, comes from somebody else's body, or some other object's movements.

GG Exactly.

JK And we're always carrying that other with us through sound.

In our conversation we've been focusing on the relationship of sound to migrants in the sea or in the desert, but music and sound, as so much recent scholarship has argued, aren't just tools of witnessing or empowerment or struggle; they can also be forces of domination, surveillance, torture, and control.

GG Of course. More and more, music can be an instrument of cultural imposition and domination. Sound can even be used as a weapon.

JK In the context of music's relationship to migration, there are many musical stories. But contemporary art is mostly focused on the sonic evidence of the resistance of the migrants. What about the sound and music of the Border Patrol? The sound and music of Frontex? The sound and music of smugglers, of cartels?

GG Yes, imagine the example of *Devil's Highway*: the sound of the radio blasting in the Border Patrol car means something different to the Border Patrol agent than to the migrant. It's the same sound, just different perspectives on what's going on at the moment.

JK A few years ago the Border Patrol hired a Hispanic advertising company to create a series of *corridos* to try to warn migrants of the dangers of the migrant trail and to deter people from crossing the border. They used a migrant musical form against itself and its listeners, telling them, "Stop immigrating. Don't come here."

GG Yeah. It's easier to insert the poison pill inside styles of music that people have already assimilated. Everybody lets down their guard when listening to something familiar. This is yet another form of manipulation.

JK I was recently watching [Richard Mosse's video installation] *Incoming* [2014–17, discussed on pp. 52–53], which has a score by Ben Frost. The music is used to force us to feel and react, manipulating us with a heavy musical hand. I don't necessarily mean that in a negative way, but I was very conscious of the way I was being made to feel.

GG I think the best film music influences our mood without us even realizing. The film score becomes experiential and even visceral. We think we only listen with our ears, but that's not true: we listen with our bodies, especially at low frequencies. We interpret through our experiences. If you're a musician, especially in percussion or bass, you hear with your body. You're not hearing only with your ears.

JK And the person receiving it is positioned in a different way.

GG We could be in the same room, perceiving the same sounds, and having completely different experiences. Our perception can be influenced by anything from the mood we're in that day to our memories, or simply the space of the room we're occupying. When listening to sound, everybody perceives similar yet different phenomena.

JK I think this is why music and sound are so important in thinking about larger political and social issues. We've been unable in this conversation to talk about sound and music outside of life, outside of death, and outside of questions of positionality and directionality—where are we coming from, where are we standing, who are we in the moment in which we're standing and being directed, and where is our place in the world. We can't separate any of that from the experience of sound and the experience of music.

— — — — — — — —

Recorded via Skype on October 9, 2018.

1. Daniel Barenboim, *Music Quickens Time* (Brooklyn: Verso, 2009).

2. Nicolas Collins, *Handmade Electronic Music: The Art of Hardware Hacking*, 2006 (reprint ed. New York: Routledge, 2009), p. 14. The passage reads, "Fans of what is known as VLF (Very Low Frequency) radio make big coils by wrapping yards of wire around big wooden crosses and then camp out on remote hilltops like hermit Klansmen. Get far enough from civilization's ubiquitous 50/60 Hz. hum and you may be lucky enough to pick up the Aurora Borealis, 'whistlers' induced by meteorites self-immolating as they enter the earth's atmosphere, the pipping of GPS satellites, or top-secret submarine radio communication."

Tania Bruguera

B. 1968, Havana, Cuba;
lives and works in Queens, New York

Cuban artist and activist Tania Bruguera is steadfast in her commitment to using art to shape the political imaginary. Associated with the New Cuban Art movement, she embraces political and cultural dissent through long-term projects that manifest as public interventions, ongoing social movements, and new-found educational institutions.[1] Having come of age in the wake of the Cuban Revolution (1953–59), Bruguera is critical of its legacy, which—despite the revolution's many failed promises—she observes to have retained people's faith with its own language and ideology, sustained through propaganda and media.

For the duration of *When Home Won't Let You Stay*, the ICA/Boston will fly Bruguera's banner *Dignity Has No Nationality* inside the entrance hall.[2] The work, which also exists as a flag, shows the image of Pangaea, the borderless supercontinent that formed over 300 million years ago, in the late Paleozoic era, before breaking apart into the continents we know today. This is the logo of Immigrant Movement International (IMI), a political movement that Bruguera, long concerned with issues of migration, launched in 2011 [fig. 1]. The ICA/Boston is sited on Boston Harbor, an important historical site of immigration and currently home to shipyards, commuter ferries, cruise-ship docks, and Logan International Airport. The harbor remains integral to the movements of goods and people in this port city, and the presentation of the banner—which bears the IMI slogan "Dignity Has No Nationality," a public proclamation of affiliation and identity—moves the topos of the exhibition outside of the gallery walls in the spirit of the work's call for a borderless world consciousness.

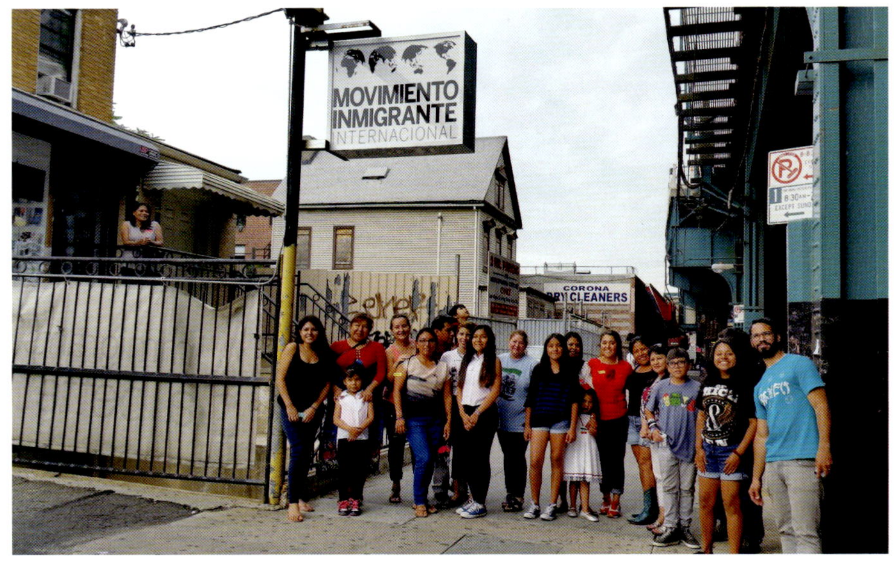

Fig. 1. Immigrant Movement International Corona (2010–18) council members outside IMI Corona office, Queens, New York, 2014

The graphic was also translated in the material language of propaganda: a subway advertisement, a postcard, a vinyl campaign banner, and a T-shirt. In *The Francis Effect* (2014), Bruguera spent fifteen weeks outside New York's Guggenheim Museum collecting over 14,000 signatures on a petition to request Pope Francis to grant Vatican City citizenship to undocumented immigrants. Her most recent large-scale project, *10,148,451*, in the Turbine Hall at Tate London (2018–19), marks the scale of mass migration in its changing numeric title, arrived at by adding the number of international migrant deaths recorded worldwide in 2018 to the number of people who migrated from one country to another in 2018.[3] Multi-sensory and immersive, it features a heat-sensing floor, a low-frequency soundscape that vibrates the body, and a strong eucalyptuslike odor that fills the huge hall, evoking corporeal presence on an environmental scale.

Bruguera began her career as a performance artist before turning to more conceptually oriented work that could be experienced by multiple publics. She still identifies as a performance artist, moving energetically in the space between art, activism, and social change. Examining political and economic power and its social effects, her works position themselves in relation to the general public more than to an informed art audience: they take place in highly visible public areas or require participation, activating the audience through what Bruguera calls "behavior art." In *Destierro* (Displacement, 1998–99), which has been staged in various locations with different materials, Bruguera wears a sculptural suit covered with Cuban earth and studded with nails, textiles, and other symbolic materials. In wearing this suit she embodies the *nkisi n'kondi*, a Congolese religious object believed to grant wishes to those who make offerings to it, or to punish those who make promises in its presence but fail to fulfill them. The *nkisi* is recognizable to those versed in Afro-Cuban religious beliefs, and when Bruguera performed *Destierro* in the streets of Havana on Fidel Castro's birthday in 1998, the faithful among the bystanders formed a procession behind her.

Retaining the body as an instrument of public disturbance, Bruguera's later works take the form of organizational models adaptable for use by others. Adhering to a central concept of *arte útil* ("useful art," or "art as a tool"), she works to develop social and political movements.[4] These projects have long lifespans and are realized in collaboration with multiple individuals and institutions in a range of contexts. To follow the principle of *arte útil* is to seek answers to the question "What use is art?," and has led Bruguera into an intense process of institution-building. She founded IMI, for example, in partnership with the Queens Museum of Art, to engage social-services organizations and artists devoted to immigration reform in an exploration of the political and social circumstances facing immigrants, both in the museum's immediate community and internationally. IMI runs on four pillars: as a community space open to all, regardless of legal status, a place where practical and creative knowledge meet through *arte útil*; a think tank that recognizes immigrants' role in the advancement of society and envisions a different legal reality for human migration; a lab for activism aimed at transforming social affect into political effectiveness; and an educational platform for creating alternative economies based on a culture of reciprocity rather than economic advantage.[5]

Bruguera's activist tactics have put her into a long-standing and vexed relationship with the Cuban government, exposing her to significant risks. In 2014–15 she was arrested and detained in Cuba three times as she was planning a performance called *Yo También Exijo* (I also demand), which was to be a reprise of her famous piece *Tatlin's Whisper #6*. The latter work, originally staged in Havana's Plaza de la Revolución for the 2009 Biennal de la Habana, gave audience members a platform to speak for one minute each about anything on their minds—a risky proposition in a political culture that regularly exercises censorship [fig. 2]. During an eight-month house arrest in 2015, Bruguera staged a 100-hour performance during which she stood on her doorstep and read from Hannah Arendt's book *The Origins of Totalitarianism* (1951). In 2017 in Havana, she established the Instituto de Artivismo Hannah Arendt (INSTAR), devoted to the study of totalitarian systems—a form of institutional redress for the suppression of her free speech in 2014. Her political feelings intensifying, Bruguera announced her intention to run for president in the Cuban elections of 2018.

Bruguera has said, "The first right an immigrant is stripped of is the right to be political."[6] IMI provides an adaptable global platform for commitment to the political rights of migrants and refugees. Its form morphing from pedagogical structure to political party, it spun off from an earlier idea, the Migrant People Party, which would secure political representation for those without citizenship to participate in the 2012 Mexican presidential elections. But as Bruguera clarifies, "*Arte Útil* is not NGO art. Its aesthetics is the ethics of social transformation. *Arte Útil* is about a collective ethics; therefore it can't involve another person's exploitation."[7] —ET

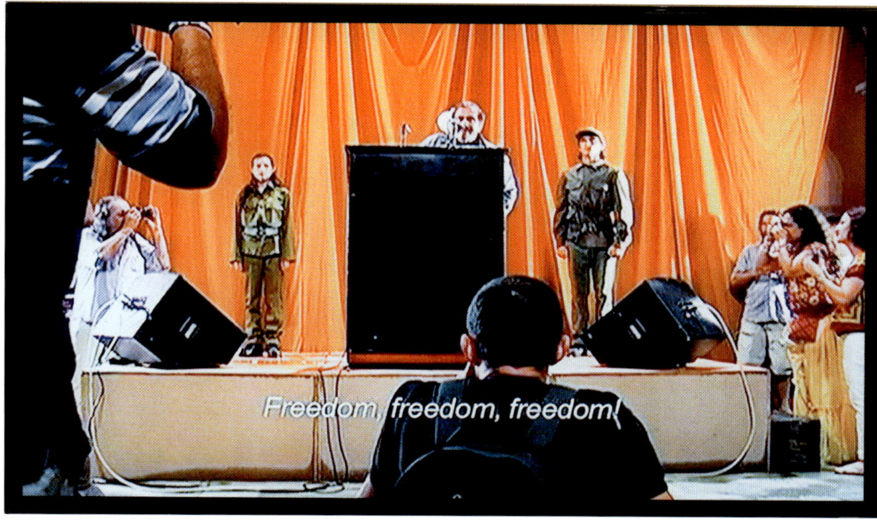

Fig. 2. Tania Bruguera, *Tatlin's Whisper #6 (Havana Version)*, 2009. Stage, podium, loudspeaker, video camera, microphones, and video (color, sound; 40:32 minutes), dimensions variable. Solomon R. Guggenheim Museum, New York, Guggenheim UBS MAP Purchase Fund, 2014, 2014.11

1. See Rachel Weiss, *To and from Utopia in the New Cuban Art* (Minneapolis: University of Minnesota Press, 2010).

2. Tania Bruguera created the flag for the project *Pledges of Allegiance*, organized by Creative Time in 2017, during which several versions were flown atop buildings in New York and Miami.

3. Bruguera derived these statistics from the website http://missingmigrants.iom.int/ (accessed March 5, 2019). The title as articulated in this text reflects the number as of March 19, 2019. The Missing Migrants Project tracks incidents involving migrants, including refugees and asylum-seekers, who have died or gone missing in the process of migration toward an international destination.

4. In developing various manifestations of *arte útil*, Bruguera encountered both the Italian artist Pino Poggi's *Arte Utile* manifestos from 1965 and the Argentine artist Eduardo Costa's *Manifiesto de Arte Util* from 1969, documents confirming the global salience of this approach to art practice.

5. See Immigrant Movement International's mission statement on its website: http://immigrant-movement.us/wordpress/mission-statement/ (accessed March 5, 2019).

6. Bruguera, in "Migrations," Creative Time Summit: Stockholm, 2014. Recording available online at www.youtube.com/watch?v=4rpFoXdqGZY (accessed January 29, 2019).

7. Bruguera, quoted in "Tania Bruguera: A conversation between Bruguera, Paul O'Neill, and graduate students from the Center for Curatorial Studies at Bard College," *Bomb* no. 128 (Summer 2014):132.

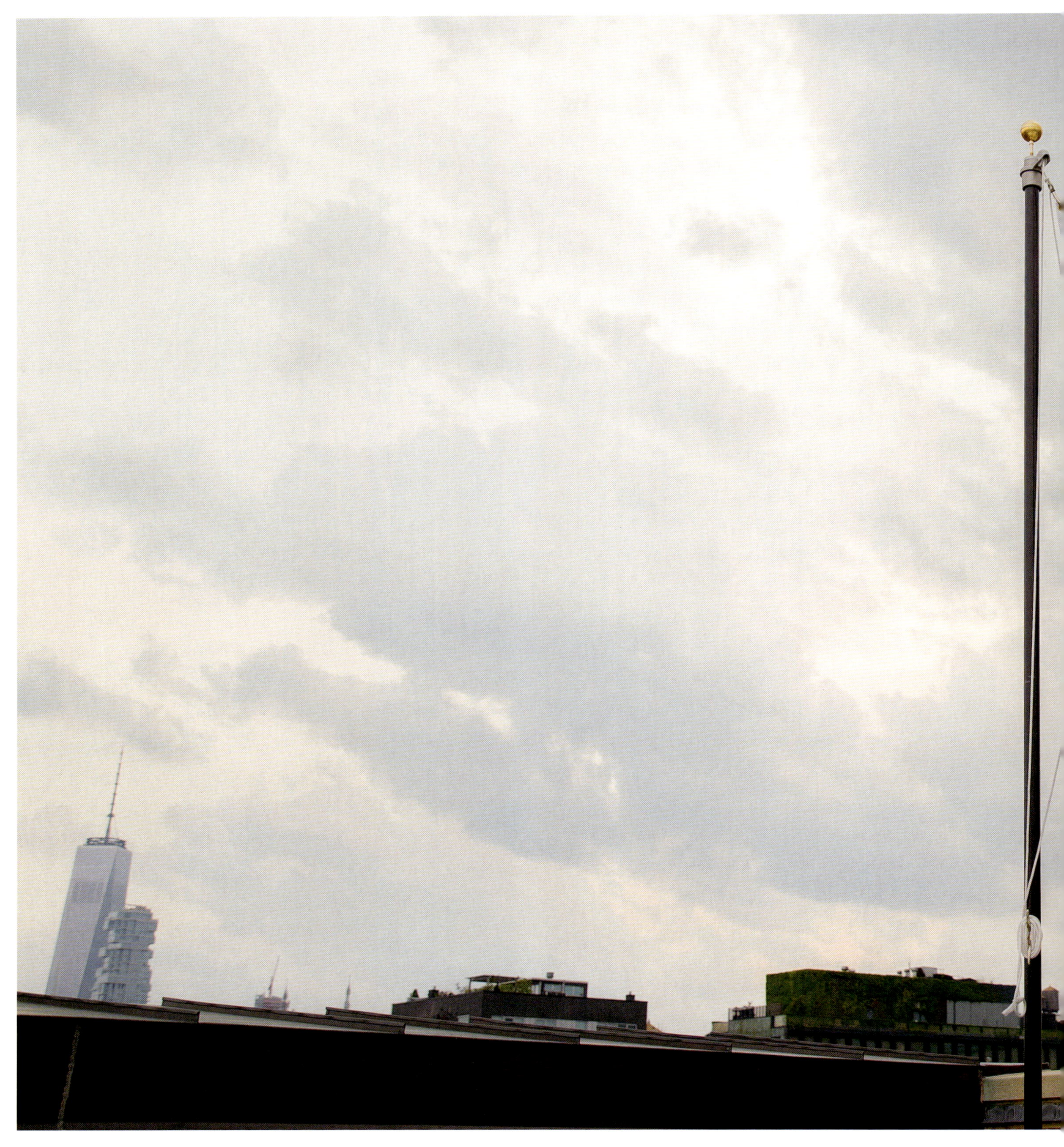

Tania Bruguera, *Dignity Has No Nationality*, 2017.
Installation view, *Pledges of Allegiance*, Creative Time Headquarters, New York, 2017

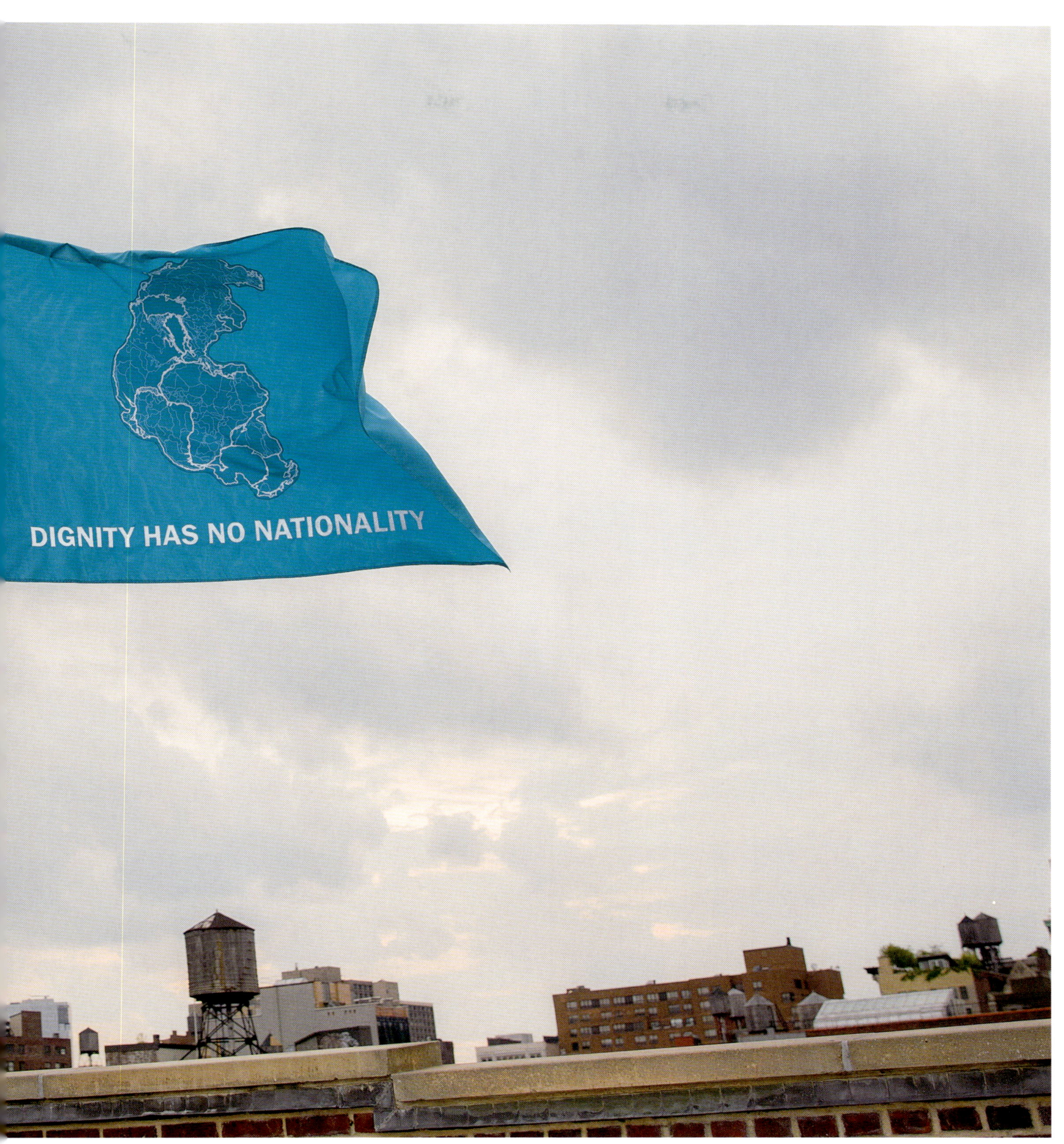
DIGNITY HAS NO NATIONALITY

Richard Misrach

B. 1949, Los Angeles, United States;
lives and works in Berkeley, California

As captured by Richard Misrach's camera, the environment of the American West is under duress, simultaneously divided and interconnected, caught between historical visions of the American frontier and the altered landscape today. In 2004 Misrach began photographing around the nearly 2,000-mile-long U.S.-Mexico border, examining both official structures, such as walls and fences, and unofficial interventions in the landscape, such as makeshift structures and lost belongings, whether abandoned by migrants or by the U.S. Border Patrol. While photographing, Misrach collects objects—inner tubes, backpacks, water bottles—used by people crossing such barriers as the Rio Grande and the Sonoran Desert. While initially more anthropological and environmental in nature, his project has gained political urgency as the physical infrastructure of border policing and surveillance has intensified with heightened desires for security and increased militarization.

A pioneer of color photography in the 1970s, Misrach both recognizes and challenges the vision of the American West championed by photographers such as Ansel Adams and before him Carleton Watkins. Seeing the emergence of American identity in the collision of civilization and nature, he is devoted to cataloguing the environmental change generated by human impact. Poetic and often eerie in tone, his large-scale photographs, made with a large-format camera, capture the intersection of the landscape with the forces that transform it, whether environmental, cultural, or political. His most recent project, Border Cantos (2004–16), addresses how the social and political contingencies of cross-border migration have transformed the landscape.

In both structure and style, Border Cantos has a key precedent in Desert Cantos, which Misrach began in 1979 with a philosophical question: what makes the desert the desert? Photographing landmarks such as Monument Valley and the Grand Canyon, Misrach also focused on more paradoxical sights such as California's Salton Sea, an artificial lake now too polluted and saline for either agricultural or recreational use. Informed by the then burgeoning environmental movement in the United States, the project claimed the desert as both cultural metaphor and social phenomenon. Misrach organized it in independent but related subseries such as "The Terrain" and "The Flood," calling these sections "cantos"—a section of a song, or of an epic poem—to suggest a musical structure. In the soft-hued desolation of these images, Misrach reveals unexpected signs of human occupation in landscapes that are often depicted as remote and untouched. The land is already lost—"stained and trampled, franchised and fenced, burned, flooded, grazed, mined, exploited, and laid waste," in Reyner Banham's words—but it remains beautiful.[1]

Misrach's interest in the border as a photographic subject began in 2011, when he met the musician Guillermo Galindo, who was making instruments assembled from materials he had found in the region. As it became riskier for Galindo, who is of Mexican descent, to navigate that territory, Misrach began photographing and collecting such objects to send to Galindo. Border Cantos developed into a collaborative installation and book project that includes photographs by Misrach, musical scores by Galindo inspired by the photographs, and Galindo's sound objects.[2]

The photographs in Border Cantos focus on areas marked by human presence: the security-industrial complex, alternative infrastructures of mobility, and remnants of human movement. Misrach shows the wall—which has loomed large in U.S. political discourse since the signing of the 2006 Secure Fence Act under President George W. Bush, and larger still since the election of Donald Trump to the presidency—as a paradoxical structure: physically menacing on the ground, it reads as aesthetically sublime in Misrach's photographs, which are devoid of human occupants and situate the wall in the mythology of the western American landscape. In some images, such as *Wall, east of Nogales, Arizona/El muro, al este de Nogales, Arizona* (2014) [p. 120], it cuts through the landscape like a road or river, blending with pathways along which humans have moved immemorially. In others, such as *Wall, Los Indios, Texas/El Muro, Los Indios, Texas* (2015) [fig. 1], an inert fragment of wall—whose construction costs have been estimated at $4–12 million per mile—looms alone, a metonym for the unequal allocation of resources that promises security for some but not others.[3]

What do these traces say about migration? The found objects photographed in Border Cantos are wayfinding tools, used both by migrants traveling their routes and by the Border Patrol to track the migrants' movements. Water barrels in the California desert are marked by flags left by immigrant-aid organizations such as Water Stations, Inc., which refills the barrels with drinking water to offset the dangers to migrants funneled by the Border Patrol into inhospitable parts of the desert. Misrach sent flags that were no longer in use to Galindo, who transformed them into musical scores with markings [p. 124] informed by the visual content and tone of Misrach's existing Border Cantos photographs taken in the same region. Other, more haunting photographs picture makeshift effigies often found near underpasses—scarecrowlike sentinels, made of agave stalks, wire, and discarded clothing, that may be markers of migrants' routes, or decoys to throw off the Border Patrol [p. 123]. These images inspired Galindo to make sonic sculptures in the form of stringed instruments. The ambiguity of these possessions, abandoned under unknown circumstances, points to the unknowable journeys of the people who depended on them.

Artifacts found from California to Texas between 2013 and 2015/Artefactos encontrados entre California y Texas de 2013 a 2015 (2013–15) [pp. 118–19] presents a sampling of objects found along the border. Set in a forensic grid, each of the work's forty-eight photographs is a mystery that indexes the particular exigencies of being-in-motion; together this long horizontal arrangement of frames constitutes an abbreviated lexicon of border objects, from junk to keepsakes. Misrach's consciously objective approach acknowledges the limitations of the objects' representational power: "Every single one of these personal belongings has an incredible story of a human being. The journey that they took is all embedded in there, but there is no way that you can actually transcribe that."[4] His cataloging process also visualizes transformations in immigration patterns: he was puzzled by the plethora of children's items in the border area near Brownsville, Texas, until news broke of the surge of unaccompanied minors migrating to the United States. In this sense, *Artifacts* . . . is a time capsule of immigration history during the two-year period it covers.

For Misrach and Galindo, Border Cantos counters mainstream narratives of migration and immigration that render humans as mere data points in a larger system, while also recognizing the impossibility of knowing every migrant's individual story. Misrach uses the tropes of color landscape photography as a tactic of allure:

> I've come to believe that beauty can be a very powerful conveyor of difficult ideas. It engages people when they might otherwise look away. Recent theory has been critical of the distancing effect of artistic expression—"Create solutions, not art." But the impact of art may be more complex and far-reaching than theory is capable of assessing. To me, the work I do is a means of interpreting unsettling truths, of bearing witness, and of sounding an alarm. The beauty of formal representation both carries an affirmation of life and subversively brings us face to face with news from our besieged world.[5]

—ET

1. Reyner Banham, "The Man-Mauled Desert," in Misrach, *Desert Cantos*, exh. cat (Wellington, NZ: National Art Gallery, 1988), p. 1.

2. See Misrach and Guillermo Galindo, *Border Cantos* (New York: Aperture, 2016).

3. See Josh Kun, "Misrach|Galindo," in ibid., p. 11.

4. Misrach, quoted in April Kincrease, "Art out of Artifacts." *East Bay Express*, April 20, 2016. Available online at www.eastbayexpress.com/oakland/art-out-of-artifacts/Content?oid=4755854 (accessed January 21, 2019).

5. Misrach, in an interview with Melissa Harris, in Misrach, *Violent Legacies* (New York: Aperture, 1992). Available online at https://aperture.org/blog/archival-interview-richard-misrach/ (accessed March 6, 2019).

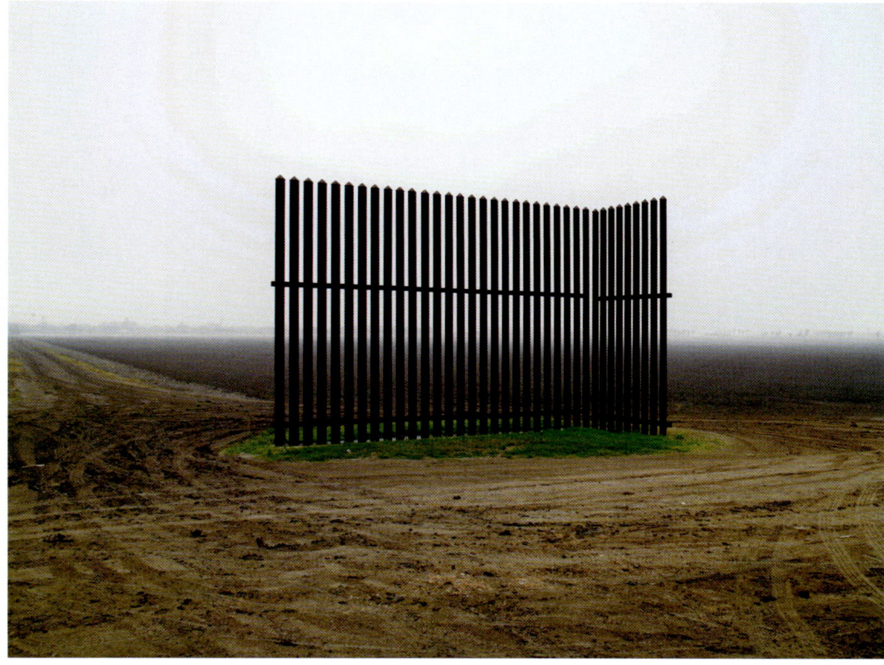

Fig. 1. Richard Misrach, *Wall, Los Indios, Texas/El Muro, Los Indios, Texas*, 2015, from the series Border Cantos, 2004-16. Pigment print, 60 x 80 inches (152.4 x 203.2 cm)

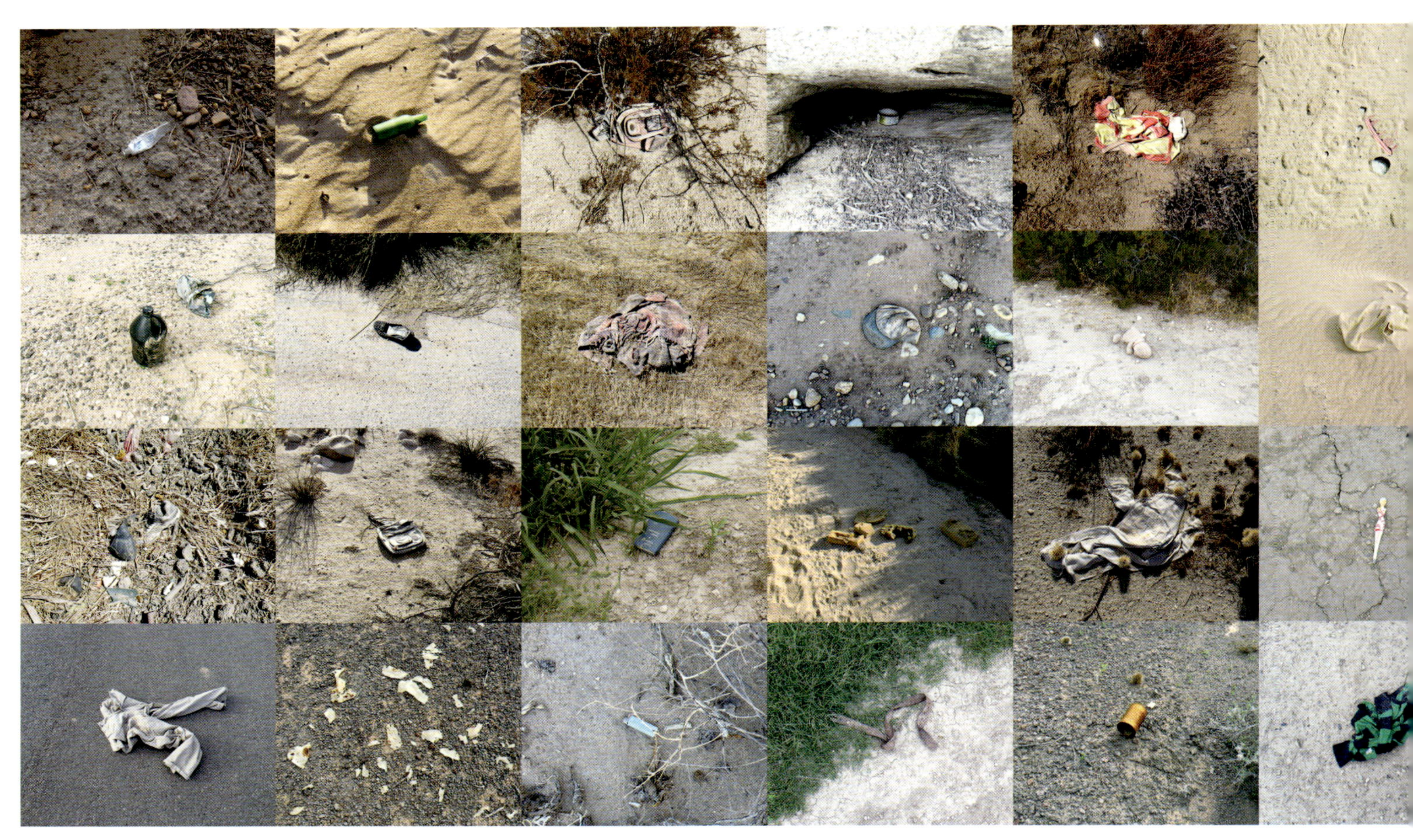

Above and following two spreads:
Richard Misrach, from the series Border Cantos, 2004–16. Pigment prints

Above: *Artifacts found from California to Texas between 2013 and 2015/ Artefactos encontrados entre California y Texas de 2013 a 2015*, 2013–15.
Six parts, each 86 x 57½ inches (218.4 x 146.1 cm);
86 inches x 28 feet 9 inches (218.4 x 876.3 cm) overall

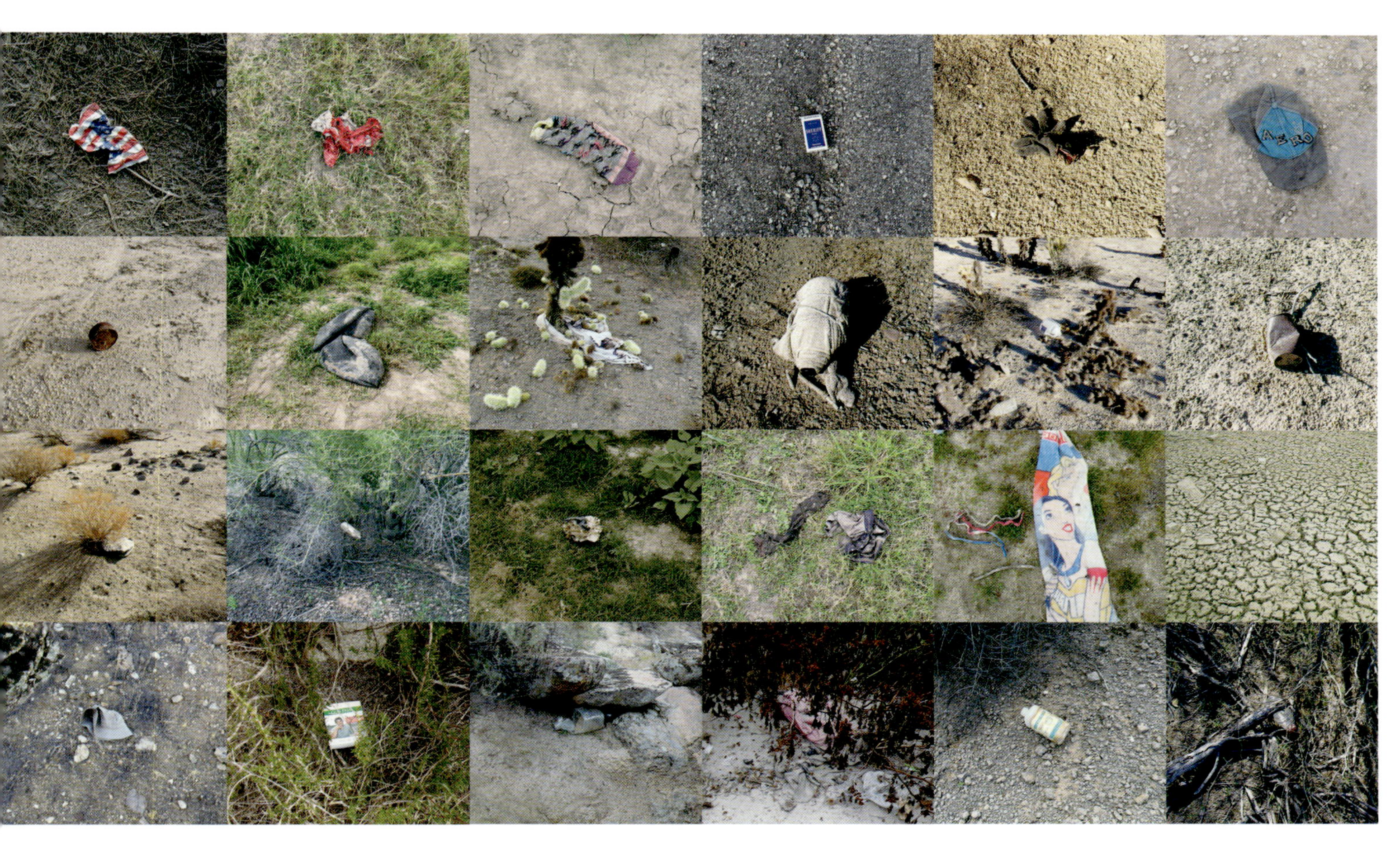

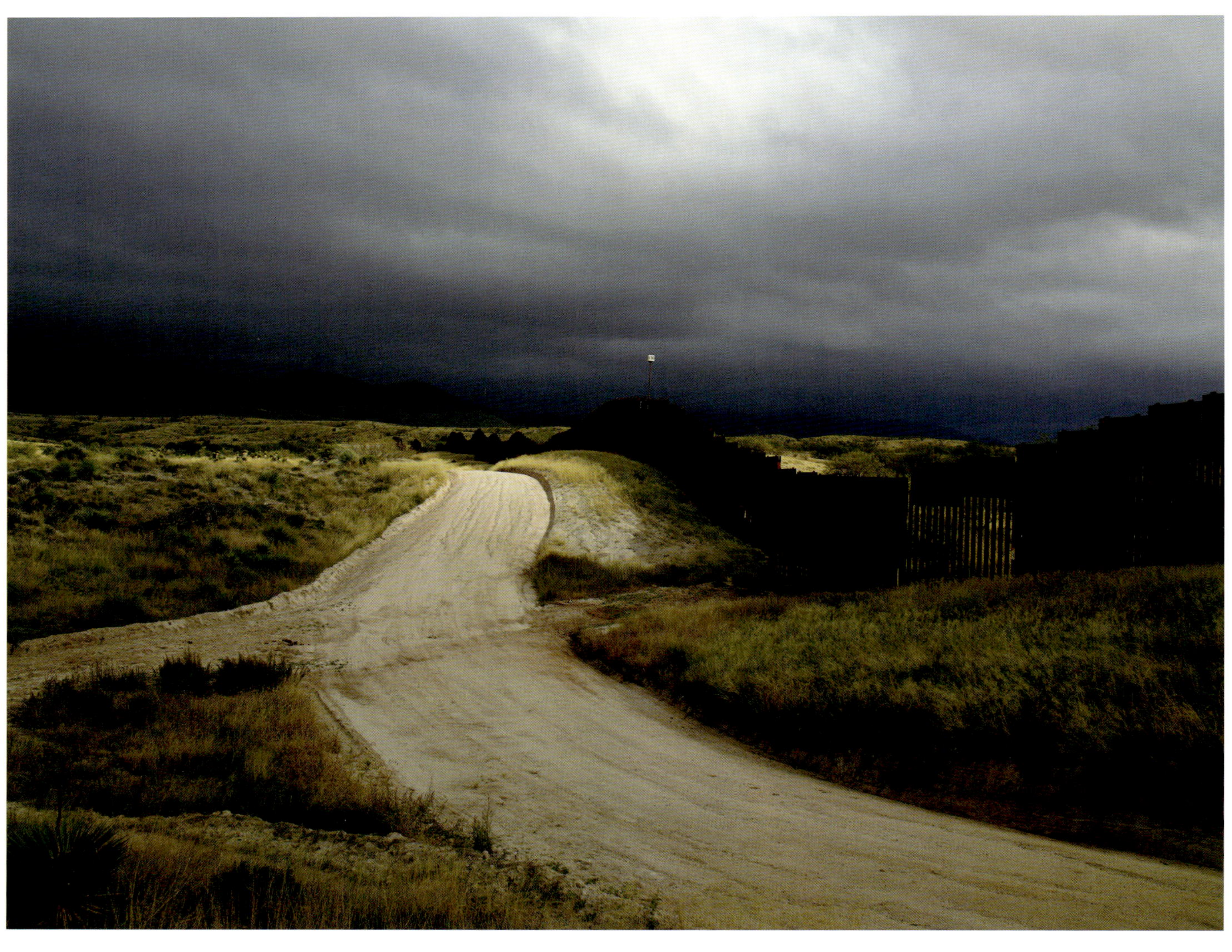

Wall, east of Nogales, Arizona/El muro, al este de Nogales, Arizona, 2014.
60 x 80 inches (152.4 x 203.2 cm)

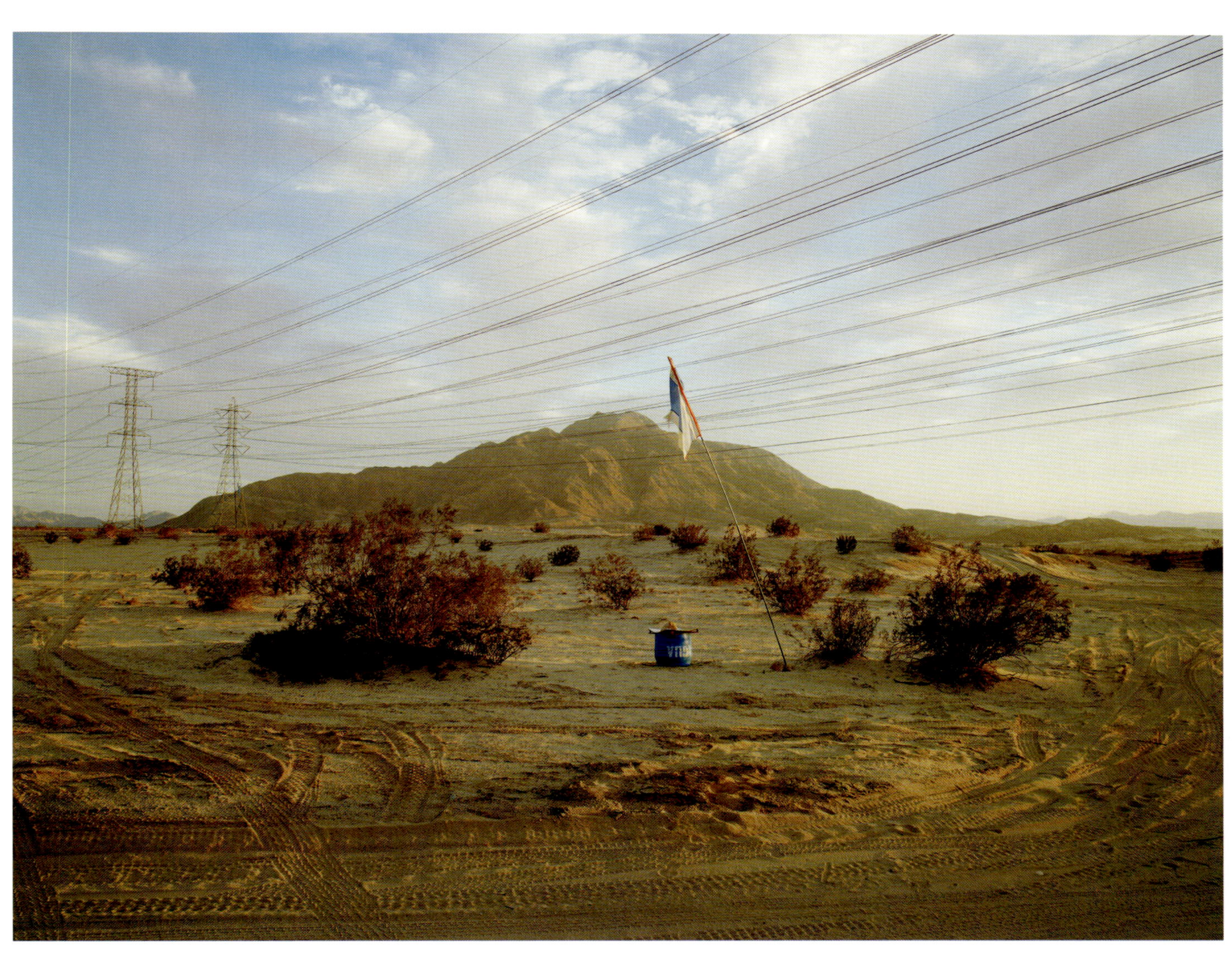

Agua #10, near Calexico, California/Agua nº 10, cerca de Calexico, California, 2014.
60 x 80 inches (152.4 x 203.2 cm)

Effigy #7, near Jacumba, California/Efigie nº 7, cerca de Jacumba, California, 2009.
60 x 80 inches (152.4 x 203.2 cm)

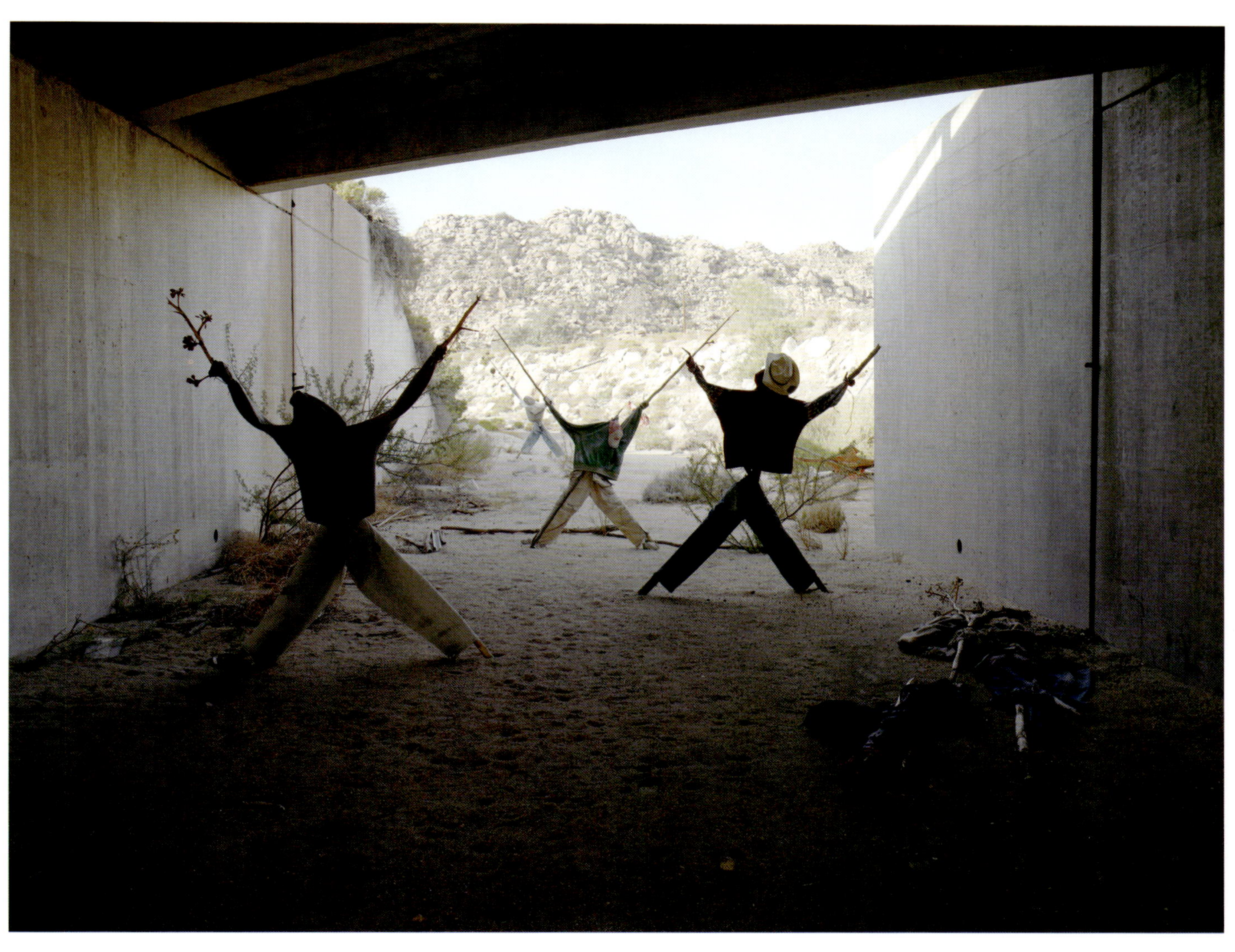

Guillermo Galindo

B. 1960, Mexico City, Mexico;
lives and works in Oakland, California

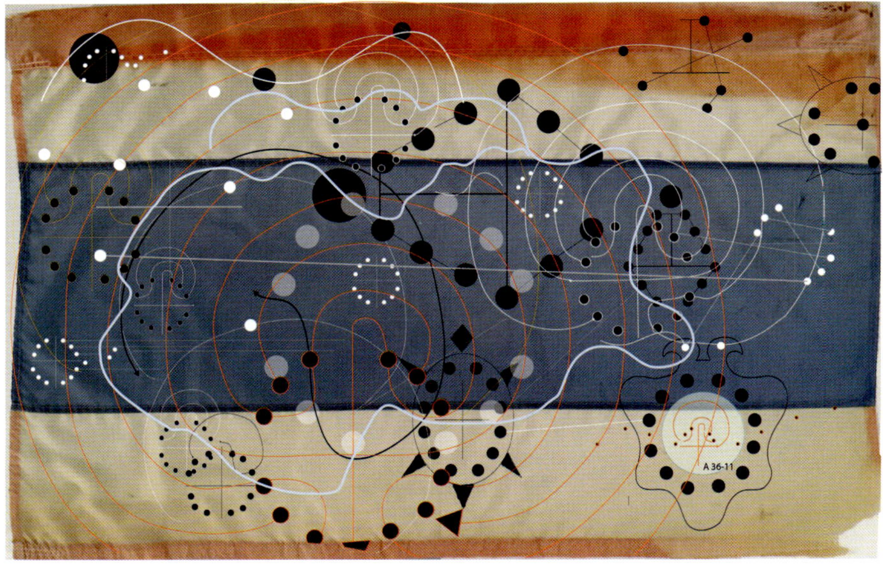

Fig. 1. Guillermo Galindo, *Cartografía del Espíritu/Cartography of the Spirit*, 2017. Acrylic on beacon flags used by humanitarian aid group Water Stations, 29½ x 47 inches (74.9 x 119.4 cm)

Guillermo Galindo is an experimental composer and performance artist who explores the link between sound and physical presence through musical compositions, performances, and what he calls "sonic devices," sculptures designed for sound activation. His work redefines conventional limits between music, the art of musical composition, and the intersections of visual art, politics, humanitarian issues, spirituality, and social awareness. Classically trained, he is also informed by the work of European and American avant-garde composers such as Karl Stockhausen, Iannis Xenakis, Harry Partch, and John Cage, and he is a long-time collaborator with the cross-disciplinary performance-art group La Pocha Nostra, cofounded by Guillermo Gomez-Peña in 1993.

Galindo began to build instruments in 2006 after identifying a link between music-making and healing, both of which are treated as embodied ritual practices in his Mexican and Mesoamerican heritage, and inspired in part by the "psychomagic" healing techniques of Alejandro Jodorowsky.[1] Bringing the aesthetics of Western classical music into conversation with such practices, he began to consider the concatenation of colonialism, memory, and nationhood through the medium of sound. Using objects he has found or received from the area of the U.S.-Mexico border, he builds devices whose relationship to both a moving body and a physical site evokes what the musical historian R. Murray Schafer describes as an "acoustic ecology" of migration.[2] In Galindo's hands, the everyday materiality of water bottles, clothing, shotgun shells, and even the border wall itself takes on a musical function.

In 2011, while performing with his border-relic sculptures at a *Pop-Up Magazine* event in San Francisco, Galindo met the photographer Richard Misrach, who has photographed the border landscape of the American southwest and traces of migrant movement since 2004 [pp. 118–23]. Together they developed Border Cantos, a collaborative installation and book project comprising photographs by Misrach, musical scores by Galindo inspired by those photographs (works such as fig. 1, made independently by Galindo after the series ended), and Galindo's sound sculptures, many of them incorporating objects found by Misrach during his travels.[3]

Zapatello (2014) [p. 127] is based on Leonardo da Vinci's fifteenth-century design for a *martello a camme*, a mechanical hammer. In the original plan, the turning of a crank attached to a notched wheel causes a lever connected to the hammer to rise and then drop when the wheel catches on a stop. Galindo's version replaces the single hammer with two levers bearing a glove and a boot, both found at the border. When the wheel turns, the glove and boot land on a drag tire—an auto tire that U.S. Border Patrol agents drag through the desert so that migrants will leave traceable footprints—that Galindo fashioned into a drum using Lakota craft techniques.[4] The crank is mounted on an axle that pierces two targets of the kind used for shooting practice, while a donkey jaw and a ram's horn found in the same region as the work's other components are used as stops. *Zapatello*

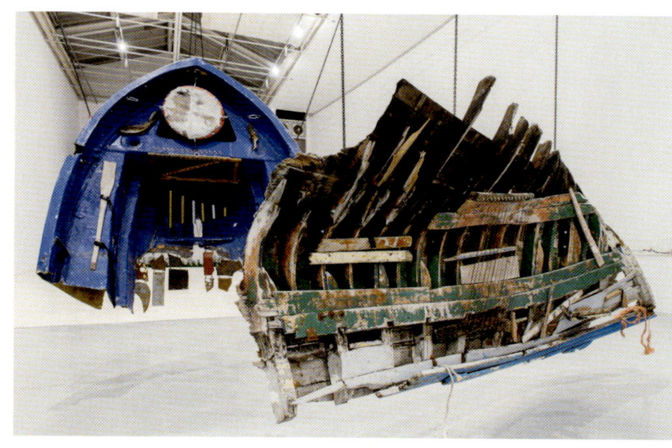

Fig. 2. Guillermo Galindo, *Fluchtzieleuropaschiffbruchschallkörper* (Escapetargeteuropeshipwrecksoundbody), 2017. Installation view, documenta 14, Kassel, Germany, 2017

establishes a link between da Vinci's machine—an early technology of mechanized labor—and border security as itself a kind of machine, clunky but effective. It thus positions the migrant body as a resonant object: on the one hand, control of that body is claimed to bring security to an imagined homeland public, and on the other, the body's material traces suggest its presence and survival.

Galindo's sculptures stem from the pre-Columbian notion that a "sonorous body" can become the medium through which the spiritual, animistic world expresses itself. In Mesoamerican history, for example, the sound of the bone flute was believed to be linked with celestial phenomena, and the flute was used to call deities into the terrestrial domain. Zoomorphic instruments signal ancient Mesoamerican beliefs that human and animal spirits could inhabit each other's bodies.[5] The intimate connection between a sonic device, the material from which it is made, and the person who plays it grounds Galindo's commitment to honoring the presence of migrants, and their traumas, by activating their former belongings through sound. He sees "making the wounds audible" as a healing practice: "What I'm trying to do here is to resonate with the viewer or listener, to give her a deeper understanding of the tragedy that is happening, every day, before our eyes.... The objects that I play are sacred. They send healing energy—not only to this border, but to all the borders in the world."[6]

Ángel Exterminador/Exterminating Angel (2015) [p. 126] adapts the functions of both a gong and gallows, obliquely referring to the 1962 film of the same title by Luis Buñuel. This monumental winged form is made out of a border-wall fragment, a piece of twisted steel repurposed from a Vietnam War landing strip. As such it has a military history, but the wall, as Josh Kun writes, is not just a product of the U.S. military-industrial complex, "it is an ideological, social, and economic pressure point where the pulls and pushes of multiple political forces, past and present, converge in volatile and often tragic ways."[7] Echo Exodus, presented at documenta 14 in Kassel, Germany, and Athens, Greece, in 2017, is a series of sculptural works made from the belongings of European refugees. For one of these, *Fluchtzieleuropaschiffbruchschallkörper* (Escapetargeteuropeshipwrecksoundbody), Galindo suspended two large broken boat-hulls found on the Greek island of Lesbos from the ceiling of the exhibition hall [fig. 2], turning nautical fragments associated with a site that hosts thousands of stranded migrants into instruments that were activated by musicians.[8]

Galindo's sonic objects engage the complexity of representing others, inviting recognition and witnessing not through imagery but rather in the act of sonorous activation. These found objects index both the physical absence and the resistant presence of migrant bodies moving through the landscape. Galindo does not craft them with the aim of producing aesthetically pleasing music, but rather to allow the materials to, in the artist's words, "sing in their own voices."[9]
—ET

1. See Josh Hall, "Lost and Found," *Frieze*, February 7, 2017, available online at https://frieze.com/article/lost-and-found-0 (accessed December 24, 2018), and Alejandro Jodorowsky, *Psychomagic: The Transformative Power of Shamanic Psychotherapy* (Rochester, Vt.: Inner Traditions, 2010).

2. See R. Murray Schafer, *The Tuning of the World* (New York: Knopf, 1977, repr. as *The Soundscape*, Rochester, Vermont: Destiny Books, 1994).

3. Guillermo Galindo writes, "Translating photographs into scores also allowed me to challenge the traditional Cartesian tradition of reading music from left to right. These photographs inspired me to think of unexpected events coming from all directions all at once or at different times: a polycentric universe where anything can happen at any given time." Galindo, "Imaginary Stories," in Richard Misrach and Galindo, *Border Cantos* (New York: Aperture, 2016), p. 195.

4. See Mikaela Lefrak and Stephanie Heimann, "Requiem for a Border Wall," *The New Republic*, June 23, 2016. Available online at https://newrepublic.com/article/132220/requiem-border-wall (accessed December 25, 2018).

5. See Sarah B. Barber, Gonzalo Sánchez, and Mireya Olvera, "Sounds of Death and Life in Mesoamerica: The Bone Flutes of ancient Oaxaca," *Yearbook for Traditional Music* 41 (Ljubljana International Council for Traditional Music, 2009):94–110.

6. Galindo, quoted in Alexander Ortega, "Songs of the Cross: Guillermo Galindo's Border-Healing Ritual." *Slug Magazine* no. 334 (October 2016). Available online at www.slugmag.com/interviews-features/guillermo-galindo/ (accessed December 25, 2018).

7. Josh Kun, "Misrach | Galindo," in Misrach and Galindo, *Border Cantos*, p. 12.

8. Two performers, Mathias Reuter and Mathias Schubert, activated these nautical fragments, using one as a percussion instrument, the other, strung with wires, as a stringed instrument. A 2016 deal between the European Union and Turkey cut off the Aegean Sea route between Turkey and Greece for asylum seekers, leaving thousands of people detained and stranded on Lesbos.

9. Galindo, "Imaginary Stories," p. 193.

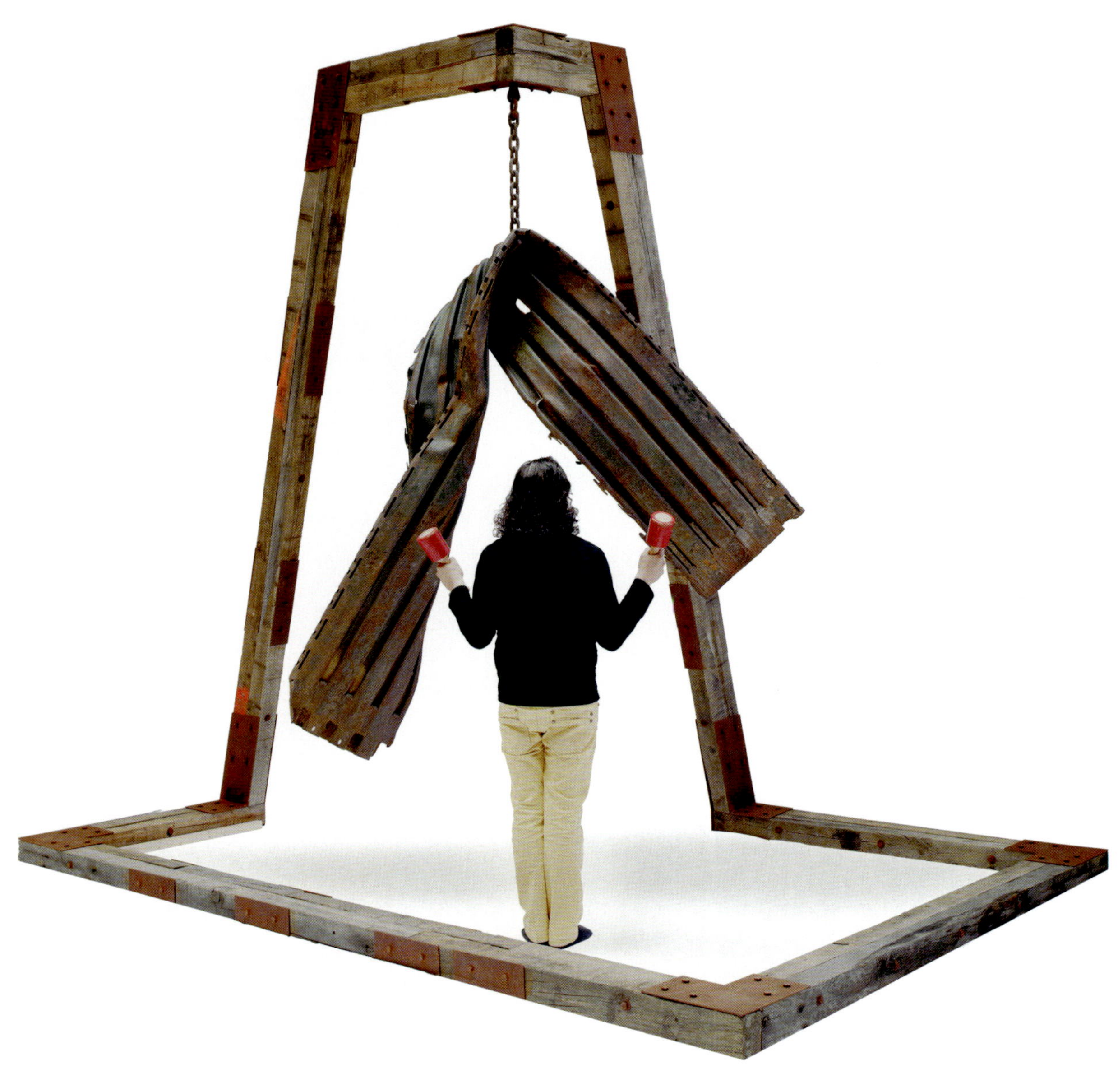

Guillermo Galindo, *Ángel Exterminador/Exterminating Angel*, 2015,
from the series Border Cantos, 2004–16.
Section of border wall, Border Patrol drag chain, and
wood blocking used in construction of wall.
9 feet x 48 inches x 12 feet 3 inches (274.3 x 121.9 x 373.4 cm)

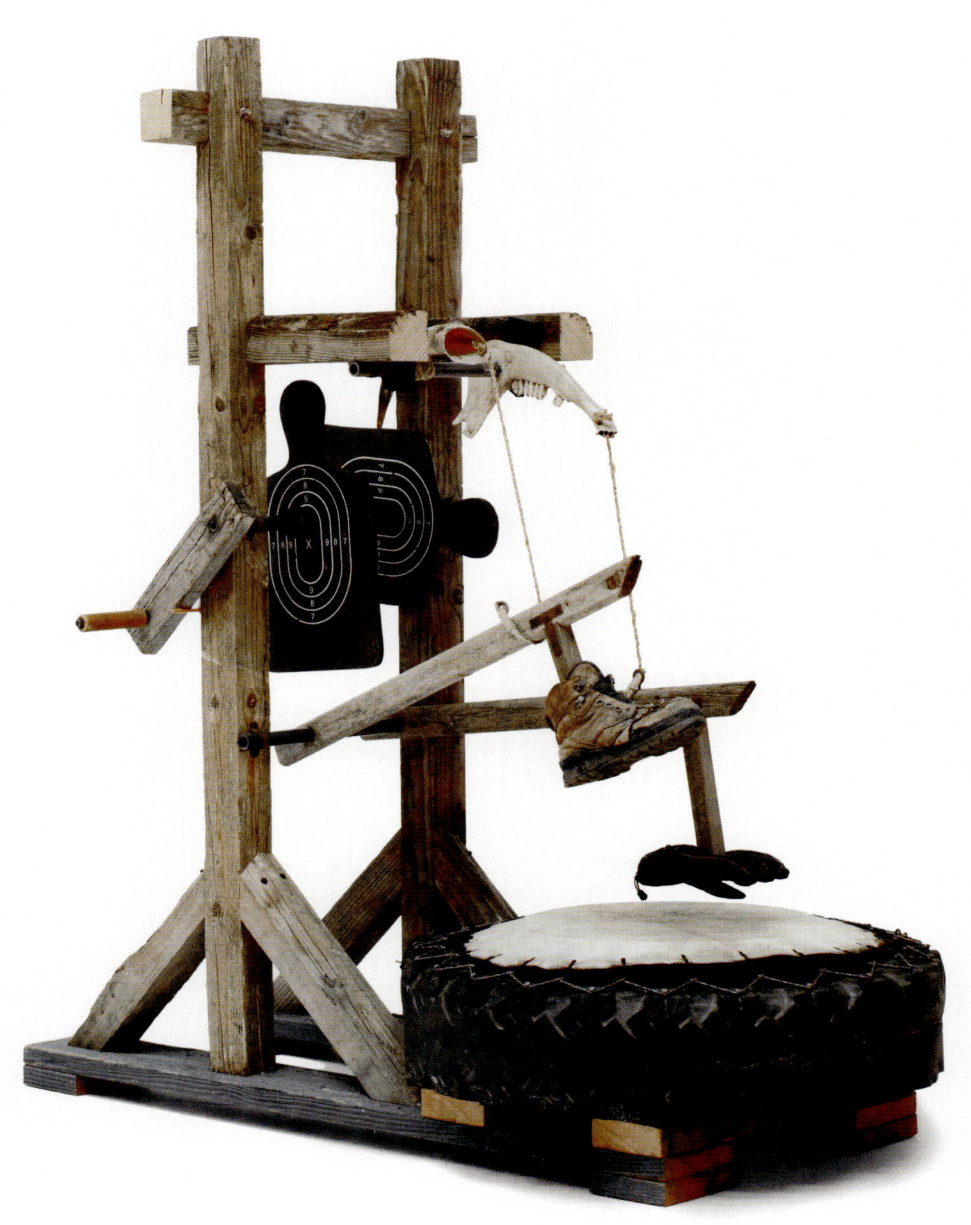

Guillermo Galindo, *Zapatello*, 2014, from the series Border Cantos, 2004–16.
Wood blocking used in construction of border wall,
tire, rawhide, boot, glove, donkey jaw, and ram's horn.
70 x 38 x 76 inches (177.8 x 96.5 x 193 cm).
Fabricated by Ross Craig and Tiffany Huey

Carlos Motta

B. 1978, Bogotá, Colombia;
lives and works in New York

Working across media, histories, and geographies, Carlos Motta exposes and challenges normative ways of thinking about identity and politics. His projects have examined how religion, capitalism, colonialism, and the mechanisms of the state create exclusionary norms that regulate ways of being. Motta's videos, performances, and online and print platforms uncover suppressed histories, using specific figures and events, both historical and contemporary, to challenge the frameworks through which we understand the world.

Motta's recent projects *The Crossing* (2017) and *The Dreamers* (working title; in progress) focus on sexuality and migration, topics Motta describes as "deeply personal" given his identification as a queer Colombian migrant. He is also highlighting the policing of queer and migrant difference and responding to the recent increase in individuals seeking refugee status based on persecution for their LGBTQI+ identities.[1] Motta's artistic engagement with the issues faced by queer migrants began in 2011 as a collaboration with the grassroots group Queerocracy and New York's Museum of Arts and Design (MAD). Held on Indigenous Peoples' Day (formerly known as Columbus Day), this multipart event, titled *A New Discovery: Queer Immigration in Perspective*, encompassed a performance at Columbus Circle in Manhattan and a panel discussion that interpreted Christopher Columbus's "discovery" of America in 1492 as an origin story of the state policing of borders and bodies.[2] It also introduced *A Timeline of Queer Migrations*, a document of over 100 entries enumerating a range of international exclusionary laws—from the U.S. Chinese Exclusion Act of 1881 to Russia's antigay law of 2012—and highlighting advances in inclusion and human rights. *A Timeline*... records the countless ways in which sexuality is contested and regulated, but also suggests how queer politics might confront, challenge, and transform those mechanisms. *A New Discovery*... shows sexual exile as systematically instituted and reinforced over centuries.

The Crossing comprises video portraits of eleven LGBTQI+ refugees from Egypt, Iran, Iraq, Morocco, Syria, and Pakistan, all currently living in the Netherlands [pp. 130–35].[3] Through engrossing monologues addressed directly to the camera and so to the viewer, the refugees speak of their experiences. Their personal narratives reveal the particularities as well as the shared patterns of religious, cultural, and political oppression that spur the often dangerous process of migration. Anwar, from Egypt [p. 133], speaks of physical and emotional abuse, as well as of the agony of being unable to accept himself through having internalized his culture's criminalization of homosexuality. He describes asking himself, "Why did god make us this way in this country?" Benham, an Iranian who identifies as trans, recounts an incessant demand to demonstrate gender differentiation in appearance and language and an arrest in Iran for not doing so. Living in a Dutch refugee center when the portrait was shot, Benham describes how intimidation and gender discrimination followed them to the center, despite its location in a country with protective laws. In addition to highlighting the restrictions placed on individuals as functions of ethnicity and religion, Motta's project speaks to the limits of the apparently liberal Dutch migration and asylum systems. Emerging from *The Crossing* is a picture of the deep-rooted discrimination faced by LGBTQI+ people throughout the world, and of their bravery in seeking to be, simply and peacefully, themselves.

Through his approaches to filmmaking and to installation in *The Crossing*, Motta forces an encounter between recorded subject and viewer, prompting identification and empathy while demarcating the limits of such emancipatory responses. The videos present first-person testimonies, drawn from interviews Motta conducted with the refugees and without the usual editing and contextualizing tactics of documentary film. Motta cites his use of the interview in his artistic practice as a means "to emphasize the construction of discursive arenas of social exchange; spaces for dialogue, which might lead to both confrontation or consent."[4] He translates this agenda to the gallery space by installing the screens out on the gallery floor and at eye level with the viewer, creating an alignment between viewer and recorded subject, and inserting these subjects into the spatiotemporal and the social aspects of the museum or gallery experience. This arrangement—which Motta has employed in other works, such as *Patriots, Citizens, Lovers*... (2015) [fig. 1]—insists on the visibility of the LGBTQI+ subjects, resisting the invisibility that often characterizes them in patriarchal society.[5] Yet this direct presentational structure does not alter the visible and invisible layers of difference between the experiences of refugees and museum visitors, of LGBTQI+ and heterosexual individuals, of social minorities and majorities; rather, it allows them a meeting, a collective—if tense and temporary—coexistence.

Motta's tactics of display engage the politics of the exhibition space, especially the museum's contrasting connections to colonialism and privilege, on the one hand, and to civic life and inclusion on the other. When first installed, at the Stedelijk Museum Amsterdam, *The Crossing* included a vitrine of historical objects from museum collections that Motta selected in order to bridge the Netherlands' contemporary involvement in issues of migration and asylum and the country's colonial history [fig. 2]. He emphasized the intersection between recent migration to Europe and the continent's burgeoning right-wing political movements, as well as a complex public debate on how museums and institutions in Holland and elsewhere might decolonize and diversify their collections.[6] His work invites us to recognize how institutions—the church, the state, the museum—organize and reproduce behavior, and to imagine alternative forms.

In order to gain protection in their new countries, asylum seekers must make a legal case for themselves, demonstrating their persecution in their countries of origin. The degree to which such testimony fits within accepted frameworks of both humanity and violence varies from country to country, from administration to administration, and from judge to judge. Given the widespread criminalization of consensual acts between same-sex adults (illegal in eighty member states of the United Nations) and the increasingly xenophobic politics worldwide (including the United States and Europe), queer migrants are doubly constrained to present themselves in ways that correspond with the dominant heteronormative and patriarchal culture. In his newest video works, Motta scratches at the layers of discrimination facing LGBTQI+ migrants, revealing the complexity and familiarity of how the nation state, law, and religion endeavor to maintain control over the lives of us all. —RE

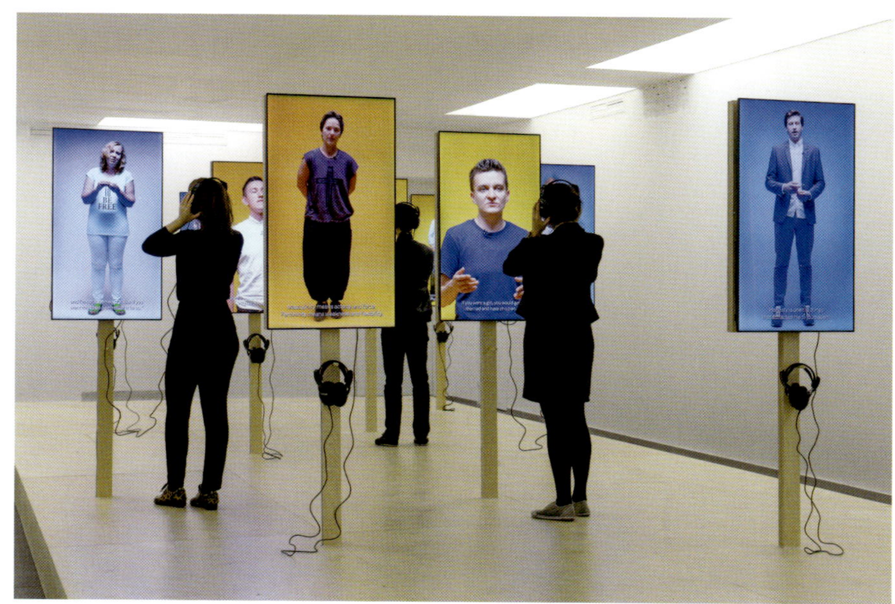

Fig. 1. Carlos Motta, *Patriots, Citizens, Lovers…*, 2015.
Installation view, *Carlos Motta: Patriots, Citizens, Lovers…*, PinchukArtCentre, Kiev, Ukraine, 2015–16

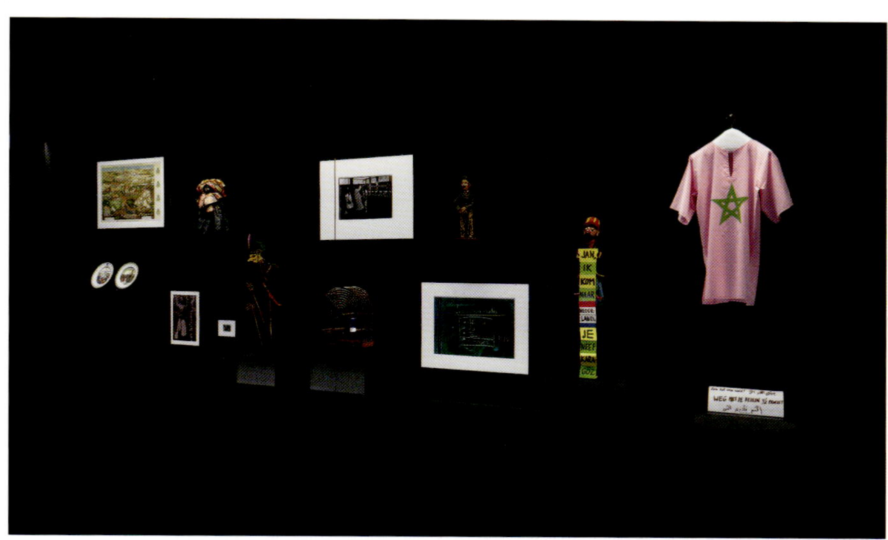

Fig. 2. Carlos Motta, *The Crossing*, 2017.
Installation view, *Carlos Motta: The Crossing*, Stedelijk Museum, Amsterdam, 2017–18

1. In 2012, the United Nations High Commissioner for Refugees (UNHCR) issued new guidelines on protection for individuals applying for refugee status based on sexual orientation or gender identity. Available online at https://www.unhcr.org/en-us/publications/legal/50ae466f9/guidelines-internationalprotection-9-claims-refugee-status-based-sexual.html?query=gender%20identity (accessed December 23, 2018).

2. See "A New Discovery: Queer Immigration In Perspective (2011)," on Carlos Motta's website: https://carlosmotta.com/project/a-new-discovery-queer-immigration-in-perspective/ (accessed December 23, 2018).

3. To make contact with the subjects, Motta collaborated with the Amsterdam organization Secret Garden, which supports LGBTQI+ refugees and assists them once they have immigrated to the Netherlands.

4. Motta, in "An Interview on the Interview: A Conversation between Carlos Motta and Eva Díaz," in *Carlos Motta: The Good Life*, exh. cat. (New York: Art in General, 2008). Available online on Motta's website: https://carlosmotta.com/an-interview-on-the-interview-a-conversation-between-carlos-motta-and-eva-diaz/ (accessed March 5, 2019).

5. See the page for *Patriots, Citizens, Lovers…* on Motta's website: https://carlosmotta.com/project/patriots-citizens-lovers-2015/ (accessed December 24, 2018).

6. See Hendrik Folkerts, "The Living Monument," *Mousse Magazine*, Fall 2018. Available online on Motta's website: https://carlosmotta.com/the-living-monument-by-hendrik-folkerts-mousse-magazine-fall-2018/ (accessed March 5, 2019).

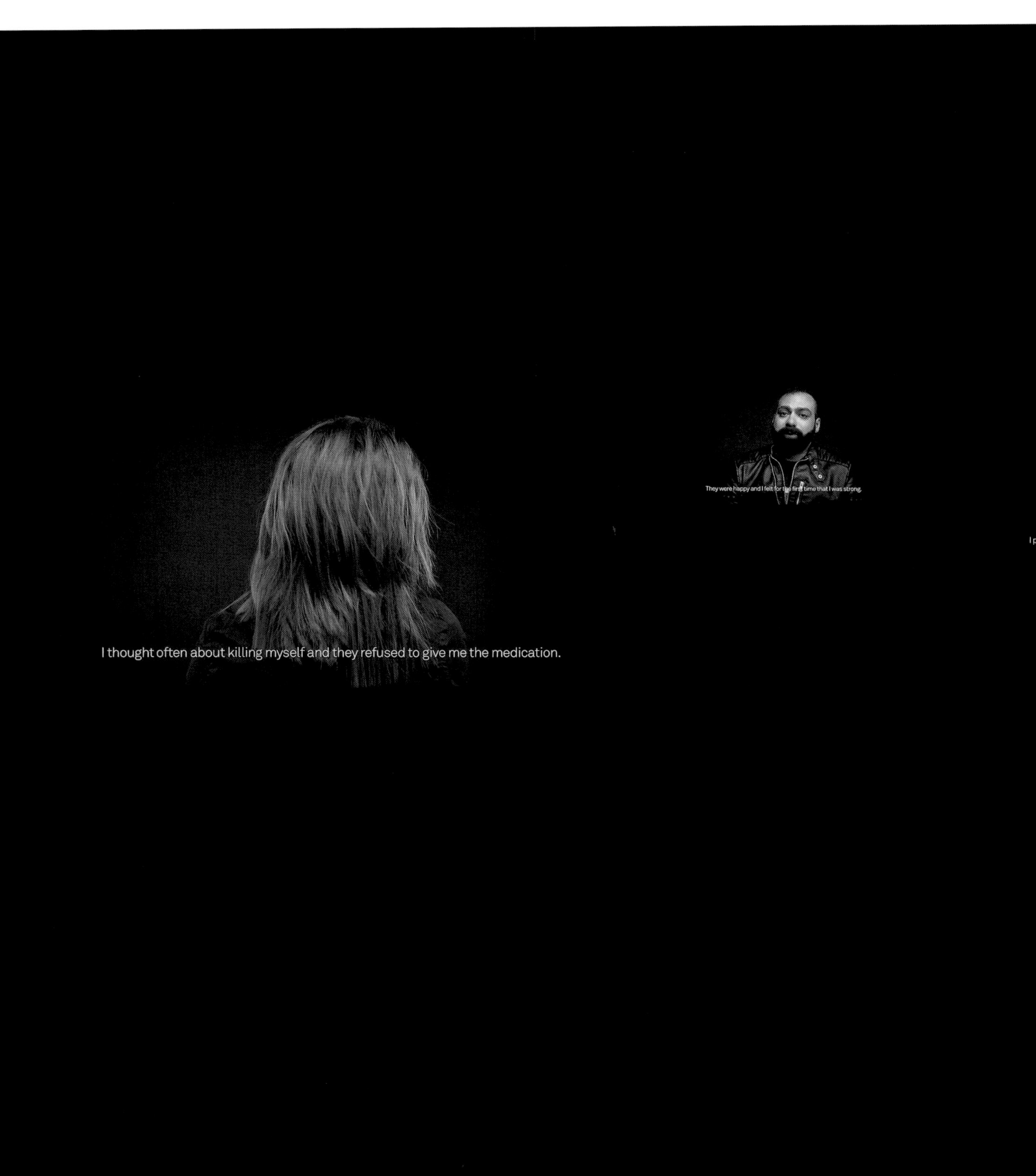
They were happy and I felt for the first time that I was strong.
I prepared myself.
I thought often about killing myself and they refused to give me the medication.

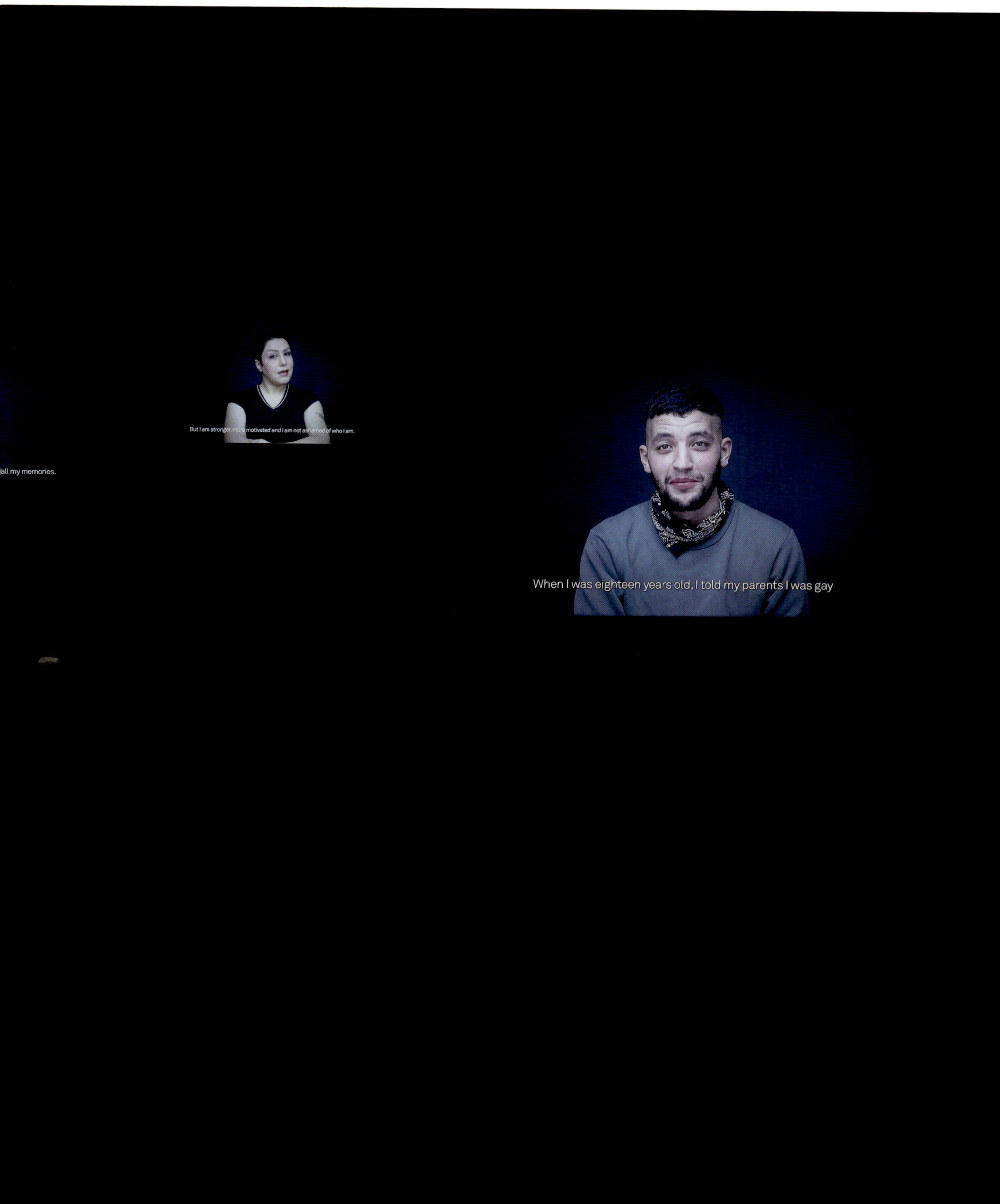
But I am stronger, more motivated and I am not ashamed of who I am.
all my memories.
When I was eighteen years old, I told my parents I was gay

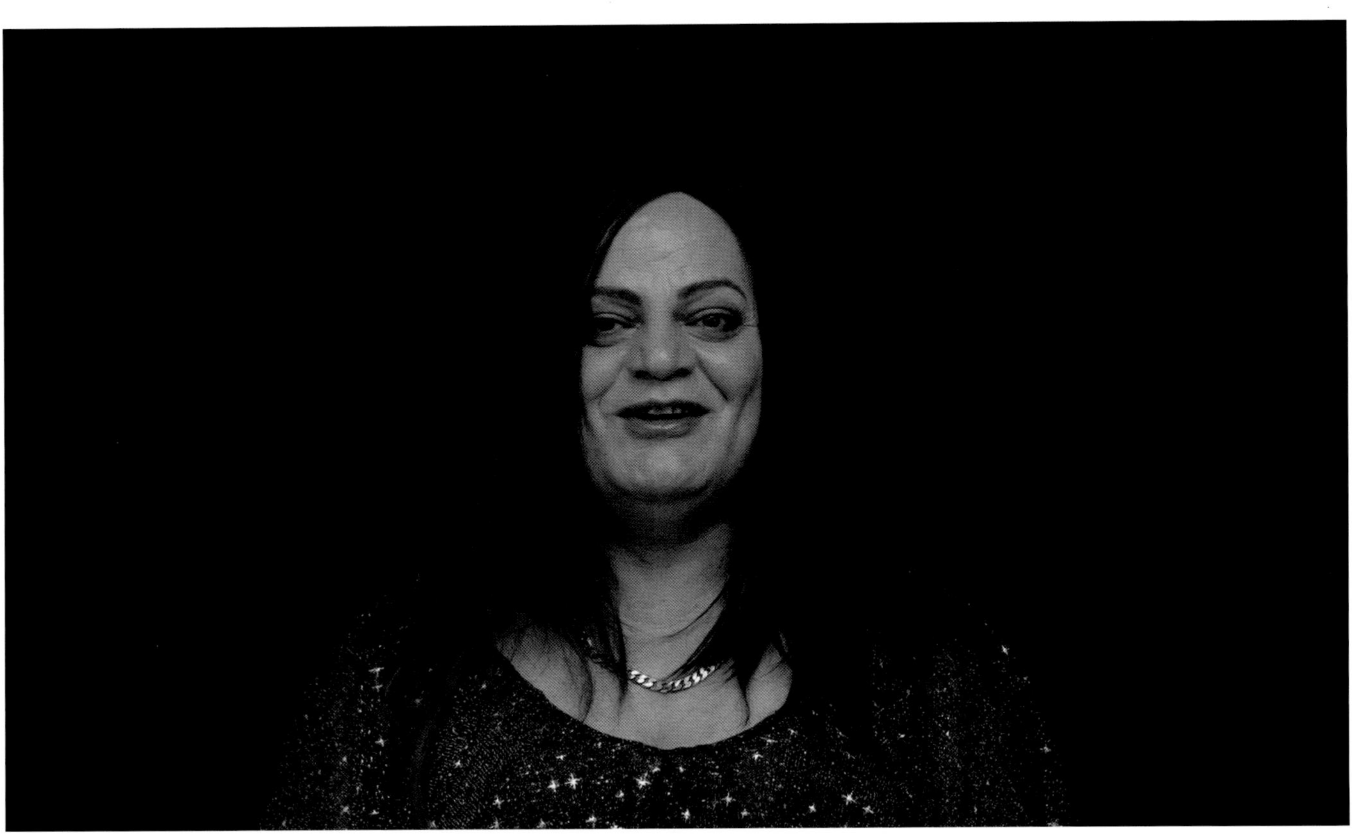

Previous spread, above, opposite, and following spread:
Carlos Motta, *The Crossing*, 2017.
Eleven-channel video installation (color, sound). Dimensions variable.
Installation view, *Carlos Motta: The Crossing*,
Stedelijk Museum, Amsterdam, 2017–18

"Raneen" (11:58 minutes)

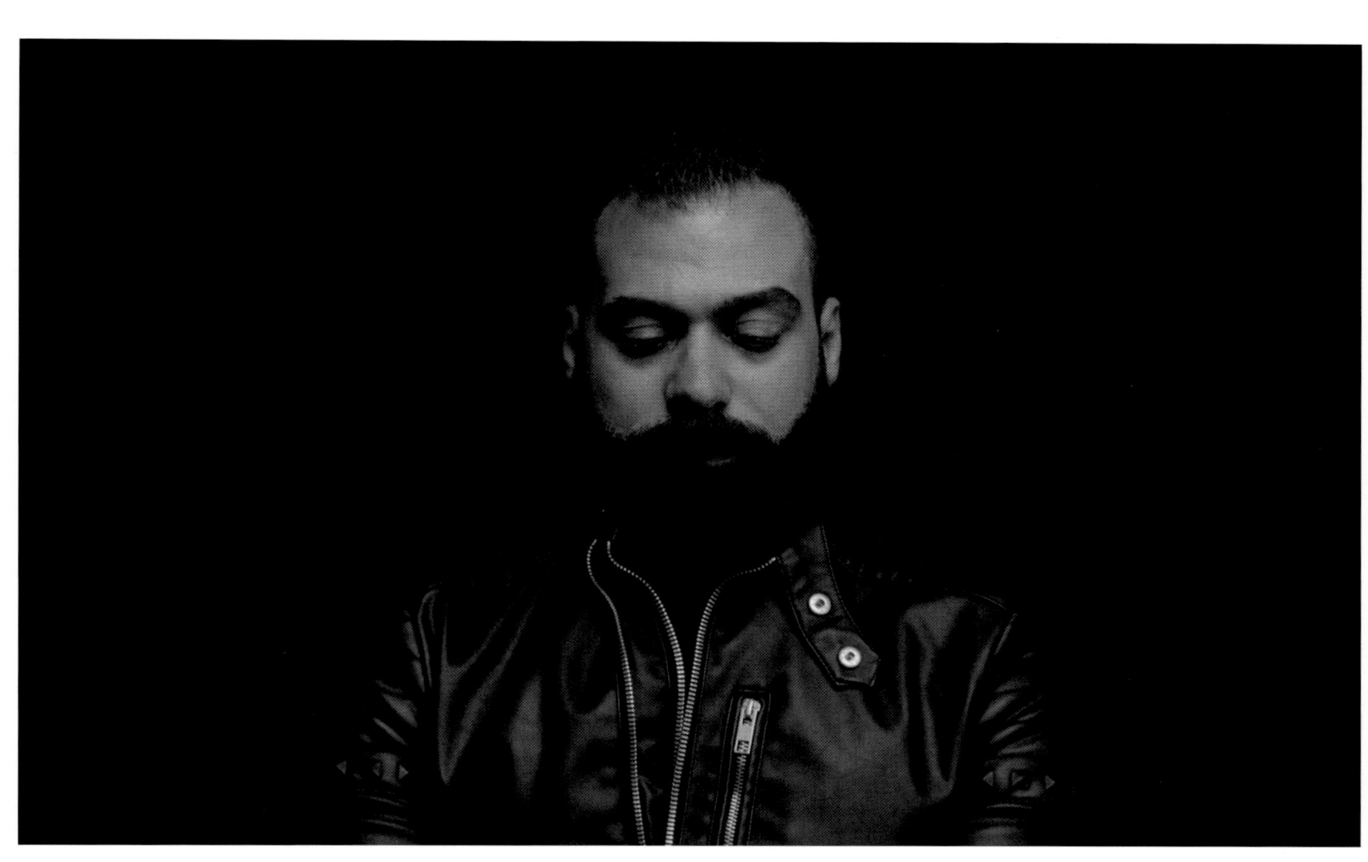

“Anwar” (12:08 minutes)

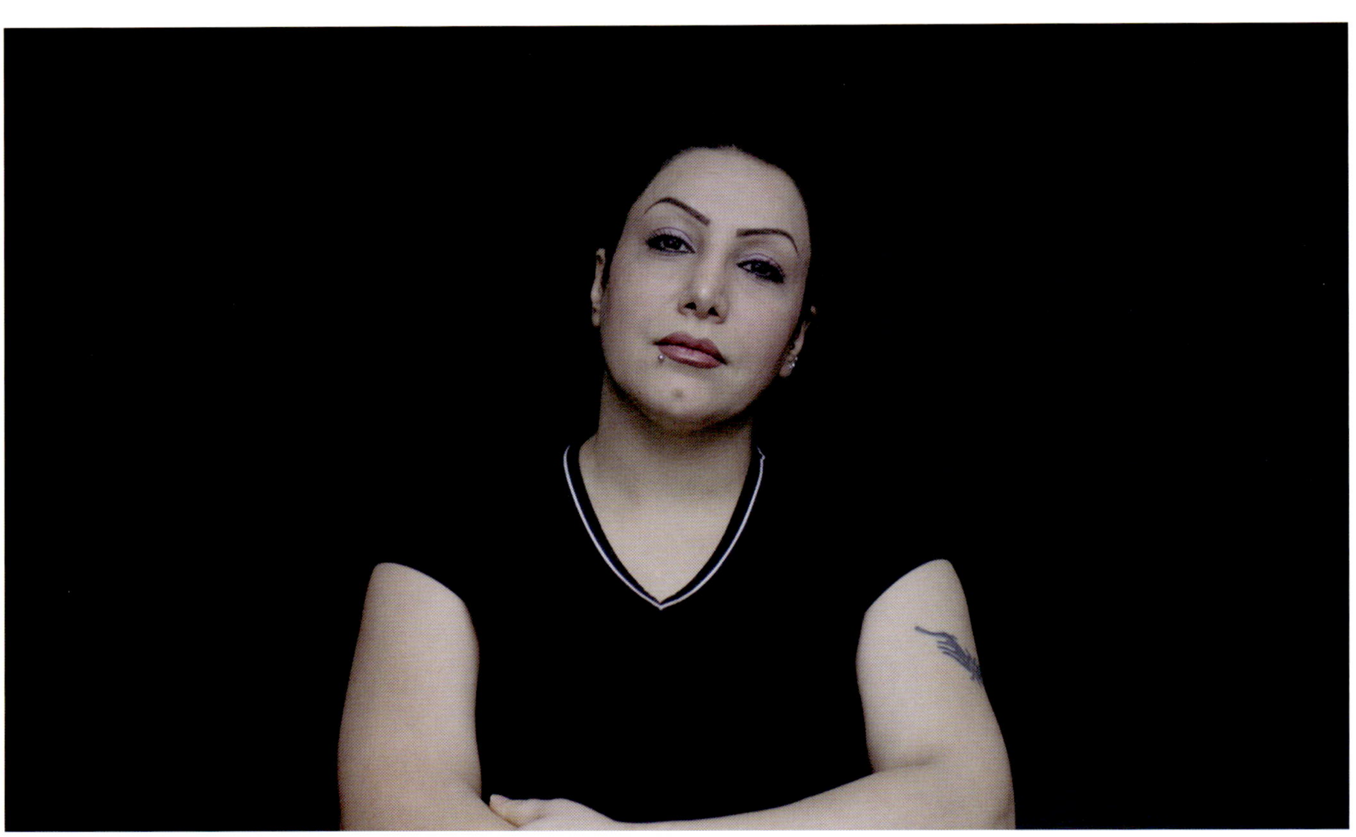

“Mahshid” (11:05 minutes)

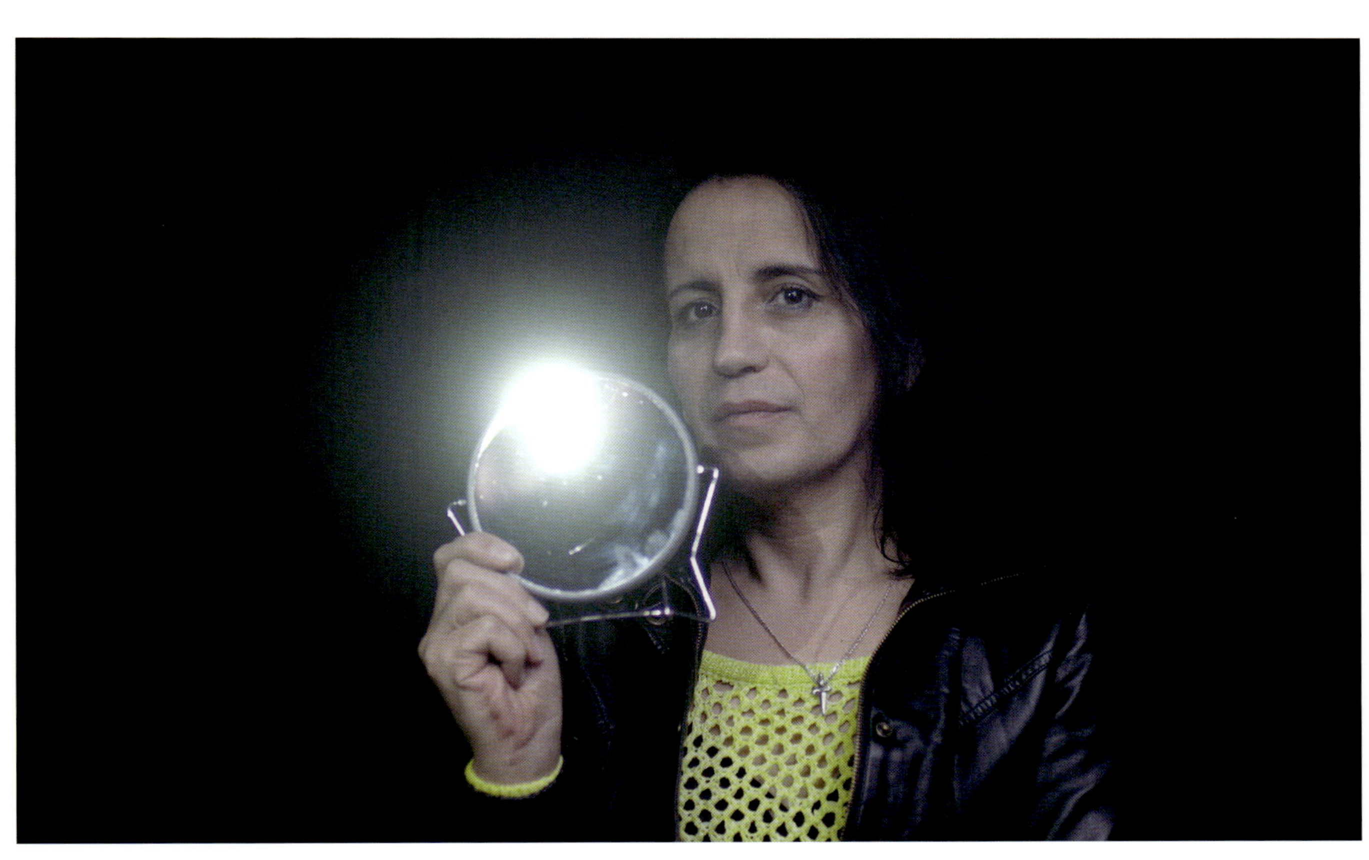

"Butterfly" (12:20 minutes)

Aliza Nisenbaum

B. 1977, Mexico City, Mexico;
lives and works in New York

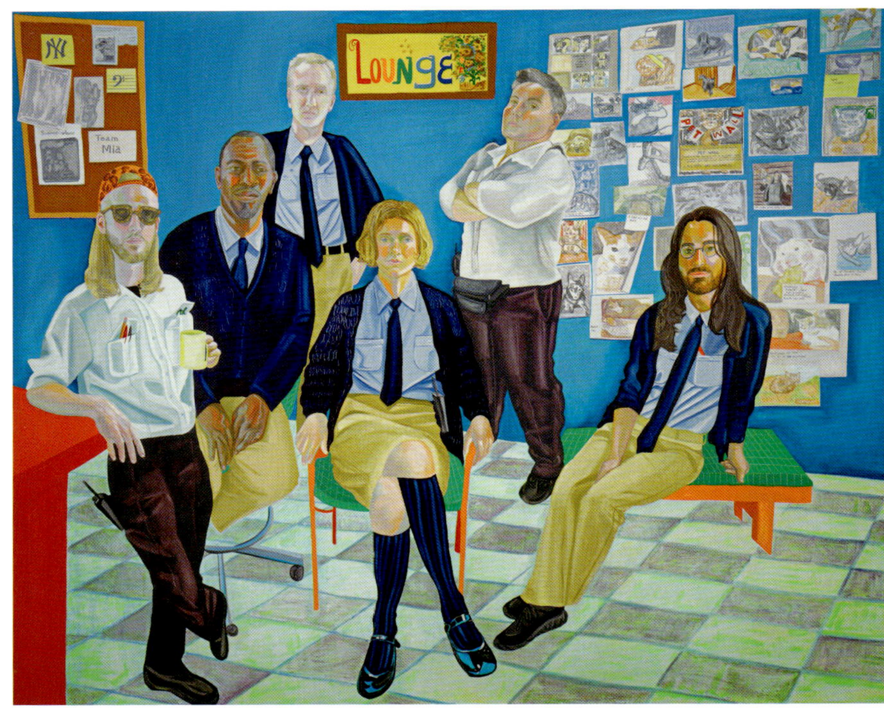

Fig. 1. Aliza Nisenbaum, *Morning Security Briefing at the Minneapolis Institute of Art, basement door open into the Guard Lounge Pet Wall*, 2017.
Oil on linen, 75 x 95 inches (190.5 x 241.3 cm). Minneapolis Institute of Art.
The Mary Ingebrand-Pohlad Endowment for Twentieth-Century Paintings

A significant part of Aliza Nisenbaum's practice is the act of paying attention. Sitting across from her subjects, she takes her time, building trust with them, attending to their needs, and ultimately rendering their likenesses in sensitive and colorful paintings. "To pay attention to someone," Nisenbaum says, "can be a political act."[1] Since 2012, Nisenbaum has focused on depicting individuals and communities that are underrepresented in the history of art and generally underserved by public institutions. She first gained attention for her portraits of undocumented immigrants, mostly from Mexico and Central America, living in New York, and she has also depicted women who work in the city's Office of Immigrant Affairs, security guards at the Minneapolis Institute of Art [fig. 1], and, recently, salsa dancers. Through the humanity, expressiveness, and individuality of her paintings, Nisenbaum complicates the narratives—whether of victimhood, criminality, or invisibility—that stereotypes associate with her subjects. Her exaggerations of color and form and her montages of both observed and imagined environments make her works hybrids of figuration and abstraction, observation and projection. Complex expressions of subjectivity, her paintings are formed through reciprocity and exchange.

Nisenbaum met many of her early sitters when she volunteered to teach a class at Immigrant Movement International, a community space in Queens, New York, started by the Cuban-born artist and activist Tania Bruguera in 2011. Teaching an English-language class there by way of feminist art history, Nisenbaum was impressed by the women taking the class and by their stories of immigration to the United States. Wanting to spend more time talking with them, she proposed to paint portraits of them and set up a small studio in the space.[2] Here she met Veronica and her family, who would become her first and longest-running sitters as well as close friends. Veronica and her husband Gustavo immigrated from Mexico over two decades ago, settling in Queens, where they had their daughter, Marissa. Nisenbaum has painted eight portraits of the family, and her canvases capture Marissa maturing from a round-faced adolescent to a teenager. When asked about her experience with Nisenbaum, Veronica reiterates the sense of value and self-confidence it stirred in her: "I felt a feeling of importance. Being taken into account."[3]

The time and attention Nisenbaum spends on her portrait sessions form the foundation of not only compelling pictures but close relationships. She feels that her slow process "generates the conditions for a very specific encounter and conversational exchange between myself and sitters."[4] The intimacy of observing and being observed, of sharing time, space, and conversation, leads to a heightened sensitivity and self-recognition on the part of both painter and subject. Veronica has talked about gaining self-knowledge by being painted: "I feel that I learned to know myself more, to value more my own characteristics."[5] Both she and Marissa have described how closely Nisenbaum attended to their needs and made them comfortable throughout. Many of the figures in her paintings are visibly relaxed, a necessity if they are to hold a pose for a long time and a condition enabled by Nisenbaum's hospitality. In *Veronica, Marissa, and Gustavo* (2013) [p. 139], the seated father is a stable armature upon whom Veronica and Marissa rest and drape their limbs, forming a tenderly intertwined family portrait. Relaxation suffuses the poses of the figures in *Las Talaveritas* (2015) [p. 140] and *La Talaverita, Sunday Morning NY Times* (2016) [p. 138] and extends to the way their bodies intersect, the child's head resting on the mother's shoulder, or the father's hand resting on his daughter's feet, which lie on his lap. The naturalism with which Nisenbaum's subjects inhabit their bodies speaks to the atmosphere she endeavors to create *through* rather than *despite* the scrutiny of close looking. Rather than a method of control, observation becomes a means of care and consideration.

Also invested in fair economic exchanges, Nisenbaum compensates her sitters for their time. The very first paintings Nisenbaum made of Veronica and Gustavo hang in their apartment above their couch, early gifts from the artist to the family. Visiting this apartment in Queens, I was struck by how Nisenbaum's art, like the artist herself, has become part of the family's quotidian life, joining the other framed pictures, bric-a-brac, and plants in the tidy, crowded space.

Patterned wallpapers and textiles, plants and everyday objects, embellish the environments in which Nisenbaum places her subjects. These individualized settings, both observed and imagined, enhance the character of the sitters. *Marissa's Room* (2015) [fig. 2] overflows with patterns and colors, from the overlapping rugs on the floor, through the batik cloth covering the couch, to the crowded wall of drawings and posters and the guitar. This kind of personalized and decorative glut is common in the bedrooms of teenagers, those early spaces of self-expression. Marissa's white high-top sneakers and bared midriff or ripped jeans in *Las Talaveritas* engender a similar effect—a sense of familiarity with the teen's expression of her persona. In *Veronica, Marissa, and Gustavo*, Veronica's black-and-gray patterned shirt and hat visually merge with the gridded background, rendering the matriarch's body notably abstract, as if floating or, perhaps more symbolically, as the foundation of the family portrait. Many of the objects depicted, such as the indigenous Mexican tiles covering the walls in *Las Talaveritas* and *La Talaverita, Sunday Morning NY Times*, reference the sitters' cultures of origin. By integrating a range of patterns and objects—some chosen by the sitters, others by Nisenbaum's sharp eye—the artist generates a visual play within her compositions and points up the hybridity of her subject matter. She extends this experimentation to her mark-making techniques, achieving a remarkable range of textures in her sixteen-by-sixteen-inch portrait of Marissa (2014) [p. 141], the individual strands of whose hair contrast with her smooth brown face, while her denim jacket stands out against the patterned ground. Nisenbaum's paintings encompass pictures within pictures, still life vignettes and abstractions that augment the portraits.

When asked how seeing a portrait of herself and her family in a museum made her feel, Veronica replied, "I feel as part of this beautiful country although I wasn't born here. I feel as part of this place and with the same rights as anyone."[6] In recognizing people many of whom live in some way at the margins of recognition, Nisenbaum's paintings imply a change in the way we acknowledge the lives of others. "I'm interested in the politics of visibility—who and why someone is depicted," Nisenbaum has said.[7] She pursues this interest through the most ethical of terms: a commitment to coming face-to-face with another person, to bearing witness to that person's humanity and translating it through her own hand. An arduous process, it is also a necessary one in order to reimagine how to portray each other today. —RE

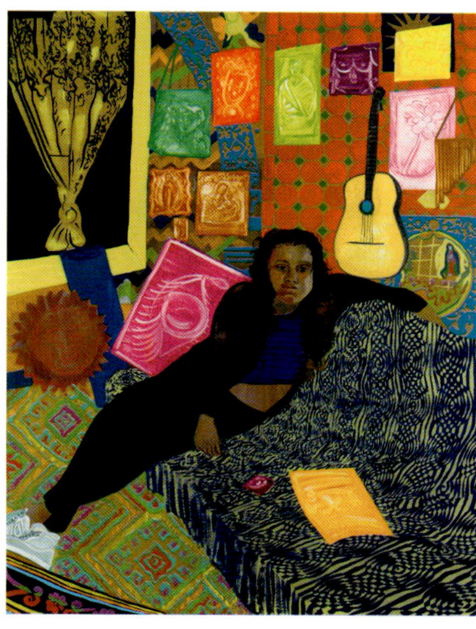

Fig. 2. Aliza Nisenbaum, *Marissa's Room*, 2015. Oil on linen, 66½ x 51 inches (169 x 130 cm)

1. Aliza Nisenbaum, quoted in Dodie Kazanjian, "Who Says Painting Can't Be Political?," *Vogue*, January 31, 2017. Available online at www.vogue.com/article/aliza-nisenbaum-artist-immigration-political-portraits (accessed November 26, 2018).

2. See Scott Indrisek, "Aliza Nisenbaum on Why Her Intimate Portraits of Immigrants Aren't about Empathy," *Artsy*, September 25, 2017. Available online at www.artsy.net/article/artsy-editorial-aliza-nisenbaum-intimate-portraits-immigrants-empathy (accessed November 26, 2018).

3. Veronica, interview with the author, August 9, 2018.

4. Nisenbaum, "Why I Paint," October 26, 2016, *Phaidon*. Available online at www.phaidon.com/agenda/art/articles/2016/october/26/aliza-nisenbaum-why-i-paint (accessed November 29, 2018).

5. Veronica, interview with the author.

6. Ibid.

7. Nisenbaum, "Why I Paint."

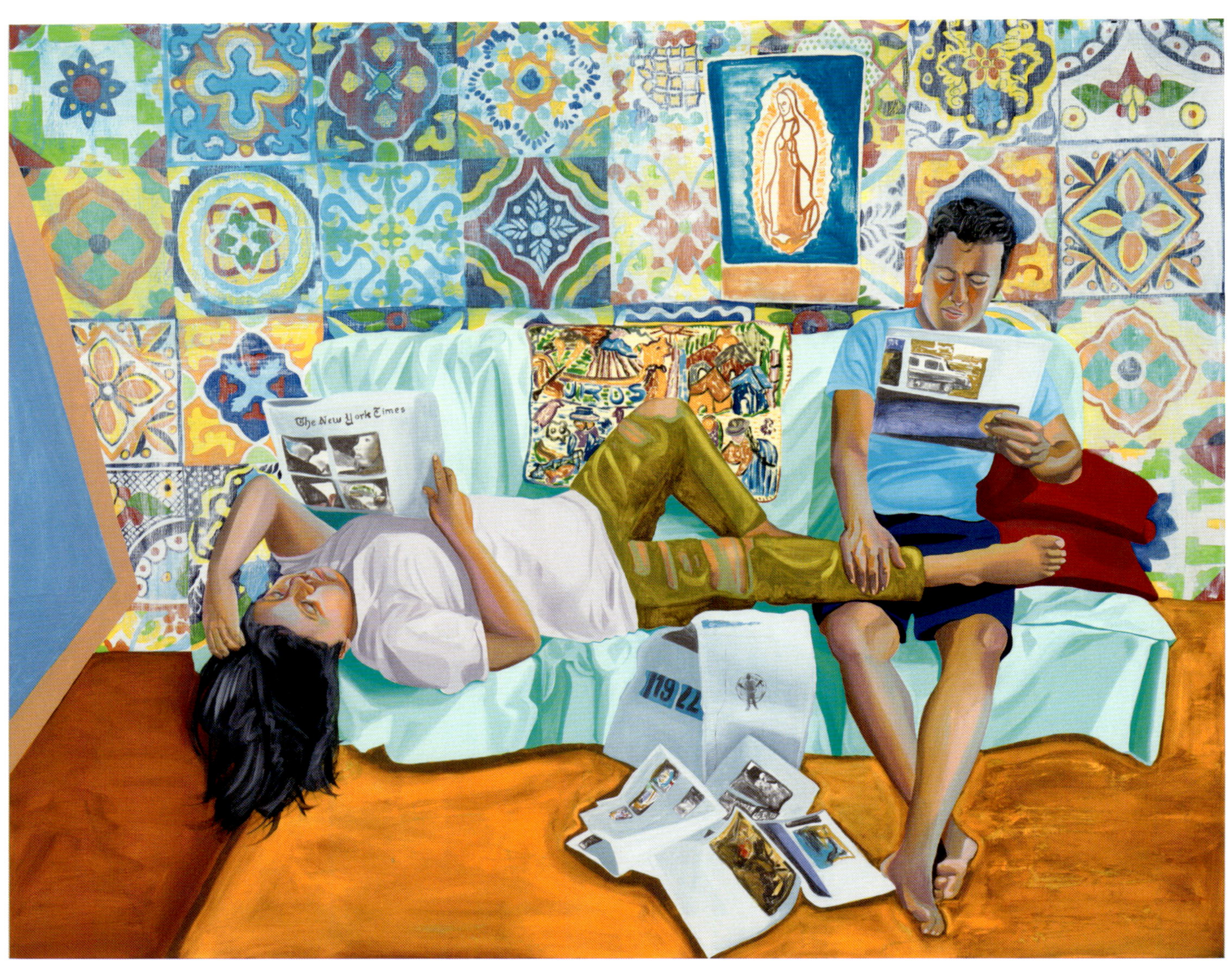

Aliza Nisenbaum, *La Talaverita, Sunday Morning NY Times*, 2016.
Oil on linen. 68 x 88 inches (172.7 x 223.5 cm)

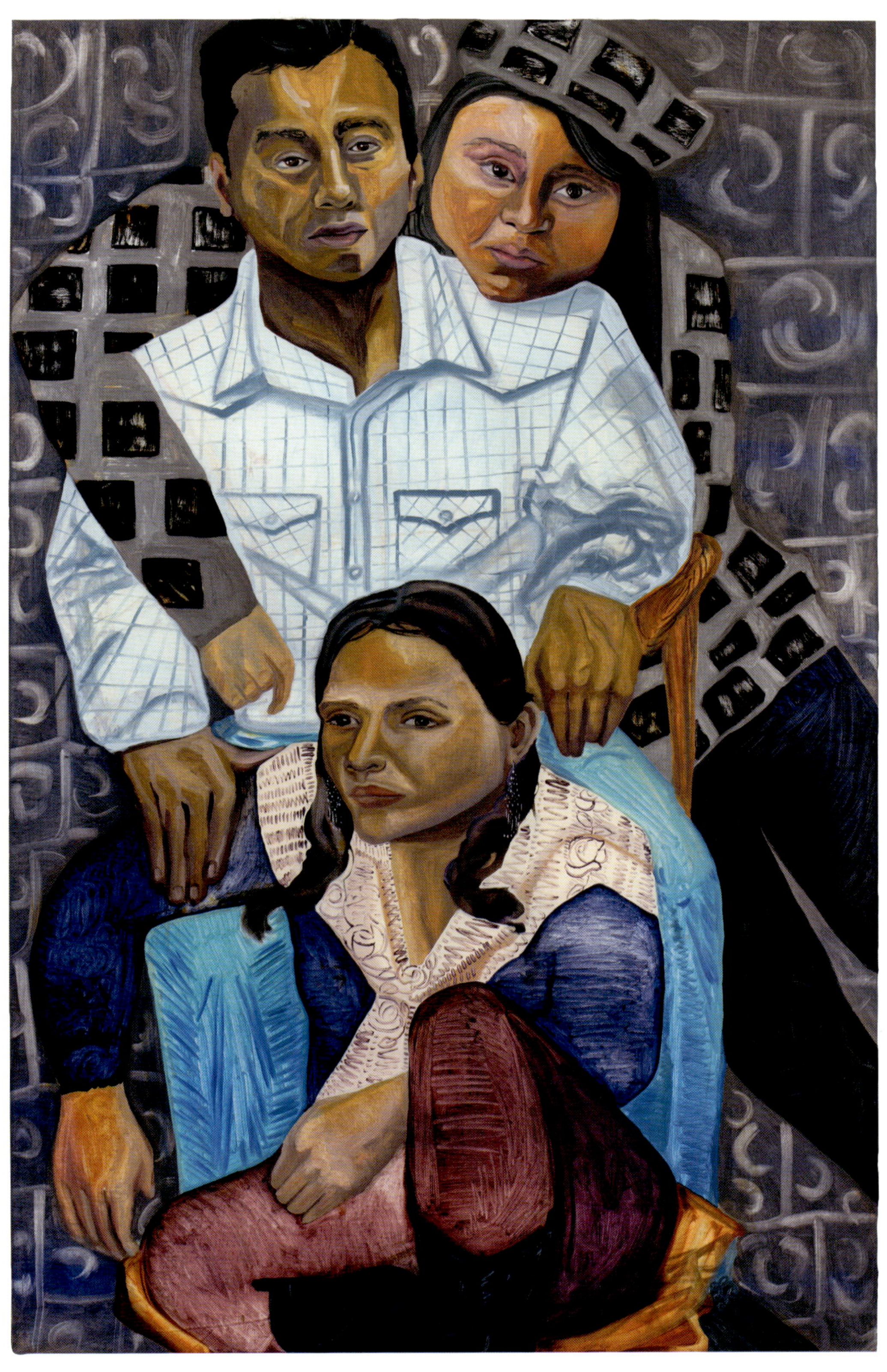

Aliza Nisenbaum, *Veronica, Marissa, and Gustavo*, 2013.
Oil on linen. 51 x 33 inches (129.5 x 83.8 cm)

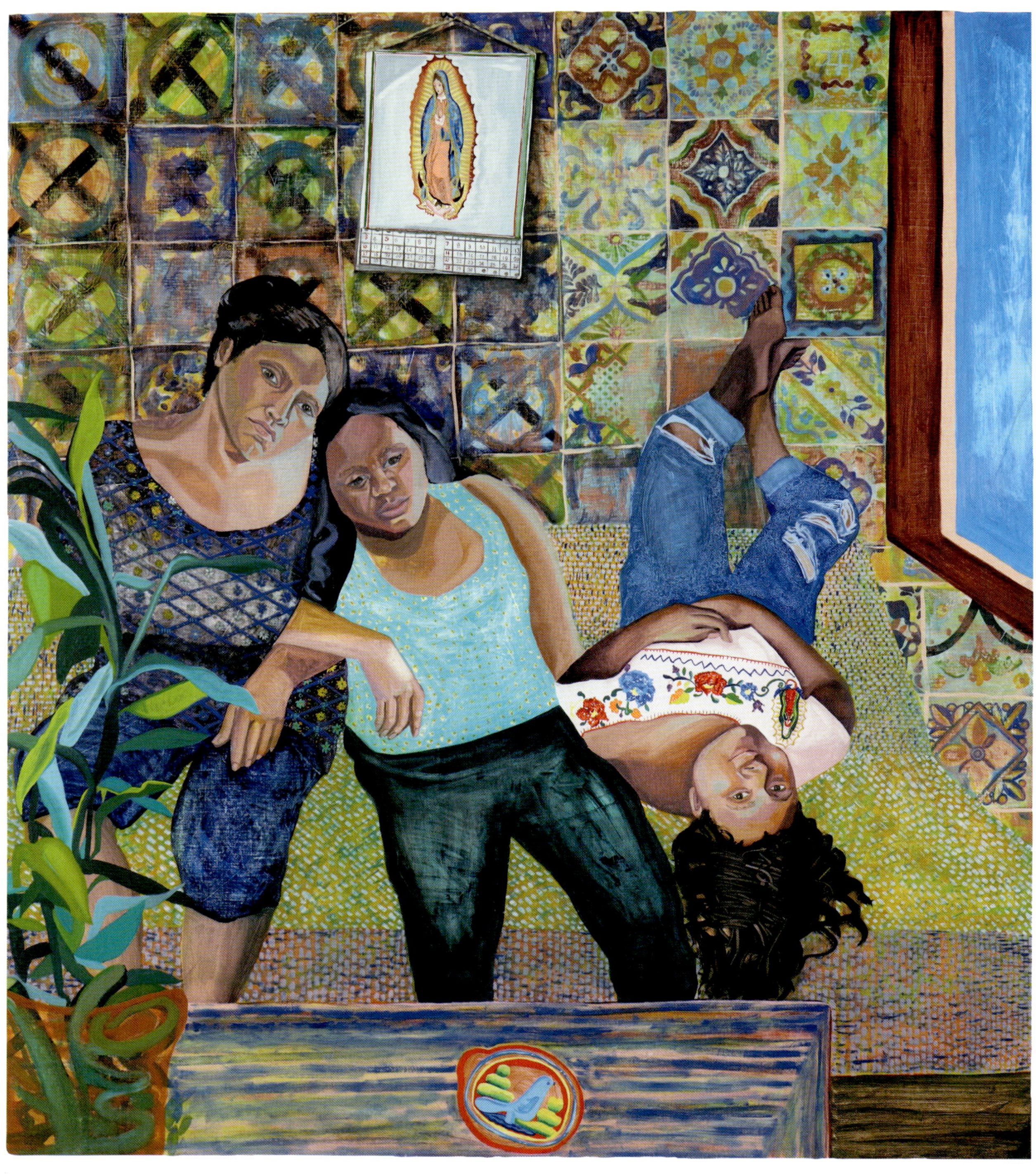

Aliza Nisenbaum, *Las Talaveritas*, 2015.
Oil on linen. 64 x 57 inches (162.6 x 144.8 cm)

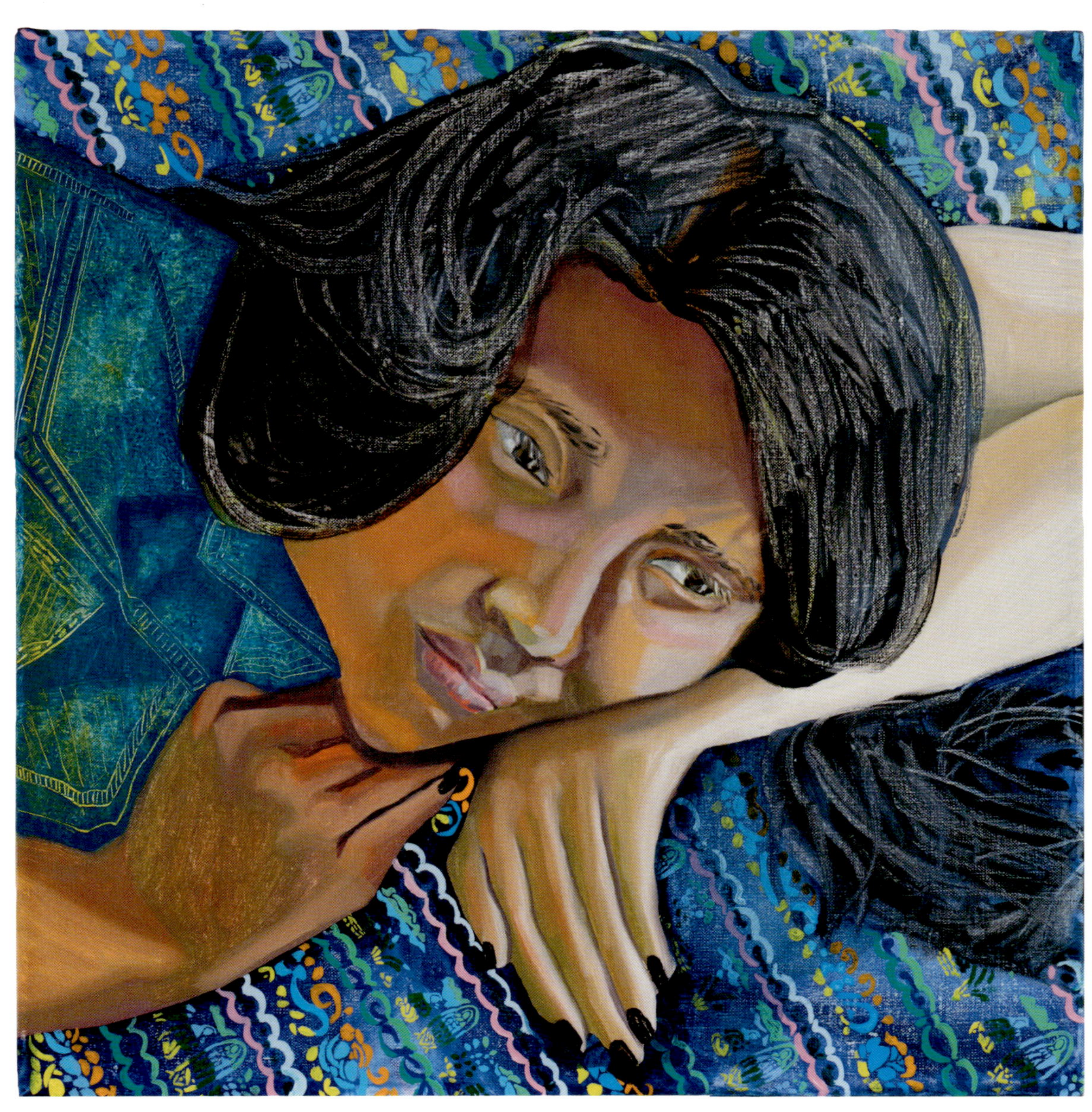

Aliza Nisenbaum, *Marissa*, 2014.
Oil on linen. 16 x 16 inches (40.6 x 40.6 cm)

Anthony Romero

B. 1983, Austin, United States;
lives and works in Boston

Anthony Romero is an organizer, educator, artist, and writer whose performance-based installations combine speech acts—public, academic, political—with their institutional structures of support to reanimate Chicano/a histories in the United States. His performances often combine a public reading of a text with visual elements that expand its context—a range of site-responsive props, artworks referencing other histories or cultures, or ephemera selected to constitute a living archive. Romero explores the complications that race introduces to sociality: how it troubles the limits of participation, how group identities based on exclusion are created around it, and how the art world upholds structures that support racism.[1] The project that he has developed for *When Home Won't Let You Stay* includes community gatherings, legal-empowerment workshops, and performance events at the ICA that offer both participants and audiences spaces for understanding the various impacts of immigration law and policy.

Romero comprehends space and architecture as supplements to authority, and his installations often include various armatures, such as a podium or a screen, as platforms that channel those structures. He activates these devices by reciting well-known texts that, when performed, refract the Chicano/a histories emergent in the spaces between modern and postcolonial histories. Recitation, for Romero, involves more than verbalizing language; it is activated through the supplementary knowledge produced by the movements and postures of the body as it interacts with space. "The speech act allows for simultaneity," Romero notes, "an experience of the text and its embellishment by the voice and the body."[2] In an environment where accented speech all too readily suggests foreignness or threat, speech-based performance offers a culturally specific formal language to express the Chicano/a experience.

For his ICA/Boston commission, *...first in thought, then in action* (2019) [p. 144], Romero collaborated with Dan Jackson and Jules Rochielle Sievert of NuLawLab, an innovation laboratory within Northeastern University Law School focused on legal empowerment.[3] In this work Romero links the frustrations of asylum seekers lost in a judicial labyrinth with the central themes in Franz Kafka's 1914–15 novel *The Trial* [fig. 1]. In the book, a man awakes one morning having committed an unknown crime, and the novel unfolds through a series of dystopian scenes in which the man navigates an unnerving juridical process, endless bureaucracy, and secrecy about his alleged crime. Romero activates Kafka's text in tandem with different objects in the galleries to reflect the unique carceral particularities of migrating to the United States, where the first entry space for new migrants is often a jail or detention center. The work's second component is a series of workshops and community gatherings organized in partnership with NuLawLab that focus on legal literacy, specifically in areas that impact the lives of immigrant residents of East Boston and elsewhere. In its nomadic and political qualities, the project invokes the role of guerilla theater in the era of the Civil Rights Movement, namely *El Teatro Campesino* [fig. 2], co-founded by Luis Valdez and Agustin Lira in 1965 as the cultural wing of the United Farm Workers union in the central valley of California.[4]

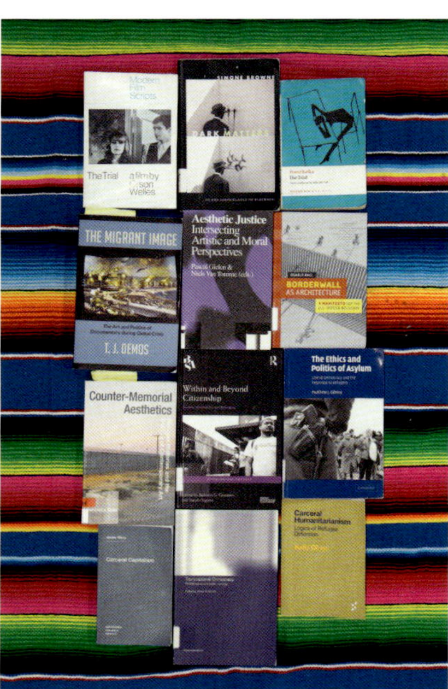

Fig. 1. Anthony Romero, reading list for *...first in thought, then in action*, 2019

In *I am American: I Speak English* (2015), Romero and collaborator Josh Rios used found text, mediation, performance, and sculptural props to explore the systematic erasure of native tongues in the United States and the effects of this erasure on subsequent generations. Reading from an English-language learning text from behind a chicken-wire screen—which evokes a fence or a coop, as well as the formal language of border walls, detention centers, migrant encampments, and other such sites—Romero approaches the performance from the perspectives of translation, multilingualism, interpretation, and the tools of language acquisition.

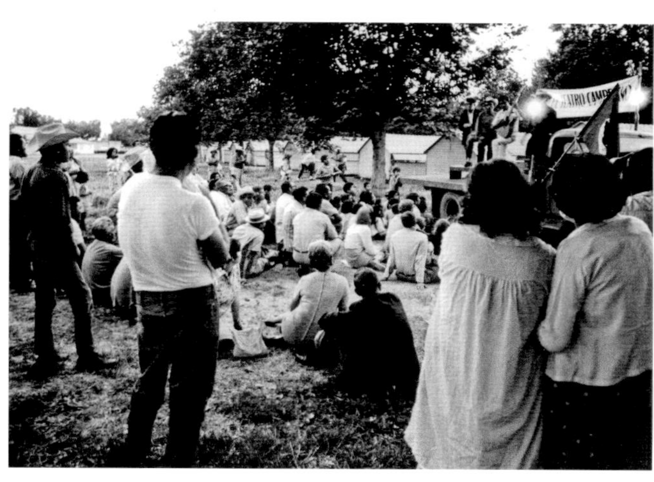

Fig. 2. Jon Lewis, *From the bed of a flat bed truck, El Teatro Campesino performs at a farm labor camp*, c. 1966–68. Farmworker Movement Documentation project, University of California San Diego Library

Romero's and Rios's *Please, Don't Bury Me Alive!* (2015), a performative lecture and art installation, took inspiration from Efraín Gutiérrez's film of the same title, from 1976.[5] This independent film follows a young Chicano struggling with the death of his brother, and of many other Latinos, in the Vietnam War, combining that era's broad scope of grief with the political, cultural, and familial contexts in which the protagonist comes of age.[6] Romero's and Rios's performance features two readers. One, flanked by historical photographs of San Diego's Chicano Park, reads the artist Robert Smithson's lecture "Hotel Palenque," which Smithson delivered in 1972 to graduate students at the University of Utah, Salt Lake City. The lecture describes the art, architecture, and culture of Mexico as mesmerizing inspirations, but at moments, as when Smithson asserts a psychic and ontological danger supposedly present in the land of Mexico itself, it suggests to Rios and Romero the presence of a colonialist fantasy.[7] The other performer plays the main character in an abridged version of Samuel Beckett's *Waiting for Godot* (1953), which Romero and Rios site in an unnamed detention center along the U.S./Mexico border. These discursive conditions articulate the experiences of waiting that are unique to many migrants and other racialized subjects whose relationship to the state or prison is framed by methods of visual surveillance and spatial control.

Romero's and Rios's resiting of Beckett's dystopian play in the context of U.S. immigration debates advanced a contemporary fascination with the play's continuing bleak relevance and proposed the salience of waiting as a metaphor for the migrant experience. In 2007, for example, artist Paul Chan created *Waiting for Godot in New Orleans*, a multifaceted project inspired by a visit to New Orleans the previous year in the wake of Hurricane Katrina [pp. 164, 168].[8] Perhaps the most significant thread in Romero's practice is his nuanced understanding of the social as central to the life of the work of art, and the significance of the social realm to our lives as well. "Art," he writes, "is at its core a social event, from the museum to the stage, the apartment gallery to the performance arena. Even when spectators believe themselves to be fully alone in their experience, they are in fact always in the company of others. Whether it is the other mediated through the object, the event, or the body, art relieves us of our solitude and returns us to the multitudes."[9] —ET

1. See Anthony Romero and Dan S. Wang, *The Social Practice That Is Race* (Minneapolis: Beyond Repair, 2016).

2. Romero, in Risa Puleo, "A Conversation with Anthony Romero and Josh Rios," *Glasstire*, November 3, 2015. Available online at https://glasstire.com/2015/11/03/a-conversation-with-anthony-romero-and-josh-rios/ (accessed November 29, 2018).

3. See www.nulawlab.org (accessed March 5, 2019).

4. Teatro Campesino used the mode of commedia dell'arte, performing outdoors on flatbed trucks, as a method of entertaining workers in the fields, and later as a tool of political and social organizing. Their work is considered central to the crystallization of the Chicano/a arts movement in the 1960s and '70s.

5. *Please, Don't Bury Me Alive!* debuted at the Andrea Meislin Gallery, New York, in 2015, and has appeared in a number of places since.

6. Considered the first Chicano feature film, *Please, Don't Bury Me Alive!* was shot in the barrios of San Antonio, Texas, where Efraín Gutiérrez was a community-theater director.

7. Romero, quoted in Puleo, "A Conversation with Anthony Romero and Josh Rios."

8. Chan's project comprised several performances of the play by local performers trained by actors from the Classical Theatre of Harlem. Chan's project also included a "field guide," published later, containing ephemera, photographs, articles, and essays, and other collaborative resources in the form of seminars, educational programs, and a "shadow" fund to support rebuilding efforts in the New Orleans neighborhoods where the play was presented. Chan notes, "There is a terrible symmetry between the reality of New Orleans post-Katrina and the essence of this play, which expresses in stark eloquence the cruel and funny things people do while they wait: for help, for food, for tomorrow." Chan, quoted in "Creative Time Presents Paul Chan's Waiting for Godot in New Orleans. A Play in Two Parts, a Project in Three Parts," New York: Creative Time, 2007. Available online at http://creativetime.org/programs/archive/2007/chan/welcome.html (accessed November 29, 2018). See also Chan's artist statement: http://creativetime.org/programs/archive/2007/chan/artist_statement.pdf.

9. Romero, "Utopian Impulse and Social Practice," *Performa*, January 11, 2013. Available online at http://performa-arts.org/magazine/entry/utopian-impulse-and-social-practice (accessed November 29, 2018).

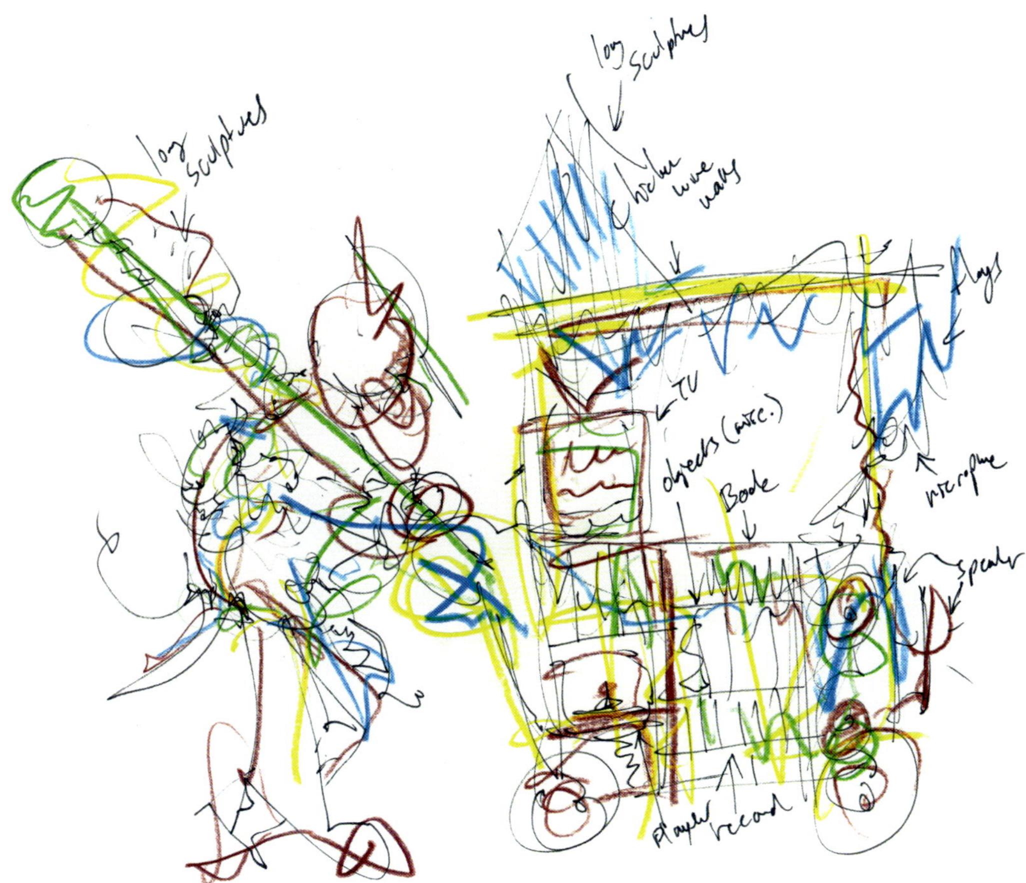

Above:
Anthony Romero, *... first in thought, then in action*, 2019.
Preparatory sketch for sculpture and performance

Opposite:
Anthony Romero, *Not Peaceable and Quiet*, 2018.
Performance collaboration with Matt Joynt and Josh Rios.
M:ST Mountain Standard Time Performative Art Biennial 9, Calgary, Alberta

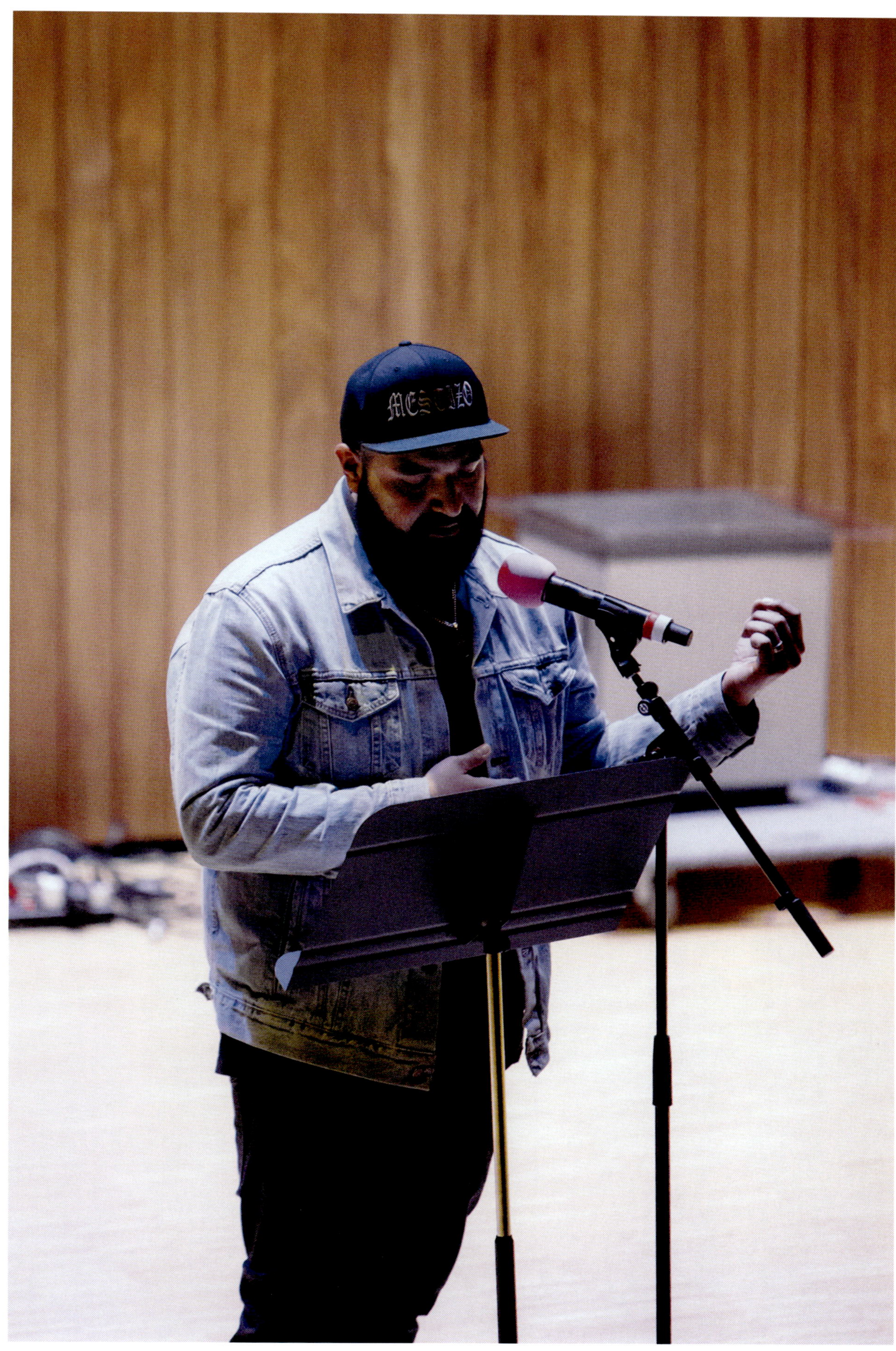
MESTIZO

Conversation

Aliza Nisenbaum and Anthony Romero

ANTHONY ROMERO In talking about your work, I think care is a good place to start, because it's certainly one of the things I've been ruminating on for our project in East Boston.

ALIZA NISENBAUM Care is paying attention to a person's materiality. I always paint people from life, and when somebody comes to me, they're vulnerable. Maybe it's the first time they've entered an art studio, or the first time for sure that they've been painted. How do I make them comfortable? How does one pay attention to the materiality of another person's body? I'm curious to hear how you approach this. How do you start to warm up to your audiences?

AR Hospitality feels so much a part of Mexican culture and Mexican family—this sense of sharing, this sense of communal collective experience, particularly around meals. I approach so much of my collaborative work from that place. It's also the place I want institutions to move into. With this project for the ICA [p. 142], for example, there are two things happening, or that I hope to make happen. One is more symbolic, aesthetic things happening in the galleries (sculptures, performances, etc.); the other exists in the space and time of the communities I'm working with and in, leveraging institutional resources as an opportunity to develop a network of care. We can also think of this in terms of what Martin Luther King, Jr., referred to as a "network of mutuality." I hope to build this kind of hospitality by creating situations of listening.

AN Your work is pure presence. You have people enacting their situation and stepping outside of it right there in front of you. Myself I've been very influenced by Tania Bruguera [p. 112], I got close to her and her practice early on, and I wanted to understand how a painter can approach direct social action. It kind of happened organically: I just told her I wanted to teach a class on English through feminist art history. I think there are different levels of authorship with socially engaged practices: some are more authored than others, and painting stands symbolically for the most authored thing. A painter working in isolation in a studio—that's the symbolic realm, but the aesthetic in my work happens through the social interactions I have with people. The paintings develop as my relationships with people develop. The works in *When Home Won't Let You Stay* show a family I've worked with for six years [pp. 136–41]. The paintings really happened through interaction [over a period of time].

AR To what extent could any one particular work—a painting, a performance, a sculpture—really capture the scale of the thing?

AN I guess the relation of the archive to the body is that painting ends up entering the symbolic realm. It's a theatrical stage in which you enact a certain gesture.

AR I was working with the performance group Teatro Línea de Sombra on a project for the Museum of Contemporary Art Chicago [MCA] for a couple of years, and we were meeting with Mexican-American folks and Mexican immigrants, mostly folks that had immigrated. We were just listening and learning about their experiences and over the course of talking with these folks in this community you sort of amass stories, some of which can be quite violent or traumatic. Performance art can't quite articulate that experience, but I'm less concerned with creating a situation where a museumgoer would suddenly become interested in the experience of immigrants, because of the violence and trauma of that experience, than with investing in their neighbors, the folks that are around them all the time. I imagine that you also collect these stories. The organic experience of getting to know someone—how much of that moves into the work?

AN When I was looking at your performances, I felt a certain level of opacity. They don't want to be totally legible; they're like a negation of being perfectly legible. Your work has a very modernist quality of turning your back on legibility, which is something that Fred Moten talks about as well.

That's a really important space of resistance in any artwork, where part of the process is disclosed and legible and others are secret. I don't mind that the frame of my work can be expansive in that way. It starts to enter into different economies that aren't necessarily those of the museum, which I think is the exciting part that you can't predict.

AR I think I get a little bit conflicted about it. For better or worse, I have a sense of shifting responsibility in regard to practice. I think there are certainly works that exist purely symbolically and aesthetically in their engagement with particular histories, but I also feel an immense sense of responsibility to resist my own exceptionalism by stretching the museum to include a collective "us." The work as a whole is situated across these points, both as an experience [of a given artwork] and as a network of actions, experiences, gestures, etc..

AN That's why I paint groups. I started painting individuals first, and then I started to think about how necessary it was to paint groups who have started to coalesce and form a community, a shared group of interests or alliances. Even by bringing people together in the same group, there's a kind of contagion of ideas and political purposes that you can't predict.

AR How do you think of yourself as an artist? How do you think about yourself in relationship to this particular body of work?

AN I didn't start making this work around the issue of immigration to start out. It came organically from working with a particular group of people, and teaching them, and the outcome of that teaching was these paintings. I've been a teacher for fifteen years, so pedagogy is a really important part of my painting practice. Every institution I start working with, I expand out into the networks they've sometimes already built with their education partners. For example, after being in the 2017 Whitney Biennial with work that I had been doing for six years, I started teaching a class at Hamilton-Madison House in Lower Manhattan, and I started a series of paintings from that experience.

AR So your practice progresses through these various teaching engagements?

AN And from various very personal interests. I'm actually working with dancers now. I've been salsa dancing since I was a kid, so I was thinking about the space of dance as a place where identities fall off or get confused in many ways. Do you think about how one defines oneself as an artist in terms of one's identity? Because identity can be quickly commodified into being this type of artist or that. Identity is always fraught because it is a story we tell ourselves. I think you have a complex way of thinking about that in your work, the way you mine that through your history.

AR When I was working on the MCA project, the curator paired me with Teatro Línea because I'd been doing this work trying to understand the legacy of the Chicano civil rights movement. I was trying to understand the Mexico that I know here, in the borderlands, and the Mexico in Chicago.

AN Myself, I'm Jewish-Mexican, and I grew up in Mexico until I was twenty-one, so I'm perfectly fluent in Spanish, yet people are always, "You're not Mexican, because you don't look Mexican." These kinds of conversations remind me of how people are choosing to work nowadays—who can speak for whom. But it's our work as artists to make identity complex, and I think the more you work with immigrant subjects, the more you realize how infinite the stories are.

AR You know, as soon as I got to Boston, I was reaching out to folks, I was trying to understand, for my own level of comfort, where all the Mexicans are [*laughter*]. Where are the grocery stores? Where are the bakeries? Where's the culture? And it's very small, I mean, it makes up 1 percent or

0.5 percent of the total population of the Boston metropolitan area. When the invitation came from the ICA to do a project, I was thinking a lot about that, because the Spanish-speaking populations in East Boston are Salvadoran, or Colombian, or Dominican. It underscores a question for me which I wrestle with regularly: what, if anything, do brown folks share with each other? I wonder if opacity or the insistence on the illegibility of our collective brown experience isn't at the heart of the question. Perhaps in some ways, brownness is already a kind of abstraction?

AN Abstraction has become commodified in some ways, but I think it's about breaking through these identities over and over again. I'm interested in thinking about abstraction as that kind of space, or about how Barnett Newman would talk about the encounter between a viewer and a painting: "I hope," Newman said, "that my painting has the impact of giving someone, as it did me, the feeling of his own totality, of his own separateness, of his own individuality." It's not an aesthetic situation where you break up the parts, it's a total unity that happens in one second. For a long time I was an abstract painter, because I thought that was the way to get at these kinds of difficult ethics that I was interested in.

AR I think about abstraction in dance. For example, I just connected with Rudy Perez, who's of Puerto Rican descent. He's from New York and he's the only brown choreographer who was part of the Judson Church. I reached out to Rudy because I want to think about the expectations that are put on brown bodies and the effect of those expectations over time. As Latinx folks, we have access to a kind of abstraction that's unique to our lived experiences as people who, if nothing else, share the history of Spanish colonization. Could we deploy this, and would it be legible to audiences? Or would it still be read in relationship to our particular histories or lived experiences as the audience understands them? Or, another example, I've become really interested in the narrative of Frantz Fanon coming to the U.S. to receive medical treatment, and the way Homi Bhabha writes of this kind of delirium and madness that sets into him.[1] We can think of this as the cumulative effect of colonial domination upon him over the course of his life. Fanon writes up until his death, but the writing from this period is filled with paranoia, anxiety, delirium, and a kind of remorse over, as he writes, how he could have been killed fighting imperialism on the battlefield, but he wasn't. Instead he's in the seat of imperialism. Thinking through Fanon, we can see how oppression produces the conditions of a certain kind of madness. It's related to the sense that once one crosses a border, one ceases to be what one was previously. You used to be doctor, lawyer, engineer, sister, child, whatever, and then you become a migrant, an immigrant, and as a result you are now this new subject, because the border made you a new subject. It's a dehumanizing transformation. For me, that's like delirium, the delirium of the experience, or the incomprehensible parts of it. One's relationship to power affects one's internal or psychological life as it does one's social life.

AN It's a kind of madness, but a transformative one as well, as you mentioned. Portraiture, which has always been a medium about power in some ways, is by default the medium that's mostly about depicting the victors or the powerful.

AR Some of my favorites of your paintings are the still lifes, because it's not a body, it's an object.

AN Those works came from a person I was very close to who was incarcerated. They were inspired by my painting practice. I was making portraits of people while they were in a correctional institution; they'd send me letters over two years—Christmas letters, Easter letters, Halloween letters—and I would transcribe the letters and make a portrait of this person out of the two years' worth of letters. We would kind of help each other in some ways. And then I went to the market in Mexico, and you know those board games, like *Serpientes y Escaleras* [Chutes and Ladders]? I painted that along with the letters.

AR Is there a difference to you between the treatment of those objects and the treatment of the body?

AN That's interesting. I mean, I think that when I paint people oftentimes they're either by themselves or somehow not engaging the viewer. Sometimes they do, but I allow a certain kind of in-turnedness, I guess. And since I always paint people from life, there's a kind of urgency of whether they're helping me along with the painting by being relaxed, or whether they're nervous and want to get out of there. So there's a reciprocal, real-time situation that happens when you're painting someone from life, because they're literally collaborating with you in terms of how they give themselves over in terms of their energy, their time, and how they're being with you. And when you're making a still life you can obviously compose, say, a memento mori, or create a narrative or a metaphor in some ways; you can exert so much more control over it, I guess. What about you? Do you feel there are urgencies when you're working with real people?

AR Yeah, totally. And the process is always a little bit different. You know, in Chicago the process was initially just getting to know folks in the community, and introducing them to folks that I already knew, and then those folks introducing us to other folks. But we didn't know if we were going to make something for a while. We didn't know what it would be. We settled on a performance, but the idea was always that we were going to produce something in collaboration with whoever wanted to collaborate with us from those communities. We had to become comfortable with the idea that nothing might happen and, in turn, attempt to make the museum comfortable with the same thing.

AN That's exciting when it's almost totally out of your control and you have enough time to just let it be an organic process. The outcome is always really surprising, I'm sure.

AR Yeah, in Boston it's similar in the sense that I've set out to collaborate with the NuLawLab and together we have begun to meet with folks in different parts of the neighborhood without any real expectation about what's going to happen. The work is situated between the city, the museum, and the sociopolitical conditions of both, which have a direct effect upon the folks in East Boston, and for that reason the project requires a kind of slowness and intentionality around the process. I think you have to be ready to fail to do the work. In some ways, this project for the ICA has me becoming more comfortable with the fact of faith. By that I mean that I am wanting to have faith in this underlying network of mutuality that we are building across cultures, experiences, neighborhoods.

AN Well, I hope I can participate in your [project] at some point when I'm in Boston. That would be really fun.

AR That would be great.

– – – – – – – –

Recorded via Skype on December 28, 2018.

1. See Simone Browne, *Dark Matters: On the Surveillance of Blackness* (Durham, NC: Duke University Press, 2015), p. 3. Browne references Homi Bhabha's preface to the 2004 reprint of Fanon's *Wretched of the Earth.*

Michelle Angela Ortiz

B. 1978, Philadelphia, United States;
lives and works in Philadelphia

Interested in how public art can embolden, uplift, and serve the underrepresented, Michelle Angela Ortiz makes art for the public realm. Her work often incorporates community-centered strategies such as participant collaboration and grassroots organization. Perhaps her best-known project is *Familias Separadas* (Separated families) (2015–), an ongoing series of public artworks addressing the detention and deportation of immigrant communities in Pennsylvania. As of 2018, two phases of this project have taken shape, the first begun in 2015, in three highly trafficked public sites in Philadelphia, and the second in 2018, in various public locations in Harrisburg. Both projects center the words and experiences of incarcerated people in the Berks Family Residential Center, which stands between the two cities and is one of three prisons in the United States specifically used for the detention of immigrant and migrant families. Conversations with the detained at Berks both inspire and serve as source material for Ortiz's mural works, which are staged at public sites such as Philadelphia's City Hall [fig. 1], or in commercial districts, and are often overwhelmingly large in scale, a tactic she has described as "taking over vision" to force another perspective.[1]

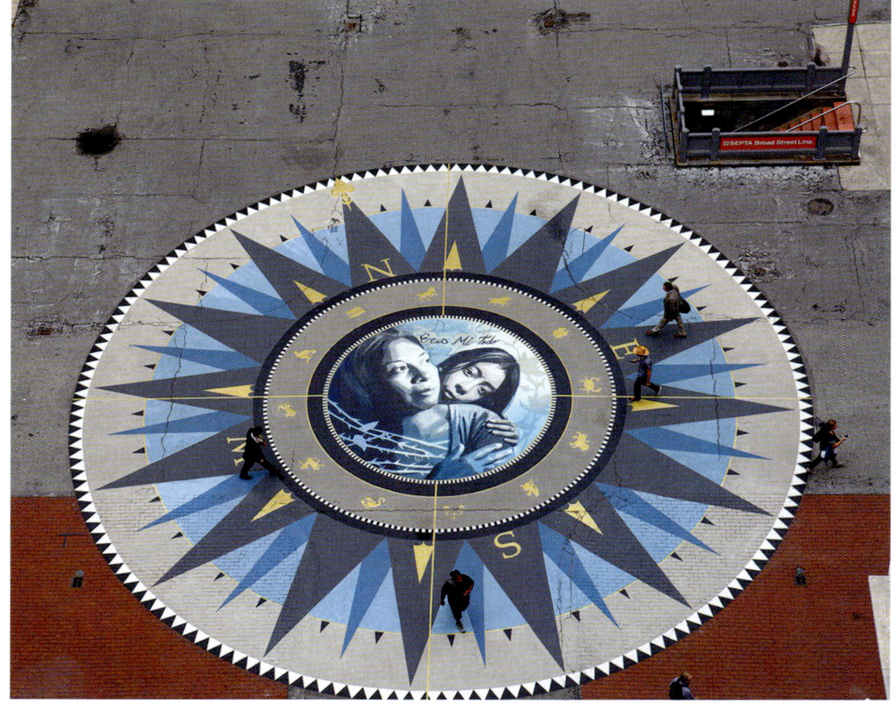

Fig. 1. Michelle Angela Ortiz, "*Eres Mi Todo*" ("You're my everything"), from the *Familias Separadas* (Separated families) project, 2015– . Installation view, Compass Rose, Philadelphia City Hall, 2015

Ortiz approaches her public work with the goal of "amplifying existing voices and energizing existing power."[2] This position is pointedly different from what she learned as an art student: "What we are taught in art school is that our vision is the most important. But what is important is to acknowledge our own privileges and use our vision and creative process to energize the existing power of the community."[3] Ortiz usually begins each public work through collaboration with local organizations active in areas important to her political beliefs, such as the immigrant-rights group Juntos or the Shut Down Berks Coalition. Juntos was her community partner for "*Somos Seres Humanos*" ("We are human beings") (2015) [pp. 152–53], which took place outside the U.S. Immigration and Customs Enforcement (ICE) building in Philadelphia on October 12, 2015—Indigenous Peoples' Day (formerly known as Columbus Day). Accompanied by a team of over thirty community volunteers [fig. 2], Ortiz stenciled onto the ground directly in front of the building, in bright yellow spray paint, "WE ARE HUMAN BEINGS, RISKING OUR LIVES, FOR OUR FAMILIES AND OUR FUTURE." The text was a quotation from Ana, an undocumented woman who was detained at Berks when Ortiz met and interviewed her through her lawyer. Having obtained Ana's permission to use her words, Ortiz chose the public pavement outside Philadelphia's ICE headquarters because of its proximity to the building's exit, through which not only ICE agents but those detained inside would eventually have to pass in order

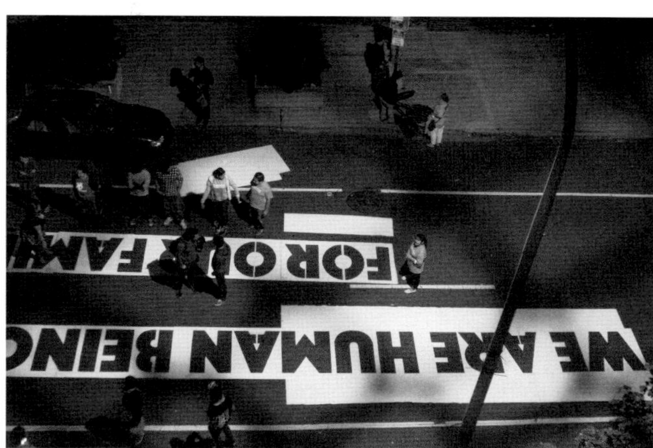

Fig. 2. Michelle Angela Ortiz, "*Somos Seres Humanos*" ("We are human beings"), 2015, from the *Familias Separadas* (Separated families) project, 2015– . Cut stencil and chalk spray on asphalt, 90 feet (2743.2 cm)

to continue their detention in centers such as Berks.[4]

As an artist who often works in public space, Ortiz is interested in how such spaces change in meaning under specific social and political conditions. Her murals, often begun as collaborations with neighborhood communities, include "*Nuestro Andar Florece*" ("Our journey begins") (2016), made with Federico Zuvire to honor Mexican women immigrants living in Brooklyn, and "*Somos Regla*" ("We are Regla") (2016), a public art project in Havana, Cuba among a mostly Afro-Cuban community, made with the Meridian International Center. *Familias Separadas* included public art works created mostly on the ground, including "*Eres Mi Todo*" ("You're my everything") (2015), in the courtyard of the Compass Rose, Philadelphia City Hall, as well as "*Te Amo*" ("I love you") (2015) and "*Se Siente El Miedo*" ("You feel the fear") (2015), respectively at Philadelphia's Love Park and 9th Street outdoor market. Like the work placed on the street in front of the ICE building, these works were staged at sites open to everyone, including those who might be subject to the politics of immigration law. "*Eres Mi Todo*" drew from an interview Ortiz conducted with a woman named Maria whose husband had been deported. The location at the Compass Rose put the work in conversation with prominent public sites—City Hall, and the statue of the colonist and Quaker politician William Penn, the city's founder. Ortiz chose the location for precisely these intersections: "What does Maria's story mean in the context of all these symbols of liberty and freedom?"[5] In presenting the work here, Ortiz fulfills what she sees as her social responsibility as an artist, using tactics such as street art (often made horizontally on the pavement), murals, and, later, billboards and bus-shelter signs to site her work in areas where anyone can participate in the visual conversation.[6]

Ortiz's public-art practice also questions the role of the monument in memorial landscapes, drawing attention to whose histories and experiences it is that are preserved in public spaces. The choice to install her murals and collaborative artworks in highly trafficked areas is driven by an understanding of the political power of public space. In the United States, individuals have rights of speech and assembly to protest for political and social causes. But Ortiz has also described her struggle to develop a practice whose material draws from the very real, lived experiences of vulnerable communities. She explains, "I take it with a lot of care because this is their story. I need to make sure that they are 100 percent on board on how their story is being told, how their images are going to be seen, who is seeing these images."[7] For similar reasons, Ortiz often includes resources for those viewers of her public works who are moved into taking action. In her collaboration with Juntos, for example, she often directs visitors to time-lapse videos showing how collaboration played a role in both the inspiration and the installation of the piece (she almost always stages her large-scale pieces with the help of volunteers).

Installing a site-specific work such as "*Somos Seres Humanos*" in a location such as the ICA, located on Boston's busy harbor, invites a reflection on the pathways that connect notions of place. Ortiz recalls that Ana crossed many borders to arrive in the United States as an immigrant fighting for her family, in much the same way that those who traveled through and to Boston over the city's long history may have crossed the waters outside the present-day port.[8] For Ortiz, this has a powerful resonance, even as all migration experiences cannot and should not be conflated. Rather, Ortiz's mural and community-art practice carries out the ongoing work of bringing change: "If we see ourselves as a thread in the larger fabric of change in our country, we see the purpose in our work."[9] —AP

1. Michelle Angela Ortiz, in an interview with the author, December 7, 2018.

2. Ibid.

3. Ibid.

4. Ibid.

5. Ibid.

6. These Philadelphia murals were part of the first phase of the *Familias Separadas* project, featured in the Mural Arts Program's Open Source city-wide exhibition in 2015.

7. Ortiz, in Paul Farber, "Episode 05: Michelle Angela Ortiz," Monument Lab podcast, 2018. Available online at http://monumentlab.com/podcast-1/2018/10/28/episode-05-michelle-angela-ortiz-artist-sy7b9?rq=ortiz (accessed January 21, 2019).

8. Ortiz, interview with the author.

9. Ibid.

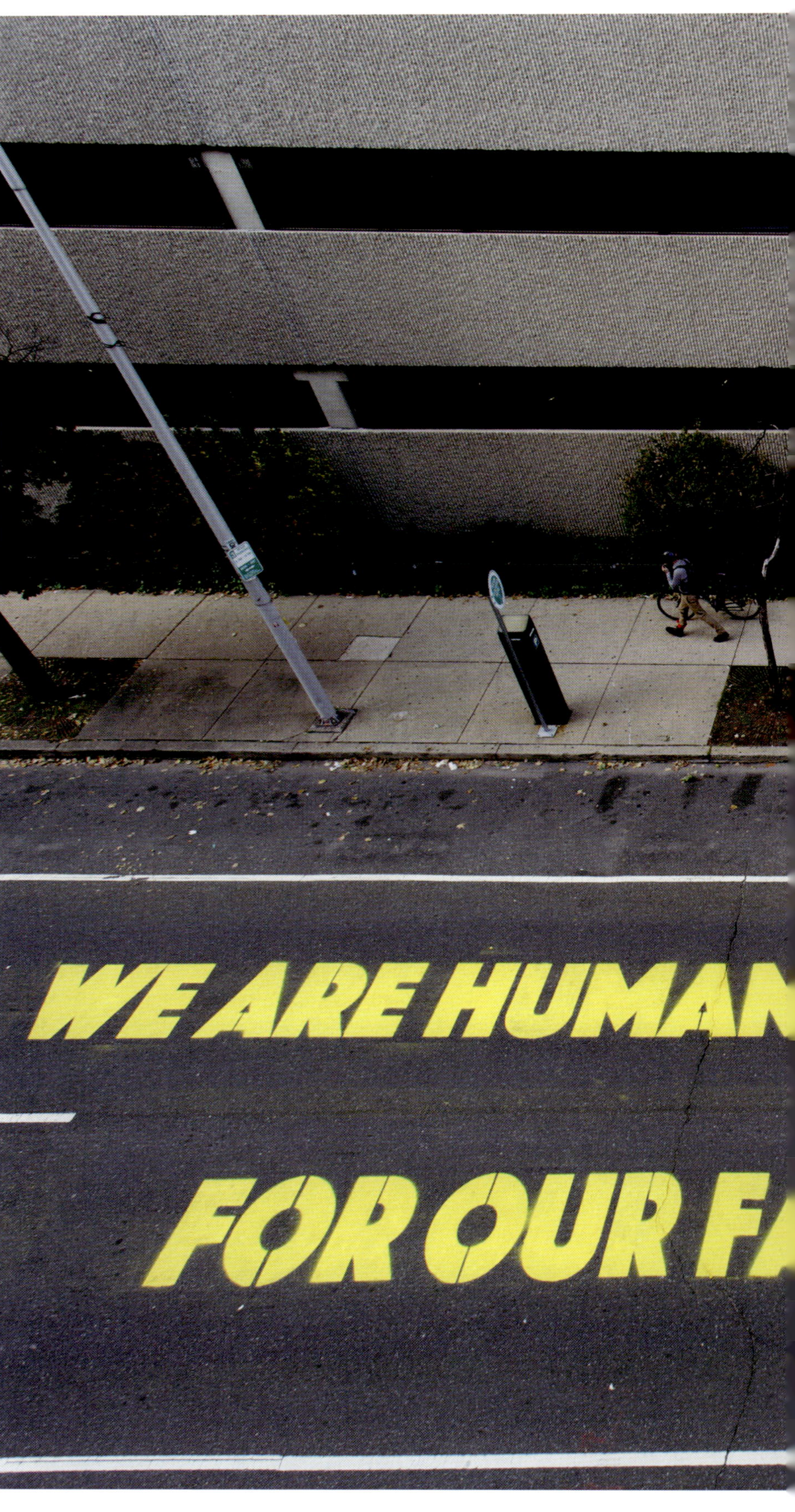

Michelle Angela Ortiz, *"Somos Seres Humanos"* ("We are human beings"), 2015, from the *Familias Separadas* (Separated families) project, 2015– . Cut stencil and chalk spray on asphalt. 90 feet (2743.2 cm) wide. Site-specific installation, Immigration and Customs Enforcement Agency, Philadelphia, PA

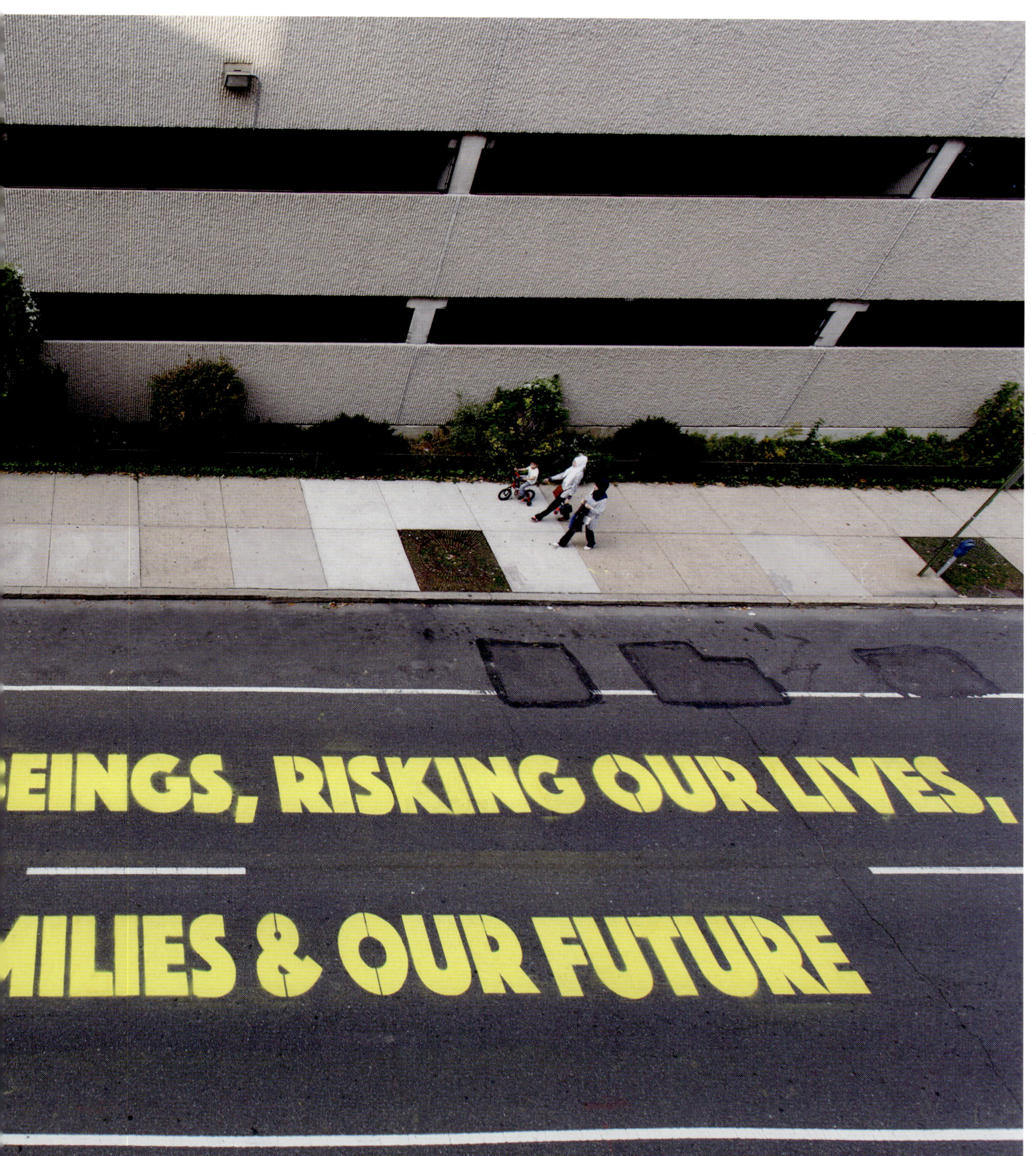
EINGS, RISKING OUR LIVES,
MILIES & OUR FUTURE

Yinka Shonibare CBE

B. 1962, London, United Kingdom;
lives and works in London

Yinka Shonibare CBE's practice encompasses the expansive hybridity of a globalized world. His sculptures, installations, and film and video works focus not on an idyllic representation of post-colonial multiculturalism but on the ambiguities, fissures, and erasures that such narratives reinforce. In *The American Library* (2018) [pp. 156–59], Shonibare enfolds these shifting cultural registers in an installation of over 6,000 books wrapped in brightly colored Dutch wax print fabric.[1] Their spines bear the names of first- and second-generation immigrants to the United States, and of descendants of some of those who moved from the South to the North or West in the country's Great Migration in the first half of the twentieth century. All those named have made a mark on American culture; they include writers ranging from W. E. B. Du Bois to Grace Lee Boggs, Toni Morrison, and Teju Cole, artists such as Ana Mendieta, and the Apple innovator Steve Jobs. The names listed in *The American Library* span occupation, race, gender, class, and politics, recasting how ideas of the "other," the "citizen," and even "home" or "nation" acquire their complex meanings.

Born in Britain but raised in Lagos, Nigeria, Shonibare is known for his use of Dutch wax-print fabric, a mill-printed derivative of patterned batik cloth that has become synonymous with West African fashion. In fact, these prints were introduced to the region in the nineteenth century through colonial-era trade with English and Dutch merchants, who acquired vibrantly patterned batik cloth from Indonesia and went on to mass-produce similar designs in Europe for sale in West African colonies. Today, Shonibare purchases Dutch wax-print cloth in bulk from London markets and uses it to fabricate brightly theatrical works ranging from mannequins in colonial-era costumes to wrapped objects such as the books in *The American Library*. He makes no attempt to trace a literal history of the material; rather, he enjoys its connotations of inauthenticity and stereotype: "I like the fact that the fabrics are multilayered. They have this interesting history that goes back to Indonesia. And then they're appropriated by Africa and now represent African identities. Things are not always what they seem.... I enjoy working with that."[2]

Shonibare believes that to be an artist, "you have to know how to fabricate, how to weave tales, how to tell lies, because you're taking your audience to a nonexistent space and telling them that it does exist."[3] *The American Library* follows his earlier work *The British Library* (2014), which similarly featured significant contributors to British cultural history, including Mick Jagger, George Frideric Handel, Anish Kapoor, Kazuo Ishiguro, and Helen Mirren. Both works cater to the promise of multicultural ingenuity, even inviting visitors to add their own stories of immigration through interactive media stations. Yet Shonibare's selection for *The American Library* of more controversial figures, such as politicians Barack Obama and Donald Trump, as well as his use of Dutch wax fabric—a colonialist trade good—suggests an ultimately ambiguous perspective on narratives of national history and their instability. This timely installation may also offer a visual critique of how public discourses on immigration often center on what immigrants can offer a host nation. The names included in both *The British Library* and *The American Library* may make us question who may be entered into such archives, if inclusion is based solely on subjective ideas of contribution and value, an oversimplification that can be politically dangerous. In bringing these complexities to the forefront, but without insisting on any definitive readings, Shonibare asks how these rhetorical frameworks shape our ideas of who is valued in national histories, as well as how these valuations change.

As an installation, *The American Library* categorizes national culture in much the same way that museums institutionalize national history. Many of the first public museums were national museums, or collections amassed by state or monarchical authorities as a kind of official record of state history. In many cases they incorporated natural and ethnographic spoils of colonial-era expeditions. These institutions, including the Smithsonian Institution in Washington, DC, and the British Museum in London, established public collections that served both to organize the way national histories were preserved and to discipline the audiences for whom they were presented. *The British Library* and *The American Library* utilize the taxonomic and encyclopedic grammar of national collections, individuating each object by the name of the "author." Yet in printing these names on Dutch wax fabric—itself as much a colonialist invention as the museum—Shonibare weaves artifice with archive, calling attention to how we reconcile state and personal histories in the ongoing work of building a nation.

Shonibare has said that he makes art "about power, the so-called establishment," and the way our social, political, and economic institutions confront us with their inherent and ultimately transparent contradictions.[4] If contradiction is one element of Shonibare's work, then juxtaposition becomes a necessarily enriching device. In his sculptural practice, Shonibare often creates headless mannequins outfitted in Western garb cut from batik cloth. He sometimes positions these robed figures in unusual, graphic, and exaggerated poses, as in *Gallantry and Criminal Conversation* (2002) [fig. 1], an installation of five "scenes" staged as a fantastical evocation of the experience of the Grand Tour, a popular sojourn among wealthy Europeans in the eighteenth century. In *Scramble for Africa* (2003) [fig. 2], Shonibare reimagines the Berlin Conference of 1884–85 as a dinner conversation wherein European colonial powers, all robed in Dutch wax cloth, dissect the African continent between the imperial states of Belgium, Germany, France, Britain, and others. These works, which involve incisive, tongue-in-cheek critiques of empire, might contrast with the fantasy of multicultural inclusion embodied in *The American Library*, but cautious ironies remain. While no costumed mannequins appear in *The American Library*, the work nonetheless dresses its contributors as collectible cultural volumes, conveying little about whose library this accumulative collection might constitute.

Shonibare's interest in the cinematic, the decadent, and the excessive conflates ideas of class, difference, and power through playful yet graphic interjections. Uninterested in didactic messaging, his art instead works as a subversion of and through fantasy: "As a black person in this context, I can create fantasies of empowerment in relation to white society, even if historically that equilibrium or equality really hasn't arrived yet.... This is something that art is able to do quite well, because it's a space of transformation, where you can go beyond the ordinary."[5] *The American Library* is seemingly boundless in its imaginative projection of a nation of immigrants, yet foregrounds how these complexly entangled ideas of the nation, the archive, and collective memory continue to affect these same histories.
—AP

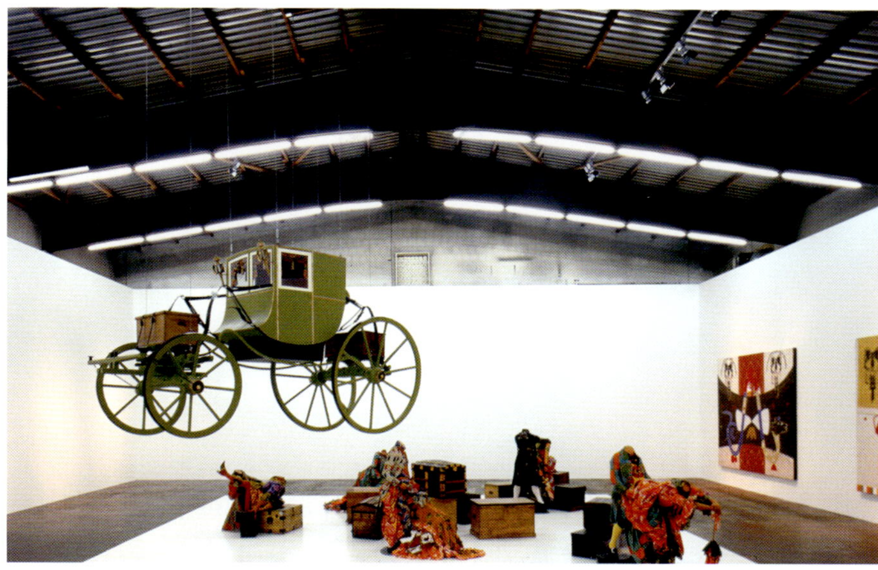

Fig. 1. Yinka Shonibare CBE, *Gallantry and Criminal Conversation*, 2002.
Installation view, documenta 11, Kassel, Germany, 2002

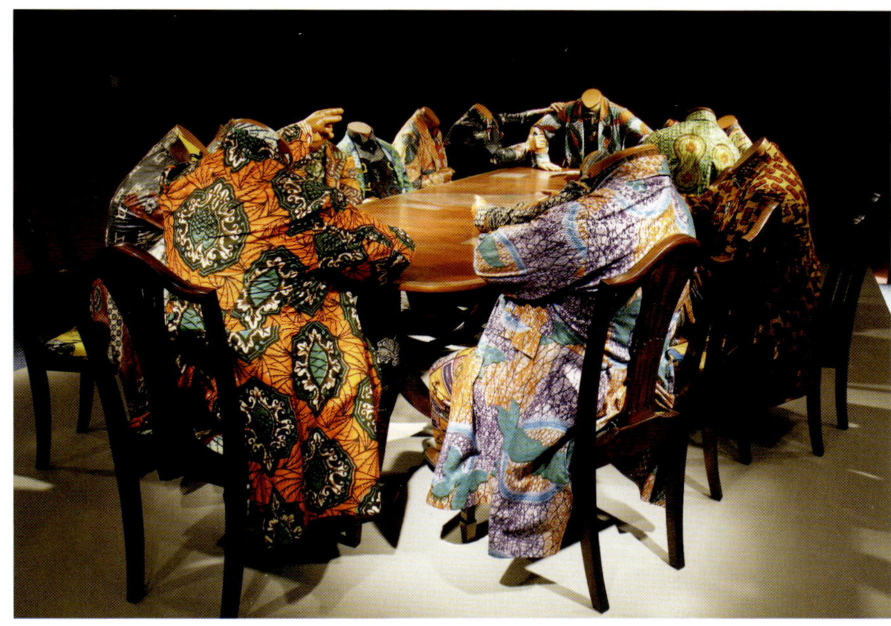

Fig. 2. Yinka Shonibare CBE, *Scramble for Africa*, 2003.
Fourteen life-size fiberglass mannequins, fourteen chairs, table, and Dutch wax-printed cotton, 52 inches x 16 feet ⅛ inches x 9 feet 2¼ inches (132.1 x 488 x 280 cm).
Guggenheim Abu Dhabi

1. *The American Library* was co-commissioned by Front International: Cleveland Triennial for Contemporary Art, VIA Art Fund, and James Cohan Gallery, New York.

2. See Art21, "Yinka Shonibare MBE (RA) in 'Transformation,'" 2009. Available online at https://art21.org/watch/art-in-the-twenty-first-century/s5/yinka-shonibare-mbe-in-transformation-segment (accessed December 23, 2018).

3. Yinka Shonibare, in Anthony Downey, "Yinka Shonibare by Anthony Downey," *Bomb* 146 (Winter 2019). Available online at https://bombmagazine.org/articles/yinka-shonibare/ (accessed December 23, 2018).

4. Ibid.

5. Ibid.

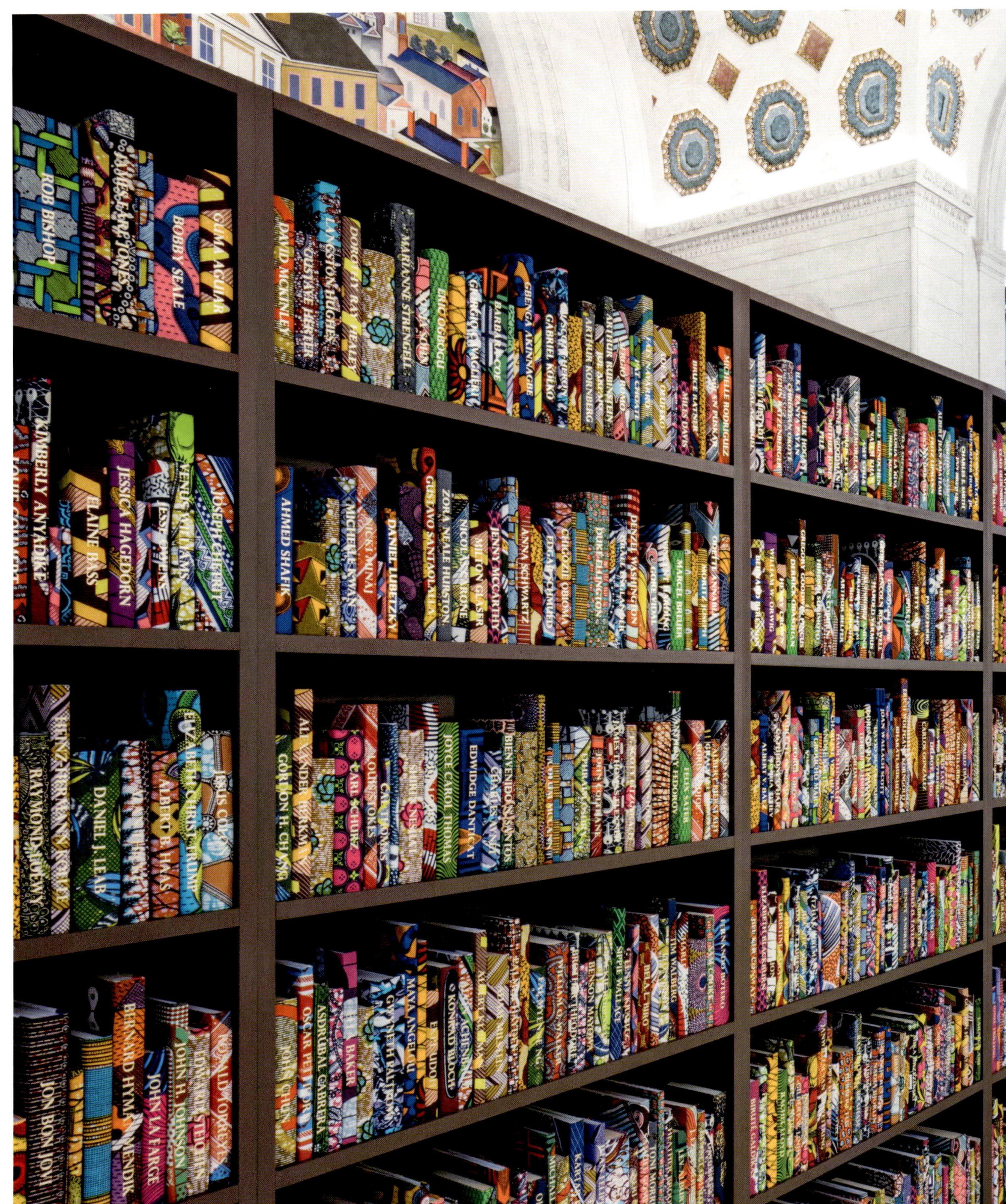
ROB BISHOP
BOBBY SEALE
DAVID MCKINLEY
MARIANNE STRENGELL
GABRIEL KOLKO
ARTHUR KORNBERG
MICHELLE RODRIGUEZ
KIMBERLY ANYADIKE
ELAINE BASS
JESSICA HAGEDORN
VENUS WILLIAMS
AHMED SHAFIK
MICHEL KHAN
DANIEL LUBETZKY
GUSTAVO SANTAOLALLA
ZORA NEALE HURSTON
ANNA SCHWARTZ
DENZEL WASHINGTON
MARCEL BREUER
RAYMOND LOEWY
DANIEL J LEAB
ALBERT E HAAS
GORDON H. CHANG
EDWIDGE DANTICAT
OSCAR PELLIGRINO
ADRIBAL GARBER
MAYA ANGELOU
JON BON JOVI
BERNARD HYMAN
JOHN LA FARGE
JOHN H. JOHNSON

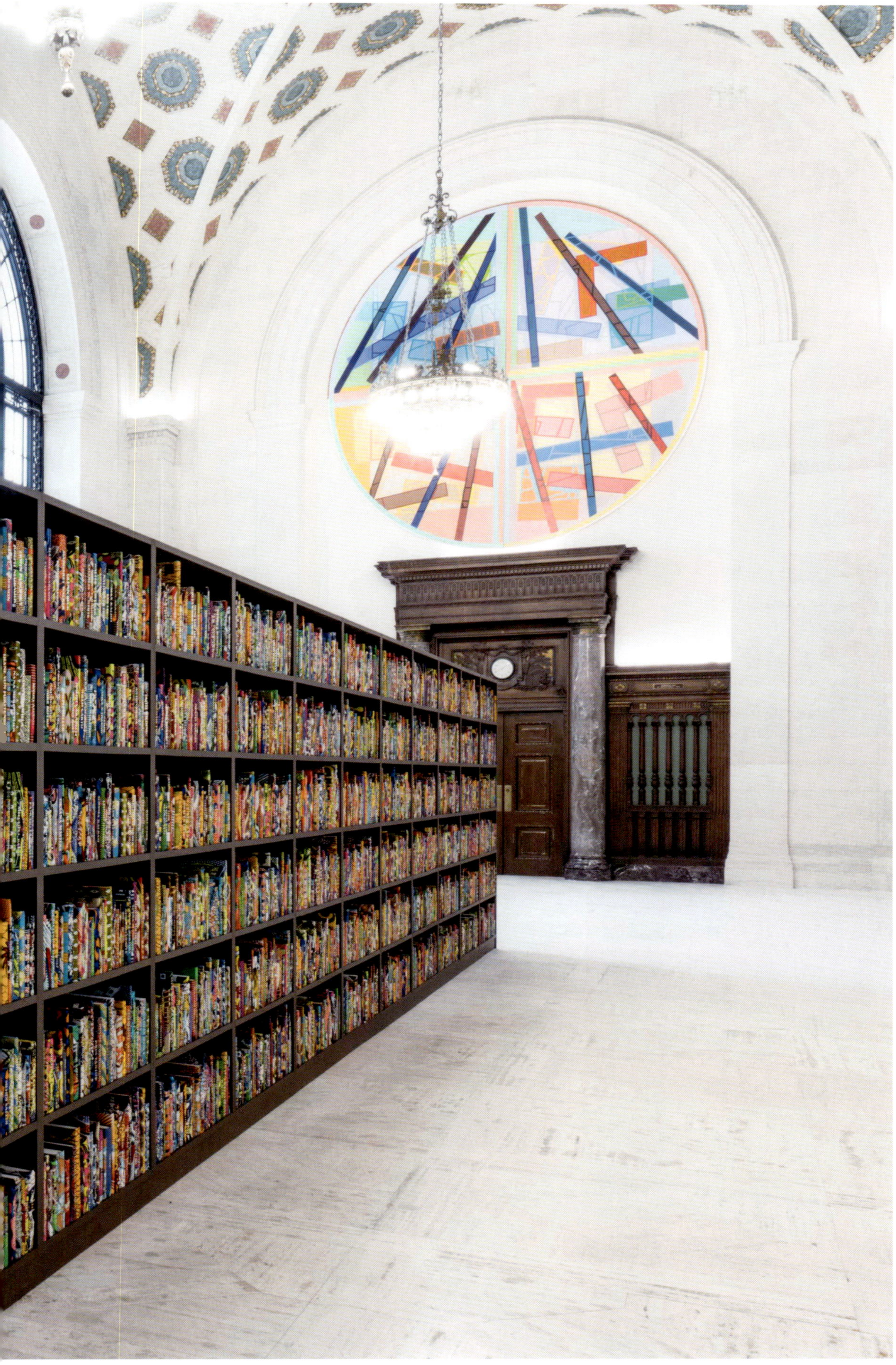

Previous spread and opposite (detail):
Yinka Shonibare CBE, *The American Library*, 2018.
Hardback books, Dutch wax-printed cotton textile, gold-foiled names, and website.
Dimensions variable. Installation view, FRONT International, Cleveland, Ohio, 2018

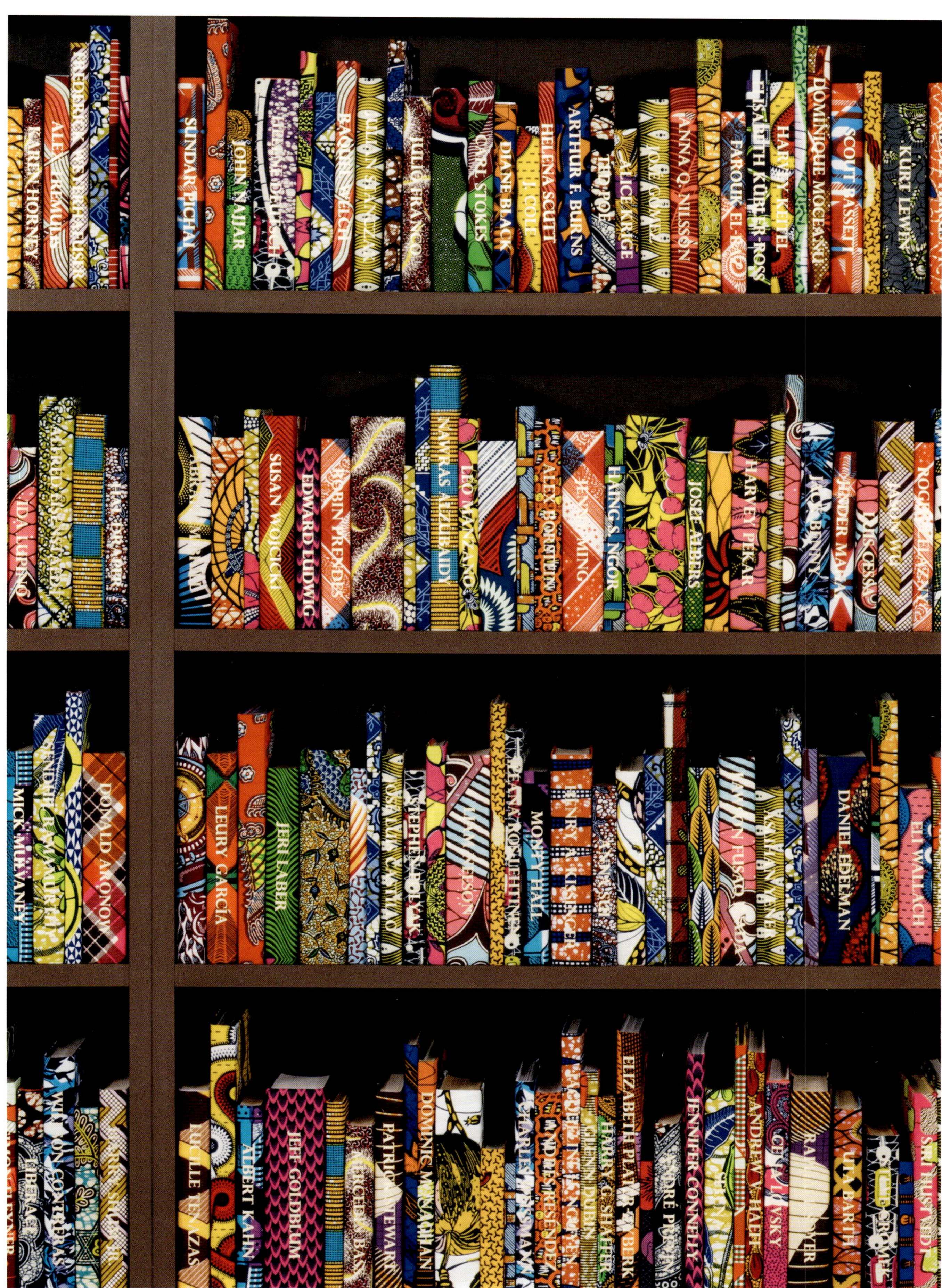
SUNDAR PICHAI
JOHN NAJJAR
JULIO FRANCO
CARL STOKES
DIANE BLACK
HELENA SCOTT
ARTHUR F. BURNS
ALICE KRIGE
ANNA Q. NILSSON
DOMINIQUE MOCEANU
SUSAN WOJCICKI
EDWARD LUDWIG
HARVEY PEKAR
MICK MULVANEY
DONALD ARONOW
LEURY GARCÍA
JERI LABER
MONTY HALL
HENRY A. KISSINGER
DANIEL EDELMAN
ELI WALLACH
ALBERT KAHN
JEFF GOLDBLUM
DOMINIC MONAGHAN
JENNIFER CONNELLY

Essays

Waiting to Go

Aruna D'Souza

Appalled....
The Dead Sea was pale blue....
We've no rights anymore....
The truth of the first water....
My clothes dried in the sun....
Where he lived it was warm it was dry....
Everything oozes....
To all mankind were addressed those cries for help....
What do we do now.... Wait....
He does nothing sir....
And if he comes tomorrow.... We'll be saved.

—Samuel Beckett, *Waiting for Godot*, 1952[1]

In 2007, in the wake of Hurricane Katrina's devastation of New Orleans in 2005—and, more tragically, in the wake of the failure of the U.S. government to prevent the devastation, and of national, state, and local governments to mitigate the suffering that the storm caused, and of the free rein given to corporations to exploit these regions in the name of "rebuilding"—the artist Paul Chan staged Beckett's *Waiting for Godot* in the city. The play took place on a street corner in the impoverished and still ravaged Ninth Ward, and then again in the middle-class neighborhood of Gentilly. Chan was inspired, he said, by the landscape, how eerily it echoed every production of the play he'd ever seen—a setting Beckett described tersely as "A country road. A tree. Evening."

Chan's *Waiting for Godot in New Orleans* (2007) [figs. 1–2] cannot be reduced to the production of a play, mind: it was, on the contrary, a many-tentacled form of social practice, fueled by a commitment to political activism and grassroots organizing. The artist moved to New Orleans for four months, as did his production team and members of the Classical Theatre of Harlem; they taught free and open classes at local universities, worked with schools and community groups, met with organizers and individuals, hosted potlucks for local residents, and listened. The goal was not simply to stage a play, but to see if by staging a play an artist could produce something meaningful in a place that had become a ground zero of disaster capitalism, a place that people pointed to as a sign of the failure of civil society, a place into which many had parachuted to demonstrate their social-justice cred without making meaningful change. As Chan put it, "The organizing involved in doing this project not only went into the actual production of the play, but also the production of a public, a public that is incredibly divided and tired and waiting still for things to come."[2]

Robert Green, a Ninth Ward resident who had ridden out the hurricane on the roof of his home with his three granddaughters, his brother, a cousin, and his mother, losing one of his granddaughters to the water and his mother shortly after, spoke to the perpetual waiting that marked a post-Katrina New Orleans: "Everybody knows about waiting. Whether you are waiting for FEMA [the Federal Emergency Management Agency] to call you, or for The Road Home to call you, or for the Red Cross to give you an appointment three months down the line, everybody knows about waiting."[3] And the writer Kalamu ya Salaam gives a sense of what creating a public organized around the forced entropic condition might be, might always have been:

> Sometimes when it looks like we are doing nothing but waiting on the corners, sitting quietly on a well-worn kitchen chair sipping a beer in the early afternoon shade, holding court on one of the many neutral grounds, i.e. medians, that separate the lanes of major streets and avenues around Central City, sometimes those blank stares you see at a bus stop are not what you think it is.
>
> We are not waiting for the arrival of a messiah or for a government handout. We expect nothing from our immediate future but more of the past.[4]

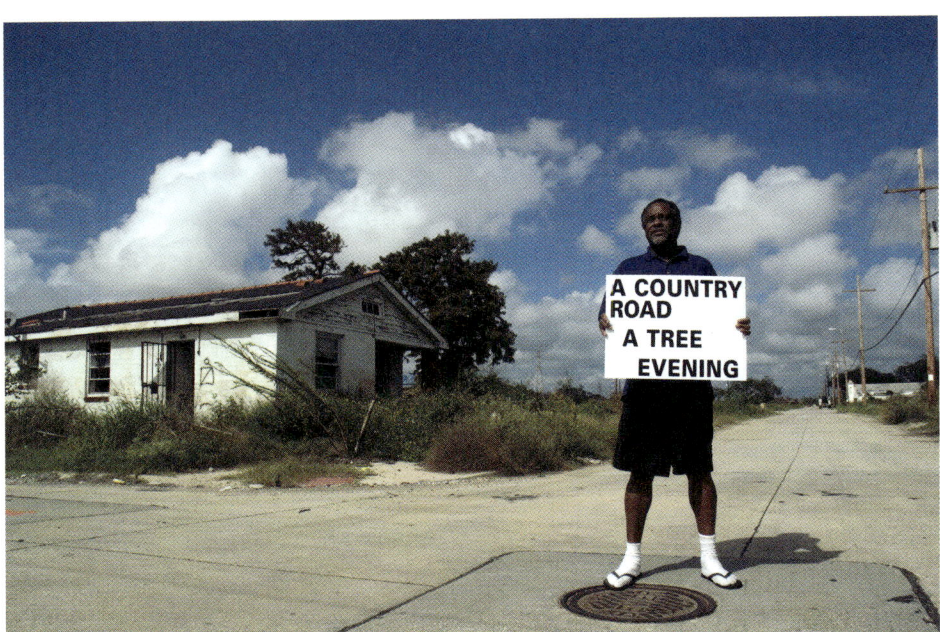

Fig 1. Paul Chan, *Waiting for Godot in New Orleans* (performance view), 2007

In the weeks leading up to the 2018 midterm elections, Donald Trump, a president fearing the loss of his party's control of both branches of Congress, whipped his base of supporters into a frenzy about a so-called "migrant caravan" about to invade the United States. In tweets and public statements, he spoke of these people as hordes, an imminent threat, even going so far as to deploy troops to the Mexican border. This latter act, especially, was a nauseatingly cynical piece of political theater, turning his metaphors of "war against illegal immigration" into an actual military operation.

Trump's rhetoric was, not surprisingly, entirely at odds with the reality of this caravan, which was traveling on foot from Central America, along the way picking up itinerants who sought safety in numbers on the perilous journey from south to north, from countries ravaged for years by ill-considered interventionist policies to the nation that was the primary source of those interventions. As Trump spoke of bracing for the onslaught, the migrants were not rushing the barricades; they were weeks, perhaps even months, from the border. The relative speeds of Trump's xenophobic hysteria and the migrants' slow progress were tragicomically out of sync.

And when they got to the border in December, what would these migrants do? They did not cross illegally, for the most part. Instead, they did what they were, by international and U.S. law, perfectly entitled to do: they waited in lines, endlessly long lines, lines that might take months and years to shorten, to apply for asylum. It was then, while they waited, that what had been political theater turned into something unbearably real: it was then that U.S. forces began teargassing these migrants legally seeking refuge. It was then that the border became a war front, at least for one side of the equation; for the other side, it became a place to endure, to survive—if only because what was back home was even worse.

It is common to think of borders as geographical boundaries. But borders are much more conceptual than that. Yes, in some cases they consist of a line drawn in the sand, or a checkpoint, or a wall, but they also consist of a waiting room in an airport, or a waiting room in a government building, or a waiting room in a foreign embassy. They consist of children's detention centers and ICE-issued ankle monitors, of visa requirements and travel bans, of troop buildups. It is common to think of borders as pathways for movement, as liminal sites. But borders are more commonly sites of stoppage and stasis and containment and incarceration. We have gotten well past the 1990s fantasy of a globalized utopia, a borderless world—we know now (perhaps always did) that that delusion involved enabling capital to skate across a flat earth unimpeded while people were to be increasingly constrained in their place. The borders for things are different from the borders for people—the former have been torn down while the latter have, increasingly, been fortified, militarized, thickened, lengthened, multiplied.

And so, in front of these barriers, visible and barely so, migrants wait.

\- - - - - - - -

A few days after I sat down to write this essay, the illustrator Molly Crabapple wrote the following words in *The New York Review of Books* to accompany her sketches of one of these conceptual borders, a room in which asylum hearings were being conducted at the Varick Street Immigration Court, New York:

> To be an immigrant in America is to wait. This goes double for the millions of immigrants who have found themselves at

> the sour end of the Immigrations and Customs Enforcement (ICE) bureaucracy—and triple in the age of Trump. If you are an immigrant in the process of deportation proceedings, you must wait for your Master Calendar, on which a bureaucrat will assign you to a check-in date several months into the future. At this check-in, you may win several more months of anxious waiting—or disappear into a detention center, where you will wait for a one-way plane ride to a country you may no longer know. And if, for instance, your paperwork is straight but, twenty years ago, you jumped a turnstile or got into a bar fight, then ICE has a mandate to hunt you down. Once snatched, you, too, will wait in a detention center, losing your job, your apartment, and possibly your health, while the months pass until a judge grants you a bond hearing. Then, you will appear in court—in chains or via video link—and learn how many thousands of dollars your family must pay for you to have the privilege of waiting outside a cage.[5]

The limbo Crabapple describes is similar for asylum seekers in Calais, in Lesbos, in Cox's Bazar, in Nauru.... Google "refugees" and "waiting" and you will find an endless string of results, describing situations in many different regions and over many years but using identical language. The bureaucratic details may differ, the conditions in which one waits may vary, but the waiting is the same. Immigration as immobilization. Immigration as a forced lingering.

It is becoming increasingly clear that waiting is a form of violence—the bureaucratic equivalent to so many state-sponsored forms of literal violence. Trump's troops did not need to teargas those asylum seekers; many would soon have succumbed (and might still) to the poverty, malnutrition, disease, and despair experienced by migrants around the world. The tear gas was simply a convenient visual iconography for Trump's war on immigrants, a more camera-ready substitute for what has become the neoliberal state's preferred method of dealing with migrants, the poor, the *inconvenient* (most easily categorized under the rubric "brown and black," if we're being honest): delay, red tape, lines, background checks, quotas, restrictions of all kinds. To people for whom "Wait your turn" more often means "We'll wait until you die, either here or at the hands of what awaits you from whence you came," the consequences do not change when the means of execution does.[6]

\- - - - - - - -

It is not beside the point that the visual materializations of Trump's war on immigrants—those teargas canisters—were manufactured by The Safariland Group, the chairman of whose parent company is also the vice-chair of the Board of Trustees of the Whitney Museum of American Art.[7] The art world is constructed to depend on capital, no matter its source. (There is no clean money.)

It is not beside the point that the vast majority of those artists, curators, and art critics we know who travel to biennials and exhibitions around the world—Venice, São Paulo, Istanbul, Miami, Basel, Karlsruhe, Gwangju, Kochi, and so on—are the privileged ones, the ones who travel on favored passports, the ones who are not impeded by visa restrictions and travel bans. That art world is constructed according to the rules and (lack of) restrictions on capital, not people. (None of us is unimplicated.)

- - - - - - - -

At the many sites of waiting that have been produced by inhumane foreign-policy decisions, capitalist greed, economic injustice, colonial and postcolonial forms of violence, racism, xenophobia, and so on (Flint, Michigan, has been waiting for clean water for 1,748 days at the time of writing), people wait for something to happen. But one of the devastating implications of Beckett's play—written in the aftermath of World War II and of Europe's first experiment with fascism on a massive scale—is the very question of what, exactly, that means. Terry Eagleton writes of Godot's world-in-abeyance,

> Everything in this post-Auschwitz world is ambiguous and indeterminate, which makes it hard to understand why sheer physical pain should be so brutally persistent. As far as indeterminacy goes, it is not just that nothing much happens, but that it is hard to be sure whether anything is happening or not, or what would count as an event. Is waiting doing something, or the suspension of it?[8]

Beckett might have seen such endless deferment as a fact of human existence itself—the most we can expect, now that we know the full horror of which we as a species are capable. But now that waiting—for Godot, for survival—has been weaponized by the capitalist state, how to imagine a politics that counters it?

- - - - - - - -

Samuel Beckett (A country road, a tree, evening, 1953):

> ESTRAGON: I can't go on like this.
>
> VLADIMIR: That's what you think.
>
> ESTRAGON: If we parted? That might be better for us.
>
> VLADIMIR: We'll hang ourselves tomorrow. (Pause.) Unless Godot comes.
>
> ESTRAGON: And if he comes?

VLADIMIR: We'll be saved.

Vladimir takes off his hat (Lucky's), peers inside it, feels about inside it, shakes it, knocks on the crown, puts it on again.

ESTRAGON: Well? Shall we go?

VLADIMIR: Pull on your trousers.

ESTRAGON: What?

VLADIMIR: Pull on your trousers.

ESTRAGON: You want me to pull off my trousers?

VLADIMIR: Pull on your trousers.

ESTRAGON: *(realizing his trousers are down)* True.

He pulls up his trousers.

VLADIMIR: Well? Shall we go?

ESTRAGON: Yes, let's go.

They do not move.
Curtain.[9]

Kalamu ya Salaam (New Orleans, 2007):

We expect nothing from our immediate future but more of the past.[10]

Zakya Daoud (Gibraltar, 2002):

Everything is hiatus.[11]

– – – – – – – –

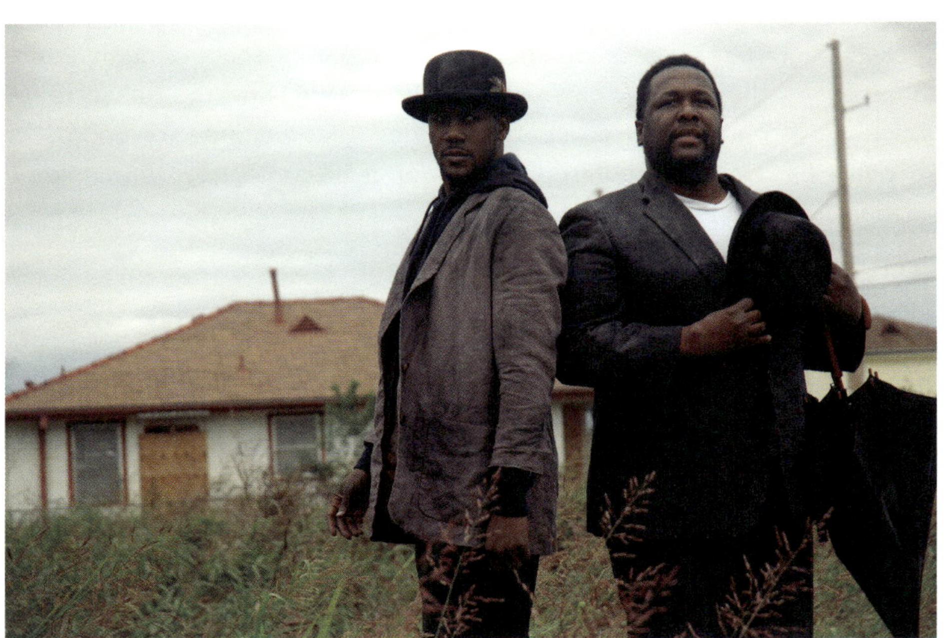

Fig 2. Paul Chan, *Waiting for Godot in New Orleans* (performance view), 2007

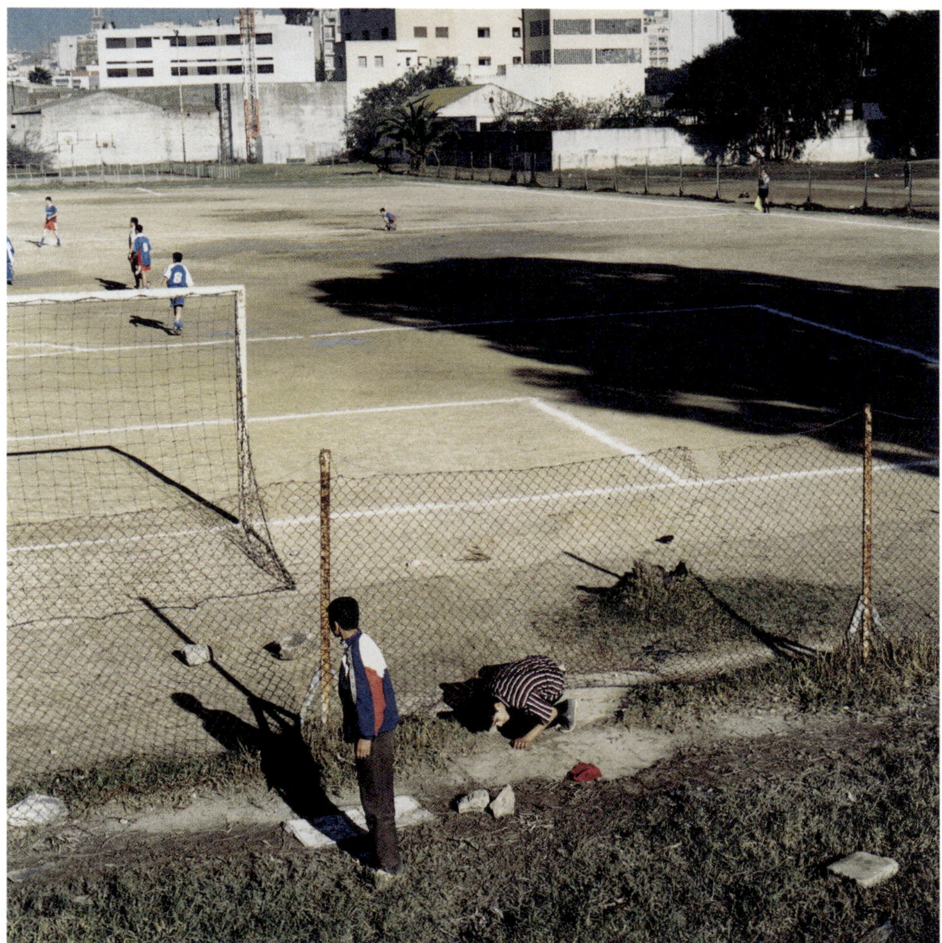

Fig. 3. Yto Barrada, *Trou dans le grillage—Tanger 2003 [Hole in the fence—Tangier 2003]*, 2003, from the series A Life Full of Holes: The Strait Project, 1998–2003. Chromogenic color print, 31 ½ x 31 ½ inches (80 x 80 cm)

In one work from Yto Barrada's photographic project A Life Full of Holes: The Strait Project (1998–2003), the marks left by a soccer ball repeatedly kicked against a whitewashed surface are an index of the migrant's time. So is a small boy stopped on the street, viewed from above, a toy boat occluding his head, with no water in sight—all we see is concrete (street, sidewalk) rising up to the top edge of the image. And likewise another boy, looking through a chain-link fence, transfixed by a soccer game going on at the upper edge of the photograph; nearby, his friend, crawling through a small opening at the bottom of the fence, is eerily still, holding his crouched pose, neither coming nor going [fig. 3]. So too the sheep that loll about on the grass in front of a concrete apartment building. Or, with less humor, more pathos, the two children, seen only in silhouette, who plaster themselves against a light box advertisement of a ferry on the sea.

These images of Tangier—a city just ten miles from Spain across the Strait of Gibraltar, the site of departure for many African migrants who dream of escape to Europe, the site of not a few disappointments for those unable to make the journey—show people for whom waiting is a way of life. Barrada describes her vision of her hometown as "a kind of Beckettian waiting-room, a jumping-off place for thousands of hopes," in which the condition of the refugee is not only experienced by those who leave but also by those who wait:

> People are standing there thinking all day how you're going to make enough money to be able to cross, to pay your passage through. That state that I've described in my body of work creates a sort of floating figure...as a consequence of spending your time on the edge, on the jumping-off place of Africa, trying to get to the other side, you are turning your back on whatever is happening where you are.[12]

Until 1991, Moroccans with a passport could travel freely to Europe—their movement, like those of the thousands of European travelers who make the reverse journey as tourists, was unrestricted. That is no longer the case. What does it mean for a generation, now two, to see themselves as would-be immigrants, these photos ask. "The would-be immigrant forges a collective identity here, by dint of being legally obstructed from crossing the Strait," Barrada writes. "This obstacle is not without consequences—this position is one of dispossession and indignity."[13]

It is not a coincidence, I think, that so few of Barrada's images in this series show the sky. When they do, it is sometimes seen through the rust holes of a shipping container as a blue archipelago—a strange, accidental map in which what contains us is the ocean and what we dream of is the ether.

Kader Attia's light box-mounted photographs of *les rochers carrés* [pp. 96–97], a beach near Algiers, are dominated by skies, cloudy pale gray and blinding azure by turns. The beach is filled with massive concrete blocks, three and four yards high, put there to make it untenable as a landing spot—to make it difficult, in other words, for people to take illegal boat trips across the Mediterranean. This does not prevent the young men pictured in Attia's images from dreaming of leaving. They go to *les rochers carrés* to loiter—to smoke, to socialize, maybe to sell themselves. We see them, almost always, from behind—they turn away from us and toward the water, toward the massive ships visible in the distance. Those ships carry the goods and things that are given free passage, while they, these boys, stay in place. The longing is palpable here—as with Caspar David Friedrich's *Woman at a Window* (1822), we share their romantic visions of escape.

But what, exactly, is the reality on the other side of the dream? The concrete barriers are jumbled together like the ruins of a demolished fortress, or, perhaps as trenchantly, of the decrepit urban architecture that they will find in the Paris banlieues. What waits for these boys and young men on the other side of that ocean is more of the same; Attia knows this from experience, having made the same journey from here to there and back again. "The hard existence of these young Algerian people reminds me of that experienced by young people in the French banlieues," Attia writes. "The same lack of hope in the future, same sexual misery, same frustration, same lack of social acknowledgement, same feeling of failure and same suffering."[14]

"We expect nothing from our immediate future but more of the past." Or, perhaps: the only escape is revolution.

\- - - - - - - -

> Let us not waste our time in idle discourse! (*Pause. Vehemently.*) Let us do something, while we have the chance! It is not every day that we are needed. Not indeed that we personally are needed. Others would meet the case equally well, if not better. To all mankind they were addressed, those cries for help still ringing in our ears! But at this place, at this moment of time, all mankind is us, whether we like it or not. Let us make the most of it, before it is too late! Let us represent worthily for once the foul brood to which a cruel fate consigned us! What do you say?[15]

The only escape is revolution. And yet the question, as ever, is what to do, now that we recognize that Penelope represented the migrant's condition as much as Odysseus ever did? Even she, who was forced to unravel her loom every night she waited for her deliverance, had no image of what she endured, and for how long, and at what expense.[16] For everyone who is forced to leave, there is someone who is forced to stay. Their time, too, must be accounted for.

But let us not waste our time in idle discourse! Let us do something.

\- - - - - - - -

1. Lines from Samuel Beckett's play *Waiting for Godot* (1952), quoted and arranged by Christopher McElroen. See McElroen, "Directing a Post-Katrina *Godot*," in Paul Chan, ed., *Waiting for Godot in New Orleans: A Field Guide* (New York: Creative Time, Inc., 2010), p. 51.

2. Chan, quoted in Nato Thompson, "Destroyer of Worlds," in Chan, ed., *Waiting for Godot in New Orleans*, p. 43.

3. Robert Green, quoted in ibid., p. 42.

4. Kalamu Ya Salaam, "What to do with the negroes?," in Chan, ed., *Waiting for Godot in New Orleans*, p. 13.

5. Molly Crabapple, "Waiting with Immigrants," *NYR Daily*, January 29, 2019. Available online at https://www.nybooks.com/daily/2019/01/29/waiting-with-immigrants/ (accessed February 22, 2019).

6. Giorgio Agamben's notion of the "state of exception" may be useful here: "the state of exception is not defined as a fullness of powers, a pleromatic state of law, as in the dictatorial model, but as a kenomatic state, an emptiness and *standstill of the law*." Emphasis mine. Agamben, *State of Exception*, trans. Kevin Attell (Chicago and London: The University of Chicago Press, 2005), p. 48.

7. See my article "The Recent Protests at the Whitney Show Museum Trustees' Dealings Cannot be Ignored," *Art Newspaper*, December 21, 2018. Available online at www.theartnewspaper.com/comment/museum-trustees-dealings-cannot-be-ignored (accessed February 22, 2019).

8. Terry Eagleton, "Political Beckett?" *New Left Review* 40 (July–August 2006):60.

9. Beckett, *Waiting for Godot: A Tragicomedy in Two Acts* (New York: Grove Press, 1954), p. 110.

10. Salaam, "What to do with the negroes?," p. 13.

11. Zakya Daoud, *Gibraltar croisée de mondes* and *Gibraltar improbable frontière: de Colomb aux clandestines, d'Hercule à Boabdil*, both Paris: Séguier, 2002.

12. Yto Barrada, quoted in Hamza Walker, "Riffs," The Renaissance Society, 2012. Available online at http://renaissancesociety.org/publishing/16/riffs/ (accessed February 23, 2019).

13. Barrada, untitled text on *The Strait Project*, 2005. Available online at https://www.warwickartscentre.co.uk/mead-gallery/previous-exhibitions/2005/yto-barrada-a-life-full-of-holes-the-strait-project/ (accessed February 23, 2019).

14. Kader Attia, "Rochers Carrés, 2008." Available online at http://kaderattia.de/rochers-carres-2/ (accessed February 23, 2019).

15. Beckett, *Waiting for Godot*, p. 90.

16. For this alternative reading of Penelope, I take inspiration from Margaret Atwood's alternative reading of the Odyssey, *The Penelopiad: The Myth of Penelope and Odysseus* (Toronto: Vintage Canada, 2006).

Tebbit's Ghost: Migration and the Conundrum of Belonging

Okwui Enwezor

Introduced
in conversation with
Eva Respini

An early version of "Tebbit's Ghost" appeared in 2005 in *The Manifesta Decade: Debates on Contemporary Art Exhibitions and Biennials in Post-Wall Europe*, edited by Barbara Vanderlinden and Elena Filipovic and published by The MIT Press.[1]
It is republished in this volume with minor updates by the author.
The following interview with Enwezor, conducted by telephone in January 2019 and edited for clarity and length, serves as an introduction to the republished essay.

EVA RESPINI In the opening paragraph of "Tebbit's Ghost," you write, "Europe is in the convulsive throes of a collision of worlds, cultural values, and shifting historical currents." You also reference "political hysteria" over immigration. As I read this in 2019, these words aptly describe our current moment. How do you place your republished essay from fifteen years ago in the context of today? How has the situation of art in an era of migration and nationalism changed, and not changed, in the intervening years?

OKWUI ENWEZOR Without wanting to sound prophetic, it's quite clear that in the last thirty years, since the fall of the Berlin Wall, the demise of the Soviet Union, and increasing demographic shifts across the globe, we have observed communities collapsing and the very model of cosmopolitanism become a model of social negation. We have seen terrible genocidal wars in Rwanda and the former Yugoslavia, and failed states such as Somalia, but we have also witnessed the end of apartheid in South Africa—something to be hopeful about.

What is interesting to me is, the European response to these historical shifts has been twofold: one, there's a response that is euphoric about the creation of new possibilities in Europe through the expansion of the European Union that not only affects Europeans but also other populations: immigrants, minorities, and refugees. On the other hand, there's a response that has to do with immigration, which is related to the collapse of communities and nation-states that I mentioned. How do we deal with such issues, which have not confronted the world on such a scale since the end of World War II?

Reflecting on these questions now, I think it was quite clear when I wrote this text that I was responding to these twofold ideas about change—specifically, the kind of unevenness of experience that Europeans have with immigration, and the willingness to demonize migrants and immigrants in specific contexts in a continent that witnessed the largest group of displaced people and refugees in history. I relate this to a fundamental fear of the other, which in many ways is a kind of anticosmopolitan view of the world. There are several things that the world has not really dealt with: we've had pandemics (diseases in Africa and Asia), we've had ethnic cleansing in many areas of the world, we've had wars of choice (the destruction of Iraq, the war against terror, and the war in Syria), and their repercussions in general global politics are very big, but there's no system in place to actually deal with these issues. Today, demagogues have taken over.

We now see institutions and curators thinking more globally, and about the relationship between roots and routes—the convergence of these two things, of people who are rooted but also people who are uprooted, who are en route, who are going somewhere, and whether that somewhere represents a place of hospitality or hostility, as we saw in Europe in the summer of 2015 and now the daily enactments on the U.S. border spurred on by a cruel demagogic administration. Of course many artists have dealt with these questions in very meaningful and powerful ways.

ER I want to shift to the U.S. context. There is some anxiety, and even desperation, among curators and artists regarding relationships between the work that we do, the work that artists make, and politics, especially given the current administration's conservatism, nationalism, and Donald Trump's self-described "war" on immigration. Although it's been a while since you've lived in the United States, you're a U.S. citizen, and I wonder if you could share some reflections on how the contemporary art world has intersected with the numerous so-called "migrant crises."

OE I think it's an important question. We are not doomed not to try in the curatorial world, but we have to find new strategies of solidarity across our institutions to make things happen so there could be impact. I am a citizen of the United States. I've spent most of the last twenty-five years living in other parts of the world but for some reason I've made it a point to keep a place in the United States. Why? Maybe it has to do with the specificity of not being uprooted, not being a stranger constantly in each iteration in which one moves. This is the challenge that we face: how not to become strangers even in our own homes, simply because of our difference, because of our social formation, gender, and so on.

I'm currently putting together an exhibition that reflects on the second half of the twentieth century. In looking at the period 1960 to 1980, and specifically at the notion of the postcolonial, we see the rise of social movements that were about the decolonization of everyday life—the environmental movement, the antiwar movement, civil rights, feminism, antiracist movements, indigenous movements, gay rights, you can go on and on. Think of all the amazing work that came out of that. Today we should focus more on the extragovernmental strategies of the '60s. A lot can be achieved—it might take a long time but it's needed. I think that curators and artists have a very significant role to play in that.

The preoccupation with diversity in the United States is really great, and I think more diverse programs will also give them a spirit, and reflect on the fact that communities are not monolithic. I like what's happening in the U.S., the amazing consciousness, the election of Barack Obama, the way voters rallied to put the Democrats in office in Congress. What I'm not seeing are the same kind of responses in the arts. That's why I'm thrilled by the show that you are doing, because it's important to lead the conversation and important that the space of the art institution remains a civic space.

ER Thank you for those words. In "Tebbit's Ghost" you cite Hans Haacke's work as a proposal for overcoming exclusive nationalist paradigms. Is there an artist or artwork from recent years who comes to mind, who probes relationships between nationalism or belonging in really powerful ways?

OE It's difficult to answer this question. I've worked with so many great artists, from Alfredo Jaar to Mona Hatoum [p. 78]. Walid Raad, for me, is so important and intelligent in his practice. Whether he's really probing nationalism or not... it's a different issue. I think about Amar Kanwar, and his films, and John Akomfrah has also addressed similar questions. I also think of artists who have located their practice in focused contexts, such as Emily Jacir, who deals with the question of the homelessness of the Palestinians. Or younger practitioners such as Bouchra Khalili, or Tiffany Chung and Emeka Ogboh, who have addressed the travails of migration and displacement. These issues have become a vital part of the artists' moral imagination. But very few artists deal with these questions in the bigger terms that we want to see, simply because it also has to do with experience. Few artists are able to imagine work in that arena with what I will call a "surplus of insight" that could really produce very powerful work.

I've been reading Kwame Anthony Appiah's recent book *The Lies That Bind*, about belonging. The story deals with the notion that national space is constructed. Jaar was born in Chile, educated in Martinique in French, went back to Chile, moved to New York, and lived elsewhere. Hatoum left Beirut in 1976 and couldn't go back because the war broke out, and that completely changed her world. So the personal stories of the artists themselves might be where we can look for clues on these questions of nationalism.

ER On the topic of biography, I have a personal question, if I may. You yourself were a refugee. Nigeria was in a civil war at the end of the 1960s and your family fled from one place to another. How does that personal experience inform your work, and your return to this essay?

OE It took me many years to feel confident to talk about my personal experience in public, in other words to bear witness to the trauma and rupture it created in our lives. I was six when the war ended in Nigeria. The war itself became the unspeakable. I had to learn the question of how to deal with that opacity, that opacity of the unspeakable, to be able to talk about it in public. It always surprises me, the way certain experiences of refugees get erased from their accounts, maybe because they have been through so much. It took me a long time to have the courage to speak about it, and as I started thinking more about it, it came to inform my work.

The first time I reflected on it (although I didn't specifically mention it) was in my catalogue essay for the second Johannesburg Biennial. If you read that essay now you would think again, My goodness, the world is never going to change. But I was also in the middle of an amazing transformation. This was two years after the first elections in South Africa. I was a witness to something changing before my eyes. Africa was also dealing with Rwanda, and that was when it forced me to become a witness, and to talk about having had that experience. Narratives of the civil war in Nigeria are only just beginning to come out, in the last decade. There are so few of them, but there is a momentum among many people now to find a way to break the silence, and to bear witness to it. Intellectually it's given me a vantage point from which to think about the complicated issues of displacement and migration, but not to make it all only just personal.

ER Is there anything you would like to add before we wrap up?

OE For me, "Tebbit's Ghost" remains a fundamental text. Brexit is nearly dead, and Britain might remain in Europe, but what is very clear is that the immigration gate is going to slam shut in front of people. This reconsideration of the text couldn't have come at a better time. Last year I was watching the BBC and saw Lord Tebbit himself, eighty-six years old, in the House of Lords during the debate for Brexit. I looked up in shock and I thought that Lord Tebbit was like a character from the nineteenth century, but there he was! I'm very happy to have this text republished and read more widely—thank you for giving me the opportunity.

ER Thank you, Okwui, it's been a pleasure to speak with you today. This project is in your debt in so many ways.

> *In coping with identity crisis, what counts for people are blood and belief, faith and family. People rally to those with similar ancestry, religion, language, values, and institutions and distance themselves from those with different ones.*
>
> —Samuel P. Huntington, *The Clash of Civilizations and the Remaking of World Order*, 1996

These are days of great anxiety in Europe and for Europeans. Samuel Huntington has located this anxiety in the clash of values between the Western world, its identity, culture, religion, and beliefs, against the cultures, identities, and religious beliefs of non-Western societies. This clash is today supposed to be exacerbated by the tension that has arisen in the wake of global cosmopolitanism, multiculturalism, and postcolonial migration, which have created hybrid identities and non-European ethnic communities that have become increasingly visible across Europe. These changes, which have demographic implications for a Europe undergoing a low birthrate, have pitted the identity of Europeans against nonnative Europeans who have recently settled on the Continent. But what exactly is the basis for this clash? Is it the resurrection of old antagonisms between Western norms and non-Western alternatives? Is it the historical return of the repressed in the relationship between the colonized and the colonizer? Like the rest of the world, Europe is deep in the convulsive throes of a collision of worlds, cultural values, and shifting historical currents. And like all the rest, it is bewildered by the immense challenge of making the European Union into a cohesive, federal superstate to rival the United States. To understand why the European Union is worried about this convulsion in the global order, we would do well to understand Huntington, who believes that the proper response to the identity crisis that Europe is undergoing is a return to some pure atavistic past, to a sense of an unadulterated Europeanness before the advent of the hordes that threaten its sense of cultural cohesion. He writes:

> In the new world, cultural identity is the central factor shaping a country's associations and antagonisms. While a country can avoid Cold War alignment, it cannot lack identity. The question, "Which side are you on?" has been replaced by the much more fundamental one, "Who are you?" Every state has to have an answer. That answer, its cultural identity, defines the state's place in world politics, its friends, and its enemies.[2]

Could there be a more enervating sense of cultural relationship in a globalizing world than the one sketched above, in which contact between peoples is grounded in some nativist understanding of friend and foe? It would appear that the political task of the state, henceforth, is to be based precisely on the characteristics of a fundamental separation within the body of the polity, between the friend to be protected and sheltered and the enemy who must be dominated and deracinated. Within this bleak scenario, Europe has gone to search for answers and perhaps to discover the enemies who so trouble its cultural coherence. In this quest, the immigrant has emerged as the spectral epiphany of its self-doubt, its cultural integrity, its very identity. The immigrant has emerged in the name of the postcolonial subject across the territories of the European Union as a figure of deep suspicion and anxiety.

Increasing hostility toward this figure in Europe has moved beyond the threshold of phenomena to that of a norm. It appears that a once cosseted Western modernity is out of sorts, deeply disturbed by this postcolonial mongrel in its midst. The non-European immigrant who first arrived in the late 1940s and 1950s as cheap labor, or, in more fanciful parlance, as "guest worker," on factory floors and in menial jobs after World War II to help rebuild a ruined continent has now become a pariah. The guest workers, from countries like Turkey and regions such as the Caribbean, South Asia, and Africa, filled crucial labor shortages throughout Western Europe following World War II. They were often enticed to make the journey with promises of residency and economic opportunity. Moreover, as "guests," they were expected to reside only temporarily; in time, it was assumed, they would return to their respective lands. While many of these workers went back home, many others stayed and settled into their new cultures, and in many instances remained attached to their pasts and native lands: to the cultures they had left behind.

Today, many of the guest workers now living productive lives in Europe have grown old enough to have children and grandchildren who carry seeds of their parents' and grandparents' cultural heritage but who know no other home but Europe. Fifty years later, globalization has added to this social transformation of codes of cultural attachment and fractured cultural identity, as well as a sense of social belonging in societies that are often hostile to the multicultural identities that have become the normative experience of a new generation of European citizens. But no longer will that old idealism, "Give me your tired, your poor,/Your huddled masses," suffice. *Liberté*'s beckoning call also comes with a demand for *égalité*, even if the third component of the liberal trinity, *fraternité*, has long been discounted, producing an antagonism that has engulfed Europe in debates about its political future and social networks. In this examination of the relationship between friends and enemies, hosts and guests, integration and resistance, identity and belonging, a shift in the cultural ecology of the European Union has produced its own countermeasures, such as tough immigration rules, deportation laws, detention in hostel barracks, denial of entry at ports for illegal boats smuggling human cargo, and, finally, the creation of a vast *cordon sanitaire*, which in a sense is a blockade in international waters to prevent those wanting to land on the European continent from reaching its shores.

These are extreme measures, and there are more. And they are growing increasingly dire. Let us take the recent French law proscribing all religious symbols from state schools, but most especially headscarves worn by Muslim girls. Paradoxically, the French policy of banning religious paraphernalia in its public schools was done in the name of *laïcité*, the bedrock principle of French state secularism. In order to maintain the apparent neutrality of the secular state, as well as a clear boundary between the church and the state or, as some see it, the mosque and the state, it effectively bans practices of conscience and freedom of personal religious expression guaranteed by European law. But in spite of the seeming evenhandedness of the new policy, Muslims, the most recalcitrant of all European immigrant groups, were clearly the principal target of the French law. Under the law, while Christian students can wear discreet crosses to class, Islamic girls are not allowed to don headscarves, which are deemed far too conspicuous for the Catholic taste of the supposedly secular state. What this law portends for future cultural politics in the European Union remains to be seen, especially if Turkey joins in the coming years.

Though there have been attempts to mediate the fallout from this law through calls for tolerance and intercultural dialogue, it is impossible not to recognize that in European countries Islam is perceived as a threat (according to Huntington's historical diagnosis) to the secular traditions and Christian identity of the Continent. And if Islam is a threat, one must then view it through the prism of immigration. Effective immigration policies constitute the first line of defense against Islam's incipient radicalism. But to frame the state's antagonism to Islam as an enemy requires a certain form of willful agnosia, given the recent atrocities against Muslims in Bosnia and Islamic history in European cultural traditions. But that is another matter. For now, I want to concentrate on the effects the debates on immigration have had on political and cultural discourse.

I will begin with politics. If the immigration question in Europe has produced a growing disenchantment with the auguries of pluralism, once celebrated by globalization, and the insouciant presence of postcolonial identities, the events surrounding the attack on the United States on September 11, 2001, and the combined wars on "terror" in Afghanistan and Iraq have rent the fragile fabric that formerly held out the possibility for those who persist in their daydream of a multicultural Europe. For many Europeans already opposed to or suspicious of multiculturalism or pluralism, 9/11 made clear that immigrants, especially Muslims, are anathema, as Huntington argued, to the survival of a stable European identity. Populist politicians such as Pim Fortuyn in the Netherlands, Jörg Haider in Austria, Jean-Marie Le Pen in France, Filip Dewinter in Belgium, and Nick Griffin in Britain, along with a motley crew of far-right political parties working across Europe, all united in their singular hatred of immigrants, have exploited this electorally. On the one hand, there is the insurgent rhetoric of nativism on the part of certain groups, wielding xenophobic discourse, and on the other, a rising jihadism among young Muslims insistent on the purifying ethos of Islam as cultural identity. With equal vehemence, these young Muslims, enacting their own nativist retreat to some pure past, have engaged the spectacle and speciousness of right-wing attacks on immigrants. This is perhaps what Tariq Ali meant by "the clash of fundamentalisms" in his book of that title.[3]

The paroxysm of fear and loathing that often accompanies anti-immigrant attitudes and policies is not new. Xenophobia has always had great appeal on the Continent, despite attempts at papering over its cracks, as the 2004 murder of the Dutch filmmaker Theo van Gogh and the public reaction to it clearly remind us. His murder, by a young Dutch Muslim assailant, precipitated a great deal of soul-searching, spawning anew reassessments and reevaluations of integration programs. Do they go far enough or are they hopelessly doomed to failure? Again, a new urgency surrounds the debate—decades old already—across the Continent: What is to be done with Europe's immigrant populations, the ranks of which continue to grow at a prodigious rate?

Europe's immigrant community is vast and varied, ranging from South Asians, such as Indians, Pakistanis, and Bangladeshis, to North, East, and West African, Middle Eastern, and Caribbean populations. Muslims are currently the most visible of these groups, for obvious reasons. According to population and demographic studies, Muslims constitute the largest group of immigrants living in Europe today and are often committed to their ethnic and religious identities. While their host cultures perceive many of them as hostile to the ideals and values of Western modernity, further testing the ideal of tolerance long cherished (perhaps in delusion) as part of Europe's heritage of political liberalism, a majority, it is often noted, are comfortable with such ideals and values and see no contradiction whatsoever between their cherished Muslim identities and their European identities. This credo of multiculturalism, however, has come under increasing strain. It certainly has done little to assuage the fear that Islamic radicalism has eaten more deeply into the lives of young European Muslims, a matter of both political and cultural concern.

The debate on immigration and immigrants is a complex one, to be sure, even if much of it has been reduced to cultural and loyalty tests. What to do with immigrants is not only a matter of how to assimilate them culturally and instill in them European values, it also raises the question of how to live with them as neighbors, with full recognition of their cultural and political rights as Europeans. While laying bare the ethical limits that mark the topology of European tolerance along with its myths of openness to other cultures, strange and abhorred neighbors make for uncomfortable shared space.

However, the immigration question, like "the Other question," is one side of the coin of dissension being played out in the relationship between Europeans and foreigners.[4] The other side concerns the eastward expansion of the European Union. As the Union expands to the east, moving ever closer to the edge of the Levant in Turkey, it is also experiencing another profound shock: a crisis of identity within its territorial map. The U.S. Secretary of Defense Donald Rumsfeld's slashing dissection of this crisis during the Munich Security Conference of January 2003, just as the George Bush administration was getting ready to invade Iraq, allowed him to frame

Europe less in the monadic fantasy of Euro bureaucrats based in Strasbourg and Brussels than in the oppositional terms of realpolitik: as a struggle between "new Europe" and "old Europe," a distinction, no doubt, with which Huntington would have agreed. In other words, taking a page from Huntington, Rumsfeld sought to express Europe's confusion as the difference between the inchoate and the outmoded. My metaphor of "slashing" for Rumsfeld's mode of discourse is apt, for his sword is not originary but merely an expressive power implement unsheathed to remind Europeans of the terrible tear at the core of their Union. French President Jacques Chirac, knowing firsthand the terrible truth of Rumsfeld's claims of an old sclerotic continent, more than obliged the pugnacious defense secretary with his Gallic condescension toward his seemingly subservient Eastern partners in the Union, who, rather than keep quiet and maintain the facade of European solidarity, sided with the American and, therefore, missed a vital opportunity to "keep quiet" in the debate surrounding the Iraq war.

Of course, one can also read the American defense secretary's Munich insult as calculated and deliberate, intended to dramatize and to highlight not just European weakness in the politics of power, but also its weakness as an effective superstate speaking with one voice. If Europe is in disarray, unable to unify behind a common foreign policy, how can it ever hope to manufacture a common culture with shared values among its disparate peoples? Is it not delusional to conceive of culture in the same manner as common currency, markets, foreign policy? Aren't culture and its other cognate, identity, far more resistant to any totalizing, common bureaucratic discourse? And how does citizenship fit within this map?

With due deliberateness, Rumsfeld carefully exposed and cruelly exploited this weakness in the present conception of European identity. As he knew and we all know, when we take a grand tour of Europe, from Istanbul to the Russian steppe, Cardiff to Lillehammer, Lille to Bucharest, what we encounter is not consensus as to what constitutes its identity, but dissensus: Europe as multiplicity, a concatenation of traditions that no officious fenestration manufactured in Brussels will ever bring to a totality. But how did this once powerful imperial force come to be so blind to the profound set of cultural differences that inhabit the multiple traditions of its various nation-states, not to mention the visibly present immigrant communities produced as a result of its violent colonial adventures? The contortions and agonies that Europe is now undergoing in its difficult attempt to integrate the "Other" within its borders are not unexpected. But they do beg the question, given the political hysteria surrounding immigration and religious minorities, whether all the public flagellation is not a case of amnesia or arrogance.

I will now turn to the second part of this discussion: culture. What follows is partially set in the conflagration that is Huntington's conception of identity. I shall examine how a politician frames social relations within a cultural topography and how an artist does the same. It is important, in this context, to note Europe's recidivism in response to its non-European communities: during moments of unease, it tends to revert to political hysteria, oppose the value systems of Europe and its immigrant communities, prove them irreconcilable, and test the loyalty of those who may be deemed dangerous to the res publica. In so doing, suddenly the enemy is revealed. Lord Norman Tebbit's "cricket test," a shibboleth of blatant racialized connotation, offers a useful precedent and is worth revisiting. Tebbit conceived his cricket test not just as a test of Britishness or, as it were, Englishness but also as a means by which to discover the enemy within. The full scope of the British peer's test hinges on two notions: the first is tribal, given his ethnocentric instincts; the second, which is more profoundly disabling, disarticulates the nontribal British person through a test of loyalty. To test not only whether a British immigrant belongs to Britain, but his or her loyalty to it, we are called to adjudicate which side he or she should support during a cricket match between England and, say, Pakistan, India, or the West Indies. If the immigrant supports any team other than the British one, he or she fails the test of loyalty. Amartya Sen has shown the fundamental flaw of this thinking. He was correct to take Lord Tebbit to task, pointing out,

> The plurality of competing as well as non-competing identities is not only not contradictory, it can be part and parcel of the self-conceptions of migrants and their families. For example, the tendency of British citizens of West Indian or South Asian origin to cheer their "home" teams in test cricket has sometimes been seen as proof of disloyalty to Britain. This phenomenon has led to Lord Tebbit's famous "cricket test" (to wit, you cannot be accepted as English unless you support England in test matches). This view involves a remarkable denial of consistent pluralities that may be easily involved in a person's self-conception as well as social behaviour. Which cricket team to cheer is a completely different issue from the demands of British—or any other—citizenship, and different also from a socially cohesive life in England. In fact, in so far as Tebbit's "cricket test" induces an exclusionary agenda, and imposes an unnecessary and irrelevant demand on immigrants, it makes social integration that much more difficult.[5]

The cricket test points to the tenuous concept of what constitutes "home" for immigrants living in Europe. It articulates the possibility of their exclusion from home's banner of protection, should they fail its test of loyalty. As Sen makes clear, this evident distrust of immigrants erodes the networks of goodwill necessary for social integration. But let us turn the cricket test around and place the spotlight on a country like Germany, where the consequences of the literalization of home and a people has left a lasting impression on the possible abuse of the notion of home and a common heritage shared by a people. How should the Turkish or African immigrant living in Germany interpret the unambiguous inscription *Dem Deutschen Volke* (To the German people), etched on the facade of the Reichstag in Berlin [fig. 1]? Is the *Volk* of the Nazi past the same as the *Volk* of today? If they are the

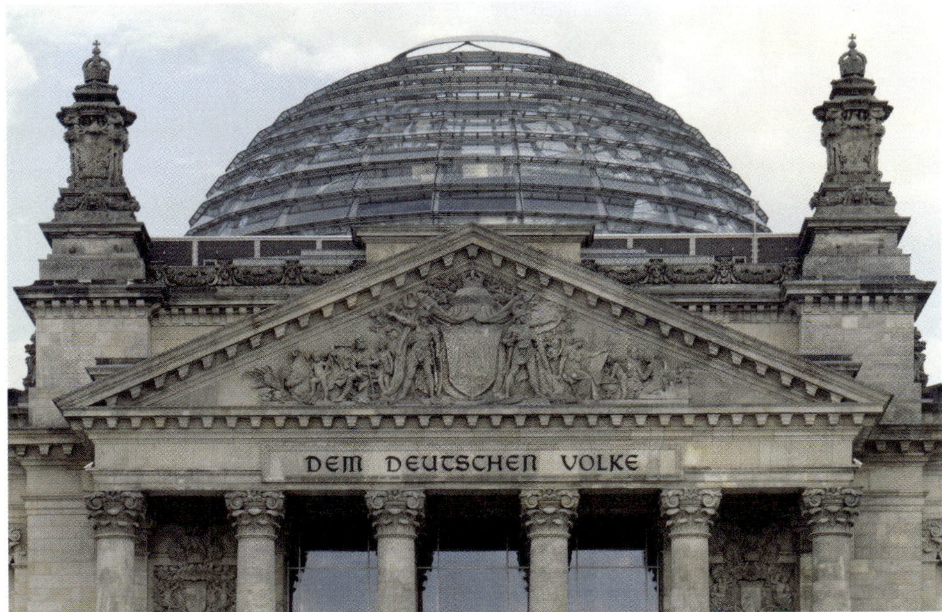

Fig. 1. Tympanum of the Western portico of the Reichstag, Berlin, 2000

same, what are the lessons learned from the Nazis' murderous denationalization of its Jewish populations in an attempt to exclude them from protection and thereby thoroughly annihilate them from their erstwhile "home"? If the *Volk* of the Nazi past is different from the one of today, what is the appropriate designation for those who came in the aftermath of National Socialism from elsewhere and settled in Germany?

In an exhibit in the courtyard of the German parliament in Berlin, Hans Haacke takes up precisely these questions in *Der Bevölkerung* (To the population) (2000) [fig. 2], a permanent sculpture installation. Haacke's sculpture, in the form of a public garden composed of soil procured from all the federal German states, is both iconographic and symbolic, representational and discursive, political and cultural. On its rectangular shape Haacke deploys a single compound phrase: *Der Bevölkerung*, spelled out in illuminated white neon lettering on top of the green bedding. The idea of the project was that over time, as the garden grew, it would incorporate the lettering. It, however, performs a crack in the mirror that seemingly reflects the self-image of the German people. The cool white lettering spelling the words *Der Bevölkerung* produces both a soothing and an acidic effect. It is soothing in its attempt at historical responsibility and acidic because it wounds and shocks memory. The specificity of the wording is both the subject and the object of the work; word and image, text and object, are intertwined in rendering the open terrain of cultural citizenship in Germany. This work simultaneously evokes the memorial and the monument. In a city like Berlin, littered with memorials and monuments of all kinds, this double resonance is crucial to the work's explicit artistic efficacy. But what was the reason for Haacke's gesture, and what are its other ramifications?

Haacke's proposition is a meditation on the Holocaust and what it means to be German today (between German identity and German citizenship), where all references to cultural heritage are darkened by the stain of the Nazi racial interpretations of belonging and citizenship. In conceiving the sculpture, it would appear that Haacke's principal aim was to confront and transform the phrase *Dem Deutschen Volke*, which has come to haunt German public memory and the question of inclusion. Transforming *Dem Deutschen Volke*, and its connotations of blood and soil, with the more open, inclusive concept *Der Bevölkerung* was not, however, a fait accompli, as the debate surrounding its approval in the Bundestag proved. To view the sculpture, the visitor has to traverse the corridors (of power), come to an expansive glass window, and look down into the courtyard where the piece is installed. Seen from the top, the sculpture declares its counter-discourse of citizenship, opposing the Nazi exploitation of the *Volk* for the *Bevölkerung*, an alternative, putatively more inclusive ideal of social

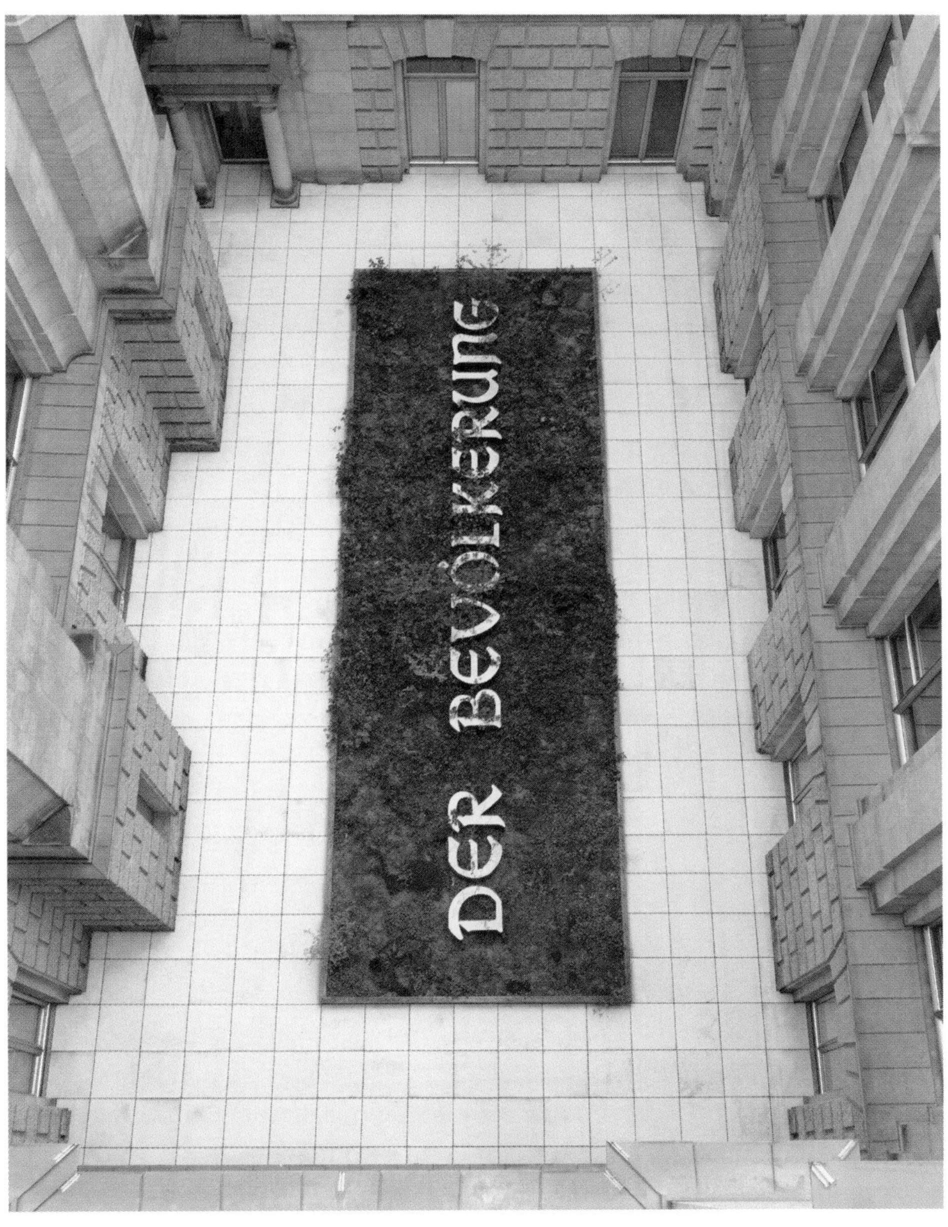

Fig 2. Hans Haacke, *DER BEVÖLKERUNG* (To the population), 2000– .
Installation view, Reichstag, Berlin, 2000

belonging. Much debate surrounded this critical work because it addressed both the matter of German reunification and its postwar immigrant identity. But Haacke's intervention in the debate on immigration presents a striking irony. If, in the act of naming, the designation "people" calls up traumatic events in European history, the seeming neutrality of "the population," rather than serving as an inclusive and welcoming designation due to its neutral benignity, calls up other uses of the term in relation to population control. More specifically, the move by right-wing political parties to curtail the rising population of immigrants, to block their entry into the Union, to deny them protection and access to legal recognition and equality, all reveal the dark side of the concept of population. Michel Foucault has shown the modern biopolitical deployment of the population at a time when the state saw that, henceforth, its power was no longer defined along the limit of life and that it had to direct its attention to the health of the population.[6] This would then mean cleansing the European body of the infesting migrant rubbish. As such, if the immigrant population in Europe is a threat to the health of the Union, then Haacke's *Der Bevölkerung* is essentially an aporia. Rather than population, should *Der Bevölkerung* not be focused instead on the concept of citizenship? It seems that in citizenship one is able to trespass, conceptually and figuratively, the ideas of identity and belonging simultaneously.

We can then ask the question: are Britain and Germany home to the immigrant families spread across their territorial boundaries today? Or is home elsewhere, in some native land? Bolstering the argument on the idea of nonbelonging by European immigrants and their recognition as citizens, Huntington argues,

> The forces of integration in the world are real and are precisely what are generating counterforces of cultural assertion and civilizational consciousness.
>
> The world is in some sense two, but the central distinction is between the West as the hitherto dominant civilization and all the others, which, however, have little if anything in common among them. The world, in short, is divided between a Western one and a non-Western many.[7]

It is this difference between the West and non-West, between the one and the clamoring many, that serves as the mordant emblem of exclusion, as the apartheid wall of racial, ethnic, and civilizational separation, especially in the atomized scattering that has sent populations across different national borders. Yet the concept of home and the cultural values attached to it are complex—not a straightforward matter. It neither defines the point of proper belonging nor should it disqualify a person from its protection, even if such a person has a divided sense of home. The cricket test and the concept of population, each in its own manner, induce a state of nonconcordance for a unified European identity.

This nonconcordance, often taken as a danger sign in the state's inability to properly integrate and assimilate immigrants into Europe, is rarely viewed as the strength of contemporary Europe. The importance of immigrants and their cultural effects on Europe continues to retail at deep discount. But for those like Lord Tebbit who continue to marginalize immigrants, C. L. R. James makes an obvious and salient point:

> What is important to me is that there are now three million black people or more in Britain today. In 10 or 15 years there will be a whole generation of black people who were born in Britain, who were educated in Britain and who grew up in Britain. They will be intimately related to the British people, but they cannot be fully part of the English environment because they are black. Everyone including their parents is aware that they are different.
>
> Now that is not a negative statement.... Those people who are in western civilization, who have grown up in it, but yet are not completely a part (made to feel and themselves feeling that they are outside) have a unique insight into their society. That, I think, is important—the black man or woman who is born here and grows up here has something special to contribute to western civilization. He or she will participate in it, see it from birth, but will never be quite completely in it. What such persons have to say, therefore, will give a new vision, a deeper and stronger insight into both western civilization and the black people in it.[8]

With this insight from James, I want to turn to another space of culture to observe how this interplay between those within and outside European culture or Western civilization have fared in its institutions, or rather how transcultural investments within the European context have been recognized in institutional formations. Whatever the case may be, many institutions across Europe today are grappling with several questions: What is Europe, and who is European? Is there a "new Europe," as opposed to an "old Europe"? Is European identity singular and unique or is it plural and multicultural? Is European cultural influence in the world waning or not? These questions have multiplied since the fall of the Berlin Wall.

Manifesta, a roving, nomadic biennial exhibition initiated by the Dutch government in 1995 as a pan-European platform for contemporary art, is one of the institutions that emerged in the wake of the dissolution of the Soviet Empire. Its mission was to reiterate these questions and elaborate possible answers to them. The goal of Manifesta is to build a network that plaits together various strands of institutional and artistic production within territorial Europe. Furthermore, the goal of integrating the newly "liberated" Eastern European countries into the Western European context was equally clear from the outset, not so much as an expansionist project but more in an assimilationist logic: to make the seemingly "backward" East more like the "advanced" West. The expansionist/assimilationist conjunction plays up the kind of image politics necessary to blend old and new Europe into one seemingly cohesive civilizational realm, even in the face of the brutal ethnic massacres in the Balkans at the time. But the definition of the topology is not only abstract, it is unhelpfully vague when it comes to other communities such as the Roma, who are not represented as nation-states within Europe. Perhaps this is intentional. Or perhaps the founders of Manifesta, in their search for a European ontology, deliberately chose to avoid illuminating identity as such. Or it may owe to the extreme conservatism of European institutions regarding this matter. For some time, we have heard from the neurotics of political incorrectness, who have lately become culturally intolerant as well, that identity politics is foreign to Europe, it being a specifically Anglo-American obsession.

Yet the challenge of identity politics to European cultural discourse cannot be overstated, especially now that tolerance alone is not sufficient for inclusion. Articulating the inherent tension in both its identification and its cognitive atlas, Manifesta has resolutely repressed "the Other question" and the presence of "Other people" working within the European artistic context.[9] This repression has one striking quality; it exposes the inherent provincialism in current discursive formations in the European artistic sphere. And no document illustrates this better than the text on the website of the International Foundation Manifesta regarding the history of its initiative. It is reproduced here in its entirety:

> Manifesta grew out of an early Dutch initiative, to create a pioneering, pan-European platform for the contemporary visual arts. The concept of an itinerant Manifesta first took shape in Rotterdam, in consultation with a specially appointed International Advisory Board (the forerunner of the present International Foundation) and with the support of thirty National Governmental Arts organisations and Ministries of Culture in Europe.
>
> Manifesta developed into a fast growing network for young professionals in Europe and one of the most innovative biennial exhibition programme [*sic*] to be held anywhere. This is due, in no small measure, to its pan-European ambitions and its uniquely nomadic nature. Both the network and the exhibition, with its related activities, are equally important components of this itinerant event. Manifesta offers a platform for emerging artists, on the basis of a networking organisation, which is able to respond flexibly to new artistic, technological and cultural developments. The most obvious aspects of Manifesta's inbuilt flexibility is the fact that a new, pan-European theme or concept is developed on each occasion by a team of outside curators, working in close consultation with representatives of all kind [*sic*] of cultural, social, academic institutions in the host city. In other words, each new edition aims to establish a close dialogue between a specific cultural and artistic situation

> and the broader context of European visual contemporary art. At the same time, Manifesta provides strong continuity, through its ever-expanding network of contacts.[10]

From the foregoing statement, given its initial existence as an initiative of the Dutch government, Manifesta may appear to be complicit in the current official disappearance of immigrants in Europe from its cultural institutions. Every goal Manifesta articulates eerily echoes the kind of vapid bureaucratspeak that characterizes Brussels's communication strategy. Despite this official discourse, which has been pervasive from the first Manifesta in Rotterdam in 1996 to the most recent one in Donostia/San Sebastián, Spain, in 2004, the so-called innovative exhibition turned its face resolutely to the peripheries of Europe and its back to the anomalous migrant communities that have had no "real" ties to the investment in the nation-states of its supposedly pan-European network. This called into question what actually defines such a network and the critical issue of European citizenship and identity in the context of the fiery discourse surrounding migration. Manifesta's resolutely conservative European agenda in relation to this question has indeed been surprising. Rather than being open and outward looking, it barricades itself, without suspecting it, behind the idealism of a form of neo-European nationalism, a model of exhibition-making long discarded by most progressive biennials across the world. In accordance with this limiting national model, all its curators have been, without exception, ethnically European, and the vast majority of artists exhibited have been of similar origin. This policy seems to stem from an inability or refusal to make an interrogation of what constitutes "Europe" in the shifting discourse on citizenship, nationality, and identity part of the process. Given such realities, and the tension between indigenous and exogenous identities that presently define Europe, one wonders what is so pioneering in its so-called new model of exhibition practice, beyond the fact that it entrenches itself as an extension of Brussels's cultural policy. What if Manifesta were to move from what has been essentially a logic of *die Europäer Volk* to an active commitment to *der Bevölkerung*, in other words to exhibiting the artwork of the European population in all its multiplicity? Or even more, what if Manifesta opened up the exhibition to all international artists, regardless of their European affiliation? Through such an extension of both its programmatic and its territorial outlook, perhaps Manifesta will recognize, however late, as James Clifford has cogently argued, that in Europe today "culture is migration as well as rooting within and between groups, within and between individual persons," not just an institutional gambit.[11]

What I have traced here is not necessarily a critique of Manifesta alone, as an extension of European Union cultural policy along with its bureaucratic cultural managerialism. I have chiefly delineated a pervasive amnesia in certain forums of contemporary cultural discourse, its blindness to the difficult terrain of European culture, its repression of immigrant communities. Today, there is a radical disorientation of the dead certainties of

Western modernity, not just in the context of Europe. At the same time, immigrant particularism cannot simply be embraced as the response to discrimination and marginalization. Immigrant essentialism and ethnic ghettos too require critical scrutiny and careful interrogation. Immigrants are responsible for opening themselves up to their host cultures, for working to understand the values of their new homes and the importance of those values as a way to build an open society. I am interested in how a careful historical examination of Europe's relationship to its immigrant communities can, at the level of the curatorial agenda of Manifesta, generate a more engaging, open exhibition model that does not confine itself to building networks with official institutions, but can equally extend itself into communities long denied proper recognition as part of the reality of contemporary Europe.

New networks of cultural participation, such as Manifesta, can articulate what is possible in contemporary Europe's relationship to its immigrant communities, while directing us to the instability of any fixed meaning of identity. But they require the recognition, as well, of the bankruptcy of the antagonistic and exclusionary view of identity and culture offered by Huntington and Lord Tebbit: between enemies and friends, between loyalty and disloyalty, between flags and cultural symbols, crosses and head scarves. The upheavals taking place in different cultural communities in Europe alert us to this.

As we rethink the radical potential of a politics of difference and the impact of migration in restructuring national and social identities and citizenship, the task then is how to demolish the paradigm of the concentration camp (as it morphed in recent years into detention camps and deportation trials of migrants and refugees) that has been dominant in the conception of citizenship and immigration in Europe.[12] In *Der Bevölkerung*, Haacke offered one possible proposal to overcome the paradigm of the concentration camp that has haunted German memory from the rise of the Nazi regime in the 1930s to the end of World War II. However, *Der Bevölkerung* falls well short of its own goal, for it merely proposes inclusion and tolerance rather than the assimilation of other forms of difference into the norms of belonging, those that can never be wholly or ethically absorbed into the discourse of the state and its institutions. The future radicality of Manifesta in European cultural discourse is to make possible and viable those forms of difference that cannot be ethically incorporated into the predetermined rules of its official networks. The goal for Manifesta, therefore, should be to surpass the institutional limit (the concentration camp) and enter the polis (the community) composed entirely out of a tremulous politics of difference. Such an exhibition model will then allow it to vanquish the ghosts of Lord Tebbit's cricket test and Huntington's antagonistic politics of civilizational clashes, as well as guide it past the treacherous path of a nativist impulse that argues for an identity secure in the fantasy of a coherent European cultural past.

— — — — — — — —

1. Okwui Enwezor's essay "Tebbit's Ghost" was originally published in Barbara Vanderlinden and Elena Filipovic, eds., *The Manifesta Decade: Debates on Contemporary Art Exhibitions and Biennials in Post-Wall Europe* (Cambridge, MA: The MIT Press, 2005). Reprinted by arrangement with the author with minor revisions.

2. Samuel P. Huntington, *The Clash of Civilizations and the Remaking of World Order* (New York: Simon and Schuster, 1996), p. 125.

3. Tariq Ali, *The Clash of Fundamentalisms: Crusades, Jihads, and Modernity* (London: Verso, 2002).

4. See Homi Bhabha, "The Other Question: Stereotype, Discrimination, and the Discourse of Colonialism," in *The Location of Culture* (New York: Routledge, 1994), pp. 66–84.

5. Amartya Sen, "Other People," Annual British Academy Lecture, delivered November 7, 2000. Available online at https://www.thebritishacademy.ac.uk/sites/default/files/09-sen.pdf (accessed February 12, 2019).

6. Michel Foucault, "Right of Death and Power Over Life," in *The Foucault Reader*, ed. Paul Rabinow (New York: Pantheon Books, 1984), pp. 258–72.

7. Huntington, *Clash of Civilizations*, p. 36.

8. C. L. R. James, "Africans and Afro-Caribbeans: A Personal View," 1984, quoted in Kobena Mercer, *Welcome to the Jungle: New Positions in Black Cultural Studies* (New York: Routledge, 1994), p. 1.

9. The Biennial of the Whitney Museum of American Art, New York, is the closest American exhibition to Manifesta in its national orientation. Yet even the Whitney has began to wrestle with what "American" means in the exhibition's designation, through self-questioning, and to transgress its previous national frontier to include nonnative immigrant artists living and working in the United States. Manifesta unfortunately still has not reflected on these issues sufficiently.

10. Formerly available online at http://www.manifesta.org/frame3.html. A very similar text appears at https://wanderlustmind.org/2008/08/31/chernobyl-matrioska-and-manifesta-7/ (accessed April 26, 2019).

11. James Clifford, "The Others: Beyond the 'Salvage' Paradigm," *Third Text* 6 (Spring 1989):75.

12. For a more succinct reflection on the concentration camp as a dominant paradigm of our time, see Giorgio Agamben, *Means without End: Notes on Politics*, trans. Vincenzo Binetti and Cesare Casarino (Minneapolis: University of Minnesota Press, 2000).

Aspirational and Operational Maps of Migration

Thomas Keenan

Images of migration are dominated by photojournalism, by documentary forms of reportage or commemoration. Images from the ruins, the beaches, the boats, the paths, the camps, the highways have an undeniable power and privilege in representing the catastrophe that we uncomfortably name the "refugee crisis." Sometimes these static images, though, can underplay the journey itself, the fact and experience of movement. They can lose sight, most important, of the ruptures and demands inherent in the act of migration: the claim to the right to move that is implied, and sometimes made explicit, when people take flight from where they live and set out for a better place.

Maps can help make these things evident, but there is more than one kind of map and it's important to see a range of them. Like other images, maps can move from context to context, acquiring different meanings and powers in that reframing.

In 2005, the filmmaker Charles Heller made a film, *NEM-NEE*, about Africans living, or at least staying alive, in the streets and parks of the Swiss city of Solothurn. In the film, the migrants testify to the hardships of their lives, activists supply legal and political analysis, and politicians go about their work of exclusion. Heller distributed the film through activist and NGO networks, including a screening before the United Nations Human Rights Council in Geneva.[1] He described the testimonial strategy as typical of "migration films": "they are grounded in the belief that if these voices are heard and the political condition that led to them grasped by the public, this will lead to mobilization and, eventually, change in policy."[2]

Three years later, Heller learned of a so-called "perception management campaign" run by the International Organization for Migration (IOM) in sub-Saharan Africa. Under the title "This is how we scare Africans," a Swiss newspaper published an IOM video on its website: a young Cameroonian migrant, calling home from Europe on a dark rainy night, lies to his father about his new life, while the film shows us the reality of living on the street, begging, and police harassment. The story's moral, appearing onscreen at the end, is "Leaving is not always living: don't believe everything you hear."[3] The video shows a grim European scene, with housing and jobs nonexistent, people hostile, police omnipresent—exactly the effects of the policies that Heller had aimed to stigmatize in *NEM-NEE*. The images are remarkably similar, too; you might even imagine that the IOM's production team had watched Heller's film. With more or less the same gestures, Heller says, "The shocking spectacle of the suffering of migrants was used not to denounce, but to justify and deepen the migration regime that produced it in the first place, all the while covering it with a humanitarian varnish."[4]

The counter-moral of Heller's story is direct: there is nothing automatically emancipatory, revelatory, or even simply critical about pictures of migration. The migrant caravan and the invasion are always just one step apart. As Thomas Laqueur writes of humanitarian narratives, images too, "sentimental or otherwise, do not come with built-in moral gyroscopes."[5] What matters, as always, is the context, the framing, the deployment, the projects in which images are inscribed—and even those contexts can never secure their contents absolutely against appropriation or reversal. An image can function very differently in different contexts; nothing holds it in place.

With that in mind, I want to discuss a range of cartographic representations of migration made over the last few years, which I've gathered and studied, with a group of colleagues, under the general title "It is obvious from the map." Now if anything is obvious about maps, practicality is at the top of the list: although they can always evade this definition, maps are instrumental images, devices for getting you from here to there, or helping you understand where "here" is, or warning you what's around the bend, or keeping track of your property. They mark land and sea with lines that put places into relationship with one another. The relation is not always benign: maps have a long colonial and imperial history as instruments of domination, exploitation, classification, invasion, exclusion, surveillance,

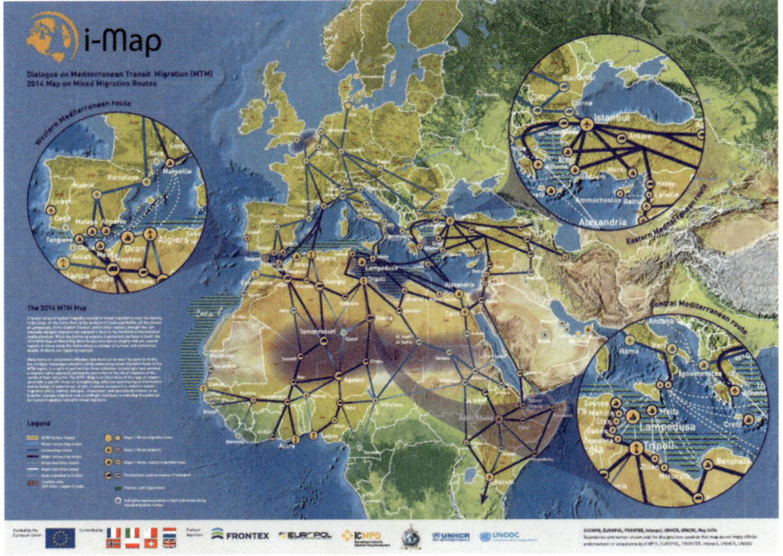

Fig 1. International Centre for Migration Policy Development (ICMPD), "MTM Map on Mixed Migration Routes in the MTM Region," 2014.
The i-Map was developed in 2006 by ICMPD, Europol, and Frontex as a "support instrument" to the Dialogue on Mediterranean Transit Migration

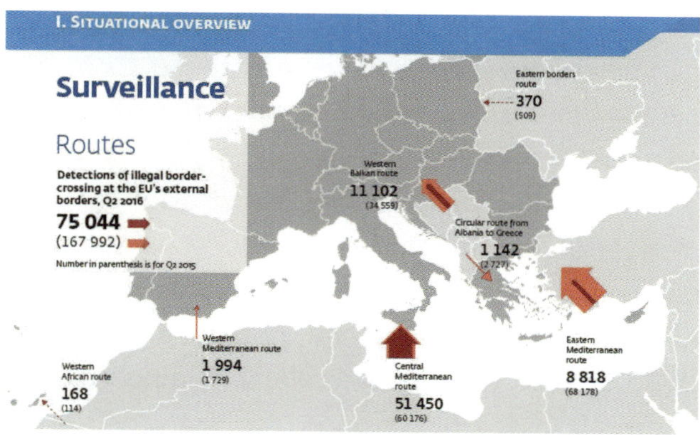

Fig 2. "Surveillance: Routes, Detections of Illegal Border-crossing at the EU's External Borders, Q2 2016," from *Frontex Risk Analysis Network Quarterly 2* (April–June 2016)

and control. They almost always have an interventionist dimension. As Laura Kurgan has shown, maps make choices, carry assumptions, argue and claim things.[6]

This has certainly been the case in the construction of both Europe's and North America's border regime in recent decades. Maps have not simply marked borders, they have been essential to those borders' enforcement. Their functions run along a spectrum from public relations icons to interactive devices for real-time intervention.

Frontex, the European Border and Coast Guard Agency, has been a prodigious producer and consumer of maps. The most extraordinary product, at once a research tool and an intervention, is the interactive i-Map [fig. 1], developed by an EU unit called the International Centre for Migration Policy Development (ICMPD). Images of the i-Map are static representations of an interactive database that tracks migration data in real time, but they figure Frontex's investment in surveillance, data collection, trend spotting, and route identification, both toward and within Europe [fig. 2]. Rogier van Reekum and Willem Schinkel write that "I-Map's visualizations reduce the multiplicity of migration data into more readily understandable maps that display common migration routes and tactical points of intervention in light of which new visa policies, risk profiles, codes of conduct at checkpoints, or border technologies may be selected, justified, or implemented."[7] The map aims to describe the territory of Europe and its southern neighbors in order to control and channel people's movements. It aspires to spatial and temporal accuracy, but it is, as van Reekum and Schinkel say, "far from disinterested." This is the world seen from the checkpoint: "typically, lines and arrows indicate people on the move, providing the onlooker with clues about 'hot spots,' 'hubs,' and 'high risk.'... They do not merely display Europe but do so from the particular vantage point of securitized mobility."[8]

The focus on what lies outside Europe is notable: as Maribel Casas-Cortés and Sebastian Cobarrubias insist, the maps show graphically what has come to be called "border externalization," the extension of the Schengen border—and of the responsibility for its policing—beyond the northern edge of the Mediterranean into Africa and the Middle East.[9] The European border-control regime acts far past its legal borders thanks to a series of arrangements, some cooperative and some imposed, that often follow pathways laid out in the colonial era: France works with its former colonies, Italy with Libya, and so on.

These cartographic visualizations are efforts to gain a certain control over what is, often intentionally, a disorderly, clandestine, ad hoc process. The maps seek, as Van Reekum and Schinkel write, to "create coherent pictures of quite incoherent phenomena," not just to represent them but to intervene in them, and not to stop them, which is impossible, but to manage and channel them.[10]

– – – – – – – –

The state is not alone in making maps. (Nor is the state alone in *using* the state's maps, but that's another story.) Migration-rights activists have a long history of counter-mapping. Among the most advanced are the representations of cross-Mediterranean migration developed by Forensic Oceanography, a group headed by Heller and Lorenzo Pezzani that emerged out of the Forensic Architecture project at Goldsmiths, University of London. Pursuing a practice it calls "disobedient sensing," the group has aimed to represent complex interactions on the high seas, where human activity often leaves few traces.[11]

They first explored the case of the so-called "left-to-die boat," a small craft from Libya that, despite encounters with NATO warships and aircraft, was abandoned to drift in the waters between Lampedusa and Libya for two weeks in the spring of 2011, at the cost of sixty-three lives [fig. 3].[12] They moved from this story of nonassistance to what might seem its opposite, the catastrophe that ensued when the EU outsourced its search-and-rescue operations in the Mediterranean to commercial vessels. Forensic Oceanography called this episode "Death by Rescue," marked as it was by two shipwrecks that killed more than 1,200 people in a single week in April 2015.[13] Their most recent work has documented the pushback of refugees to Libya and the criminalization of NGO search-and-rescue operations by European governments.

These and later case studies center around detailed, time-based, data-rich maps. In the "left-to-die boat" case, Forensic Oceanography collected, assembled, extracted, produced, and visualized an extraordinary range of data to describe two weeks in which seventy-two people first sailed and then drifted across a large stretch of the south-central Mediterranean. Starting with the testimonies of the nine survivors, which had barely been heard, they brought together documents, signals, photos, and video from the NATO naval assets in the region, including the sole photograph available of the migrants' boat (taken by a French military helicopter) and information about the deployments of NATO warships in the area; photos from plane-spotter hobbyists that enabled the identification of aircraft that the survivors said they had encountered; historical

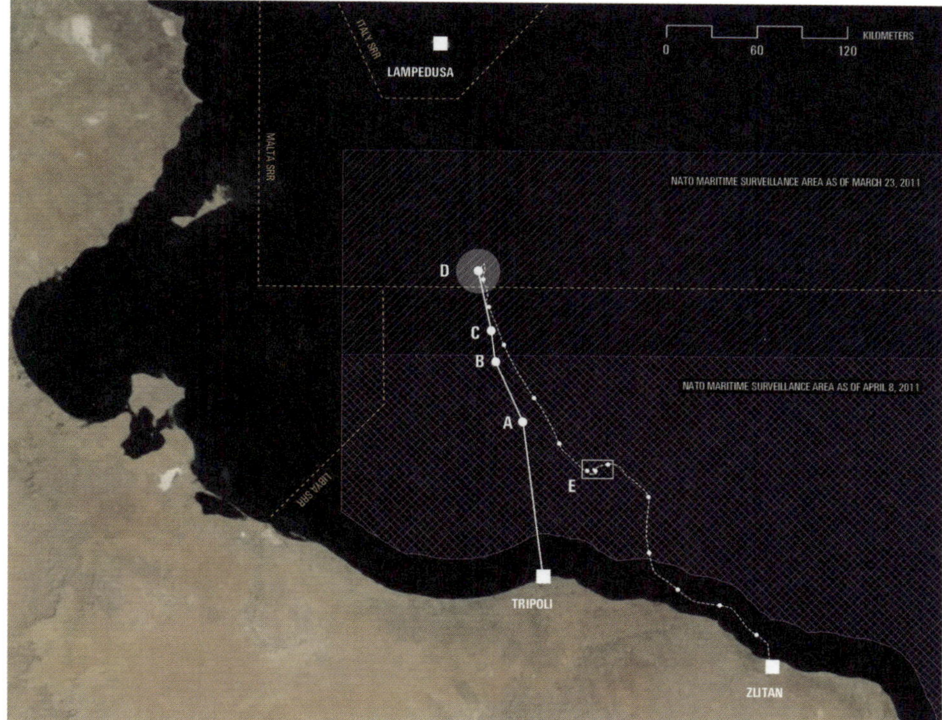

Fig 3. Forensic Oceanography, map showing the locations of key events in the "left-to-die boat" case (March 27–April 10, 2011), 2012

maps and charts describing fishing and travel routes; government maps of search-and-rescue zones; records of the distress signals sent by the migrants and relayed by government agencies; GPS data from the satellite telephone the migrants used in their first days at sea, and the testimony of the people they called; automated tracking data of the commercial vessels in the region; radar satellite imagery, also showing large vessels; and, perhaps most important, the current and wind data that allowed the calculation of the probable path of the boat after it ran out of fuel and began to drift. As the group writes, "We sought to put into practice a *disobedient gaze* that used some of the same sensing technologies of border controllers, but sought to redirect their 'spotlight' from unauthorised acts of border-crossing, to state and non-state practices violating migrants' rights."[14]

The map is complex yet simple: it shows a more-or-less linear journey from Libya north toward Lampedusa, and then the sudden displacement of that path by a wandering drift that ultimately leads back to the Libyan coast. That simple story reflects not only vast resources of testimony, imagery, and data, but also the stakes: the map demonstrates the high probability that the survivors, who told of repeated encounters with NATO warships and aircraft in what were at the time probably the most intensively surveilled waters on earth, told the truth about the capacity, and the failure, of those ships to rescue them. And the stories of the survivors need that corroboration, because NATO and the governments whose ships were most likely involved have denied responsibility for the nonrescue. The map and its data form the core of a series of lawsuits filed in European courts against

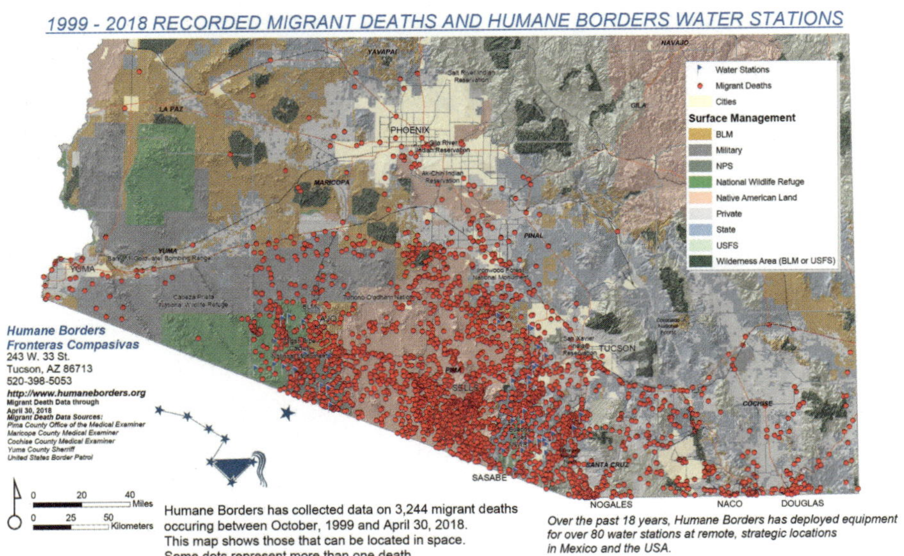

Fig 4. Humane Borders/Fronteras Compasivas, "1999–2018 Recorded Migrant Deaths and Humane Borders Water Stations," 2018

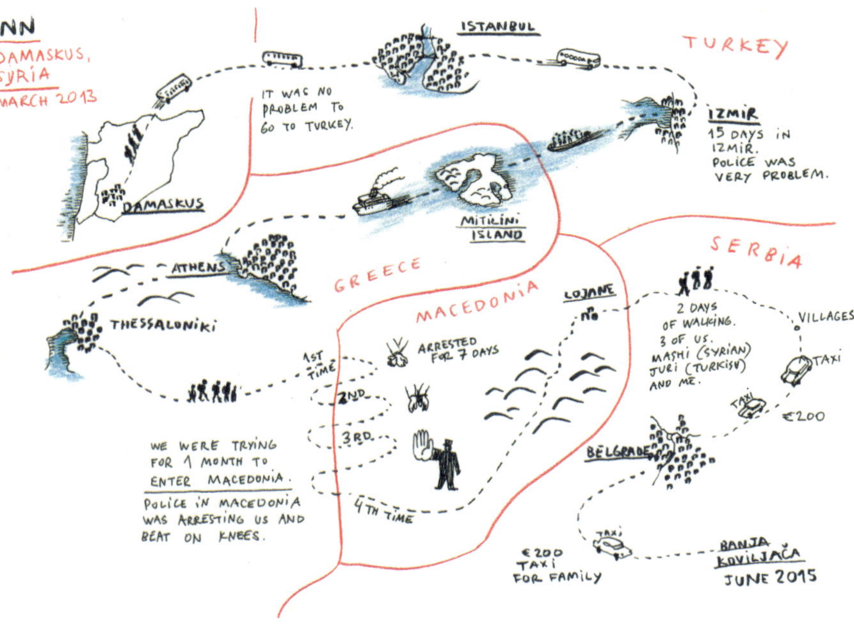

Fig 5. Đorđe Balmazović (Škart collective) in collaboration with asylum seekers in the Banja Koviljača center, Serbia, *NN: Damaskus, Syria, March 2013*

the navies in question. The map shows the traces of a crime that was supposed to leave next to none, and indicts the border policies that have forced people into small boats in the first place.

The desert has commonalities with the sea, and the one that stretches across the U.S.-Mexico border has likewise been the scene of migration, death, and a state strategy that makes the environment a weapon of deterrence. There, too, activists are confronting that strategy. The Arizona-based NGO Humane Borders/Fronteras Compasivas, for example, working with local governments, has compiled maps marking the locations of thousands of deaths in the Sonoran Desert [fig. 4]. The maps have a brutal factuality; the group describes them as "stark and perhaps unsettling."[15] "Viewers may see the exact location where each migrant body has been found, along with other information, such as the name and gender of the deceased (if known and if the family has been notified), date of discovery, and cause of death."[16] The maps are at once a memorial, a call to action, a gesture of sympathy, and a practical tool: the patterns of death that emerge over the two decades that they cover can guide the humanitarian project of providing resources, particularly water stations, to prevent deaths in the future.

Activist maps are not always high tech; artisanal strategies can tell equally complicated stories. Members of the Serbian art collective Škart, working with the human-rights NGO Group 484 in a number of centers for asylum seekers, have developed an innovative protocol. As Škart's Đorđe Balmazović puts it, they wanted to approach those stuck in the camp not as victims but "as courageous people who, by the very fact that they had decided to set out for such a journey, made a radical change in their life fleeing from wars, conflicts and poverty." Škart's strategy was narrative: "we asked them—why they had embarked on such a journey, what troubles they had survived, how they had crossed the borders, how much they had paid the smugglers, about their experience with the police, with people of the countries they had passed through."[17] These questions generated a rich representation of the journeys, becoming an investigative rubric the results of which were maps [fig. 5]. "We sketched the answers," Balmazović says, "in the form of maps, in order to piece together their routes, which in some cases lasted up to 7 years. Sometimes the maps lack details, sometimes they are unclear, and sometimes they would skip parts of the journey. We wanted to avoid pathos and the illustration of their sufferings. We wanted to show them their routes factually, by facts, and thus draw attention to the lack of humane asylum policy in Europe."[18]

With their commitment to both factuality and denunciation, all of these projects aim—not despite the patience and matter-of-factness with which they chronicle catastrophe, but through it—to leap over pathos and describe what happened, in order to point directly at *why* it happened. It's as if reconstructing the migrants' journeys so painstakingly might focus our attention on challenging the circumstances that brought them into existence in the first place.

– – – – – – – –

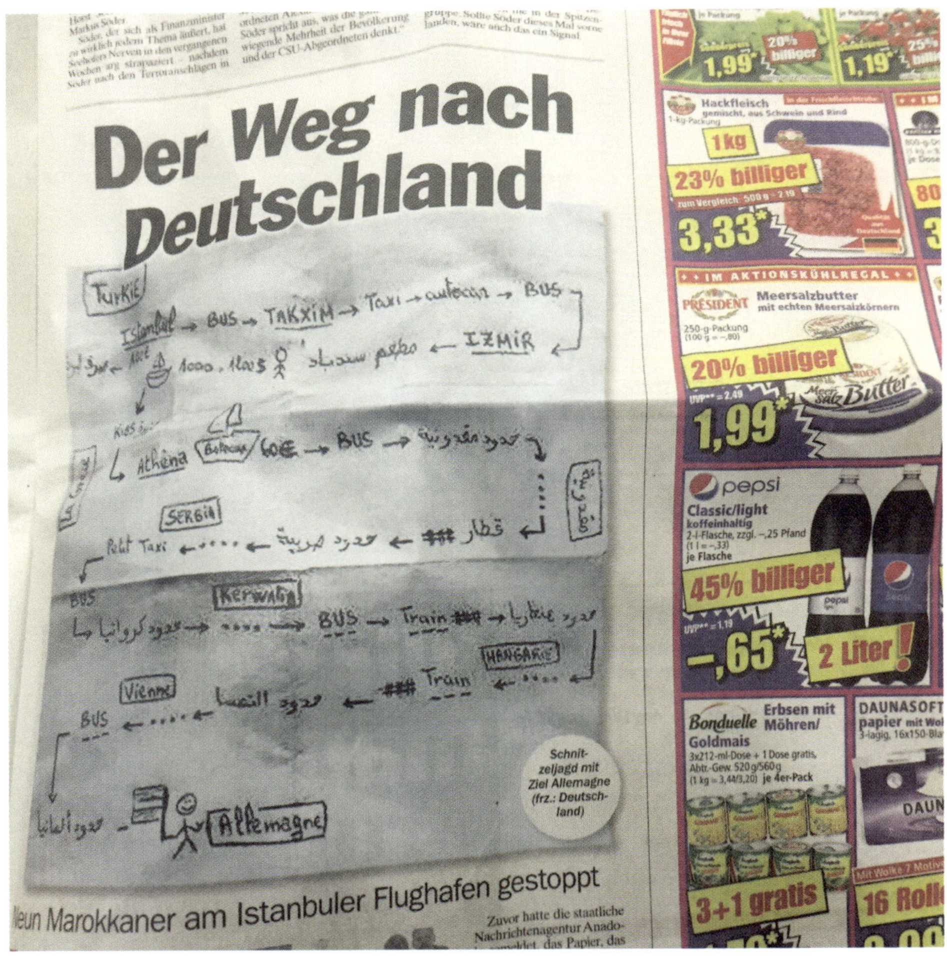

Fig 6. Thomas Dworzak, photograph of a German newspaper showing a hand-drawn diagram of a route from Turkey to Germany, seized by police in the Istanbul airport and distributed to the media, 2015

There remains a third sort of map, in a way the most immediate: the maps made by and for the travelers themselves. These need to be treated not only as signs, representations, documents, but also as a form of action. They are pictures of pathways, instructions for movement, predictions and records of journeys, as other maps are, but they are also operators of that movement and articulations of the claim to a right to move, to exercise agency.

Images made by ordinary people—militants, protesters, bystanders—have dominated the visual landscape of the Middle East for the last decade at least. When a lot of Iraqi and Syrian phone cameras started to take flight in 2015, they were not hard to notice. What was different, though, was that the images that emerged were not simply pictures of people, documents of destruction or recovery, narratives of the sort that cameras have long generated. Instead, many took advantage of specific capacities provided by smartphone and larger digital devices. So, in late August 2015, we could read the following on the front page of the *New York Times*: "'Every time I go to a new country, I buy a SIM card and activate the Internet and download the map to locate myself,' Osama Aljasem, a 32-year-old music teacher from Deir al-Zour, Syria, explained as he sat on a broken park bench in Belgrade, staring at his smartphone and plotting his next move into northern Europe. 'I would never have been able to arrive at my destination without my smartphone,' he added.... In this modern migration, smartphone maps, global positioning apps, social media and WhatsApp have become essential tools."[19]

Soon maps bearing witness to this phenomenon started to appear online and in the media. One set displayed their practically metastatic spread. In early September, Ginanne Brownell, a journalist based in Belgrade, showed on her blog a professionally drawn diagram, something like a flow chart, of the journey from Turkey to Germany.[20] A month later, writing in the *London Review of Books*, Ghaith Abdul-Ahad showed a very similar but hand-drawn map of the same journey, this one posted on Facebook by "a Kurdish friend of mine in Sulaymaniyah in northern Iraq....With little arrows and stick figures and pictures of a train and boat or two, the diagram shows how to get from Turkey to the German border in twenty easy steps."[21] In November, more or less the same route plan showed up in the news when it was seized from a group of eight men arrested in the Istanbul airport and charged as terrorists: "REVEALED: Childish map of route to Germany on scrap of paper hidden on ISIS suspect," read the headline in Britain's *Daily Express*, while a German paper titled the story more simply: "*Der Weg nach Deutschland*," or "The way to Germany" [fig. 6].[22] My colleagues and I later found the first two maps on Facebook, posted on August 8, 2015, by an Arabic-speaking user, and a fourth version, with even more elegant icons, posted by another user on August 24, 2015.

It soon became clear that Facebook, WhatsApp, and Instagram were serving not simply as spaces of exchange for these images but also as inadvertent archives. One could look around and over time assemble a collection of these maps, in a dazzling array of styles, aesthetics, graphics, formats, and software. Their scales range from the intercontinental to the hyperlocal. Some are pictorial, some tracings, some diagrams. Screen shots are annotated with directions, pins are dropped as testimonies. The maps offer coordinates, place names, real-time tracking, guidance on weather, winds, and tides, and warnings about police and other authorities. One sequence of six maps offering a route across the border from Serbia to Hungary exemplifies the granularity of detail, the confident self-assertion, the instructional rhetoric, the hybrid visual language of map and text and annotation, and the embedded experience that characterize these images [figs. 7–9]. An annotation announces, "It is obvious from the map."

If activist images are generally designed to document, to "raise awareness" (a phrase to be suspicious of), to testify, to narrate or represent an event or a harm or an experience, these images seem different—not simply in their visual language but in their structure and mode of functioning. They are, in two words, both operational and aspirational [fig. 10].

The German filmmaker Harun Farocki used the term "operational images" to denote images created in order to make something happen.

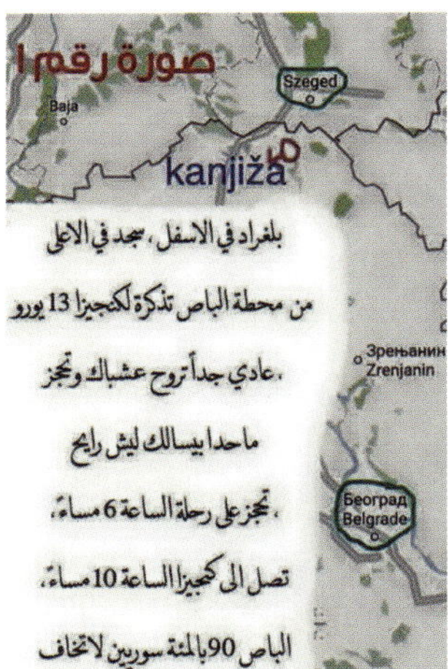

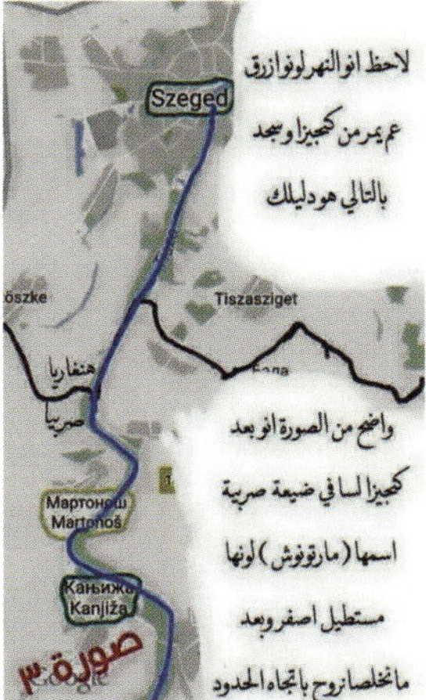

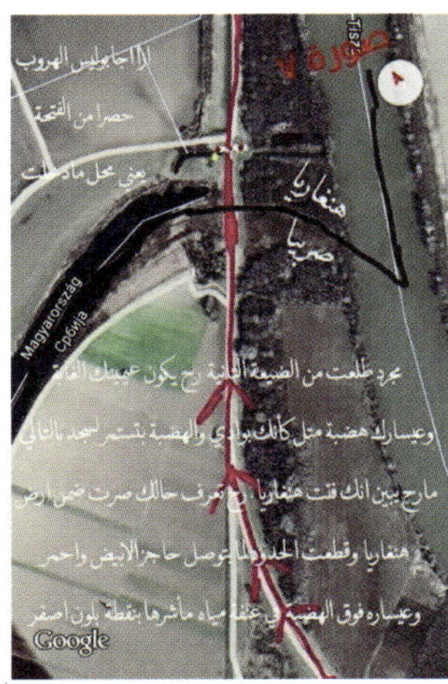

Figs. 7–9. Three from a sequence of ten maps and instructions titled "The way from Serbia to Hungary." The first annotation reads: "Belgrade is at the bottom, Szeged is at the top, from the bus station a ticket to Kanjiza is 13 euros, it is totally normal and okay to go to one of the ticket windows to buy a ticket, no one will ask you why you're going there, you book a ticket for 6 pm trip, you get to Kanjiza at 10 pm, the bus is 90% Syrians, don't worry" (translation by Basel Al-Yazouri). Posted on Facebook, June 14, 2015 (accessed July 15, 2016)

Farocki's examples were the digital images that drive robotic assembly machines in factories, or that allow cruise missiles in flight to direct their routes by matching stored maps with nose-cone video. He referred to these images as "not really intended for human eyes," not about representing something but about accomplishing it.[23] The migration maps, of course, are made very much for human eyes, but they nonetheless function in something like the way Farocki proposed. They are not created just to represent or narrate but to guide. To move without maps in this context is nearly impossible—they are constitutive of the journey itself. In the hands of the traveler, the phone and its map function like a remote control for the person who holds it. These maps are instructional, tutorial, something like recipes or algorithms. Today they are sometimes generated automatically by plotting newly collected data against stored information.

These images are also aspirational. Arjun Appadurai has written eloquently about what he calls "aspirational maps." For him these maps are a metaphor, a vision of a pathway out of the traps of the nation-state and its inevitable production of refugees, but the word tells us something important about how these maps function. He writes,

> There is no doubt that migrants today, as migrants throughout human history, move either to escape horrible lives, to seek better ones, or both. The only new fact in the world of electronic mediation is that the archive of possible lives is now richer and more available to ordinary people than ever before. Thus, there is a greater stock of material from which ordinary people can craft the scripts of possible worlds and imagined selves. This does not mean that the social projects that emerge from these scripts are always liberating or even pleasant. But it is an exercise in ... "the capacity to aspire."[24]

These possible worlds start with the route of the journey itself. The aspiration, like the claim to freedom and rights, is instantiated, articulated, and enacted in the journey and its image. The map is the aspiration, the declaration of independence, the claim to the right to refuse an intolerable situation. The activist maps, and the maps made by migrants themselves, are part of the claim that the journey constitutes. They enact, demonstrate, put into action, the claim for rights and recognition.

Some years ago Jacques Rancière wrote that the subject of human rights came into being when people enacted what had previously been a mere claim, when "they acted as subjects that did not have the rights that they had and had the rights that they had not." The strength of these rights, he said, "lies in the back-and-forth movement between the first inscription of the right and the dissensual stage on which it is put to test."[25] "Even," he said, "the clandestine immigrants in the zones of transit of our countries or the populations in refugee camps, can invoke them. These rights are theirs when they can do something with them to construct a dissensus against the denial of rights they suffer. And there are always people among them who do it."[26]

This link between aspiration and operation, between the claim to freedom and rights and the practical reappropriation of mobility, may not always succeed. The crisis—not the "refugee crisis" but the crisis of the European and U.S. border and migration regimes—is clearly just getting started, and the challenges faced by people seeking recognition and rights are enormous. Some documentary images bear witness to that. But there are other images, too, made by those "people among them," and the least we can do is to pay attention to the things they say and the images they create.

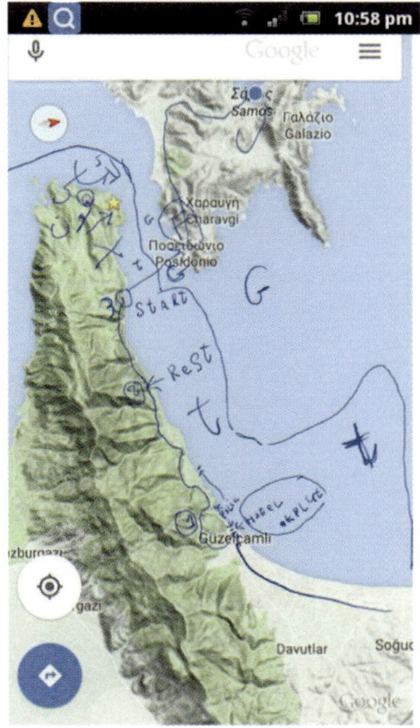

Fig 10. Screenshot from a mobile phone displaying a hand-annotated Google map of the land-and-sea route from Güzelçamlı, Turkey, to Posidonio, on the island of Samos (Greece). "This person posted that he got to Greece by swimming, and he explains how" (translation by Raghad Adwan). Posted on Facebook, September 22, 2015 (accessed March 8, 2019)

\- - - - - - - -

This essay reflects ongoing research I am conducting with Sohrab Mohebbi. We are grateful for the essential assistance of Beatrice Abbott and Basel al-Yazouri and the invaluable collaboration of Maribel Casas-Cortés, Sebastian Cobarrubias, Charles Heller, and Lorenzo Pezzani, pioneers of much of the research discussed here. Sohrab and I presented much of this material in a series of exhibitions entitled *It is obvious from the map*, most recently at Galerija Nova, Zagreb, November 2017–March 2018. I presented earlier versions of this essay at the symposium "Producing Image Activism after the Arab Uprisings" at the University of Stockholm, an inspiring event organized by Kari Andén-Papadopoulos in September 2017, and in a lecture sponsored by Interventions: Research Network on Humanitarian Politics and Culture, and the Uncertain Archives Research Group, at the University of Copenhagen in November 2018, where Devika Sharma and her group offered helpful comments and criticisms.

\- - - - - - - -

1. *NEM-NEE* can be seen online at https://vimeo.com/128189652 (accessed February 9, 2019).

2. Charles Heller, "Perception management—Deterring potential migrants through information campaigns," *Global Media and Communication* 10, no. 3 (December 2014):305.

3. Ibid., p. 306.

4. Ibid., p. 307.

5. Thomas Laqueur, "Mourning, Pity, and the Work of Narrative in the Making of 'Humanity,'" in Richard Ashby Wilson and Richard D. Brown, eds., *Humanitarianism and Suffering: The Mobilization of Empathy* (Cambridge: Cambridge University Press, 2009), p. 35.

6. Laura Kurgan, *Close Up at a Distance: Mapping, Technology, Politics* (Brooklyn, NY: Zone Books, 2013).

7. Rogier van Reekum and Willem Schinkel, "Drawing Lines, Enacting Migration: Visual Prostheses of Bordering Europe," *Public Culture* 29, no. 1 (January 1, 2017):30.

8. Ibid., pp. 30–31.

9. Casas-Cortés, Cobarrubias, Heller, and Pezzani, "Clashing Cartographies, Migrating Maps: Mapping and the Politics of Mobility at the External Borders of E.U.rope," in *ACME: An International Journal for Critical Geographies* 16, no. 1 (2017):1–33.

10. Van Reekum and Schinkel, "Drawing Lines," p. 30.

11. See Heller, Lorenzo Pezzani, and Maurice Stierl, "Disobedient Sensing and Border Struggles at the Maritime Frontier of EUrope," *Spheres: Journal for Digital Cultures* 4, *Media and Migration* (June 2017):1–15.

12. See Heller, Pezzani, and SITU Research, "Case: 'Left-to-Die Boat,'" in Forensic Architecture, ed., *Forensis: The Architecture of Public Truth* (Berlin: Sternberg Press, 2014), pp. 637–56, and Heller and Pezzani, "Liquid Traces: Investigating the Deaths of Migrants at the Maritime Frontier of the EU," in ibid., pp. 657–84.

13. See Forensic Oceanography, "Death by Rescue: The Lethal Effects of the EU's Policies of Non-Assistance," April 2016. Available online at https://deathbyrescue.org/ (accessed February 10, 2019).

14. Heller, Pezzani, and Stierl, "Disobedient Sensing," p. 5.

15. Humane Borders/Fronteras Compasivas, "Arizona Open GIS Initiative for Deceased Migrants," n.d. Available online at www.humaneborders.info/ (accessed February 10, 2019).

16. Humane Borders/Fronteras Compasivas, "Migrant Death Mapping," n.d. Available online at https://humaneborders.org/migrant-death-mapping/# (accessed February 10, 2019).

17. See Đorđe Balmazović and Škart, "Maps," in Marija Aleksić et al., *The Border Is Closed*, exh. cat. (Belgrade: The Museum of African Art and Group 484, 2015), pp. 28–29. Available online at http://grupa484.org.rs/wp-content/uploads/2016/10/granica_je_zatvorena_katalog_eng.pdf (accessed February 10, 2019).

18. Ibid., p. 29.

19. Matthew Brunwasser, "A 21st-Century Migrant's Essentials: Food, Shelter, Smartphone," *New York Times*, August 25, 2015. Available online at www.nytimes.com/2015/08/26/world/europe/a-21st-century-migrants-checklist-water-shelter-smartphone.html (accessed February 10, 2019).

20. Ginanne Brownell, "First Person: Europe's Refugee Crisis, 'I Will Follow the Light,'' September 6, 2015. Available online at https://ginannebrownell.com/first-person-europes-refugee-crisis/ (accessed February 10, 2019).

21. Ghaith Abdul-Ahad, "Some Tips for the Long-Distance Traveller," *London Review of Books* 37, no. 19 (October 8, 2015):39. Available online at www.lrb.co.uk/v37/n19/ghaith-abdul-ahad/some-tips-for-the-long-distance-traveller (accessed February 10, 2019).

22. Leda Reynolds, "REVEALED: Childish map of route to Germany on scrap of paper hidden on ISIS suspect," *Daily Express*, November 18, 2015, Available online at www.express.co.uk/news/world/620354/Arrested-ISIS-suspects-hand-drawn-map-Germany-showing-refugee-route (accessed February 10, 2019).

23. Harun Farocki, "Eye/Machine III," 2003, quoted in Kristin Marie Brockman, "Constructive Alienation and Terror," master's thesis, University of Cincinnati, 2015, p. 53.

24. Arjun Appadurai, "Aspirational maps," *Eurozine*, February 19, 2016. Available online at www.eurozine.com/aspirational-maps/ (accessed February 10, 2019).

25. Jacques Rancière, "Who Is the Subject of the Rights of Man?," *South Atlantic Quarterly* 103, nos. 2–3 (Spring-Summer 2004):304, 305.

26. Ibid., pp. 305–6.

The Refugee and a Different Vision of Security and Being Together

Uday Singh Mehta

That the Science of Cartography Is Limited

—and not simply by the fact that this shading of
forest cannot show the fragments of balsam,
the gloom of cypresses,
is what I wish to prove.

When you and I were first in love we drove
to the borders of Connacht
and entered a wood there.

Look down you said: this was once a famine road.

I looked down at ivy and the scutch grass
rough-cast stone had
disappeared into as you told me
in the second winter of their ordeal, in

1847, when the crop had failed twice,
Relief Committees gave
the starving Irish such roads to build.

Where they died, there the road ended

and ends still when I take down
the map of this island, it is never so
I can say here is
the masterful, the apt rendering of

the spherical as flat, nor
an ingenious design which persuades a curve
into a plane,
but to tell myself again that

the line which says woodland and cries hunger
and gives out among sweet pine and cypress,
and finds no horizon

will not be there.

—Eavan Boland, "That the Science of Cartography Is Limited," 1994

Migrants, typically, choose that condition and that identity from a cramped set of conditions. Sometimes what they see as they crane their heads back to look at what they are fleeing is the sight of their villages and towns in flames, sometimes it is the receding shoreline of a continent as they embark on a merciless ocean voyage, sometimes it is the machetes of a harrowing majoritarian crowd emboldened by nationalist fervor, sometimes it is the sight of barren fields parched by unforgiving years of drought, sometimes it is the Rio Grande that marks the boundary between uncertain hope and despair, sometimes it is a set of cultural attitudes that disparage or criminalize the shape of their bodies or the way in which they seek to love and to be held.

To speak of choice for journeys that are motivated by such tenebrous conditions is simply misleading. What they have in common is the urgency of movement and a prospect marked by risk and uncertainty. What migrants and refugees enter is a penumbra where every form of security and identity, political and psychic, is aleatory; sometimes a gift, other times an imposition, never assured, never permanent, and always surrounded by contingency. The lives of refugees, who, in the world we live in, are the most numerous kinds of migrants, are riven by these harsh and uncertain realities. They certainly deserve compassion, hospitality, and more. That should be a settled matter.

But as is so often the case with things that enter our imagination from a peripheral angle, the predicament of the refugee and the migrant may help us reimagine our own mode of collective existence along with the assurances that surround it and the identities and securities that we so comfortably presume. The humanities have always had an essential role in stretching our imagination to see connections between the familiar and the exceptional by pointing to that hazy line where the two meet and blur each other. It is what Shelley had in mind when he spoke of the imagination as the instrument of moral good, because, like poetry, it was "the receptacle of a thousand unapprehended combinations of thought." Perhaps, the migrant, precisely because of the risks and contingencies that mark her condition, can open us to forms of existence that may represent an aspirational ideal in which security in particular is understood as being provisional and experimental, and not as something that exists on one side of the fortified boundary that separates the citizen from the refugee?

From ancient times, travel has been that singular human activity where choice, suspicion, and danger are braided. Even before borders and boundaries were marked out as sites for the special vigilance of the state—always policed, always monitored—travel provoked an anxiety, as though the activity itself represented a transgressive freedom that could unsettle what was meant to be singular, stable, and familiar. Travel has always embodied the possibility of an excess, captured by the very act of movement, of changing places, of being in transition, and of not having identities that are clearly certifiable. It threatens the patterns of a social consensus; perhaps, by reminding that consensus of its own fragility, the arbitrary solidity on which it rests, and the complicity and darkness around which it has been forged. Even when there are no boundaries being crossed, the traveler as he or she moves is so often taken to represent the violation of a tacit limit, the potential disruption of a settled norm. The examples of such quotidian eruptions are too numerous to cite, but one is reminded of Gandhi sitting unobjectionably in a first-class compartment in a train traveling from Durban to Maritzburg, provoking by his mere presence and movement the insecurities and violent prejudices of the white train conductor. As Gandhi later noted about his experiences in South Africa, racism always had a special viciousness that was reserved for when colored and black people traveled. Thurgood Marshall, recalling a journey from Washington, DC, to Greensboro, NC, had much the same thought. African Americans were never in greater danger in the old South than when they were traveling, because that act always had the potential to inflame prejudices, which in a less fluid context had other sources of sublimation. The most macabre and horrifying images associated with the partition of India in 1947 are linked with trains and other forms of conveyance ferrying mutilated bodies in both directions across the newly demarcated boundaries of the two countries. And then of course there were the trains that blotted the conscience of Europe and the world in the 1940s.

From the standpoint of political theory, the standpoint I am most familiar with, these paroxysms of violence and prejudice that are linked with movement and the breach of boundaries are not difficult to understand. It would only be a minor exaggeration to say that the grand tradition of political thinking has typically been forged around a suspicion of the traveler and the stranger. Plato and Aristotle, in emphasizing the bounded nature of the polis and the sort of sharing it made possible and the diversity it presumed, are quite explicit that the life of the citizen is set against the image of the wanderer. In the dialogue the *Timaeus*, Socrates permits the possibility that wandering tribes may be the purveyors of philosophical knowledge, but never of political knowledge. If there is one description of people that political theory as a discipline has shown a sustained suspicion of, either explicitly or by a studied indifference, it is nomads. At the dawn of the modern era, when Locke articulates the implications of the contract through which political society is constituted, what he, like Hobbes before him, emphasizes is the clarity of the boundaries that this act of constitution and enclosure establishes—"whereby it is easy to discern who are, and who are not, in political society together." The central categories of our political lexicon—law, order, power, representation, sovereignty, the singularity of a people—are all in different and complex ways reliant on securing the contrast between boundedness and mobility.

The migrant in many ways provokes the same existential anxiety that civil war and anarchy have long provoked, and that so often is the founding contrast on which nations anchor the narratives of their identities. As a familiar heuristic, anarchy represents a condition of abject insecurity, precisely because boundaries and identities are fluid. As Hobbes famously claimed, it is a condition that points to death, and hence motivates the most basic normative postulates of modern politics, namely a hyperbolic concern for unity and security. As the post-9/11 world has made vivid, the concern with security operates as a kind of permanent, almost metaphysical backdrop for every future eventuality.

Security is the central catechism of our contemporary secular theology. It is not merely that a concern with security has been the authorizing warrant for the perpetual motion of recent foreign wars, or that security, not ideology in its traditional sense, now underwrites a global vision that needs the buttress of far-flung garrisons. Security, which until not so long ago constituted a distinct or exceptional zone of political consideration, now laces every aspect of domestic and foreign policy, ranging over food production, energy policies, the fear of viruses and diseases, the guard posts at our schools, colleges, airports, and public arenas, the integrity of our banks, the gathering of limitless information about citizens and others alike, and, of course, the people we choose to admit through our borders. At one level, this testifies to the new ways in which everything is connected, and to the fact that the designation of "separate spheres," on which liberalism relied and on whose denial totalitarianism prospered, are increasingly tenuous. But the priority that security has assumed is a distinct matter. It is now a familiar fact that officials justify even the most mundane aspects of public policies by invoking the idea of security. Terms such as justice, equality, decency, and even freedom, which once carried the hope and burden of our public ethos, have receded to the disused recesses of our shared vocabulary. Even the avowedly liberal President Barack Obama described his duty as protecting the American people and not in terms of the more complex mandate to preserve and defend the Constitution.

We are determined to be safe, as once we were determined to be free; and we subscribe to a set of fears and beliefs so that only the authorities and our political apparatuses, such as fortified borders and the dispersed paraphernalia of surveillance, can create the impression that we are in fact safe. Fear and security course through the mundane aspects of our lives with such subcutaneous and manifest ubiquity that they are now paradoxically below the threshold of our conscious anxieties. We live with them with the same mix of horror and complacency that medieval Christians lived with the presence of demons. To a considerable extent in the North Atlantic democracies (unlike the many other parts of the world where fear is the response to real and felt danger), fear has ceased to be an emotion. It is instead deployed as a policing device between what is collectively acceptable and what challenges our preestablished certainties. When fear is invoked, as it so often is, as a cant to confirm narrow group identities or to exaggerate an imminent threat to the nation, it obscures the real reasons why at least some people have genuine cause to fear—to fear a loss of health care, or the loss of jobs with a reasonable prospect of well-being and dignity, or the fear of all-too-easy incarceration that blights some communities. Ironically, the vast paraphernalia of security are now perhaps the most sustained link that ordinary citizens have with public authorities. In a perverse inversion of what is otherwise a telling absence, when it comes to being enmeshed with matters relating to security we live in a highly participatory democracy; but one that tends to amplify our sense of helplessness, and further roots us, as Roosevelt famously warned, in "nameless, unreasoning, unjustified terror which paralyzes needed efforts." This may be a premonition of the fate of democracies, which originally sought to make us safe so that we would be free to enrich our lives and our communities in myriad ways; but which through a dialectical inversion now make a concern with safety the very ground of our sense of community—a community, moreover, in which an obsession with security is coupled with mutual distrust. It is not surprising that as an administrative dictate, such a capacious anxiety has to be housed under the vague and indefinite rubric of "Homeland Security." Through a mix of coercion, paranoia, consent, neglect, and ignorance we live as inmates, under conditions that until not so long ago were reserved for the criminally consigned.

Our concern with security and political unity increasingly resembles a vision of society as a security pact pegged to the dream, the paranoid dream, of seeking complete safety, of fearing, mainly as a ruse, the slightest provocation as being a threat to life and civilization. With this as the backdrop that structures our political imagination, the migrant comes to represent the stranger, the traveler, who comes today and stays tomorrow but always remains from elsewhere. The migrant, like Gandhi or Thurgood Marshall sitting in a train compartment, triggers a threat by his mere presence, or in the case of the refugee, by the mere imagination of his presence.

A conception of political life, even of democracy, that privileges a form with such a reliance on unity and safety is liable to coalesce around the self-confirming rigidities of what is proper and what is not. It is as though our political imagination is frozen around these banal certainties. The philosopher Richard Rorty emphasized that our "final vocabularies" should be chastened by an awareness that they are always in the process of being redescribed, and that poetry and other imaginative acts have always played a significant role in that redescription. The migrant and the refugee embody poetic injunctions for a different vision of society and place of security in it.

In this other vision, safety is not wedded to the constant concern with avoiding death and to the demand of politics that it secure life at any cost. Instead it puts a limit to what individuals expect from the state and other authorities; but it also points to what they pledged to retain as inalienable, because it was internal to their self-conception as free subjects. It is related to their singularity, their expressive nature, the urges of conscience and the type of self-regard that has a spiritual and poetical aspect, for which the physical body, both of the individual and of the collectivity, is neither a stand-in nor an alibi. It refers to that kernel of the self which, even while it is touched by the conformities of time and history, retains the urge to look beyond them. It is the internal domain that sought, in the famous words of Justice Louis Brandeis, "to be left alone" to the risky adventure of living. It is predicated on the thought not only that speech, the disputation of debate, the pursuits of the imagination and the feelings they engender, do not require security but that their flourishing has an ineradicable element of risk attached to it. It considers thoughts, ideas, and feelings as belonging to a different register of existential needs than that of the body. It conceives of them as retaining that spirit that is indifferent to safety and security and to the vigilance and mediation of authorities. It vouches for a citizenry that does not take all its cues from a collective project bound together around a single catechism. It is committed to the idea that our public purposes do not have a presumptive priority over our private attempts at self-creation, and that the inevitable tensions between these two should not automatically be settled by invoking "the founding principles of the republic" or any other lofty public trumps.

The migrant, as she looks back at what she is fleeing from and as she enters a penumbra marked by risk and uncertainty, gives us a preliminary glimpse of a different, more humanist ideal and a more provisional vision of politics. Unlike the idea of a balance, between security and an expressive domain, that ultimately takes refuge in a singular political rationale, this other vision of the refugee, the nomad, the migrant, relies on an ordinary and messy heroism that values the republic not for the security it claims to ensure. Instead she values the republic because it includes spaces in which thoughts, ideas, and feelings are exempt from a collective supervision and calculus, where safety is not a grounding ideal or a Hobbesian trump that can overwhelm all else, but rather because the vision embraces the idea that the predicament of the citizen and the refugee are, however improbably, twined.

This vision is crucial to any vibrant form of collective order, because it insists that not everything worth valuing should be made subsidiary to the political rationale of security, unity, or anything else. In acute and typically brutal ways, the predicament of the refugee and the migrant is simply thrust upon them. But in part because theirs is an existence that in so many crucial respects was just arbitrarily given to them, they can potentially rejuvenate that Kantian and Gandhian conception of enlightenment that was associated not with security or uniformity or even collective purposefulness, but rather with courage, risk, adventure, and compassion.

Theirs is a vision of democracy at the edges of its familiar and clichéd affirmations that recalls a sort of truancy, a vital dream, that draws on the patterns of shared existence without obsessively relying on the demarcations of clear boundaries with policed points of entry and egress. The predicament of the refugee as one who travels, who is displaced, who lives in camps, whose identity is precarious, who must imagine the future in provisional terms, who thinks of safety as something with that is never assured and never free of risk, and of hope as something crafted within this aleatory horizon—this predicament shares something with, and yet, of course, is also starkly different from, that of the tourist, who also moves, seeks out adventure, embraces risks, relies on the hospitality of others, and imagines a condition in which identity is lifted from its familiar assurances.

Perhaps one can only speak of it as a poetic vision, of a wildflower that flourishes amidst the wheat. The humanities as they reflect on the migrant and the refugee have an essential role in drawing out the lineaments of this vision.

- - - - - - - -

This essay is derived from a talk entitled "Identity and Dignity," prepared for the Conference on Migration and the Humanities, Mahindra Humanities Center, Harvard University, February 8–9, 2018. Printed by arrangement with the author.

Eavan Boland's poem "That the Science of Cartography Is Limited" was originally published in *In a Time of Violence* (New York: W. W. Norton & Company, Inc., 1994). Reprinted by arrangement with W. W. Norton & Company, Inc., and Carcanet Press Limited.

Words That Make Worlds

Peggy Levitt

Immigration has never been an easy subject to discuss in the United States. Our debates are now more divisive than ever. They reveal that words make worlds that empower or silence, that inspire empathy or fear. The terms that we use to speak about migrants and refugees serve particular social and political interests, influencing public opinion and policy-making and the entitlements and protections offered to some groups and denied to others.

Let me begin with some examples of words we use to describe different kinds of people on the move. When individuals are granted legal refugee status, it is because they have proved that they have a "well-founded fear of persecution" because of their race, religion, nationality, or membership in a particular group.[1] They are given access to a set of rights and services, depending upon where they settle. They are distinguished from the many other asylum seekers who also move in response to violence, persecution, or war but have not yet been granted refugee status. They also stand apart from the many "voluntary" migrants who move because they cannot make enough money to support themselves and their families—a kind of economic violence in its own right. The public often uses terms such as "asylum seekers," "voluntary migrants," or "illegal aliens" to distinguish between the "deserving" and the "undeserving," although each of these labels includes all kinds of people who voluntarily or forcibly flee their homes, and the line between them is frequently quite blurred. Yet some terms inspire compassion and generosity while others provoke defensive gestures, including literally trying to build walls to keep migrants out.

My second point concerns notions of "race." The categories used to classify racial differences in, for example, the U.S., the Dominican, and the Brazilian censuses vary considerably. This does not mean that people in those countries are phenotypically different; it means that the diversity-management regimes in each place vary with respect to how race gets talked about and counted, and what resources, opportunities, and power are available to people depending on how they are classified. Meanwhile, in some countries in Europe, a culture of silence about race permeates, especially in the shadow of World War II and the Holocaust. Yet racial distinctions are of course incredibly salient. They map unequally onto labels such as "citizen," "refugee," and "migrant," powerfully influencing both official and personal responses to those to whom they are assigned, and affecting those people's rights and privileges. Again, the categories we use, and the power dynamics that produce them, are socially constructed. They express not an unchanging fact or truth but a set of values and priorities that privilege the rule-makers in charge of the dictionary at a particular moment.

This essay focuses on another set of word choices that influence our understanding of nations, of who belongs in them, and of what newcomers must do to become full members of the national community. I draw primarily on examples from the United States—a settler colonial state created by the displacement of indigenous communities and the enslavement of Africans—but my arguments hold true for many contexts across the globe.

We tend to imagine that most people in the world stay put, and that migration is the exception rather than the rule. This is why we often talk about "emigrants" (people who leave a place) and "immigrants" (people who are then incorporated into another place) instead of "migrants." We expect that people may want to, and can, leave one place and settle permanently in another and we assume that they make a definitive break, trading in one membership card for another. Yet in 2018, 244 million people, or 3.3 per cent of the world's population, were international migrants.[2] Global displacement was at a record high, with the number of people who were internally displaced within their own countries reaching over 40 million and the number of refugees who were forced to leave their countries at more than 22 million.[3] This means that, by some estimates, one out of every seven people in the world today is on the move.[4]

These data beg us to reconsider our vocabulary and to see some form of transnational movement—whether voluntary or involuntary, leading to great success or great struggle—as the norm. How would we understand the world differently if we turned our conventional wisdom on its head? What might we see about nations and belonging that is currently hiding in plain sight? What new kinds of social and political institutions would we need to create in response? Let me make this concrete by "redefining" some important words.

Nation

No doubt some migrants want to settle permanently and become naturalized citizens of the countries to which they move, and some will be able to do so. Others are what economist Michael Piore calls "birds of passage": they simply want to earn enough money to support themselves and their families and return home.[5] Many more are permanently impermanent. I'm talking not just about the estimated 11 million undocumented within U.S. borders but about the many other countries with increasing numbers of long-term *residents without membership*, people who live for extended periods without full rights or representation. More and more people are also long-term *members without residence*, living outside the country where they are citizens but participating in its economic and political life, if often without being able to fully access their rights there. In both cases, these migrants make their sending and receiving societies—the societies they come from and the societies they go to—more diverse, not only racially, ethnically, and with respect to religion but also in terms of membership, rights, and representation. There are professional-class migrants who carry two passports and know how to make claims and exercise their voices in multiple settings; there are many more poor, labor-class migrants, disadvantaged in both the country they have come from and the country where they are. A new form of stratification distinguishes those who are fully politically integrated in two places from those who are not protected anywhere. Migration redistributes inequality rather than decreasing it.

These dynamics challenge basic assumptions about what a nation is and who its members are. They also call into question ideas about how family life gets lived, where livelihoods are earned, and where citizenship is enacted. In parts of Mexico, there are many villages with few residents between the ages of eighteen and sixty-five because so many people are working in the United States to support the young and the elderly back home.[6] The more remittances they send, the more Mexico's regional economic base weakens, because the state has little incentive to fix the country's high unemployment rates when such large numbers live off migrants' remittances.[7] Likewise, migrant contributions build roads, schools, and health clinics, doing what the dysfunctional state cannot or will not do. Migrants' communities of origin enjoy better infrastructure and social services, but cannot sustain them without migrants' continuing support.

It does not stop there. The transnational ties that link families and communities change how supposedly sovereign nation-states get things done. Since Mexico depends upon migrant remittances, it wants to ensure they continue. To reinforce migrants' enduring loyalty and nationalism, the government offers incentives such as dual nationality and the right to vote from abroad. The government also steps in when the U.S. government does not provide. For example, because many migrants have no health insurance, Mexican consulates throughout the United States have opened clinics that provide very basic health care. In addition, the government issues a *Matrícula Consular*, an official ID card that, as of 2013, was accepted as formal proof of identity by more than 371 American counties, 356 financial institutions, and 1,036 police departments.[8] And when Donald Trump became U.S. president, in 2017, Mexico opened legal clinics at its consulates to defend its citizens against impending crackdowns.

These examples challenge the idea that migrants can and want to settle permanently, and that they will enjoy full rights and be able to fulfill their responsibilities once they do. They also challenge the idea that migrants will have little to do with their sending states once they move. In the case of Mexico, the government is working both to ease the difficulties migrants face in the United States and to reinforce their ties to Mexico. It believes that well-educated, integrated, English-speaking migrants are good for both Mexico and the United States. Nor is Mexico unique; more and more people are pushed or choose to belong to more than one nation. At different stages of their lives, or when there is an election, an economic downturn, or a climatic disaster, their national attachments ebb and flow. Dual loyalties are not a kind of bigamy; they give people a way to support themselves and their families in contexts of economic restructuring and shrinking social supports. No border wall or anti-immigrant crackdown will sever these attachments because they are part of the world's economic, social, and political institutional fabric.

Borders

Nations are not discrete, contained cultural and political spaces to which members pledge singular loyalty. Instead, they are continuously constructed and reconstructed. This means that we need to revisit the notion of the border. Most of us think of borders as relatively fixed or impermeable, as announcing logical divisions between one people and another. That logic pushes us to think in false dichotomies—to assume a clear distinction between ideas of good and evil, black and white, between someone who migrates and someone who is settled. But these distinctions are never so crystal clear.

Take the long-standing immigrant-rights slogan "We didn't cross the border, the border crossed us." In the case of the U.S.-Mexican border, the territory of Mexico, Texas, and the United States shifted rapidly over several short decades in the early nineteenth century. In the 1820s, Mexico, fresh from the revolution that won it independence from Spain, invited Anglos to settle in its northern territories including Texas, which was part of Mexico at the time. Texas was to be a buffer between the United States and the Mexican heartland. Some settlers came in good faith and became Mexican citizens. Others came to stake a claim to a territory that they hoped would someday become part of the Anglo, Protestant United States. "The first problem with illegal immigration in Texas," says American-history Professor Frank Cogliano, "was Anglo Americans coming into Mexican Texas as opposed to the border going the other way."[9] In losing the Mexican-American war of 1846–48, Mexico lost a large swath of its territory, including present-day California, Arizona, New Mexico, Texas, Utah, and part of Colorado.

This historical example drives home that borders are not fixed lines dividing nations and cultures but intense zones of contact that change with the social and political winds. In 2016, 42 million people regularly crossed the sixteen bridges between the United States and Mexico to work, go to school, visit family, or shop.[10] The ties that bind families, friends, and communities are creating new institutions of transnational social protection. These include private and state-run health maintenance organizations (HMOs) that offer binational health-insurance plans to migrants who live near the border in California. A network of providers offers emergency care in California and primary care in Mexico, where it is cheaper.[11] Mexican residents living on the Mexican side of the border can join too. According to Patricia Gándara, who codirects the Civil Rights Project at the University of California, Los Angeles, over 55 percent of the public school population in California are Latinx, making California a "semi-Mexican state."[12] Since 1982, the Mexican and U.S. governments have cooperated through the Programa Binacional de Educación Migrante/Bi-National Migrant Education Program (PROBEM), which aims to ensure that young people who spend part of the school year in Mexico and part in the United States still get a quality education.[13]

This intertwining of home and host-country identities and institutions often extends way beyond the border. In neighborhoods in Los Angeles, Chicago, and Houston, and also, increasingly, in small towns throughout the Southeast and Midwest, money-wiring and travel agencies, home-country political-party headquarters, immigrant churches, and grocery stores selling products from back home testify to migrants' transnational lives and daily bridging of here and there across allegedly impermeable borders.

Assimilation

My last point concerns the term "assimilation," the word generally used in the United States to describe the process by which migrants become part of the places to which they move and, after several generations, (hopefully) achieve socioeconomic parity with their native-born counterparts.

An unpacking of the intellectual and political genealogy of cultural assimilation, and of the way it has changed over time, makes clear the national project it drove forward and the changes it was devised to prevent. The initial expectation in the United States, prevalent through the mid-1960s, involved the principle of the melting pot—the idea that immigrants would and should lose their customs and language of origin and melt into the predominant white, Anglo-Saxon, Protestant culture. The civil and women's rights movements of that decade reimagined the melting pot as a multicultural mosaic in which each group could maintain aspects of its unique character but also become fully integrated into the political and economic mainstream. Instead of seeing assimilation as a one-way street, some policy-makers and pundits acknowledged that migrant and native-born cultures mutually transformed each other.

Part of the reason this plays out the way it does in the United States is that this nation, like Canada and Australia, defines itself as a nation of immigrants. Many European countries, in contrast, also talk about multiculturalism and pluralism, but because their histories of migration and enslavement differ, they define the nation and what it takes to fully belong to it differently. In Mexico, the struggle has been between the descendants of Spanish colonizers and those of the indigenous civilizations they conquered. Just after the Revolution in 1917, and during the presidency of Lázaro Cárdenas (1934–40), when the *Indigenismo* movement was particularly strong, leaders made serious efforts to bring Mexico's indigenous roots into the national narrative. Although indigenous history has been central to Mexico's national imagination, the competing image of *ranchera* culture—

a rugged life, beautiful women, macho cowboys, Catholicism, mariachi music, and tequila—has usually won out, especially in regions where indigenous communities are a minority.[14]

Back in this country, more than fifty years after the Immigration and Nationality Act of 1965, the idea that newcomers can and should become full members of the nation still holds but we continue to disagree strongly about how.[15] Full incorporation remains beyond the reach of many. The voices of anti-immigrant critics who oppose bilingual education, support "English-Only" laws, and want to restrict voting rights are loud and clear.

The experience of migration and marginalization, however, can produce unique strengths and tools. Cultural-studies scholar Gloria Anzaldúa described the geography of the Texas-Mexico border as a political, cultural, and spiritual borderland. When the border moved, making those who had been Mexicans into Americans, they became strangers in their own land. Over time, a survival strategy that Anzaldúa calls a "*mestiza* consciousness" took shape: "Indigenous like corn, like corn the *mestiza* is a product of crossbreeding, designed for preservation under a variety of conditions."[16] Mestiza consciousness embraces ambiguity and contradiction, the ability to see yourself as you are and to understand the way others see you. Though produced by hardship, this dual perspective is a powerful way of being in the world that should be cultivated, not abandoned.

Challenging power by demanding to be judged on one's own terms is also reflected in the idea of *rasquachismo*. The Spanish word *rasquache*, Nahuatl in origin, was once used disparagingly to refer to poor people who lacked taste. Chicano arts-movement activists have reclaimed it to describe artists who turn social and economic precariousness into a creative advantage. They use what is quickly and cheaply available, "creating the most from the least"—a gesture that is irreverent, deviant, and inventive.[17] For cultural-studies scholar Tomás Ybarra-Fausto, this "bi-cultural" sensibility involves an "underdog" perspective that turns power on its head.[18] The idea was not to pursue a cleaner, newer approach to art-making or to necessarily get displayed in the nation's centers of artistic power. It was to build upon *rasquachismo*'s unique cultural contribution and to honor it in its own right.

Conclusion

It is because words have the power to make worlds that our choices of them matter. As I write, the United States is fighting bitterly over border-wall funding. Every day, President Trump fires up his supporters by calling immigrants "drug dealers," "criminals," and "rapists." His words are intended to inspire hatred and fear, and they are working. It was this very rhetoric that got him elected in 2016.

But there is a counterargument, seemingly so popular that you can buy T-shirts on which it is printed at any number of outlets online: it is "We are all immigrants." This is not to say that coming to the United States voluntarily to seek a better life is the same as coming in the hold of a slave ship, or as being forced to leave your native land. It is to say, as President John F.

Kennedy did when he told a massive crowd at the Berlin Wall in 1963, "*Ich bin ein Berliner*" (I am a Berliner), that we stand with immigrants with compassion and solidarity. It is to say that we know that the immigrant experience is an invaluable, essential part of who we are as a nation. This is the kind of world I want to make. I, for one, am buying my T-shirt.

— — — — — — — —

1. UN Convention and Protocol Relating to the Status of Refugees, 1951. Available online at www.unhcr.org/3b66c2aa10 (accessed February 17, 2019).

2. See International Organization for Migration, "World Migration Report," chapter 2, "Migration and Migrants: A Global Overview," 2018. Available online at www.iom.int/wmr/chapter-2 (accessed February 7, 2019).

3. Ibid. Internally displaced persons have not crossed a border to find safety or shelter; they are "on the run" in their country of origin. See UNHCR, the UN Refugee Agency, "Internally Displaced People." Available online at www.unhcr.org/internally-displaced-people.html (accessed February 7, 2019).

4. See International Organization for Migration, "Migration in the world," June 21, 2018. Available online at www.iom.sk/en/migration/migration-in-the-world.html (accessed February 17, 2019).

5. See Michael J. Piore, *Birds of Passage: Migrant Labor and Industrial Societies* (Cambridge: Cambridge University Press, 1979).

6. It is important to note, however, that since 2012, the net flow of both legal and undocumented migration from Mexico into the United States has decreased. The Pew Charitable Trust has estimated that between 2009 and 2014, 1 million Mexicans and their families (including U.S.-born children) left the United States, while 870,000 Mexicans arrived. See Max Bearak, "Even before Trump, more Mexicans were leaving the U.S. than arriving," *Washington Post*, January 27, 2017. Available online at www.washingtonpost.com/news/worldviews/wp/2017/01/27/even-before-trump-more-mexicans-were-leaving-the-us-than-arriving/?noredirect=on&utm_term=.3fdccd730be8 (accessed February 9, 2019).

7. Between January and November of 2017, Mexican migrants sent home a record $26.1 billion, making that income one of the country's top sources of foreign currency. See Patrick Gillespie, "Mexicans in U.S. send cash home in record numbers," January 3, 2018. Available online at https://money.cnn.com/2018/01/02/news/economy/mexico-remittances/index.html (accessed February 17, 2019).

8. See National Immigration Law Center, "Basic Facts about the *Matricular Consular*," December 2015. Available online at www.nilc.org/wp-content/uploads/2015/11/Basic-Facts-about-the-Matricula-Consular.pdf (accessed February 9, 2019).

9. Frank Cogliano, speaking on "The Mexican-American War," an episode of the BBC 4 radio program *In Our Time*, aired June 28, 2018. Available online at www.bbc.co.uk/sounds/play/b0b7d18j (accessed February 17, 2019).

10. See Rosalina Nieves, "The places where thousands cross the US-Mexico border on foot each day," CNN World, available online at https://edition.cnn.com/2017/05/31/us/us-mexico-pedestrian-bridges/index.html (accessed February 9, 2019).

11. See, e.g., the website of Sistemas Medicos Nacionales, S.A. de C.V. (simnsa), as www.simnsa.com/simnsa/index.html (accessed February 9, 2019).

12. Patricia Gándara, "Policy Report—Informe: L@s estudiantes que compartimos/The Students We Share," *Mexican Studies/Estudios Mexicanos* 32, no. 2 (Summer 2016):357–78 (DOI: 10.1525/mex.2016.32.2.357).

13. See Global Forum on Migration & Development, "Bi-national Migrant Education Program (probem), January 15, 2014. Available online at www.gfmd.org/pfp/ppd/455 (accessed February 17, 2019).

14. See Claudio Lomnitz-Adler, *Las Salidas del laberinto. Cultura e Ideología en el espacio Nacional Mexicano* (Mexico City: Joaquín Mortiz/Planeta, 1995).

15. Also known as the Hart-Cellar Act, this legislation replaced the earlier national-origin quota system with a focus on family reunification and attracting skilled labor. As a result, many more Latin American and Asian migrants settled in the United States, slowly changing the face of the nation. See Muzaffar Chishti, Faye Hipsman, and Isabel Ball, "Fifty Years on, the 1965 Immigration and Nationality Act Continues to Reshape the United States," in "Migration Information Source," Migration Policy Institute, October 15, 2015. Available online at www.migrationpolicy.org/article/fifty-years-1965-immigration-and-nationality-act-continues-reshape-united-states (accessed March 9, 2019).

16. Gloria Anzaldúa, *Borderlands/La Frontera: The New Mestiza* (San Francisco: Aunt Lute Books, 1987), p. 103.

17. Sofia Quintero Art and Culture Center, "Rasquachismo," n.d., available online at https://www.rasquacheresidency.com/rasquachismo (accessed February 9, 2019).

18. Tomás Ybarra-Fausto, "Rasquachismo: A Chicano Sensibility," 1989. Available online at https://icaadocs.mfah.org/icaadocs/THEARCHIVE/FullRecord/tabid/88/doc/845510/language/en-US/Default.aspx (accessed February 17, 2019).

Works in the Exhibition

Kader Attia
La Mer Morte (The Dead Sea), 2015
Clothes
Dimensions variable
Courtesy the artist and Lehmann Maupin, New York, Hong Kong, and Seoul
Pp. 96–97

Yto Barrada
Usine 1—Conditionnement de crevettes dans la zone franche, Tanger 1998 [Factory 1—Prawn Processing Plant in the Free Trade Zone, Tangier 1998], 1998
From the series A Life Full of Holes: The Strait Project, 1998–2003
Chromogenic color print
40 9⁄16 x 40 9⁄16 inches (103 x 103 cm)
Courtesy the artist and Galerie Polaris, Paris
P. 93

Rue de la Liberté, Tanger 2000, 2000
From the series A Life Full of Holes: The Strait Project, 1998–2003
Chromogenic color print
49 3⁄16 x 49 3⁄16 inches (125 x 125 cm)
Courtesy the artist and Galerie Polaris, Paris
P. 92

Panneau—Publicité de lotissement touristique—Briech 2002 [Hoarding—advertising for a tourist development—Briech 2002], 2002
From the series A Life Full of Holes: The Strait Project, 1998–2003
Chromogenic color print
31½ x 31½ inches (80 x 80 cm)
Courtesy the artist and Galerie Polaris, Paris
P. 93

Salon de première—Ferry de Tanger à Algesiras, Espagne—2002 [First class lounge—Ferry from Tangier to Algeciras, Spain—2002], 2002
From the series A Life Full of Holes: The Strait Project, 1998–2003
Chromogenic color print
33 x 33 inches (83.8 x 83.8 cm)
Private collection
P. 91

Caisson lumineux—Lieu de transit—Tanger 2003 [Advertisement light box—Ferry port transit area—Tangier 2003], 2003
From the series A Life Full of Holes: The Strait Project, 1998–2003
Chromogenic color print
23⅝ x 23⅝ inches (60 x 60 cm)
Courtesy the artist and Pace Gallery
P. 90

Le Détroit de Gibraltar—Reproduction d'une photographie aerienne—Tanger 2003 [The Strait of Gibraltar—reproduction of an aerial photograph—Tangier 2003], 2003
From the series A Life Full of Holes: The Strait Project, 1998–2003
Chromogenic color print
23⅝ x 23⅝ inches (60 x 60 cm)
Courtesy the artist and Galerie Polaris, Paris
P. 92

Arbre généalogique [Family Tree], 2005
Chromogenic color print
59 x 59 inches (149.9 x 149.9 cm)
Courtesy the artist and Pace Gallery
P. 91

A Guide to Trees, 2011/2019
Wallpaper
Dimensions variable
Courtesy the artist

Tania Bruguera
Dignity Has No Nationality, 2017
Nylon, polyester poplin, and thread
16 feet 4⅞ inches x 9 feet 10⅛ inches (506 x 300 cm)
Courtesy the artist

Rineke Dijkstra
Almerisa, 1994–
Chromogenic color prints
Fifteen parts, each 14 15⁄16 x 11 13⁄16 inches (38 x 30 cm)
Courtesy the artist and Marian Goodman Gallery
Pp. 66–69

Guillermo Galindo
Zapatello, 2014
From the series Border Cantos, 2004–16
Wood blocking used in construction of border wall, tire, rawhide, boot, glove, donkey jaw, and ram's horn
70 x 38 x 76 inches (177.8 x 96.5 x 193 cm)
Fabricated by Ross Craig and Tiffany Huey
Courtesy the artist and Pace/MacGill Gallery, New York
P. 127

Ángel Exterminador/Exterminating Angel, 2015
From the series Border Cantos, 2004–16
Section of border wall, Border Patrol drag chain, and wood blocking used in construction of wall
9 feet x 48 inches x 12 feet 3 inches (274.3 x 121.9 x 373.4 cm)
Courtesy the artist and Pace/MacGill Gallery, New York
P. 126

Mona Hatoum
Exodus II, 2002
Compressed card, leather, metal, human hair, and beeswax
19¾ x 26 x 26 inches (50 x 66 x 66 cm)
Private collection
P. 81

Isaac Julien
Western Union: small boats, 2007
Three-channel video installation, 35mm film transferred to HD video (color, 5.1 surround sound; 18:22 minutes)
Dimensions variable
Courtesy the artist and Metro Pictures, New York
Pp. 10, 100–105

Hayv Kahraman
Bab el Sheikh, 2013
Oil on wood
9 feet 3 inches x 11 feet 10 inches (281.9 x 360.7 cm)
Private collection
Pp. 8, 62–63

Reena Saini Kallat
Woven Chronicle, 2011–16
Circuit boards, speakers, electrical wires, and fittings; single-channel audio (10:00 minutes)
Approximately 11 x 38 feet (335.3 x 1158.2 cm)
Courtesy the artist and Nature Morte, New Delhi
Pp. 34–37

Richard Misrach
Effigy #7, near Jacumba, California/Efigie nº 7, cerca de Jacumba, California, 2009
From the series Border Cantos, 2004–16
Pigment print
60 x 80 inches (152.4 x 203.2 cm)
Courtesy the artist; Pace/MacGill Gallery, New York; Fraenkel Gallery, San Francisco; and Marc Selwyn Fine Arts, Los Angeles
P. 123

Artifacts found from California to Texas between 2013 and 2015/Artefactos encontrados entre California y Texas de 2013 a 2015, 2013–15
From the series Border Cantos, 2004–16
Pigment prints
Six parts, each 86 x 57½ inches (218.4 x 146.1 cm); 86 inches x 28 feet 9 inches (218.4 x 876.3 cm) (overall)
Courtesy the artist; Pace/MacGill Gallery, New York; Fraenkel Gallery, San Francisco; and Marc Selwyn Fine Arts, Los Angeles
Pp. 118–19

Agua #10, near Calexico, California/Agua nº 10, cerca de Calexico, California, 2014
From the series Border Cantos, 2004–16
Pigment print
60 x 80 inches (152.4 x 203.2 cm)
Courtesy the artist; Pace/MacGill Gallery, New York; Fraenkel Gallery, San Francisco; and Marc Selwyn Fine Arts, Los Angeles
P. 121

Wall, east of Nogales, Arizona/El muro, al este de Nogales, Arizona, 2014
From the series Border Cantos, 2004–16
Pigment print
60 x 80 inches (152.4 x 203.2 cm)
Courtesy the artist; Pace/MacGill Gallery, New York; Fraenkel Gallery, San Francisco; and Marc Selwyn Fine Arts, Los Angeles
P. 120

Richard Mosse
Incoming, 2014–17
Three-channel HD video (black and white, 7.3 surround sound; 52:10 minutes)
Dimensions variable
Produced in Europe, the Middle East, and North Africa
Co-commissioned by the National Gallery of Victoria, Melbourne, and Barbican Art Gallery, London
Director/Producer: Richard Mosse
Cinematographer/Editor: Trevor Tweeten
Composer/Sound Designer: Ben Frost
Colorist: Jerome Thelia
Production Assistants: Marta Giaccone, John Holten, and Daphne Tolis
Courtesy the artist; Jack Shainman Gallery, New York; and carlier | gebauer, Berlin
Pp. 2–3, 54–59

Carlos Motta
The Crossing, 2017
Five channels from an eleven-channel video installation (color, sound)
"Anwar" (12:08 minutes)
"Butterfly" (12:20 minutes)
"Mahshid" (11:05 minutes)
"Mala" (11:47 minutes)
"Raneen" (11:58 minutes)
Dimensions variable
Courtesy the artist and P·P·O·W Gallery, New York; Galeria Filomena Soares, Lisbon; Galeria Vermelho, São Paulo; and mor charpentier, Paris
Pp. 130–35

Aliza Nisenbaum
Veronica, Marissa, and Gustavo, 2013
Oil on linen
51 x 33 inches (129.5 x 83.8 cm)
Collection of Josh Lilley, London
P. 139

Marissa, 2014
Oil on linen
16 x 16 inches (40.6 x 40.6 cm)
Collection of Barbara Hirsch and
Mark A. Reich, New York
P. 141

Las Talaveritas, 2015
Oil on linen
64 x 57 inches (162.6 x 144.8 cm)
Valeria and Gregorio Napoleone
Collection, London
P. 140

La Talaverita, Sunday Morning NY Times,
2016
Oil on linen
68 x 88 inches (172.7 x 223.5 cm)
Collection of Jackson Tang, New York
P. 138

Camilo Ontiveros
Temporary Storage: The Belongings of Juan Manuel Montes, 2017
Personal belongings of Juan Manuel
Montes, rope, metal sawhorse,
aluminum base, and wood
Approximately 72 x 72 x 18 inches
(182.9 x 182.9 x 45.7 cm)
The Museum of Fine Arts, Houston.
Museum purchase funded by the
2017 Latin American Experience
Gala and Auction
Pp. 45–47

Michelle Angela Ortiz
"Somos Seres Humanos" ("We Are Human
Beings"), 2019. Recommission from
the *Familias Separadas* (Separated
families) project, 2015–
Site-specific installation
Overall dimensions variable
Courtesy the artist
Pp. 152–53

Adrian Piper
Everything #4, 2004
Oval mirror with gold leaf-engraved text
in traditional mahogany frame
13 x 10 inches (33 x 25.4 cm)
Collection Adrian Piper Research Archive
Foundation Berlin
P. 41

Anthony Romero
With Dan Jackson and Jules Rochielle
Sievert of NuLawLab
...first in thought, then in action, 2019
Site-specific performance and installation
Courtesy the artist
P. 144

Yinka Shonibare CBE
The American Library, 2018
Hardback books, Dutch wax-printed cotton
textile, gold-foiled names, and website
Dimensions variable
Courtesy the artist and James Cohan
Gallery, New York
Pp. 14, 156–59

Xaviera Simmons
Found the Sea Like the River, 2018
Acrylic on wood panel
72 x 96 inches (182.9 x 243.8 cm)
Courtesy the artist and David Castillo
Gallery, Miami
Pp. 6–7, 84–85

Sundown (Number Twelve), 2018
Chromogenic color print
60 x 45 inches (152.4 x 114.3 cm)
The Institute of Contemporary Art/Boston,
Jeanne L. Wasserman Art Acquisition Fund
and Anonymous Acquisition Fund
P. 87

Do Ho Suh
Corridor-4, Wielandstr. 18, 12159 Berlin, Germany, 2015
Polyester fabric and stainless steel
11 feet 4¾ inches x 92⅜ inches x
48⅛ inches (347.3 x 234.5 x 122.1 cm)
Courtesy the artist and Lehmann Maupin,
New York, Hong Kong, and Seoul
Pp. 74–75

Hub-1, Entrance, 260-7, Sungbook-Dong, Sungboo-Ku, Seoul, Korea, 2018
Polyester fabric and stainless steel
11 feet ¼ inch x 12 feet 6 inches x
8 feet 1¼ inches (336 x 381 x 247 cm)
Courtesy the artist and Lehmann Maupin,
New York, Hong Kong, and Seoul
P. 77

Hub-2, Breakfast Corner, 260-7, Sungbook-Dong, Sungboo-Ku, Seoul, Korea, 2018
Polyester fabric and stainless steel
8 feet 10½ inches x 10 feet 8⅜ inches x
11 feet 8½ inches (271 x 326 x 357 cm)
Courtesy the artist and Lehmann Maupin,
New York, Hong Kong, and Seoul
P. 76

Selected Bibliography

Books

Agamben, Giorgio. *Homo Sacer: Sovereign Power and Bare Life.* Trans. Daniel Heller-Roazen. Stanford, CA: Stanford University Press, 1998.

———. *Means without End: Notes on Politics.* Trans. Vincenzo Binetti and Cesare Casarino. Minneapolis: University of Minnesota Press, 2000.

Ahmed, Sara, Claudia Castada, Anne-Marie Fortier, and Mimi Sheller, eds. *Uprootings/Regroundings: Questions of Home and Migration.* London: Bloomsbury, 2003.

Alberro, Alexander, and Blake Stimson, eds. *Conceptual Art: A Critical Anthology.* Cambridge, MA, and London: The MIT Press, 1999.

Ardizzoni, Michela, and Valerio Ferme, eds. *Mediterranean Encounters in the City: Frameworks of Mediation between East and West, North and South.* Lanham, MD: Lexington Books, 2015.

Anzaldua, Gloria. *Borderlands/La frontera: The New Mestiza.* San Francisco: Spinsters/Aunt Lute, 1987.

Azoulay, Ariella. *Civil Imagination: A Political Ontology of Photography.* London: Verso, 2012.

Bal, Mieke, and Miguel Á. Hernández-Navarro. *Art and Visibility in Migratory Culture: Conflict, Resistance, and Agency.* Amsterdam: Rodopi, 2012.

Barenboim, Daniel. *Everything Is Connected: The Power of Music.* London: Weidenfeld & Nicolson, 2008.

———. *Music Quickens Time.* London: Verso, 2009.

Baronian, Marie-Aude, Stephan Besser, and Yolande Jansen, eds. *Diaspora and Memory: Figures of Displacement in Contemporary Literature, Arts, and Politics.* Amsterdam: Rodopi, 2007.

Barrowclough, Diana, and Zeljka Kozul-Wright. *Creative Industries and Developing Countries: Voice, Choice and Economic Growth.* London and New York: Routledge, 2008.

Bauder, Harald. *Migration, Borders, Freedom.* New York: Routledge, 2017.

Bejarano, Carolina Alonso, et. al. *Decolonizing Ethnography: Undocumented Immigrants and New Directions in Social Science.* Durham: Duke University Press, 2019.

Bernier, Celeste-Marie. *Stick to the Skin: African American and Black British Art, 1965–2015.* Oakland: University of California Press, 2018.

Bhabha, Homi. *The Location of Culture.* New York: Routledge, 1994.

Byrd, Jodi A. *Transit of Empire: Indigenous Critiques of Colonialism.* Minneapolis and London: University of Minnesota Press, 2011.

Casid, Jill H., and Aruna D'Souza, eds. *Art History in the Wake of the Global Turn.* Williamstown, MA: Sterling and Francine Clark Art Institute, 2014.

Charhadi, Driss ben Hamed. *A Life Full of Holes: A Novel Tape-Recorded in Moghrebi.* Trans. Paul Bowles. New York: Grove Press, 1964.

Demos, T. J. *The Migrant Image: The Art and Politics of Documentary during Global Crisis.* Durham, NC: Duke University Press, 2013.

Doherty, Claire. *Public Art (Now): Out of Time, Out of Place.* London: Art Books Publishing, 2015.

Durant, Sam, and Catherine M. Lord, eds. *Essays in Migratory Aesthetics: Cultural Practices between Migration and Art-Making.* Amsterdam: Rodopi, 2007.

Elkins, James, Zhivka Valiavicharska, and Alice Kim, eds. *Art and Globalization.* University Park: Pennsylvania State University Press, 2010.

Estefan, Kareem, Carin Kuoni, and Laura Raicovich, eds. *Assuming Boycott: Resistance, Agency, and Cultural Production.* New York and London: OR Books, 2017.

Foucault, Michel. *The Order of Things: An Archaeology of the Human Sciences.* New York: Vintage, 1970.

Glick Schiller, Nina, Linda Basch, and Christina Blanc-Szanzon, eds. *Towards a Transnational Perspective on Migration.* New York: New York Academy of Science, 1992.

Gourievidis, Laurence, ed. *Museums and Migration: History, Memory and Politics.* New York: Routledge, 2014.

Hall, Stuart. *The Fateful Triangle: Race, Ethnicity, Nation.* Cambridge, MA: Harvard University Press, 2017.

Ianniciello, Celeste. *Migrations, Arts and Postcoloniality in the Mediterranean.* New York: Routledge, 2018.

Johung, Jennifer. *Replacing Home: From Primordial Hut to Digital Network in Contemporary Art.* Minneapolis: University of Minnesota Press, 2011.

Jones, Reece. *Violent Borders: Refugees and the Right to Move.* London: Verso Books, 2017.

Köhn, Steffen. *Mediating Mobility: Visual Anthropology in the Age of Migration.* New York: Columbia University Press, 2016.

Kurgan, Laura. *Close Up at a Distance: Mapping, Technology, Politics*. Brooklyn, NY: Zone Books, 2013.

Kwon, Miwon. *One Place after Another: Site-specific Art and Locational Identity*. Cambridge, MA: The MIT Press, 2004.

Levin, Amy K., ed. *Global Mobilities: Refugees, Exiles, and Immigrants in Museums and Archives*. New York: Routledge, 2016.

Lomnitz-Adler, Claudio. *Las Salidas del Laberinto: Cultura e Ideología en el espacio Nacional Mexicano*. Mexico City: Joaquín Mortiz and Planeta, 1995.

Mathur, Saloni, ed. *The Migrant's Time: Rethinking Art History and Diaspora*. Williamstown, MA: Sterling and Francine Clark Art Institute, 2011.

Mercer, Kobena, ed. *Exiles, Diasporas & Strangers*. London: Iniva, 2008.

———. *Travel & See: Black Diaspora Art Practices since the 1980s*. Durham, NC: Duke University Press, 2016.

Merrill, Heather. *Black Spaces: African Diaspora in Italy*. New York: Routledge, 2018.

Meskimmon, Marsha. *Contemporary Art and the Cosmopolitan Imagination*. New York: Routledge, 2011.

Mignolo, Walter D., and Catherine E. Walsh. *On Decoloniality: Concepts, Analytics, and Praxis*. Durham, NC: Duke University Press, 2018.

Min-ha, Trinh T. *Woman, Native, Other: Writing Postcoloniality and Feminism*. Bloomington and Indianapolis: Indiana University Press, 1986.

Nguyen, Viet Thanh. *The Refugees*. New York: Grove Atlanta, 2017.

Oliver, Kelly. *Carceral Humanitarianism: Logics of Refugee Detention*. Minneapolis: University of Minnesota Press, 2017.

Papastergiadis, Nikos. *Spatial Aesthetics: Art, Place, and the Everyday*. London: Rivers Oram Press, 2006.

Petersen, Anne Ring. *Migration into Art: Transcultural Identities and Art-Making in a Globalized World*. Manchester: Manchester University Press, 2018.

Piper, Adrian. *Adrian Piper: A Reader*. New York: The Museum of Modern Art, 2018.

———. *Out of Order, Out of Sight*. Volume 1: *Selected Writings in Meta-Art, 1968–1992*. Cambridge, MA, and London: The MIT Press, 1996.

———. *Out of Order, Out of Sight*. Volume 2: *Selected Writings in Art Criticism, 1967–1992*. Cambridge, MA, and London: The MIT Press, 1999.

Romero, Anthony, and Dan S. Wang. *The Social Practice That Is Race*. Minneapolis: Beyond Repair, 2016.

Romero, Anthony, and Daniel Tucker. *Organize Your Own: The Politics and Poetics of Self-Determination Movements*. Chicago: Soberscove Press, 2016.

Said, Edward W. *Culture and Imperialism*. New York: Vintage, 1993.

Sassen, Saskia. *The Global City: New York, London, Tokyo*. Princeton: Princeton University Press, 1991.

Schafer, R. Murray. *The Tuning of the World*. New York: Knopf, 1977.

Sheehan, Tanya, ed. *Photography and Migration*. New York: Routledge, 2018.

Shire, Warsan. *Teaching My Mother How to Give Birth*. London: Flipped Eye Publishing, 2011.

Smithers, Gregory D., and Brooke N. Newman, eds. *Native Diasporas: Indigenous Identities and Settler Colonialism in the Americas*. Lincoln: University of Nebraska Press, 2014.

Tello, Veronica. *Counter-Memorial Aesthetics: Refugee Histories and the Politics of Contemporary Art*. New York: Bloomsbury Academic, 2016.

Thompson, Nato. *Living as Form: Socially Engaged Art from 1991–2011*. New York: Creative Time, 2012.

Triulzi, Alessandro, and Robert Lawrence McKenzie, eds. *Long Journeys: African Migrants on the Road*. Leiden and Boston: Brill, 2013.

Urrea, Luís Alberto. *The Devil's Highway: A True Story*. New York: Little Brown, 2004.

Vanderlinden, Barbara, and Elena Filipovic, eds. *The Manifesta Decade: Debates on Contemporary Art Exhibitions and Biennials in Post-Wall Europe*. Cambridge, MA: The MIT Press, 2005.

Verhagen, Marcus. *Flows and Counterflows: Globalization in Contemporary Art*. Berlin: Sternberg Press, 2017.

Weibel, Peter. *Global Activism: Art and Conflict in the 21st Century*. Cambridge, MA, and London: The MIT Press, 2014.

Weiss, Rachel. *To and from Utopia in the New Cuban Art*. Minneapolis: University of Minnesota Press, 2010.

Whitehead, Christopher, et al., eds. *Museums, Migration, and Identity in Europe: Peoples, Places, and Identities*. New York: Routledge, 2016.

Wilson, Richard Ashby, and Richard D. Brown, eds. *Humanitarianism and Suffering: The Mobilization of Empathy*. Cambridge: Cambridge University Press, 2009.

Exhibition Catalogues

Adams, Deidre. *Stories of Migration: Contemporary Artists Interpret Diaspora*. Storrs: Studio Quilt Art Associates, 2016.

Aleksić, Marija, et al. *The Border Is Closed*. Belgrade: The Museum of African Art and Group 484, 2015

Al-Khudhairi, Wassan. *Third-Space: Shifting Conversations about Contemporary Art*. Birmingham: Birmingham Museum of Art, 2017.

Attia, Kader, and Ralph Rugoff. *Kader Attia: The Museum of Emotion*. London: Hayward Gallery Publishing, 2019.

Attia, Kader, et al. *Kader Attia: Sacrifice and Harmony*. Bielefeld: Kerber, 2016.

Bancroft, Sarah C. *2010 California Biennial: Orange County Museum of Art*. Munich: Prestel, 2011.

Barrada, Yto. *Yto Barrada*. Zurich: JRP Ringier, 2013.

Barrada, Yto, et al. *Riffs*. Ostfildern: Hatje Cantz, 2011.

Beil, Ralf, et al. *Facing India*. Ostfildern: Hatje Cantz Verlag, 2018.

Brielmaier, Isolde. *Signs Taken for Wonders*. New York: Jack Shainman Gallery, 2009.

Burris, Jennifer, et al. *Foreclosed: Between Crisis and Possibility*. New York: Whitney Museum of American Art, 2011.

Bruguera, Tania, et al. *Tania Bruguera: Talking to Power = Tania Bruguera: hablándole al poder*. San Francisco: Yerba Buena Center for the Arts, 2018.

Byers, Dan. *The Artist's Museum*. Boston: Institute of Contemporary Art, 2016.

Chang, Alexandra. *Circles and Circuits: Chinese Caribbean Art*. Los Angeles: Chinese American Museum, 2018.

Cherix, Christophe, et al. *Adrian Piper: A Synthesis of Intuitions, 1965–2016*. New York: The Museum of Modern Art, 2018.

Decker, Julie, et al. *Unsettled: Art + Environment Conference 2017*. Reno: Nevada Museum of Art, 2017.

Devon, Marjorie, ed. *Migrations: New Directions in Native American Art*. Albuquerque: University of New Mexico Press, 2006.

Dijkstra, Rineke, and Katy Siegel. *Rineke Dijkstra: Portraits*. Boston: Institute of Contemporary Art, 2001.

Dijkstra, Rineke, et al. *Rineke Dijkstra: The Louisiana Book*. Humlebæk: Louisiana Museum of Modern Art, 2017.

Ellegood, Anne, et al. *Made in LA 2012*. Los Angeles: Hammer Museum, University of California, 2012.

Enwezor, Okwui. *All the World's Futures: La Biennale di Venezia, 56th International Art Exhibition*. Venice: Marsilio, 2015.

Garnett, Jane, and Sunil Shah. *Doh Mix Meh Up: Diaspora and Identity in Art*. Oxford, UK: The Oxford Diasporas Programme, 2015.

Gioni, Massimiliano. *Here and Elsewhere*. New York: New Museum, 2014.

———. *The Restless Earth*. Milan: Electa, 2017.

Gregos, Katerina, and Elena Sorokina. *Newtopia: The State of Human Rights*. Antwerp: Ludion, 2012.

Grenville, Bruce, and Deanna Ferguson. *Home and Away*. Vancouver: Vancouver Art Gallery, 2003.

Hatoum, Mona. *The Entire World as a Foreign Land*. London: Tate Gallery Publishing, 2000.

Hatoum, Mona, and Laura Steward Heon. *Mona Hatoum: Domestic Disturbance*. North Adams: MASS MoCA, 2001.

Iosifidis, Kiriakos. *Mural Art: Murals on Huge Public Surfaces around the World. From Graffiti to Trompe l'oeil*. Mainaschaff: Publikat, 2008.

Julien, Isaac. *Isaac Julien: Riot*. New York: The Museum of Modern Art, 2014.

———. *Isaac Julien: Western Union: small boats*. Aarhus: ARoS Aarhus Kunstmuseum, 2018.

Kahraman, Hayv. *Acts of Reparation: Hayv Kahraman*. St. Louis: Contemporary Art Museum St. Louis, 2017.

Latimer, Quinn, and Adam Szymczyk. *The Documenta 14 Reader*. Munich: Prestel, 2017.

Lew, Christopher, and Mia Locks. *Whitney Biennial 2017*. New York: Whitney Museum of American Art, 2017.

Maharaj, Sarat, and Ulrika Sten. *Pandemonium: Art in a Time of Creativity Fever*. Göteborg: Göteborg Biennalen, 2011.

Malagamba-Ansótegui, Amelia. *Caras Vemos, Corazones No Sabemos = Faces Seen, Hearts Unknown: The Human Landscape of Mexican Migration*. Notre Dame: Snite Museum, University of Notre Dame, 2006.

Martin, Courtney J. *Four Generations: The Joyner/Giuffrida Collection of Abstract Art*. New York: Gregory R. Miller, 2016.

Massie, Annetta. *Away from Home*. Columbus: Wexner Center for the Arts, Ohio State University, 2003.

McGrew, Rebecca, et al. *Hayv Kahraman*. Claremont: Pomona College Museum of Art, 2018.

Mikki, Akiko, et al. *Chalo! India: A New Era of Indian Art*. Munich: Prestel, 2009.

Misrach, Richard, Josh Kun, and Guillermo Galindo. *Border Cantos*. New York: Aperture, 2016.

Misrach, Richard, and Reyner Banham. *Desert Cantos*. Albuquerque: University of New Mexico Press, 1990.

Mosse, Richard. *The Enclave*. New York: Aperture, 2013.

———. *Incoming*. London: MACK, 2017.

Motta, Carlos, and Eva Diaz. *Carlos Motta: The Good Life*. New York: Art in General, 2008.

Motta, Carlos, and David Getsy. *Carlos Motta: Deviations*. New York: P·P·O·W, 2016.

Muller, Nat, and Ghalia Elsrakbi. *Foundland: Escape Routes and Waiting Rooms*. Brooklyn: International Studio & Curatorial Program, 2014.

OMA and Ippolito Pestellini Laparelli, et al. *Manifesta 12—Palermo Atlas: A Project*. Milan: Humboldt Books, 2018.

Pirouz, Kiana, and Mahya Soltani. *Before We Were Banned*. Brooklyn: ArtHelix, 2018.

Posner, Helaine, et al. *Tania Bruguera: On the Political Imaginary*. Milan: Edizioni Charta, 2009.

Puleo, Risa. *Monarchs: Brown and Native Contemporary Artists in the Path of the Butterfly*. Omaha: Bemis Center for Contemporary Art, with [NAME] publications, 2018.

Scarborough, Klare, and Colleen M. Hanycz. *Border Crossings: Immigration in Contemporary Prints*. Philadelphia: La Salle University Art Museum, 2016.

Shapland, Anthony. *On Leaving and Arriving*. Cardiff: CTA, 2005.

Shonibare, Yinka, MBE, Rachel Kent, Robert Carleton Hobbs, and Anthony Downey. *Yinka Shonibare MBE*. Munich: Prestel, 2008.

Simmons, Xaviera, and Mary Lee Hodgens. *Xaviera Simmons: Accumulations*. Syracuse: Light Work, 2015.

Suh, Do Ho. *Do Ho Suh: Perfect Home*. Kanazawa: 21st Century Museum of Contemporary Art, 2013.

Suh, Do Ho, et al. *Do Ho Suh: Drawings*. Munich: DelMonico Books, 2014.

Talalay, Marjorie. *Transition/Dislocation: Images of Upheaval*. Cleveland: The Center, 1996.

Theung, Linda. *The U.S.-Mexico Border: Place, Imagination, and Possibility*. Los Angeles: Craft & Folk Art Museum, 2017.

Van Adrichem, Jan, et al. *Rineke Dijkstra: A Retrospective*. New York: Solomon R. Guggenheim Museum, 2012.

Van Tomme, Niels. *Where Do We Migrate To?* Baltimore: University of Maryland, Baltimore County, Center for Art, Design, and Visual Culture, 2011.

Vojt, Ivana. *The Border Is Closed*. Belgrade: Museum of African Art, 2015.

Wainwright, Jean. *Ship to Shore: Art and the Lure of the Sea*. Southampton, United Kingdom: John Hansard Gallery, 2018.

Articles

Agamben, Giorgio. "We Refugees." Trans. Michael Rocke. *Symposium* 49, no. 2 (1995):114–19.

Azoulay, Ariella. "What Are Human Rights?" *Comparative Studies of South Asia, Africa and the Middle East* 35, no. 1 (2015):8–20.

Barber, Sarah B., Gonzalo Sánchez, and Mireya Olvera. "Sounds of Death and Life in Mesoamerica: The Bone Flutes of ancient Oaxaca." *Yearbook for Traditional Music* 41 (Ljubljana International Council for Traditional Music) (2009):94–110.

Bowles, John. "Acting Like a Man: Adrian Piper's Mythic Being and Black Feminism in the 1970s." *Signs: Journal of Women in Culture and Society* 32, no. 3 (2007):621–47.

Cervenak, Sarah Jane. "Dignity, the Sacred, and the Ends of Black Performance." *Spectator* 30, no. 2 (Fall 2010):18–27.

Chubb, Emma. "Differential Treatment: Migration in the Works of Yto Barrada and Bouchra Khalili." *Journal of Arabic Literature* 46, no. 2/3 (2015):268–95.

———. "Small Boats, Slave Ship; or, Isaac Julien and the Beauty of Implied Catastrophe." *Art Journal* 75, no. 1 (2016):24–43.

Clifford, James. "The Others: Beyond the 'Salvage' Paradigm." *Third Text* 6 (Spring 1989):73–77.

Cross, Hannah M. "The EU Migration Regime and West African Clandestine Migrants." *Journal of Contemporary European Research* 5, no. 2 (2009):171–187.

Demerdash, Nancy N. A. "Bordering Nowhere: Migration and the Politics of Placelessness in Contemporary Art of the Maghrebi Diaspora." *The Journal of North African Studies* 21, no. 2 (2016):258–72.

Downey, Anthony. "A Life Full of Holes." *Third Text* 20, no. 5 (2006):617–26.

Espiritu, Yên Lê, and Lan Duong. "Feminist Refugee Epistemology: Reading Displacement in Vietnamese and Syrian Refugee Art." *Signs* 43, no. 3 (2018):587–615.

Ferreira da Silva, Denise. "On Difference without Separability." In Jochen Volz and Júlia Rebouças, eds. *32nd Bienal de São Paulo—Incerteza Viva*. São Paulo: Fundação Bienal de São Paulo, 2016, pp. 57–65.

Fox, Claire F. "The Fence and the River: Representations of the US-Mexico Border in Art and Video." *Discourse* 18, no. 1/2 (Fall & Winter 1995–96):54–83.

Gardner, Anthony, and Charles Green. "Biennials of the South on the Edge of the Global." *Third Text* 27, no. 4 (2013):442–55.

Glick Schiller, Nina, and Noel B. Salazar. "Regimes of Mobility Across the Globe." *Journal of Ethnic and Migration Studies* 39, no. 2 (2013):183–200.

Godfrey, Mark, T. J. Demos, Eyal Weizman, and Ayesha Hameed. "Rights of Passage." *Tate Etc.* no. 19 (Summer 2010).

Haenlein, Cathy. "Richard Mosse's The Enclave: Mediating Conflict in the Democratic Republic of the Congo." *The RUSI Journal* 159 (2014):106–10.

Munn, Nancy. "The Cultural Anthropology of Time: A Critical Essay." *Annual Review of Anthropology* 21 (1992):93–123.

Rainey, Mark Justin. "Colonus and Lampedusa: The Tragedy of the Border and the Dialectics of Repair." *Third Text* 32, no. 1 (2018):150–60.

Rancière, Jacques. "Who Is the Subject of the Rights of Man?" *South Atlantic Quarterly* 103, nos. 2–3 (Spring–Summer 2004):297–310.

Schuman, Aaron. "Sublime Proximity: A Conversation with Richard Mosse." *Aperture* no. 203 (Summer 2011):52–59.

Sheller, Mimi, and John Urry. "The New Mobilities Paradigm." *Environment and Planning A: Economy and Space A* 38, no. 2 (2006):207–26.

Siddiqi, Anooradha I. "On Human Architecture: A Story of a Border." *Humanity: An International Journal of Human Rights, Humanitarianism, and Development* 8, no. 3 (Winter 2017):519–21.

Smyczyńska, Katarzyna. "'We refugees': (Un)othering in Visual Narratives on Displacement." *Nordic Journal of English Studies* 17, no. 1 (2018):217–36.

Spivak, Gayatri Chakravorty. "Can the Subaltern Speak?" In Cary Nelson and Lawrence Grossberg, eds. *Marxism and the Interpretation of Culture* (Chicago: University of Illinois Press, 1988): 271–313.

– – – – – – – –

Compiled by Anni Pullagura and Ellen Tani

Acknowledgments

When Home Won't Let You Stay: Migration through Contemporary Art is a response to our tumultuous times. This exhibition and publication are part of ICA's long history in addressing some of the most resonant and difficult issues of our day. We are truly thankful to have realized this project here.

When Home Won't Let You Stay is the result of the collective efforts of many talented people both within and outside the ICA. We extend our heartfelt appreciation to Jill Medvedow, Ellen Matilda Poss Director, for championing this project from the very beginning, and to the ICA's fearless Board of Trustees for their continuous support. Assistant Curator Ellen Tani and Curatorial Research Fellow Anni Pullagura have been our partners in the project, providing immeasurable support for this book, exhibition, and related programs. *When Home Won't Let You Stay* belongs to them as much as it does to us.

We are grateful to the generous sponsors of this exhibition: Paul and Catherine Buttenwieser, Steve Corkin and Dan Maddalena, Alan and Vivien Hassenfeld, Kristen and Kent Lucken, the Poss Family Foundation, and Mark and Marie Schwartz. We would also like to express our deep appreciation to the lenders who graciously shared works from their collections for the exhibition. (They appear on page 238.)

This publication is intended to be an important resource for many years to come; we are proud of it, and wish to express our sincere thanks to our contributors for their insightful texts: Aruna D'Souza, writer and critic (former Associate Director of the Research and Academic Program at the Clark Art Institute); the late Okwui Enwezor, curator and critic; Thomas Keenan, Director of the Human Rights Program at Bard College; Peggy Levitt, Professor in Latin American Studies and Sociology at Wellesley College; Uday Singh Mehta, Distinguished Professor of Political Science at CUNY; Ellen Tani, Assistant Curator, ICA/Boston; and Anni Pullagura, Curatorial Research Fellow, ICA/Boston. We are thrilled to include three conversations and wish to thank the artists and scholars who participated: Guillermo Galindo and Josh Kun; Reena Saini Kallat and Hayv Kahraman; Aliza Nisenbaum and Anthony Romero. We would also like to thank and acknowledge Warsan Shire, whose poignant poem "Home" gives this project its title. Our praise and thanks go to Beverly Joel for her elegant design of this publication.

This project would not have been possible without those who represent and work closely with the artists: Adrian Piper Research Archive Foundation Berlin; David Castillo Gallery, Miami; Galerie Polaris, Paris; Jack Shainman Gallery, New York; James Cohan Gallery, New York; Lévy Gorvy, New York; Lehmann Maupin, New York, Hong Kong, and Seoul; Marc Selwyn Fine Arts, Los Angeles; Marian Goodman Gallery, New York; Mary Mary Gallery, Glasgow; Nature Morte, New Delhi; P·P·O·W Gallery, New York; Metro Pictures, New York; Pace Gallery; Pace/McGill; and White Cube, London. We are also grateful for the assistance of many studio managers who helped to realize ambitious projects.

We would like to acknowledge the invaluable insights of the individuals who gave their time and energy as members of this project's Advisory Committee (their names appear on page 237).

The exhibition was realized with the help of many in the ICA's Curatorial Department. Our sincere thanks go to: Abigail Newbold, Director of Exhibitions, and Zelana Davis, Exhibition Coordinator, for their adept oversight of many of the exhibition's logistical details; Alison Hatcher, Senior Registrar, for her good cheer despite outsized challenges; Tim Obetz, Chief Preparator, and Toru Nakanishi, Preparator, for their reliable problem-solving; and the ICA's installation crew for their often challenging work. Thanks are also due to Fabienne Keck, Curatorial Department Coordinator, for her adept planning and organization.

A number of others at the ICA have helped realize *When Home Won't Let You Stay* and have supported our efforts with the project: Liz Adrian, Director of Retail; John Andress, Bill T. Jones Director of Performing and Media Arts;

Karin France, Associate Director of Institutional Giving; Monica Garza, Director of Education; Kelly Gifford, Deputy Director for Public Engagement and Planning; Katie Mayshak, Director of Development; Colette Randall, Director of Marketing, Research, and Communications; Michael Taubenberger, Chief Operating Officer (former); Tsugumi Maki, Chief Operating Officer; Kris Wilton, Associate Director of Creative Content and Digital Engagement; and Natasa Vucetic, Chief Financial Officer.

Our final thanks must go to the twenty artists represented in the exhibition for shaping our understanding not only of resonant and complex issues of home, belonging, migration, and citizenship but also of the necessity of the arts in how we understand ourselves and our place in an increasingly divisive world.

We could not carry out our work without the incredible support of our families, as they were with us every step of the way. This book is dedicated to them.

Ruth Erickson	Eva Respini
Mannion Family Curator	Barbara Lee Chief Curator
ICA/Boston	ICA/Boston

Artists' Biographies

Kader Attia
B. 1970, Dugny, France; lives and works in Berlin and Paris
—
Kader Attia studied art at the École Supérieure des Arts Appliqués Duperré and the École Nationale Supérieure des Arts Décoratifs, Paris, in 1993 and 1998 respectively, and has exhibited in solo and group exhibitions at the Leopold Museum, Vienna (2016); the Solomon R. Guggenheim Museum, New York (2016); the New Museum, New York (2014); and Tate Modern, London (2011). In 2016 he was awarded the French Prix Marcel Duchamp; in 2017 he received the Premio Joan Miró from the Fundació Joan Miró and Obra Social "la Caixa." His work is held in several international collections, including The Museum of Modern Art, New York; the Centre Georges Pompidou, Paris; the Solomon R. Guggenheim Museum, New York; the Colección Jumex, Mexico City; and the Institute of Contemporary Art/Boston.

Yto Barrada
B. 1971, Paris, France; lives and works in Tangier, Morocco, and New York
—
Yto Barrada grew up between Paris and Tangier. She studied history and political theory at the Sorbonne, Paris, and photography at the International Center of Photography, New York. Her work has been exhibited at numerous institutions, including The Barbican, London (2018); the Walker Art Center, Minneapolis (2013); the Deutsche Guggenheim, Berlin (2011); the Fundació Antoni Tàpies, Barcelona (2004); and the Witte de With Center for Contemporary Art, Rotterdam (2004). She was the Deutsche Bank's Artist of the Year in 2011. Barrada, whose films have been presented worldwide, is the founder of the Cinéma-thèque de Tanger, Morocco's only movie theater for independent cinema and repertory programming, and was the Director of Programming there from 2006 to 2012.

Tania Bruguera
B. 1968, Havana, Cuba; lives and works in Queens, New York
—
Tania Bruguera studied at Havana's Instituto Superior de Arte and earned her M.F.A. in performance from the School of the Art Institute of Chicago in 2001. From 2003 through 2010 she was an Assistant Professor in the Department of Visual Arts of the University of Chicago. She is the founder and director of Cátedra Arte de Conducta, Havana, the first performance-studies program in Latin America. Bruguera's work has been exhibited in numerous international biennials and in institutions including Tate Modern, London (2018); the Yerba Buena Center for the Arts, San Francisco (2017); the Solomon R. Guggenheim Museum, New York (2014); and the Queens Museum, New York (2011).

Rineke Dijkstra
B. 1959, Sittard, the Netherlands; lives and works in Amsterdam
—
Rineke Dijkstra studied photography at the Gerrit Rietveld Academie, Amsterdam, from 1981 to 1986. She has been honored with the Hasselblad Foundation International Award (2017); the "Spectrum" International Prize for Photography, Stiftung Niedersachsen (2017); an Honorary Fellowship in the Royal Photographic Society, Bath (2012); the Citibank Photography Prize (1999); the Werner Mantz Award (1994); the Kodak Award Netherlands (1987), and others. Her work has been presented at the Museum of Fine Arts, Boston (2018); the Louisiana Museum of Modern Art, Humlebaek, Denmark (2017); the Stedelijk Museum, Amsterdam (2017); and the National Gallery of Art, Washington, DC (2016). A mid-career retrospective of Dijkstra's work appeared at the San Francisco Museum of Modern Art and at the Solomon R. Guggenheim Museum, New York, in 2012. Her work is held in numerous public collections.

Guillermo Galindo
B. 1960, Mexico City, Mexico; lives and works in Oakland, California
—
Guillermo Galindo received his B.A. at Mexico City's Conservatorio Nacional de Música in 1987 and his M.A. in music composition at Mills College, Oakland, in 1991. Galindo has written for orchestra, string quartet, and other ensembles; his major chamber and solo works include two symphonies respectively commissioned by the Orquesta Filarmónica de la UNAM (the orchestra of the Universidad Nacional Autónoma de México) and the Oakland Symphony, and two operas with librettos by Guillermo Gomez Peña and Anne Carson. His work has been presented at documenta 14, Kassel, Germany (2017); the Huntington Library, San Marino, California (2017); the Crystal Bridges Museum of American Art, Bentonville, Arkansas (2017); and the Amon Carter Museum of Art, Fort Worth, Texas (2016). He is a Senior Adjunct Professor at the California College of Art.

Mona Hatoum
B. 1952, Beirut, Lebanon; lives and works in London
—
Mona Hatoum was educated at London's Byam Shaw School of Art and then at the Slade School of Fine Art. She has exhibited in major group exhibitions and biennials,

including documenta 14, Kassel, Germany (2017); the 51st Venice Biennale (2005); the Turner Prize exhibition, Tate Britain (1995); and others. She has staged solo exhibitions at institutions including the Menil Collection, Houston (2017); the Centre Georges Pompidou, Paris (2015); the Kunstmuseum St. Gallen, Switzerland (2013); the Museum of Contemporary Art Australia, Sydney (2005); Tate Britain, London (2000); and the Museum of Contemporary Art Chicago (1997). She is the recipient of the 10th Hiroshima Art Prize (2017) and the Premio Joan Miró (2011), and her work is held in numerous international collections.

Isaac Julien
B. 1960, London, United Kingdom; lives and works in London
—
The child of migrants from St. Lucia, Isaac Julien earned his B.F.A. from Central Saint Martins School of Art, London, in 1984, where he studied fine art and film and cofounded the Sankofa Film and Video Collective (1983–1992), dedicated to developing an independent black film culture. He completed postdoctoral studies at Les Entrepreneurs de L'Audiovisuel Européen (EAVE), Brussels, in 1989. In 2017 he received the Royal Academy of Arts' Charles Wollaston Award and was made Commander of the Order of the British Empire (CBE). He has been making films and producing film installations for over thirty years and his work has been exhibited worldwide, at venues including the Royal Ontario Museum, Toronto (2017); MUAC (Museo Universitario Arte Contemporáneo), Mexico City (2016); The Museum of Modern Art, New York (2013); the Art Institute of Chicago (2013); the Museum Brandhorst, Munich (2009); and the Centre Georges Pompidou, Paris (2009).

Hayv Kahraman
B. 1981, Baghdad, Iraq; lives and works in Los Angeles
—
Before establishing her studio practice in the United States, Hayv Kahraman trained in painting at Umeå University, Sweden, and Cappiello-Accademia di Design e Comunicazione, Florence, Italy, respectively. Recent solo exhibitions and performance installations have been presented at the Honolulu Museum of Art (2019); the Victoria and Albert Museum, London (2018); the Contemporary Art Museum St. Louis (2017); and the Pomona College Museum of Art, California (2017). She was short-listed for the Jameel Prize at the Victoria and Albert Museum in 2018 and 2011. Her work is held in several public collections, including the Contemporary Art Museum St. Louis; the Third Line, Doha and Dubai; the Saatchi Gallery, London; the Nelson-Atkins Museum of Art, Kansas City; and the San Antonio Museum of Art.

Reena Saini Kallat
B. 1973, New Delhi, India; lives and works in Mumbai
—
Reena Saini Kallat received her B.F.A. in painting from the Sir J. J. School of Art, Mumbai, in 1996. In 2018 she had a solo exhibition at the Manchester Museum, University of Manchester, and she has exhibited in major institutions, including the Art Gallery of New South Wales, Sydney (2018); The Museum of Modern Art, New York (2016); the Vancouver Art Gallery (2015); the Kennedy Center, Washington, DC (2011); and in numerous galleries and biennials in Europe. Her works are held in the permanent collections of major institutions around the globe, including the Art Gallery of New South Wales, Sydney; the National Gallery of Canada, Ottawa; the National Taiwan Museum of Fine Arts, Taichung City; and the National Gallery of Modern Art, New Delhi.

Richard Misrach
B. 1949, Los Angeles, United States; lives and works in Berkeley, California
—
Richard Misrach earned his B.A. in psychology from the University of California, Berkeley, in 1971. He has exhibited at the Museum of Fine Arts, Houston; the Art Institute of Chicago; the Whitney Museum of American Art, New York; the Denver Art Museum; and the National Gallery of Art, Washington, DC. He was awarded a Guggenheim Fellowship in 1978, four fellowships from the National Endowment for the Arts, and in 2002 was presented with the Kulturpreis der Deutschen Gesellschaft für Photographie. His work appears in the collections of numerous museums, including The Museum of Modern Art and The Metropolitan Museum of Art, New York, and the Centre Georges Pompidou, Paris.

Richard Mosse
B. 1980, Kilkenny, Ireland; lives and works in New York
—
Richard Mosse received a B.A. in English Literature and Language from King's College London in 2001, an MRes in cultural studies from the London Consortium in 2003, a postgraduate diploma in fine art from Goldsmiths, University of London, in 2005, and an M.F.A. in photography from the Yale University School of Art, New Haven, in 2008. He has presented solo exhibitions at the San Francisco Museum of Modern Art (2019); the Joslyn Art Museum, Omaha, Nebraska (2018); The Curve, Barbican Centre, London (2017); and the Künstlerhaus Bethanien, Berlin (2012).

In 2015, shortly after winning the Deutsche Börse Photography Prize for his series Infra, he was nominated for membership of the Magnum Photo Agency. He represented Ireland at the Venice Biennale in 2013.

Carlos Motta

B. 1978, Bogotá, Colombia; lives and works in New York

—

Carlos Motta received his B.F.A. from the School of Visual Arts, New York, in 2001, his M.F.A. from Bard College, New York, in 2003, and he attended the Whitney Independent Study Program, in 2006. His work has been exhibited widely, at institutions including the Stedelijk Museum Amsterdam (2017); the Perez Art Museum, Miami (2016); the Museo de Arte Latinoamericano de Buenos Aires (2016); and the New Museum, New York (2012). He has won the Vilcek Foundation's Prize for Creative Promise (2017), the Pinchuk Art Centre's Future Generation Art Prize (2014), and a Guggenheim Fellowship (2008). Motta's work appears in numerous public collections, including The Metropolitan Museum of Art, New York; The Museum of Modern Art, New York; the Solomon R. Guggenheim Museum, New York; the Museo Nacional Centro de Arte Reina Sofía, Madrid; and the Museo de Arte Contemporaneo de Barcelona.

Aliza Nisenbaum

B. 1977, Mexico City, Mexico; lives and works in New York

—

Aliza Nisenbaum studied art at the School of the Art Institute of Chicago, receiving her B.F.A. in 2001 and her M.F.A. in 2005. She has been teaching at Columbia University since 2015. She has exhibited at the Museum of Contemporary Art, Los Angeles (2018); in the Whitney Biennial, New York (2017); the Minneapolis Institute of Arts (2017); the Museum of Contemporary Art, Denver (2015); and White Columns, New York (2014). Her work is in the collections of the Whitney Museum of American Art, New York; the University of Chicago Booth School of Business; and The Progressive Art Collection, Ohio.

Camilo Ontiveros

B. 1978, El Rosario, Sinaloa, Mexico; lives and works in Los Angeles

—

Camilo Ontiveros received his B.A. from the University of California, San Diego, in 2006 and his M.F.A. from the University of California, Los Angeles, in 2009. He is a cofounder of NOMART, a performance art space on wheels; of Lui Velazquez, an artist-residency program in Tijuana; and of Imprenta, an alternative space in the MacArthur Park area of Los Angeles. His work has been exhibited in museums nationally, including the Los Angeles County Museum of Art (2017); the Museum of Fine Arts Houston (2017); the Hammer Museum, Los Angeles (2012); and the Museum of Latin American Art, Long Beach (2010).

Michelle Angela Ortiz

B. 1978, Philadelphia, United States; lives and works in Philadelphia

—

Michelle Angela Ortiz received a B.F.A. from Moore College of Art & Design, Philadelphia, and an M.A. in the science of arts and cultural management from Rosemont College, Rosemont. Ortiz has created public works in many locations around the world, including Pennsylvania, New Jersey, Mississippi, and New York, as well as Costa Rica, Ecuador, and Cuba. She has served as a cultural envoy on behalf of U.S. embassies in Fiji, Mexico, Argentina, Spain, Venezuela, and Honduras. For her community organization and art activism she has received recognition from Americans for the Arts (Public Art Year in Review Award, 2016); the National Association of Latino Arts and Cultures Fund for The Arts (2011); the Leeway Foundation (Transformation Award, 2008); and Art & Change (2006, 2012). In 2018 she was a Fellow at The Pew Center for Arts and Heritage and a Rauschenberg Foundation Artist as Activist Fellow.

Adrian Piper

B. 1948, New York, United States; lives and works in Berlin

—

Adrian Piper studied at the Art Students League of New York as a teenager and was exhibiting her work by the age of twenty. She earned an associates in art degree from the School of Visual Arts in 1969, then studied philosophy and musicology at the City College of New York, graduating in 1974. In 1987, while teaching at Georgetown University, Piper became the first tenured African-American woman professor in the field of philosophy. In 2005 she moved to Berlin, where she edits *The Berlin Journal of Philosophy* and oversees the Adrian Piper Research Archive Foundation Berlin, which she founded in 2002. Her work has been exhibited widely around the world, including a fifty-year retrospective at The Museum of Modern Art, New York, in 2018. In 2015 she was awarded the Golden Lion for best artist in the international exhibition at the Venice Biennale.

Anthony Romero

B. 1983, Austin, United States; lives and works in Boston

—

Anthony Romero is an artist, writer, and organizer and is Professor of the Practice at the School of the Museum of Fine Arts, Tufts University, Boston. Recent projects and performances have appeared at The Bemis Center for Contemporary Arts, Omaha; the Blue Star Contemporary, San Antonio; Konsthall C, Stockholm; Tufts University Art Galleries, Boston; and the Mountain Standard Time Performative Art Biennial, Calgary. His publications include *The Social Practice That Is Race*, cowritten with Dan S. Wang, and the exhibition catalogue *Organize Your Own: The Politics and Poetics of Self-Determination Movements*, of which he was the editor. He is a cofounder of the Latinx Artist Visibility Award, a national scholarship for Latinx artists produced in collaboration with artist J. Soto and OxBow School of Art, and a cofounder of the Latinx Artists Retreat, a national gathering of Latinx artists and administrators.

Yinka Shonibare CBE (RA)
B. 1962, London;
lives and works in London
—
Yinka Shonibare CBE studied fine art at Byam School of Art, London, and received his M.F.A. from the city's Goldsmiths College. His work has been presented in many group and solo exhibitions since 1988, at institutions including Tate Britain, London (2012); the Smithsonian Institution, Washington, DC (2009); the Moderna Museet, Stockholm (2006); and documenta 11, Kassel, Germany (2002). In 2004 he was a Turner Prize nominee, and in 2010 he received the Fourth Plinth Commission for Trafalgar Square, London. He has been a member of the Royal Academy, London, since 2013 and was made a Commander of the Most Excellent Order of the British Empire (CBE) in 2019. His works are included in the collections of major institutions including The Museum of Modern Art, New York; the Smithsonian Institute's National Museum of African Art, Washington, DC; the Victoria and Albert Museum, London; the Tate Collection, London; and the Moderna Museet, Stockholm.

Xaviera Simmons
B. 1974, New York, United States;
lives and works in New York
—
Xaviera Simmons received her B.F.A. from Bard College in 2004, then completed advanced degrees in both the Whitney Museum of American Art's Independent Study Program in Studio Art and The Maggie Flanigan Studio, New York, where she trained as an actor. She has exhibited in numerous solo and group exhibitions at institutions including Prospect.4, New Orleans (2017); the Institute of Contemporary Art/Boston (2016); the Studio Museum in Harlem, New York (2010); and the Contemporary Arts Museum Houston (2007). A recipient of Agnes Gund's Art for Justice Award (2018) and Denniston Hill's Distinguished Performance Artist Award (2018), she received the Robert Rauschenberg Foundation for Contemporary Arts Grant in 2015. Her works are held in major collections around the world, including The Museum of Modern Art, the Rubell Family Collection, the Agnes Gund Art Collection, the Solomon R. Guggenheim Museum, and the High Museum of Art, Atlanta, among others.

Do Ho Suh
B. 1962, Seoul, Korea; lives and works in London, New York, and Seoul
—
Do Ho Suh trained in painting at Seoul National University, then received his B.F.A. in painting at the Rhode Island School of Design, Providence, in 1994 and his M.F.A. in sculpture at the Yale University School of Art, New Haven, in 1997. He has exhibited in numerous galleries and museums, including the Smithsonian American Art Museum, Washington, DC (2018); the Whitney Museum of American Art, New York (2017); the National Museum of Contemporary Art, Seoul (2013); and Tate Modern, London (2011). His work has been supported by fellowships at the Singapore Tyler Print Institute, the Joan Mitchell Foundation, and the Public Art Fund.

Contributors

Aruna D'Souza is a scholar of modern and contemporary art, intersectional feminism, and diaspora. She is a writer and former associate director of the Research and Academic Program at the Clark Art Institute, Williamstown, MA. Her book *Whitewalling: Art, Race & Protest in 3 Acts* was published in 2018. Her work appears regularly in *4Columns.org*, where she is a member of the editorial advisory board, and has been published in *The Wall Street Journal*, *CNN.com*, *Art News*, *Garage*, *Bookforum*, *Momus*, *Art in America*, and *Art Practical*, among other outlets.

The late **Okwui Enwezor** was a renowned curator and critic and served as director of Munich's Haus der Kunst from 2011 to 2018. He was artistic director of the 56th Venice Biennale in 2015 and its first African-born curator, and the first non-European to serve as the artistic director of documenta 11 in 2002. His long-standing commitment to art of the African diaspora and to African histories materialized in major international exhibitions. He lectured widely and wrote extensively on contemporary African art and artists; he was the founding publisher and coeditor of *Nka: Journal of Contemporary African Art*, and his writing has appeared in numerous journals, catalogues, and books including *Third Text*, *Texte zur Kunst*, *Parkett*, *Frieze*, *ArtJournal*, and *Research in African Literatures*.

Ruth Erickson is Mannion Family Curator at the Institute of Contemporary Art/Boston, where she has curated exhibitions of work by Kevin Beasley, Mark Dion, Rokni and Ramin Haerizadeh, Ethan Murrow, and Wangechi Mutu, among others. She received her Ph.D. from the University of Pennsylvania in 2014. Her writing has appeared in numerous publications, including *France and the Visual Arts since 1945: Remapping European Postwar and Contemporary Art* (2018), *Mark Dion: Misadventures of a 21st-Century Naturalist* (2017), *Leap Before You Look: Black Mountain College 1933–1957* (2015), *Critical Landscapes: Art, Space, Politics* (2015), and *Take It or Leave It: Institution, Image, Ideology* (2014).

Thomas Keenan is Director of the Human Rights Project and Associate Professor of Comparative Literature at Bard College. He is the author if *Fables of Responsibility: Aberrations and Predicaments in Ethics and Politics* (Stanford University Press, 1997) and serves on the editorial board of *Journal of Human Rights*, WITNESS, and the Scholars at Risk Network. He is the recipient of numerous fellowships, including the Joan Shorenstein Center for Press and Politics at the John F. Kennedy School of Government at Harvard University. He received his Ph.D. from Yale University.

Josh Kun is Director of the School of Communication, Professor of Communication and Journalism, and Chair in Cross-Cultural Communication at the University of Southern California's Annenberg School for Communication and Journalism. He is a 2016 MacArthur Fellow and the winner of a 2018 Berlin Prize and of a 2006 American Book Award. His research focuses on the arts and politics of cultural connection, with an emphasis on popular music, sound, the cultures of globalization, the U.S.-Mexico border, Los Angeles, and Jewish-American musical history. He also works as a journalist, essayist, and curator. He is the director of The Popular Music Project at USC Annenberg's Norman Lear Center and coeditor (with Ron Radano and Nina Sun Eidsheim) of the book series *Refiguring American Music* for Duke University Press.

Peggy Levitt is Luella LaMer Slaner Professor in Latin American Studies and Professor of Sociology at Wellesley College. Her research examines the relationship between migration and mobility and the cultural institutions and patterns that affect these global movements. She is the author of *The Transnational Villagers* (University of California Press, 2001) and *Artifacts and Allegiances: How Museums Put the Nation and the World on Display* (University of California Press, 2015). Her work has been supported by the MacArthur Foundation, the National Science Foundation, and the Radcliffe Institute at Harvard University, where she is a Senior Fellow at The Weatherhead Center for International Affairs.

Uday Singh Mehta is a political theorist and Distinguished Professor of Political Science at the Graduate Center, The City University of New York. His research explores philosophies of freedom, imagination, and liberalism within histories of empire and colonialism. He is the author of several books, including *The Anxiety of Freedom: Imagination and Individuality in the Political Thought of John Locke*, and *Liberalism and Empire: Nineteenth Century British Liberal Thought*. He is the recipient of the 2002 J. David Greenstone Prize for Best Book in Political Theory by the American Political Science Association and a 2003 Carnegie Foundation Fellowship.

Anni A. Pullagura is a Curatorial Fellow at the Institute of Contemporary Art/Boston. She is a Ph.D. candidate in American Studies and an M.A. candidate in the History of Art and Architecture at Brown University, where she received her M.A. in Public Humanities in 2016. A historian of modern and contemporary American art, she wrote her dissertation, "Seeing Feeling: The Work of Empathy in Exhibitionary Spaces," on the way the contemporary art museum reinforces racial sightlines through the rhetoric of empathetic sight. She has held positions at The Metropolitan Museum of Art, New York; the High Museum of Art, Atlanta; and the Smithsonian Institution's National Museum of African American History and Culture, Washington, DC.

Eva Respini is Barbara Lee Chief Curator at the Institute of Contemporary Art/Boston. Her recent exhibitions include *John Akomfrah: Purple* (2019), *Huma Bhabha: They Live* (2019), *William Forsythe: Choreographic Objects* (2018), and *Art in the Age of the Internet, 1989 to Today* (2018). Respini previously served as Curator at the Museum of Modern Art, New York, where she organized numerous exhibitions, including the retrospectives *Cindy Sherman* (2012), *Robert Heinecken: Object Matter* (2014), and *Walid Raad* (2015–16). She has published numerous books and her writing has appeared in many museum publications and journals on contemporary art and photography.

Warsan Shire is a Somali-British writer and poet. Her debut pamphlet, *Teaching My Mother How to Give Birth*, was published in 2011. Shire was awarded the inaugural African Poetry Prize in 2013. In 2014, she was appointed as the first Young Poet Laureate for London and was selected as Poet in Residence for Queensland, Australia. In 2018, she was elected Fellow of the Royal Society of Literature. In 2016, she provided the film adaptation of her poetry for the Peabody Award–winning visual album *Lemonade* in collaboration with Beyoncé Knowles-Carter. In 2017, she was included in the Penguin Modern Poets series alongside Sharon Olds and Malika Booker. In 2019, she wrote the short film *Brave Girl Rising*, narrated by Tessa Thompson and David Oyelowo.

Ellen Y. Tani is Assistant Curator at the Institute of Contemporary Art/Boston. Her recent exhibitions include *Nina Chanel Abney* (2019) at the ICA/Boston and *Second Sight: The Paradox of Vision in Contemporary Art* (2018) at the Bowdoin College Museum of Art, where she was the Andrew W. Mellon Postdoctoral Curatorial Fellow (2015–18). She earned her Ph.D. in Art History from Stanford University in 2015. Her writing has appeared in numerous publications, including *Art Journal*, *American Quarterly*, *Apricota*, and exhibition monographs on Senga Nengudi and Charles Gaines.

Image Credits

Front cover, pages 34–35, 36, 37: courtesy the artist. Photos by Jonathan Muzikar. Digital image © The Museum of Modern Art/Licensed by SCALA/ Art Resource, NY. © Reena Saini Kallat.
Pages 2–3, 54–55, 56, 57, 58, 59, back cover: courtesy the artist; Jack Shainman Gallery, New York; and carlier | gebauer, Berlin. © Richard Mosse.
Pages 4–5, 71 (fig. 2), 74, 75, 76, 77: courtesy the artist and Lehmann Maupin, New York, Hong Kong, and Seoul. © Do Ho Suh.
Pages 6–7, 84–85: courtesy the artist and David Castillo Gallery, Miami. Photo by Zach Balber. © Xaviera Simmons.
Pages 8, 60, 61, 62–63: courtesy the artist and Jack Shainman Gallery, New York. © Hayv Kahraman.
Pages 10, 98, 100–101, 102, 103, 104, 105: courtesy the artist; Victoria Miro, London/Venice; and Metro Pictures, New York. © Isaac Julien.
Page 14: courtesy the artist and James Cohan Gallery, New York. Photo by David Ramsey. © Yinka Shonibare CBE.
Page 18: © John Moore/Getty Images News/ Getty Images.
Page 21: courtesy Anmahian Winton Architects, Cambridge, MA.
Page 22: © Giorgos Moutafis/Reuters Pictures.
Page 24: © Hannah McKay/Reuters Pictures.
Page 33 (fig. 1): courtesy the artist. Photo by Iris Dreams. © Reena Saini Kallat.
Page 33 (fig. 2): courtesy the artist and Chemould Prescott Road, Mumbai. Photo by Anil Rane. © Reena Saini Kallat.
Page 38: vintage wall blackboards in lacquered wood frames, each mounted on wall at eye level in landscape orientation and covered with single handwritten sentence, "Everything will be taken away," repeated twenty-five times in handwritten cursive text in white chalk, four parts, each 47¼ x 98⅜ inches (120 x 250 cm). Photo by Alfredo Cacciani. © Adrian Piper Research Archive Foundation Berlin.
Page 39: various private and public collections. © Adrian Piper Research Archive Foundation Berlin.
Page 41: Collection of the Adrian Piper Research Archive Foundation Berlin. Photo by Timo Ohler. © Adrian Piper Research Archive Foundation Berlin.
Pages 42, 43: courtesy the artist. © Camilo Ontiveros.
Pages 45, 46, 47: installation photo from the exhibition *HOME—So Different, So Appealing*, Los Angeles County Museum of Art, 2017. Courtesy Los Angeles County Museum of Art. Photos © Museum Associates/LACMA. © Camilo Ontiveros.
Page 52: Courtesy the artist and Jack Shainman Gallery, New York. Photo by Tom Powel. © Richard Mosse.
Pages 65, 66, 67, 68, 69: courtesy the artist and Marian Goodman Gallery, New York. © Rineke Dijkstra.
Page 71 (fig. 1): courtesy the artist and The Stuart Collection, University of California, San Diego. Photo by Philipp Scholz Rittermann. © Do Ho Suh
Pages 72–73: courtesy the artist; Lehmann Maupin, New York, Hong Kong, and Seoul; and Victoria Miro, London/Venice. Photo by Thierry Bal. © Do Ho Suh.
Page 78: courtesy the artist. Photo © White Cube (Ben Westoby). © Mona Hatoum.
Page 79: courtesy The Menil Collection, Houston. Photo by Fredrik Nilsen. © Mona Hatoum.
Page 81: courtesy the artist and Galerie Nordenhake, Berlin. Photo by Sofia Bertilsson. © Mona Hatoum.
Page 82: courtesy the artist and David Castillo Gallery, Miami. © Xaviera Simmons.
Page 83: courtesy Virginia Museum of History & Culture, Richmond, 2000.92.432.
Page 87: The Institute of Contemporary Art/Boston, Jeanne L. Wasserman Art Acquisition Fund and Anonymous Acquisition Fund. Courtesy the artist and David Castillo Gallery, Miami. © Xaviera Simmons.
Pages 89, 90, 91, 92, 93, 169: courtesy Pace Gallery; Sfeir-Semler Gallery, Hamburg, Beirut; and Galerie Polaris, Paris. © Yto Barrada.
Page 95: courtesy the artist and Galerie Nagal Draxler, Cologne and Berlin. Photos by Simon Vogel. © Kader Attia.
Pages 96–97: courtesy the artist. Photo by Henning Rogge. © Kader Attia.
Page 99: photo by Jonathan Muzikar. Digital Image © The Museum of Modern Art/Licensed by SCALA/Art Resource, NY. © Isaac Julien.
Page 112: courtesy the Queens Museum, New York.
Page 113: Solomon R. Guggenheim Museum, New York, Guggenheim UBS MAP Purchase Fund, 2014, 2014.11. Courtesy the Solomon R. Guggenheim Museum, New York. © Tania Bruguera.
Pages 114–15: Courtesy Creative Time, New York. Photo by Guillaume Ziccarelli. © Tania Bruguera.
Pages 117, 118–19, 120, 121, 123: courtesy the artist and Fraenkel Gallery, San Francisco; Pace/ MacGill Gallery, New York; and Marc Selwyn Fine Art, Los Angeles. © Richard Misrach.
Pages 124, 126, 127: courtesy the artist and Pace/ MacGill Gallery, New York. Photo by Richard Misrach. © Guillermo Galindo.
Page 125: courtesy the artist. Photo by Nils Klinger. © Guillermo Galindo.
Page 129 (fig. 1): courtesy PinchukArtCentre © 2015. Photo by Sergey Illin. © Carlos Motta.
Page 129 (fig. 2): courtesy Stedelijk Museum Amsterdam. Photo by Gert Jan van Rooij. © Carlos Motta.
Pages 130–131, 132, 133, 134, 135: courtesy the artist; Galeria Filomena Soares, Lisbon; Galeria Vermelho, São Paulo; mor charpentier, Paris; and P·P·O·W Gallery, New York. © Carlos Motta.
Page 136, 137, 138, 139, 140, 141: courtesy the artist; Anton Kern Gallery, New York; and Mary Mary, Glasgow. © Aliza Nisenbaum.
Pages 142, 144, 145: courtesy the artist. © Anthony Romero.
Page 143: Farmworker Movement Documentation Project, University of California San Diego Library.
Pages 150 (fig. 1), 152–153: courtesy the artist. Photos by Steve Weinik. © Michelle Angela Ortiz.
Page 150 (fig. 2): courtesy the artist. Photo by Jose Mazariegos. © Michelle Angela Ortiz.
Page 155 (figs. 1 and 2): courtesy the artist and James Cohan Gallery, New York. © Yinka Shonibare CBE.
Pages 156–57, 159: courtesy James Cohan Gallery, New York, and FRONT International: Cleveland Triennial for Contemporary Art with funds from VIA Art Fund, Cleveland Public Library and The City of Cleveland's Cable Television Minority Arts and Education Fund. Photography by Field Studio. © Yinka Shonibare CBE.
Pages 164, 168: courtesy Creative Time, New York. Photos by Paul Chan. © Paul Chan.
Pages 182, 183: Photos by Stefan Müller. © Hans Haacke/Artists Rights Society (ARS), New York/ VG Bild-Kunst, Bonn.
Page 195: courtesy Forensic Oceanography (Charles Heller, Lorenzo Pezzani) and Situ Studio, with drift modeling by Richard Limeburner, Woods Hole Oceanographic Institution. Available online at https://www.forensic-architecture.org/case/left-die-boat/(accessed April 1, 2019).
Page 196 (fig. 4): available online at https://humaneborders.org/migrant-death-mapping/ (accessed April 1, 2019).
Page 196 (fig. 5): courtesy the artist and Grupa 484.
Page 198: newspaper photo courtesy Thomas Dworzak.

Advisory Committee

Every exhibition is the result of many years of collaborative work. In the process of organizing *When Home Won't Let You Stay*, the ICA convened an advisory group of local scholars, activists, artists, and individuals focused on issues of migration. Over the course of several meetings beginning in the spring of 2018, we turned to this group to help us shape the exhibition and think through its language, programming, didactics, and outreach. The committee was made up of the following individuals, who we thank for their many contributions:

Pedro H. Alonzo
Independent Curator

Celina Barrios-Millner
Director of Equity and Inclusion, Mayor's Office for Economic Development, City of Boston

Matt Cameron
Co-director, the Golden Stairs Immigration Center, and Managing Partner, Cameron Micheroni & Silvia

Monica Garza
Charlotte Wagner Director of Education, ICA/Boston

Cheryl Hamilton
Director of Special Projects, International Institute of New England

Carol León
Outreach and Community Engagement Coordinator, Mayor's Office for Immigrant Advancement, City of Boston

Noora Lori
Assistant Professor of International Relations, Frederick S. Pardee School of Global Studies, Boston University

Timothy Patrick McCarthy
Lecturer on History and Literature, Education, and Public Policy, and Core Faculty, Carr Center for Human Rights Policy, Harvard University

Anthony Romero
Professor of the Practice, School of the Museum of Fine Arts, Tufts University

Adam Strom
Director, Re-imagining Migration

Mehtap Yağcı
Executive Assistant to the Director at ICA/Boston

Lenders to the Exhibition

Kader Attia
Yto Barrada
Tania Bruguera
carlier | gebauer, Berlin
David Castillo Gallery, Miami
Rineke Dijkstra
Galeria Filomena Soares, Lisbon
Fraenkel Gallery, San Francisco
Guillermo Galindo
Barbara Hirsch, New York
James Cohan Gallery, New York
Isaac Julien
Hayv Kahraman
Lehmann Maupin, New York, Hong Kong, and Seoul
Josh Lilley, London
Marian Goodman Gallery, New York
Guillaume Malle, New York
Metro Pictures, New York
Richard Misrach
mor charpentier, Paris
Richard Mosse
Carlos Motta
Museum of Fine Arts, Houston
Valeria and Gregorio Napoleone Collection, London
Nature Morte, New Delhi
Aliza Nisenbaum
Camilo Ontiveros
Michelle Angela Ortiz
Pace Gallery
Pace/MacGill Gallery
Collection Adrian Piper Research Archive Foundation Berlin
Galerie Polaris, Paris
P·P·O·W Gallery New York
Private collection
Private collection, London
Rennie Collection, Vancouver
Anthony Romero
Reena Saini Kallat
Marc Selwyn Fine Arts, Los Angeles
Jack Shainman Gallery, New York
Yinka Shonibare CBE
Xaviera Simmons
Do Ho Suh
Jackson Tang, New York
Galeria Vermelho, São Paulo

Trustees of the Institute of Contemporary Art/Boston

This book is published on the occasion of the exhibition

When Home Won't Let You Stay: Migration through Contemporary Art

Organized by Ruth Erickson, Mannion Family Curator, and Eva Respini, Barbara Lee Chief Curator, with Ellen Tani, Assistant Curator

The Institute of Contemporary Art/Boston
October 23, 2019–January 26, 2020

Minneapolis Institute of Art
February 22–May 24, 2020

Cantor Arts Center at Stanford University
October 2, 2020–January 24, 2021

Support for *When Home Won't Let You Stay: Migration through Contemporary Art* is generously provided by Paul and Catherine Buttenwieser, Steve Corkin and Dan Maddalena, Alan and Vivien Hassenfeld, Kristen and Kent Lucken, the Poss Family Foundation, and Mark and Marie Schwartz.

Okwui Enwezor's essay "Tebbit's Ghost" was originally published in Barbara Vanderlinden and Elena Filipovic, eds., *The Manifesta Decade: Debates on Contemporary Art Exhibitions and Biennials in Post-Wall Europe* (Cambridge, MA: The MIT Press, 2005). Reprinted by arrangement with the author with minor revisions.

Uday Singh Mehta's essay "The Refugee and a Different Vision of Security and Being Together" is derived from a talk entitled "Identity and Dignity," prepared by the author for the Conference on Migration and the Humanities, Mahindra Center, Harvard University, February 8–9, 2018. Printed by arrangement with the author.

Eavan Boland's poem "That the Science of Cartography Is Limited" was originally published in *In a Time of Violence* (New York: W. W. Norton & Company, Inc., 1994). Reprinted by arrangement with W. W. Norton & Company, Inc., and Carcanet Press Limited.

The opinions expressed in this book are those of the authors and do not necessarily reflect the views of the Institute of Contemporary Art/Boston.

Publication Coordinator: Ellen Tani
Proofreading: Aimery Dunlap-Smith
Design and Typesetting: Beverly Joel, pulp, ink.
Production Manager: Sarah Henry
Printed in Singapore by Pristone

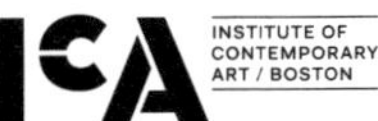

Institute of Contemporary Art/Boston
25 Harbor Shore Drive
Boston, MA 02210
icaboston.org

Yale

Published in association with
Yale University Press
302 Temple Street
P.O. Box 209040
New Haven, CT 06520-9040
yalebooks.com/art

Library of Congress Control Number: 2019934209
ISBN 978-0-300-24748-0

A catalogue record for this book is available from the British Library.

The paper in this book meets the requirements of ANSI/NISO Z39.48-1992 (Permanence of Paper).

10 9 8 7 6 5 4 3 2 1

Front cover: Reena Saini Kallat, *Woven Chronicle* (detail), 2011–16. Circuit boards, speakers, electrical wires, and fittings; single-channel audio (sound; 10:00 minutes), approximately 11 x 38 feet (335.3 x 1158.2 cm). Installation view, *Insecurities: Tracing Displacement and Shelter*, The Museum of Modern Art, New York, 2016–17
Back cover, pages 2–3: Richard Mosse, *Incoming* (still), 2014–17. Three-channel HD video installation (black-and-white, 7.3 surround sound; 52:10 minutes)
Pages 4–5: Do Ho Suh, *Wielandstr. 18, 12159 Berlin, Germany—3 Corridors*, 2011. Polyester fabric and stainless steel. Three parts, each 11 feet 6⅛ inches x 82¼ inches x 21 feet 5⅞ inches (351 x 209 x 655 cm); 11 feet 5 inches x 42½ x 9 feet 10½ inches (348 x 108 x 301 cm); and 11 feet 4¼ inches x 31 feet 11¾ inches x 92⅛ inches (346 x 975 x 234 cm)
Pages 6–7: Xaviera Simmons, *Found the Sea like the River* (detail), 2018. Acrylic on wood panel. 72 x 96 inches (182.9 x 243.8 cm)
Page 8: Hayv Kahraman, *Bab el Sheikh* (detail), 2013. Oil on wood. 9 feet 3 inches x 11 feet 10 inches (281.9 x 360.7 cm)
Page 10: Isaac Julien, *Western Union Series No. 1 (Cast No Shadow)*, 2007. Duratrans image in lightbox. 47¼ x 47¼ inches (120 x 120 cm)
Page 14: Yinka Shonibare CBE, *The American Library* (detail), 2018. Hardback books, Dutch wax-printed cotton textile, gold-foiled names, and website, dimensions variable. Installation view, Van Every/Smith Galleries at Davidson College, Davidson, NC, 2018